Isan Writers, Thai Literature

Isan Writers, Thai Literature

Writing and Regionalism in Modern Thailand

Martin B. Platt

NUS PRESS
SINGAPORE

nias
PRESS

© 2013 Martin B. Platt

First published by:

NUS Press
National University of Singapore
AS3-01-02, 3 Arts Link
Singapore 117569

Fax: (65) 6774-0652
E-mail: nusbooks@nus.edu.sg
Website: http://www.nus.edu.sg/nuspress

ISBN 978-9971-69-697-9 (Paper)

Published in Europe by:

NIAS Press
NIAS — Nordic Institute of Asian Studies
Øster Farimagsgade 5, DK–1353 Copenhagen K, Denmark
Tel: (+45) 3532 9501   Fax: (+45) 3532 9549
E-mail: books@nias.ku.dk
Website: www.niaspress.dk

ISBN 978-87-7694-129-1

The Nordic Institute of Asian Studies (NIAS) is a research and service institute located at the University of Copenhagen and collaborating closely with the wider Nordic Asian Studies community. NIAS works to encourage and support Asian Studies in the Nordic countries as well as actively participating in the international scholarly community in its own right. In so doing, NIAS has published books since 1969 and in 2002 launched NIAS Press as an independent, not-for-profit publisher aiming at a premium reputation among authors and readers for relevant and focused, quality publishing in the field of Asian Studies.

Cataloguing-in-Publication Data for the book is available from the National Library, Singapore and the British Library.

Cover image: Highway 212 heading south in Mukdahan Province, December 1986, courtesy of Paul Wagner

Cover design by Paul Wagner

Printed by: Mainland Press Pte Ltd

To my parents and my brother,
who together taught me to read

CONTENTS

Preface

This book attempts to investigate, and hopefully encourage further interest in, modern Thai literature. It examines Isan writers, the modern literature they produce, and the role that both have played in the development of Thailand's national literature. Thus this is simultaneously a literary history and a study of regionalism. It covers the second half of the 20th century, beginning when Isan writers first gained some national prominence, and ending, somewhat arbitrarily, when the century (and coincidentally my fieldwork) ended. By that time, though, Isan writers and their work had attained the highest levels of literary and cultural achievement and influence in Thailand.

I wish to acknowledge those who have touched on this project and helped bring it to fruition.

First I would like to express my deep gratitude to Ajan Manas Chitakasem, whose knowledge, experience, and humanity have made a lasting impact. David Smyth and the late Henry Ginsburg also provided advice, encouragement, and friendship that have been greatly appreciated. Colleagues in Copenhagen, especially Cynthia Chou and Denise Gimpel (who also gave valuable comments on two chapters), and Nipaporn Hansen and Alice Andersen, have been a source of inestimable support in maintaining morale as well as a sense of discovery and humor. My students in Thailand, London, and Copenhagen have provided challenge and inspiration, and have helped deepen my understanding of Thai language and literature.

In Thailand, the many people who have contributed to this project, whether directly or indirectly, knowingly or not, cannot all be counted, let alone named. Particular thanks are due to Naowarat Phongphaiboon, who provided the spark by introducing me to a number of writers. I owe an enormous debt of gratitude to Chukiet Chathaisong who took me into his circle and through whom I came to know many writers, artists, and critics. Many others in Thailand were generous with their thoughts and hospitality, especially Wira Sudsang, Manote Phromsingh, Pramote Naijit, Chaiya Wannasri, Somphong Thawi, Phaiwarin Khaongam, and Suchart Sawatsri;

also Wiwat Rotchanawan, Somneuk Phanitchakij, Surachai Janthimathorn, Raks Mananya, Prachakhom Lunachai, Phisit Phusri, the late Khamphun Bunthawi, and others. I thank two anonymous reviewers for their suggestions to improve the manuscript. *Kho'p khun* to Aphiwat for his wizardry in finding books. For their insights and camaraderie, I would also like to thank Jo and Zin, David Streckfuss, Patrick McCormick, and also Peter Koret, who has long been a fount of ideas, inspiration, and amusement (as well as skepticism). Special thanks to Paul Wagner for his friendship and artistry over many years. Let none of them be tainted by any error or weakness in this book.

Finally, many thanks to NUS and NIAS presses, especially Eunice Low for her care and patience, and Paul Kratoska for his high standards, practicality, and conviction that literature matters.

Martin B. Platt
Copenhagen, August 2013

Introduction

One learns early on in Thailand that the country is composed of four distinct regions, and that each of these has its own language and characteristics. The stereotypes surrounding the regions are so commonly held and heard as to be unquestioned: the north is inhabited by attractive, light-skinned people who speak slowly and behave graciously; southerners are dark-skinned, hot-tempered, and speak extremely quickly; northeasterners, who are simple, hardworking, and not too bright, speak a language something like Lao. The north has a respected ancient culture; the south is exotic and a little dangerous, as some of its people are Malays and Muslims; the northeast (or "Isan") is hot, dry, and poor. What about the fourth region? There are no stereotypes about the central region. It is simply normal, the standard by which the other regions are measured, and the model that they are expected to emulate.

These nearly universal views by the center obscure the complex histories and realities of the regions. Why is the northern region's culture seen to be older and of higher status than that of the other (non-central) regions? How is the language of the northeast like Lao, and does everyone there speak it? The more we investigate, the more we see the complexities of the regions, and the contradictions of the view from the center. For example, more people in Thailand speak Lao as their first language than central Thai, yet Lao is laughed at and its speakers looked down on by other Thais. Since the middle of the 20th century (if not earlier), regional languages have been diluted by the influence of Central Thai, and their written forms have nearly disappeared, due to discouragement and at times hostility from the central government.

The center, almost by definition, determines the direction of the country and has the power to dictate to the regions. What has been the reaction on the part of people of the regions? What are their own views on the stereotypes about them? How do they see themselves? What is the nature of the relationships among the regions, and between the regions and the center? How have these relationships developed? These kinds of questions have been touched upon to some extent in such disciplines as History, Anthropology, and Political Science, but what has not been considered is how these issues come to bear on literature in Thailand. What relevance does the existence of regions, and their relationships to the center, have for modern Thai literature?

This book is an investigation of the Isan region, its writers, and their role in modern Thai literature. It seems to me that of all the regions, the northeast and the south have the most distinctive literary presence in the national modern literature. I have chosen to concentrate on the northeast due to my own greater familiarity with that region and its predominant language (Lao). Although effectively all modern literature in Thailand today is written in Thai, some writers do use a certain amount of the local language in their work. Is there such a thing as modern regional literature in Thailand, and if so, how is it defined, if not by language? I believe there is a modern Isan literature, and that it is defined largely by who writes it. This obviously begs the question: how does one define "Isan writer"?

The question of who is an Isan writer is a complex and important one. Many factors are relevant, including where an author was born and grew up, where s/he lives (if alive), and what his/her native language is. How the author identifies him-/herself is also significant, as are the subject matter, setting, and readership of an author's works. Although all of these factors play a role, none is by itself decisive. The most important elements seem to be that an author identifies him-/herself as being from Isan, and that his/her work has some kind of Isan content. Being from Isan is a somewhat fluid concept. People can be born in Isan but move away as children, or spend much of their lives elsewhere, or even move to Isan from a different region. Isan content is also a broad designation, and may involve use of Isan language or culture, common themes, historical references, or landscape. In general, an Isan writer will present him-/herself as such, will likely be involved in Isan-related literary activities (see Chapter 6), and will be recognized by other Isan writers.

During a year of fieldwork in Thailand (1998–1999), I was asked any number of times what I was doing there. My answer, depending on my assessment of the questioner's level of interest, ranged from the vague and general to the specific and (I thought) clear. I was doing research, or researching literature, or researching Thai literature, or modern Thai literature, or modern Isan literature, or contemporary Isan writers and writing. Sometimes, if my answer had tended toward the non-specific end of this gradation, I was then asked if I was referring to historical chronicles, for example, or traditional Isan tales. However, if I said I was working on contemporary Isan literature, I would usually draw a blank look, and the conversation would either change subject or end. More rarely, the person would ask what I meant, perhaps assuming that I must be talking about the contemporary telling of *mo' lam* tales or local medicinal or religious lore. When I said I meant short stories and novels (and sometimes poetry) written by modern Isan writers, a glimmer of recognition at times resulted, and sometimes the name of the well-known writer Khamphun Bunthawi or his novel *Luk Isan* (see Chapter 4) was mentioned. Even then, however, I felt a certain disconnection, non-acceptance, or even disapproval.

The category of Contemporary Isan Literature does not exist in Thailand (nor outside it, judging from the lack of treatment of the subject academically). The idea of Isan writers, though, has been gaining credence for some time now, as has the idea of other regions' writers: Southern writers, Northern writers, even Eastern writers. From time to time, articles have appeared in the Thai press referring to a particular writer's regional association, or covering the activities of a particular writers' group. However, these groups, whether formally constituted or not, have been seen as assemblages of people who have in common their regions and all that might entail, as well as their occupation (or avocation) as writers. Their work, their writing, their literature has not been seen as comprising a unity of any kind, or having any particular similarity, commonality, or relationship. The general attitude seems to be that it is all simply Thai literature.

This is not to say that Isan writers are seen to exist while Isan literature is believed to not exist. Isan writing is simply not seen as such. Nonetheless, Isan writing does exist. There is such a thing as modern Isan literature, or so I will contend in this book. Certainly it is not monolithic, or entirely and absolutely different from all other Thai literature, or instantly recognizable in all its many varieties. Modern Isan writing, though, has played a significant, unique, and at times pivotal role in the development of Thai literature. Isan writers' goals and achievements have been shaped by their origins, experiences, and relationships with the Thai center. By looking at a subset of Thai literature as modern regional literature of Isan, we will, I believe, increase our knowledge and understanding of the literature and literary culture of both Isan and Thailand.

This study represents a first stab at the subject of regionalism and modern Thai literature. Since the topic has hardly been recognized, let alone investigated, the results presented here are at best only a start. I have tried to sketch the big picture and consider a wide variety of issues and writers in an attempt to give an overall view. My approach has been to consider individual writers and their works in the context of the development of Thai literature and literary movements over half a century, from about 1950 to 1999. This is because the presence and significance of modern Isan writing is most noticeable late in this period, and less noticeable the farther back in time we go. In 1950, modern Isan writing had scarcely begun, for historical and political reasons (see Chapter 1), and modern Thai literature was essentially a literature of the center. Before that, the impulse toward literary expression in Isan manifested itself in the more traditional verbal arts of *mo'lam*, palm leaf manuscripts, and other religious or secular poetic storytelling forms. While these literary arts still exist in popular performances, temple manuscripts, and commercially available recordings, they are disappearing.[1]

The modern novel and short story represent a separate tradition, and one that is largely (although not completely) discontinuous with the local literary endeavors mentioned above. Rather than arising or evolving from preexisting indigenous forms, the novel and short story were derived from the literary practices of the West and thus are without immediate, direct antecedents in Thailand. Not surprisingly, some elements of traditional forms have at times been carried over, including such norms and aesthetics of storytelling as the use of reduplicative expressions, and other traditional elements are being rediscovered (see Chapter 5). Nonetheless, modern Isan literature seems best understood in the historical context of modern Thai literature in general, rather than traditional Isan literature (although such a topic would be of interest as well).

The purpose of this book is to investigate and attempt to shed light on a particular phenomenon, specifically, modern writing based (conceptually, if not always physically) in the Isan region, and in so doing, to further an understanding of the literature and society of Isan and Thailand. I believe that a concrete and analytical examination of authors, their works, and the reception of those works, furthers knowledge about literature and the society that produces it in a way that is more valuable than an explicitly and self-consciously theoretical exploration. My conviction is that observations of details, events, and activities, and the lives and works of writers, as well as readers and critics, can provide real insight into literary culture. For this reason I have chosen to discuss particular writers, their attitudes and specific works, and even anecdotes that I think, taken together, tell a great

---

[1] See Peter Koret, "Whispered So Softly It Resounds through the Forest, Spoken So Loudly It Can Hardly be Heard: The Art of Parallelism in Traditional Lao Literature," PhD thesis, SOAS, University of London, 1994.

deal about the subject at hand: contemporary Isan writing. I do not claim to have produced a comprehensive treatment of all Isan writers, or even of any one writer among them. Instead I have concentrated on certain features that illuminate the general picture. In writing this book, I have tried to avoid fashionable theory and jargon, and attempted instead a readable and informative discussion of my topic in the hope that this effort might help lead to further study and understanding.

When I first became interested in modern Thai literature, in the mid-1980s, I wanted a book (in English, at that time) that would give some kind of overview on the subject — addressing such questions as who some of the influential writers were, what kind of work they produced, what some of the ideas that engaged the literary community were, how they had changed over time. Yet there was no such book. In the 25 years since then, some informative works have appeared, though a few might be seen as introductions to a scholar's favorite writer or an idiosyncratically chosen collection of short stories or novel excerpts, often in illustration of a social science argument or some popular "-ism." Significantly, no attempt at a coherent, methodical treatment of Thai literature of the 20th century has been made, whether in Thai or English (or any other language, to my knowledge).[2]

A study along such lines is certainly needed, in part to provide some context in which to place existing literary studies that concentrate on more narrowly defined topics. While studies of individual writers are of course valuable (and there are still so few), it seems that a fair amount of detail is beginning to accumulate but without sufficient perspective on movements and developments that have taken place over time (decades, rather than years). While obviously a book such as the current one cannot give a comprehensive consideration of modern Thai literary history, perhaps it can stand as an initial attempt, however incomplete and imperfect, to consider the topic, and might encourage others to expand and improve on its results.[3]

It is both fortunate and unfortunate that modern Thai regional literature is a scholarly field that does not yet really exist: fortunate because there is a lot to see and say, but unfortunate because there are no existing studies with

---

[2] The works of David Smyth and of Trisilp Bunkhajorn provide extremely useful insights into particular periods within the 20th century.

[3] The lack of scholarship on the topic of Thai (and other Southeast Asian) modern literary history is of course attributable in large measure to institutional failure to support this field and the consequent relative lack of training and expertise.

which to disagree, or on which to build. In Thailand, as noted above, modern literature is not conceived in regional terms. Regional literature is seen as ancient, usually written in antiquated scripts on palm leaves or mulberry paper, and not widely read. Outside of Thailand, the idea of regional modern Thai literature may not be entirely unheard of, but scholars have given little attention to it beyond noting that there is an Isan writers' group, for example, or that some southerners have formed a printing house.[4] It is an area of study waiting to be recognized, like a forest that locals regularly walk past without noticing, and outsiders, if they see it at all, do not enter.

In his useful book, *Is Literary History Possible?*, David Perkins[5] makes a strong argument which concludes with what seems like a convincing answer: no. He makes important points, relevant to any literary history, about the arbitrariness of choices of time frame, of authors and works considered, of ideas and trends acknowledged or ignored, and so on. Not only can there be no objectivity, he says, but any attempt to tell some kind of narrative of literary development can only end up as a fatally flawed reflection of the individual literary historian's biases, shortcomings, and idiosyncrasies. While there may be much truth in this point of view, if we completely accept it, we must not only cease to make any attempt to make sense of literary history, but also renounce all historical writing and the entire historiographic endeavor. Surely this argument goes too far. Thus, although the purposes and accomplishments of academics can and should be questioned and often doubted, we may still exert efforts to learn about, and even understand, however partially, the literary past.

In carrying out this study, I have relied predominantly on three kinds of materials: 1) literary texts, mainly short stories and novels, but also some poetry; 2) commentaries on these texts, mostly in Thai but also some from Western sources; and 3) interviews with many of the writers, as well as with some academics, critics, and publishers.[6] I also discuss activities in which the writers participated, and the various endeavors that made up contemporary literary culture at the end of the 20th century (see Chapter 6). My approach is to consider Isan literature in the historical context of Thai literature generally, of which it is a part.

---

[4] See Anthony Diller, "What Makes Central Thai a National Language?" in *Thai National Identity and Its Defenders: Thailand 1939–1989*, ed. C. Reynolds (Clayton, Victoria: Monash University, 1991), pp. 87–132.
[5] David Perkins, *Is Literary History Possible?* (Baltimore: Johns Hopkins U, 1991).
[6] Translations of quotations from written and oral sources are my own unless otherwise indicated.

Initially, I attempted to observe Isan writing both historically and as it continued to unfold and develop at the time of my fieldwork. However, my perspective has now shifted. Rather than trying to bring the discussion up to the present moment and incorporate the latest developments, I have decided to consider the phenomenon in a bounded period of time, up until the end of the 20th century. This is because, as with any continuing process, some cut-off date must be chosen; otherwise a manuscript can never be completed. Furthermore, the assessment of historical significance can rarely be made in the moment, but rather benefits from, nay demands, the passage of time.[7] Although 1999 is in many ways an arbitrary end, primarily marking the end of my main fieldwork, I believe that the period considered does permit elucidation of some useful aspects of the topic while admitting that changes and new developments continue beyond the artificial confines of this book. It is worth noting that nearly all of the writers discussed here were alive and presumably still writing at the time this book was being completed in 2012.[8]

Most of the sources used in this study date from the year 2000 and earlier. There are two main reasons for this. First, as this is a literary history of Isan regionalism from 1950 to 1999, I am looking at the literary activities of that period and the response to them. This is not a current events study with up-to-the-minute commentary on the latest developments. Indeed, such a project would likely be unsatisfactory, as the importance of events and literary works is hardly apparent except with hindsight. The second reason for the relative lack of 21st-century sources here relates to what O.W. Wolters called the "present-mindedness"[9] of Southeast Asia: "being up-to-date [is] a cultural trait."[10] In Thailand, literary works are read and discussed at the time they appear. Other than the rare bestseller or award winner, most

---

[7] This is evident from Danerek's 2006 doctoral study of Indonesian literature from the 2002–2006 period. See Stefan Danerek, "Tjerita and Novel: Literary Discourse in Post New Order Indonesia," Lund University Center for Language and Literature, 2006.

[8] The exceptions are Udorn Thongnoi, who seems to have stopped writing; Rom Ratiwan and Prasert Jandam, who died before this study was undertaken; and Khamphun Bunthawi, who passed away in 2003.

[9] O.W. Wolters, *History, Culture, and Reason in Southeast Asian Perspectives* (Ithaca, NY: Southeast Asian Program Publications, Cornell University, 1999), p. 267. He further notes, on page 187, "Southeast Asian cultures are well-known for their indifference to the past for its own sake."

[10] Ibid., p. 134.

newly published books disappear from bookstores after six months or a year. Thus the majority of works considered here are out of print and no longer the subject of readers' attention or critics' comments. One has only to ask around for a book (or film) that appeared a year or two ago to be told that it is "old" (เก่าแล้ว) and thus no longer of interest.[11]

Furthermore, once opinion has been expressed on a particular work, especially by recognized authorities, the assessment is rarely revised or reconsidered. Even on the rare occasions when a writer or an important work is celebrated on some kind of anniversary or at a funeral, the discussion tends to be not a reassessment but a re-statement of the established views (often by merely reprinting written comments from the past). For example, a book celebrating Lao Khamhawm's 70 years of life and work consists almost entirely of articles collected from previous decades.[12] Moreover, very few Isan writers ever receive this kind of homage or attention. In short, writers and works from even just a few years ago are considered old news and rarely hold the attention of published commentators. The sources I use in this study reflect that reality.

I assume anyone reading this to have a basic knowledge of Thailand and its modern history. A weakness I see in some discussions of Thai literature is that they generally assume an uninformed reader, and thus always feel the need to explain even the most basic background: where Thailand is, who King Chulalongkorn was, what happened in 1932, etc. While such explanations have their place and are at times necessary, I do not wish to write yet another introduction to Thailand, or give one more version of the political events of the 1970s. Such subjects have been amply introduced elsewhere. Rather than covering the same ground, I wish to go

---

[11] This phenomenon is evident even in a recent book, published in the West, on Southeast Asian fiction (a rarity which deserves praise for its mere existence). Although the book calls itself "a literary history," in fact the two chapters on Thai literature are heavily weighted toward only the last 15 years or so, emphasizing in particular a few writers who were attracting attention at the time the book was being prepared. Just two Isan writers are referred to: Lao Khamhawm, who is listed only in a bibliography, and Prachakhom Lunachai, most of whose pre-2002 work is not even mentioned (neither of these authors is discussed in relation to Isan or regionalism). See Susan Kepner, "Thai Short Fiction of the Modern Era" and Suradech Chotiudompant, "Contemporary Trends in Thai Short Fiction," both in *Modern Short Fiction of Southeast Asia: A Literary History*, ed. Terry Shaffer Yamada (Ann Arbor, MI: Association for Asian Studies, 2009).

[12] See ชาติ กอบจิตติ ฯลฯ บก, ลาว คำหอม *Khamsing Srinawk* กรุงเทพฯ: นักเขียน, 2544.

beyond the usual standard accounts and instead build and expand on them. We know (or should know) the fundamentals of Thai history, but what is less commonly known is the role Isan has played in literary history, and, further, how the Isan region and its writers and literature have influenced and been influenced by Thai society and Thai literature overall.

In this book, I discuss in detail 24 writers and their work in terms of Isan, regionalism, and modern Thai literature. I have tried to treat each writer in proportion to his or her importance or position in relation to my topic. I have not intended, nor do I claim, to provide an exhaustive or final commentary on any writer's entire *oeuvre* or its significance. That is not my purpose. Instead I have presented elements of each writer's life and work that I feel are relevant to the subject of Isan literary regionalism and are indicative of the nature of that phenomenon as it developed over a half century or so. Some writers, like Khamphun Bunthawi and Phaiwarin Khaongam, have produced a wide body of work that warrants the kind of full-length consideration that is not possible or pertinent here. Other writers, such as Somneuk Phanitchakij and Siowjan Raemphrai, have played a relatively modest (but instructive) role in Isan writing and are considered accordingly. Certainly more could be said about all of these writers (as well as others) and their work, but my goal is not an encyclopedic investigation of every work by every writer with a connection to Isan. I feel it is more productive to look at the overall subject and choose aspects of various writers, and their works and activities, that illuminate notable features of Isan literary regionalism. This is what I have tried to present.

The structure of the book is as follows. Chapter 1 discusses the factors that make Isan a region, distinct from the rest of Thailand; these include physical, cultural, historical, and attitudinal elements. Chapters 2 through 5 follow a historical trajectory, starting about 1950 and moving to the 1990s. Each of these chapters presents a short historical period, beginning with a discussion of the context (historical, political, social, etc.) as it pertains to Isan writers of that period, and then considering individually a few of those writers and their work. Specifically, Chapter 2 traces the earliest manifestations of an Isan sensibility in modern Thai literature, while Chapter 3 examines the growth of an Isan presence in literature (and related popular music) as part of an ethos of search, social consciousness, and political protest in the wider society. Two writers whose work became widely known, first nationally and then internationally through translation, are the subject of Chapter 4. Chapter 5 chronicles the rise of an explicitly expressed and organized Isan regionalism (in literature, scholarship, and the culture at large) in the aftermath of a collapsed political engagement. The state of Isan writing at the end of the 20th century is the subject of Chapter 6, which includes a discussion of literary group activities, local endeavors, and emerging young writers. Finally, the Conclusion considers questions of Isan identity, awareness, and regionalism as elements within the national literary sphere. Given the structure of the book, some readers may wish, after Chapter 1, to read the beginning sections of Chapters 2 through 6 in order to gain an idea of historical contexts and trajectories of Thai literature and Isan literary regionalism; then, the more detailed treatments of each writer's life, work, and significance can be read (or not) according to the interests of the individual reader.

CHAPTER 1

What Makes Isan a Region?

Isan is a region distinct from the rest of Thailand. Recognition of this fact is reflected in all aspects of the country and its activities: government policies, newspaper reports, television shows, music performances, political campaigns, tourism promotions, educational planning, agricultural research, religious practices, development projects, military organization, fashion design, and literary activities. Anyone in Thailand hearing or using the word *Isan* will likely have a whole complex of images, ideas, and attitudes associated with it, and these are likely to vary according to speaker, hearer, and context. Use of the word can call forth feelings of pride, shame, humor, pity, nostalgia, derision, admiration, paternalism, disgust, warmth, fear, greed, or reverence, but never draws a blank.

How has this situation come to be? How did Isan's status as a region arise, and how has it changed and developed? The word *Isan* อีสาน itself is of Pali-Sanskrit origin and simply means "northeast direction,"[1] and thus *phak isan* ภาคอีสาน is "northeast region," but its denotational meaning is only a very small part of its overall referential meaning. Isan is a region both by virtue of its physical reality and of how it is perceived, whether by those inside its borders or outside them. The measurable, observable features of Isan have helped to give rise to the perceptions and attitudes that have characterized it. Ignorance, prejudice, and other forms of bias have played a major role in determining how Isan has been viewed and treated by outsiders, particularly Central Thais, and thus also in how Isan people have reacted to such views and treatment.

There are two principal modes by which Isan is defined to be a region. The first is in comparison to other regions of Thailand. Isan has

---

[1] พจนานุกรม ฉบับราชบัณฑิตยสถาน กรุงเทพฯ พ.ษ, 2525.

characteristics of various kinds that distinguish it from the South, the Center, and the North. Contrasts with the Central region are most salient because it is the Center which sets the standard for what is Thai in Thailand. The other way in which Isan is a region is in relation to itself, that is, as an entity that is in some way cohesive. While Isan is far from homogeneous, it does contain elements that amalgamate into a whole (although an argument can be made questioning the inclusion of Korat, see below). In this chapter, rather than discussing all the many distinctive features of Isan as a region, I will concentrate on those that have significance for modern Isan literature and its place in Thailand and Thai literary life.

The Northeast region of Thailand can be referred to in Thai in a number of ways. The term *Isan* อีสาน is the most common.[2] It was first used in the 19th century under King Rama V (see below), and thus has certain political and historical roots.[3] Another term used is *thi rab sung* ที่ราบสูง, meaning "plateau" or "high flat place." Its use carries an expressive and evocative quality, with a geo-cultural referent (rather than a political or historic one). This term is used primarily in literature, often by writers who are themselves from Isan. Although it refers specifically to the Korat Plateau, it can be used metonymically to mean all of Isan, or Isan in general. Finally, the phrase *phak tawan o'k chiang neua* ภาคตะวันออกเฉียงเหนือ is Standard Thai for "northeast." It is a general and technical term which carries strictly neutral, geographic meaning.

Physical and Social Aspects

The most obvious characteristic of Isan is its location: it is the large, distinctive lobe protruding on the east and slightly north side of Thailand. Isan is bounded on the north and east by the border with Laos (most of which is demarcated by the Mekong River), on the south by the border

---

[2] Some Thais make a distinction between *Isan* with a short vowel /i/ อิสาน and *Isan* with a long vowel /ii/ อีสาน, preferring the former term due to a (perhaps misguided) belief that the long /ii/, in the word อี, carries negative connotation. I have not heard any Isan people make this distinction, which may be in part related to the fact that in Lao, the long /ii/ does not have the same negative meaning that it has in Central Thai.

[3] The term as used in the names Isanapura (the city founded in the seventh century in what is now Cambodia) and Isanavarman (its ruler) was a different word and referred to Siva.

with Cambodia and the southern extremities of Korat Province, and on the west by the western edges of Korat, Chaiyaphum, Khon Kaen, and Loei provinces. Thus Isan is the northeastern part of the country, and it is also situated northeast of Bangkok and the Center.

Topographically (and perhaps in other ways), Isan is high and dry, particularly away from the Mekong River. The region has a reputation for poor soil and an arid climate, with variable and unpredictable rains resulting in both floods and droughts. Rice, usually sticky rice (for which there is limited export demand), is the primary agricultural crop, producing one harvest of uneven yield per year (as compared to the usual two harvests in the North and often three per year in the Central region). This low productivity of the land, combined with its natural topography and climate, historically have mitigated against the rise of urban centers and accompanying powerful elites in the region, and have contributed to a lack of unity both within Isan's own borders and in its relation to the rest of Thailand.

Isan's 66,000 square mile (172,000 square kilometer) area represents close to one-third of the land area of Thailand and contains about one-third of the country's population.[4] However, while Isan is the largest region, it is also the poorest, and has been for many decades at least. In 1953 the average income per family in Isan was one-third that in the Central Plains,[5] by 1960, that figure had declined to one-quarter, and levels of education were correspondingly low.[6] From 1975 on, Isan consistently experienced the highest incidence of poverty in the country, between 36 and 48 percent.[7] According to Luther, in 1989 average GDP per capita in Isan was about one-third of the national average and one-ninth of the average in Bangkok.[8] Isan is also lacking in natural resources, other than forests, which decreased

---

[4] Charles Keyes, "Isan: Regionalism in Northeast Thailand," Southeast Asia Program Data Paper #65, Cornell University, Ithaca, NY, 1967, p. 37. This figure increased to 37% by 1989. Hans Luther, "Regional Identity versus National Integration — Contemporary Patterns of Modernization in Northeastern Thailand," in *Regions and National Integration in Thailand 1892–1992*, ed. V. Grabowsky (Wiesbaden: Harrassowitz, 1995), p. 188.

[5] Keyes, "Isan," p. 37.

[6] John Girling, *Thailand: Society and Politics* (London: Cornell University, 1981), p. 195.

[7] Pasuk Phongpaichit and Chris Baker, *Thailand Economy and Politics* (Kuala Lumpur: Oxford University Press, 1995), p. 65.

[8] Luther, "Regional Identity," p. 188.

in area by approximately two-thirds between 1961 and 1988.[9] The situation is exacerbated by the fact that:

> [M]ost children drop out of the school system after 4–6 years of basic education. Either their labor is needed on the farm and their parents cannot afford further school attendance for them or they see no reason to continue because they believe they may face unemployment anyway … But students alone cannot be blamed for their low motivation. Schools are often in bad shape and teachers are indebted because they receive their salaries late or sometimes not at all.[10]

Meanwhile,

> The Northeast of Thailand has the highest birth rate in the country which is 1.7 times the national average. Consequently, population pressure is high and unskilled labor is abundant. This corresponds to very few employment opportunities due to the absence of industrial development. Hence, the Isan region [has] traditionally supplied cheap labor for the rest of the country.[11]

Members of this pool of unskilled labor have been migrating to look for work in a pattern that has lasted for generations. In 1949 the trend was accelerated when quotas on immigrants in Thailand ended large-scale Chinese immigration and created a vacuum in the urban labor force. Migration of Isan laborers then increased, but generally they took up only temporary jobs between the planting and the harvest seasons. In Bangkok, Isan people, "employed in lowly occupations and seen as unsophisticated and uncultured provincials,"[12] found themselves considered inferior by urban Thais. The upshot is that social mobility for northeasterners has primarily been through either the civil service or the Sangha, both of which require increasing conformity to Central Thai modes of behavior.[13]

Cultural Aspects

Probably the most noticeable and significant features that distinguish Isan from the rest of Thailand are cultural ones. Between 80 and 90 percent of the population of Isan is ethnically Lao, speaking one or another dialect

---

[9] Pasuk and Baker, *Thailand*, p. 62.
[10] Luther, "Regional Identity," p. 189.
[11] Ibid., p. 186.
[12] Keyes, *Isan*, p. 38.
[13] Ibid., p. 60.

of Lao,[14] rather than Thai, as their first language.[15] The next largest ethnic group in the region are the Khmer, who in (Central) Thai have traditionally been referred to as *khamen pa dong* เขมรป่าดง, the "jungle Khmer" or "wild Khmer." In Isan itself, they are generally called *khamen sung* เขมรสูง, the "high [elevation] Khmer," distinguishing them from the *khamen tam* เขมรต่ำ, the "low [elevation] Khmer" of Cambodia proper. Ethnic Khmer make up ten percent of the population of Isan; in the three main provinces where they live, Buri Ram, Surin, and Srisaket, they comprise 40–50 percent, 70 percent, and 30 percent of the local population respectively.[16]

Another ethnic group in this southern Isan region are the Kui กุย, who in Thai are commonly called by the pejorative term *suay* ส่วย implying a subject, tribute-paying people. Grabowsky puts their number at between 150,000 and 200,000 while describing them as "aboriginal" people who "have to a great extent been assimilated by the culturally more complex Lao and Khmer."[17] In fact, many Kui people still speak Kui as their first language and practice customs related to keeping elephants and other traditions in villages in Surin and neighboring provinces. Nonetheless, some observers have spoken of a social status hierarchy in Isan in which the Kui are below the Khmer and the ethnic Lao are above both. There is also the Thai Korat ethnic group, described by Grabowsky as "a Siamese speaking minority concentrated in Korat Province" and numbering "roughly ten percent of the northeastern population,"[18] an estimate that would appear high. Finally, other ethnic groups include Vietnamese, Chinese, and Chao Bon or Nyakur, a Mon group descending from the Mon civilization that existed prior to that of early Tai peoples.[19]

A striking fact emerges when one looks at the population and language maps of Thailand. Not only is Lao (in various mutually intelligible dialects) by far the majority language spoken in Isan, but, as Diller points out, "just over one third of the local residents in Thailand speak Lao as their native or first linguistic variety," while "[s]lightly under that figure could

---

[14] This Lao designation includes Lao sub-groups such as Phuan, Phu Thai, Yo, etc.

[15] See Volker Grabowsky, "The Isan Up to Its Integration into the Siamese State," in *Regions*, ed. Grabowsky, p. 108; and Charles Keyes, "Hegemony and Resistance in Northeastern Thailand," in *Regions*, ed. Grabowsky, p. 157.

[16] Grabowsky, "The Isan," p. 108.

[17] Ibid.

[18] Ibid.

[19] William Smalley, *Linguistic Diversity and National Unity: Language Ecology in Thailand* (Chicago, IL: University of Chicago Press, 1994), p. 264.

claim varieties of Central Thai as theirs."[20] In other words, while there are complexities in counting dialect speakers and "native" speakers, it appears that Lao is Thailand's first language. This also means that there are approximately ten times as many Lao speakers in Thailand as in Laos itself. This of course does not change the fact that Central or Standard Thai "is the leading prestige dialect [in Thailand] favored by professionals and other high status individuals," and "is thus the variety that most parents would like to have their children speak well for reasons of social mobility and occupational security."[21] It is also used by officials of all kinds, and "for many religious and other ritual purposes, even where it is not the majority dialect spoken," such as upcountry Buddhist sermons, which "are routinely preached in Central Thai."[22]

Indeed, language status and hierarchy are tightly held values throughout Thai society. This was brought home to me on a trip to Lampang in December 1998. I was speaking to a native of the province who had spent all his life there and spoke the local language at home. He had traveled to Isan two or three times, he said, and, when I asked, stated that he had had no real trouble conversing with Isan people. He spoke Lampang dialect to them, and they spoke an Isan dialect back to him; except for a word here and there, they understood each other well. When I replied that the languages were virtually the same, he appeared to take offense and strongly disagreed. "No they're not," he maintained. "We speak Northern Thai, but they speak Isan." The idea that the two could both be dialects of the same language, Lao, was simply not acceptable, or even to be considered. When I wrote an article in Thailand on this incident,[23] claiming that Isan and Kam Meuang were dialects of Lao, it was received with amused interest by Isan readers and cool tolerance by others. One Bangkok friend commented, "People will not accept this." A poet from Chiang Mai, when asked his opinion about the article, replied that he was glad that people from various places could express various ideas.

These artificial terms "northern language" or "Northern Thai" and "Isan language" or "Isan Thai" are manufactured and promoted by the Thai

---

[20] Anthony Diller, "What Makes Central Thai a National Language?" in *Thai National Identity and Its Defenders: Thailand 1939–1989*, ed. C. Reynolds (Clayton, Victoria: Monash University, 1991), pp. 97–8.

[21] Ibid., p. 99.

[22] Ibid., p. 100.

[23] มาร์ติน, "คนละภาษาเดียวกัน," จดหมายข่าวสโมสรนักเขียนภาคอีสาน 4, 17 (ม.ค. - ก.พ. 2542) (1999): 28.

government to serve the myth of Thai superiority and homogeneity and to deny ethnic differences in Thailand. "Isan language" is, simply, Lao,[24] and "Northern Thai," likewise, is not Thai (that is, Siamese, or Central Thai) at all either; neither is comprehensible to an untutored or inexperienced native speaker of Central Thai. Thus, by definition, they are not dialects of Thai. Moreover, since "Northern Thai" and "Isan" are mutually comprehensible (a speaker of one can understand a speaker of the other), they can be considered dialects of the same language (although this might be disputed by some linguists as well). However, since Northern language and culture enjoy a high relative status in Thailand, while Isan language and culture are generally looked down upon, an attempt to link or equate the two goes against social norms. Grabowsky makes the observation that the political and cultural center of northern culture, Chiang Mai, lies within Thailand's borders, while such centers for Lao and Khmer culture are situated outside of Thailand.[25] This illusion of "foreign origin" may help explain why these cultures in Thailand are harder to claim as Thai, and thus are devalued and denigrated.

The distinctive customs of Isan people have at times received much attention, whether from Isan people asserting their identity, central officials justifying government policies, or outsiders promoting tourism. Certain aspects of Isan traditions and practices have contributed to Isan's being perceived as a region and have been cited or used in various ways when Isan is taken up as a subject of interest in politics, development, tourism, gastronomy, literature, and so on.

Food in Isan is immediately identified, by both outsiders and Isan people themselves, as one of its distinguishing features. Certainly the climate must be in part an explanation for why eating habits in Isan are so noticeably different from those in the rest of Thailand. Traditionally, sticky rice is the staple food, eaten with the hands. Beef, pork, and chicken are less common sources of protein than fish, amphibians, crustaceans, and insects. The distinctive *pa daek* (Lao) or *pra hok* (Khmer), known in Thai as *pla ra* ปลาร้า, is salted fish fermented in ceramic vessels (thus preserving it for daily use and times of scarcity) and eaten usually as a condiment in other dishes like *tam mak hung* (*som tam* ส้มตำ in Thai). Field crabs are often added to this dish as well. Various kinds of frogs and toads are caught and roasted, and several types of lizard are grilled, made into *lap* ลาบ, etc. Field rats and

---

[24] Actually a collection of (mostly) closely related dialects of Lao.
[25] Grabowsky, "The Isan," pp. 107–8.

many other kinds of mammals, some now rare and protected by the central government, are used in curries. Lao curries, in contrast to Thai curries, traditionally did not contain coconut milk. This is presumably due to the fact that coconuts naturally grow only in coastal areas, and both Laos and Isan are landlocked. A broad variety of insects comprise a significant part of the diet, including certain bee pupae, red ant eggs, bamboo grubs, buffalo dung grubs, silkworm pupae, water beetles, flying termites, and so on. Most of these are seasonal, and are prepared as particular dishes. All of these foods, both insect and vertebrate, are caught or gathered rather than raised or bred, the exception being the silkworm pupae. These are left over after their cocoons are unraveled in hot water to make silk thread, the silkworms having been kept and fed on mulberry leaves. The pupae, known in Lao as *dak dae*, are popped into the mouth as each cocoon is unwound, or are fried and eaten as a snack. Until recently, they were available in small plastic bags for three baht on the trains from Isan to Bangkok.

Lao music is readily distinguished from other kinds of music in Thailand. The *khaen*, a bamboo reed instrument, has become a symbol of Isan in many contexts. There are also distinctive Lao varieties of drums, *phin*,[26] and *so'*.[27] Many kinds of *mo'lam* music are still performed, whether traditional forms that tell folktales or involve witty courting banter between a man and a woman, or the more modern forms using electrical instruments and accompanied by dancing girls. Some aspects of traditional folk music have been incorporated into Thai *luk thung* ลูกทุ่ง, country music perennially popular throughout Thailand (and beyond) and of late enjoying a resurgence in Bangkok.

Certain kinds of traditional music play roles in particular festivals. The *bun bang fai* (Thai *bo'ng fai* บ้องไฟ), or rocket festival, is celebrated annually near the end of the dry season. This specifically Lao practice pre-dates the coming of Buddhism, although it is overlain with some Buddhist elements such as the public reading of (sometimes apocryphal) *jataka* tales recounting past lives of the Buddha, and is intended to insure the coming of the rains. The celebration often involves the performing of *soeng* dances,[28] drinking alcohol, dancing, cross-dressing, courting and flirting with revelers from

---

[26] A mandolin-like instrument with two or three strings.

[27] A stringed instrument played with a bow and sounding a bit like a fiddle.

[28] A type of Lao traditional dance and song (with call-and-response elements) performed on particular annual occasions including the rocket festival and boat races festival.

other villages, and of course, the firing of rockets. Certain places, such as Yasothorn and Nong Khai, are renowned for their *bang fai* festivals. Other festivals are celebrated in Isan throughout the year in relation to agricultural cycles and religious occasions, as well as for funerals, weddings, etc.

Fallon has pointed out that Isan and Lao society are less hierarchical, more egalitarian, than Central Thai society, a fact he attributes to historical lack of grain surpluses that have limited the size of villages and populations and thus resulted in the absence of powerful rulers and a *sakdina* system.[29] Isan people have a custom of sharing whatever they have, whether the meat of an animal from a hunt, fruit from a tree in the garden, or labor in the rice fields. While this may not be unique to Isan, it is seen as a strongly held and longstanding custom of the region, and plays a role in such social phenomena as weddings, migration for work, resettling to other regions, etc.

Beliefs about how to lead one's daily life, including activities relating to spirits, are common in Isan, but specific details tend to be more local than Isan-wide. A woman from Khon Kaen described to me how her mother would quietly ask permission of flowers before cutting them for use at home or as offerings at the temple. A man who I met while waiting for a train at Hualamphong remained at the station for at least an hour after his train arrived from Surin; he explained that he was waiting until the auspicious time to start off on his business in Bangkok (which he had determined to be 9 am). Fallon lists a number of such beliefs about how to behave:

> Nursing women shouldn't consume certain herbs or the meat of an albino buffalo; upon lowering a corpse from the house, water jars should be overturned to prevent bad luck; ... village ancestors must be honored in an annual ceremony (*liang phi pu ta*); ... one possessed by the *phi pob* spirit must leave the village; inviting the spirit essences (*suu khwan*) through the wrist-tying ceremony can give protection and prevent illness.[30]

Another important aspect of traditional culture in Isan involves traveling and relocating. Pasuk and Baker point out that while villages, particularly in the past, tended to be small and scattered, they were not isolated.[31] Traders, fortunetellers, and wandering monks carried goods, news,

---

[29] Edward Fallon, "The Peasants of Isan: Social and Economic Transitions in Northeast Thailand," PhD diss., University of Wisconsin-Madison, 1983, pp. 179–81.

[30] Fallon, *Peasants of Isan*, p. 298.

[31] Pasuk and Baker, *Thailand*, p. 69.

and knowledge from place to place. *Mo'lam* troupes brought entertainment and different perspectives on life and current events:

> Young men travelled for a handful of years in search of knowledge …
> to gain training in specialist skills needed in rural society … [which]
> included healing, fighting, singing and dancing, divination, and expertise
> in knowing and influencing the various forces, particularly malevolent
> forces, which controlled the environment of the village.[32]

The desired training was sought out from teachers either in the hills and forests, or in the cultural centers of Laos and Cambodia. Knowledge of herbs, tattoos, incantations, and other spiritual-medicinal practices were particularly valued for prevention and treatment of disease and injury.

Buddhist religious practices in Isan also differ in some ways from those in the rest of Thailand. For example, the forest tradition is reputed to be particularly strong in Isan. A theological comparison of Isan and other regions would be out of place here; however, there are some relevant aspects of the role of Buddhism in Isan particularly as it relates to education and literature.[33]

Until the 20th century, formal education was provided, for those who sought it out, by the temple. Young boys would ordain as novices for a season or a few years, studying Pali and the Buddhist scriptures. Some few individuals remained at the temple to become monks, or came to the temple in adulthood to ordain as monks. The Pali canon, *jataka* stories, and even local folktales (often masquerading as *jataka* stories) were recorded and transcribed on palm leaf manuscripts. These were read, actually chanted, at festivals throughout the year, and the stories were known to everyone in the community. While nearly all males would ordain for some period of time, many did not acquire and maintain the skills required to continue reading and writing. Thus literacy was confined primarily to men, and then generally only those few who remained in the monkhood for a long period.[34] There was no royal court where scribes and poets were educated and supported (as in the Central Plains). Interestingly, to this day Isan has low rates and levels

---

[32] Ibid.

[33] Details on Buddhist education in Isan can be found in Justin McDaniel, *Gathering Leaves and Lifting Words: Histories of Monastic Education in Laos and Thailand* (Seattle, WA: University of Washington Press, 2008).

[34] These monks were given titles by villagers and later retained them (or related titles) as forms of address after returning to lay status. See Fallon, *Peasants of Isan*, p. 292.

of education, and women are still rare in the writing profession (though not the teaching profession).

Now, however, general education has been taken over by the central government. While manuscripts in the Lao language and various Lao scripts still exist in temples throughout Isan, few monks stay long enough to learn the scripts, and in any case there is very little interest. Chanting recitations are sometimes still performed, but the practice is dying out since, for the most part, interest is confined to the elderly, who still hope to gain merit, as well as enjoyment, from hearing the stories. As Koret states in his monumental study of the subject, "In northeastern Thailand, even the monks cannot generally read the ancient scripts and [thus] rely on printed texts [in Thai] for their sermons. The art of transcribing manuscripts is known by few."[35] Many of the stories survive, however, as *mo' lam* recordings sold in shops all over Isan, and are still widely known.

Historical Aspects

Parts of Isan have been under the control or influence of various states, kingdoms, and empires over the last 15 centuries or so. Evidence of the different cultures that have existed in Isan remains, some weak and some strong, to this day. Cave and cliff paintings, for example, in Udorn and Ubon, and the well-known excavations of the Ban Chiang civilization, show an early human presence in the region dating back thousands of years.[36] History in the region begins in the sixth century AD, when the Chenla kingdom replaced the Funan and held sway over what is now eastern Isan and nearby areas of Laos and Cambodia. Further west in the Chaophraya valley was the Mon state of Dvaravati, and further east the Cham kingdom. In the eighth century, however, Chenla split, and by the ninth century the Angkor empire arose under Jayavarman II.[37] According to Hall, Angkor was also known as Yasodharapura;[38] this name is now used for the modern-day town and province of Yasothorn in Isan.

---

[35] Peter Koret, "Whispered So Softly It Resounds through the Forest, Spoken So Loudly It Can Hardly be Heard: The Art of Parallelism in Traditional Lao Literature," PhD thesis, SOAS, University of London, 1994, p. 17.

[36] Srisakara Vallibhotama, *A Northeastern Site of Civilization* (Bangkok: Matichon, 1997), p. 19.

[37] D.G.E. Hall, *A History of South-East Asia*, 4th edition (London: Macmillan, 1994), pp. 107–21.

[38] Ibid., p. 121.

Over the next several centuries until the 1300s, when it was attacked by Ayuthaya and subsequently abandoned, Angkor extended its territory over a huge area, reaching as far west as present-day Lopburi and even Kanchanaburi. It also provided aid to the Lao prince Fa Ngum, thus enabling him in 1353 to unify Laos and establish the kingdom of Lan Xang, including all of what today is Isan except for part of Korat.[39] Of the many monuments built throughout the Angkor empire at the time, many remain today in Korat, Buri Ram, and in fact all the way through southern Isan to Ubon. Thais often refer to this Khmer civilization in what is now Central Thailand as Lopburi civilization, and its presence in Korat, Buri Ram, etc., as ancient Isan culture.

In the meantime, Sukhothai was emerging, and in 1238 the Khmer commander was defeated at Sukhothai by two Tai princes. King Ramkhamhaeng's rule began in 1283; as Hall states, "the majority of [his] subjects must have been Mons and Khmers, and from them he adopted the … Sukodaya script … [which] had a strong influence also upon the development of writing in the Lao states."[40] An inscription, written after the purported date of the famous Ramkhamhaeng stone, claims that Ramkhamhaeng's rule reached as far east as Viengchan, but this remains unverified.[41]

Ayuthaya, the "first Siamese kingdom," was founded in the 14th century and in 1350 crowned its first king, Ramathibodi. Soon it was contesting for territory and subjects with both the Burmese and the Khmer. According to Grabowsky, much of the interior of Isan was uninhabited for centuries, from the early 1200s.[42] He suggests that only with the disintegration of Lan Xang, starting in the early 1700s, did significant migration into and settlement of central Isan occur. Then Champasak extended its influence to Ubon and Roi Et, while Kui and upland Khmer populations increased in southern Isan. Ayuthaya grew in strength as Lan Xang diminished, but even by the time of the fall of the former in 1767, "Siamese influence hardly reached beyond Korat, [which] had been founded by King Narai in 1657."[43] After the start of the Rattanakosin era in Thonburi, King Taksin had Viengchan destroyed as punishment for "disloyalty" (that is, for siding with the Burmese after the destruction of Ayuthaya). The leader of the military expedition against

---

[39] Keyes, *Isan*, p. 7.
[40] Hall, 1994, *History of Southeast Asia*, pp. 186–8.
[41] Ibid.
[42] Grabowsky, "The Isan," p. 111.
[43] Ibid., p. 115.

Viengchan was General Chakri, later Rama I, founder of the current Chakri dynasty.[44] Champasak and Viengchan became vassal states of the Siamese, but their territories, including Isan, remained distant from Siamese power, attention, and influence.

In 1827, Jao Anu, joined by the leaders of Ubon (his son) and Roi Et, led a military force against Siam.[45] The fighting lasted a year and a half, and ended with the Laos' defeat. Jao Anu was eventually captured and taken to Bangkok, where, according to Hall, he is said to have been kept in a cage for four years until he died.[46] Stuart-Fox alternatively reports that Jao Anu survived in the cage only a fraction of that time and was forced daily to avow the munificence of the Siamese king, while being accompanied in the cage by torture devices and sometimes by his own children.[47] His action against Bangkok is referred to by Thais as a rebellion, while Laotians describe it as a war either to free Lao captives from the Thai central plain or to stop further dismantling of the Lao kingdom.[48] In any case, in retaliation the Siamese "made a complete holocaust of Viengchan," utterly destroying it, and then "proceeded methodically to devastate the whole kingdom, drawing off the population to repopulate areas of their own kingdom."[49] In the 30 years after the Jao Anu war, more than 100,000 people moved from the so-called "left bank" of the Mekong (i.e., left when facing downstream). The war and its aftermath produced resentments that continued to be felt for generations. Isan, and particularly Isan elites, became tainted with suspicion in the eyes of Bangkok rulers and officials.[50] Lao and Isan people, for their part, did not forget the destruction of their capital nor the forced migration inflicted by the Siamese forces.

Even after the defeat of Jao Anu, though, Siamese control and influence in Isan remained nominal, in fact "so much so that foreigners who visited the region doubted that [they] at all existed."[51] Isan was still ruled by local noble lineages with little or no overall unity. As Fallon states:

---

[44] Keyes, *Isan*, p. 10.

[45] Hall, *History of Southeast Asia*, p. 473.

[46] Ibid., p. 474.

[47] Martin Stuart-Fox, *The Lao Kingdom of Lan Xang: Rise and Decline* (Bangkok: White Lotus, 1998), pp. 126–7.

[48] Grabowsky, "The Isan," p. 118.

[49] Hall, *History of Southeast Asia*, p. 474.

[50] Fallon, *Peasants of Isan*, p. 203.

[51] Erik Cohen, *Thai Society in Comparative Perspective* (Bangkok: White Lotus, 1991), p. 70.

These regional rulers were largely left to their own devices regarding administrative matters, their major obligations being to supply tribute to Bangkok on a regular basis and to preserve order in their domains. Strong encouragement was given to the appointed rulers of towns closer to the Mekong to attract settlers from the opposite bank, thereby denying population in areas subject to Vietnamese influence and increasing the number providing tribute to Bangkok.[52]

The reign of Rama V, King Chulalongkorn (r. 1868–1910), shaped and changed Isan more than any other period in its history up to that point, and in ways that are still acutely felt to this day. Probably the most visible development was the establishment, in the 1893 treaty with France, of the Thai border with Laos. All Lao areas on the "left" bank of the Mekong were ceded to France, and in 1904, Sanyabouly and Champasak also passed to French control.[53] This meant that Lao people in Isan became politically separated from their cultural centers of Luang Phabang, Viengchan, and Champasak,[54] and instead fell directly under the authority of the Thai monarchy. Indeed, even before the 1893 Treaty, King Chulalongkorn had begun to make his influence felt in Isan.

The administrative reforms ordered by King Rama V and implemented by Prince Damrong were to have far-reaching effects and implications. As Keyes has described, the first changes made were in nomenclature. The northern and northeastern areas of Siam had previously been called Lao country, with people of the former called "black-bellied Lao" and those of the latter "white-bellied Lao" based on whether or not the men there tattooed their abdomens and thighs. These regions were organized into *monthon* (administrative spheres) in about 1890, with the two *monthon* in the northeast called *Monthon Lao Phuan* and *Monthon Lao Khao* based on the ethnic groups living there. By 1892, however, these names had been changed to *Monthon Udorn* and *Monthon Isan* respectively, thus referring to them by their location in the kingdom, northern and northeastern[55] (as opposed to *Phayap*, the northwest, meaning the Chiang Mai region). This was in line with Chulalongkorn's stated policy that the Lao people in Thailand were really Thai and not Lao at all.[56] In fact, he "forbade the use of the word

---

[52] Fallon, *Peasants of Isan*, p. 189.

[53] Keyes, *Isan*, p. 12.

[54] Fallon, *Peasants of Isan*, p. 199.

[55] "Isan" later came to refer to the entire northeastern region, with "north Isan" and "south Isan" referring to its two parts.

[56] Charles Keyes, "Hegemony and Resistance in Northeastern Thailand," in *Regions*, ed. Grabowsky, pp. 154–6.

'Lao' in census reports."[57] Thus, through administrative fiat by the central government, the ethnic identity of the inhabitants of northeastern Siam was simply erased and replaced with a geographical identity defined with respect to Bangkok and the whole country. This became the official government position, and has remained so ever since. As Keyes states this policy:

> Such people are 'Thai', not some other distinctive group which might aspire to nationhood separate from that of the Thai ... There is nothing in Prince Damrong's account [of the reforms] which shows any indication that how peoples living in the outlying regions of the country thought of themselves had any relevance for determining how they should be integrated within the Thai nation-state.[58]

The reason behind these reforms, not surprisingly, had nothing to do with a desire to improve the lives of people in Isan. Indeed, Tej states his belief that "the achievements of the Ministry of the Interior under Prince Damrong ... was one of the factors which helped Siam to survive as an independent nation in an age of imperialism."[59] In other words, only under threat from other nations did Siam make any effort to assert real control over the distant, unproductive, and otherwise undesirable Isan region. Denying the Lao ancestry of Isan people deprived the French of their justification for claims, already opposed by Siam, that Lao people in Siam actually belonged to French Indochina.[60]

The administrative system set up by the central government to enhance its control of the northeast (and other regions), called the *Thesaphiban* system, was developed between 1892 and 1899 and implemented from 1899 onwards.[61] The core of the reform was the replacement of autonomous local nobility with civil servants who were chosen and sent from the center to fill essentially all official positions. It was at this time that the term *phu wa ratchakan*, glossed by Tej as "one who is acting in the royal service," was first used,[62] thus emphasizing that central authority was being exercised.

---

[57] Kanala Eksaengsri, "Political Change and Modernization: Northeast Thailand's Quest for Identity and Its Potential Threat to National Security," PhD diss., State University of New York at Binghamton, 1977, p. 209.

[58] Keyes, "Hegemony," p. 156.

[59] Tej Bunnag, *The Provincial Administration of Siam 1892–1915* (Kuala Lumpur: Oxford University Press, 1977), p. v.

[60] Thongchai Winichakul, *Siam Mapped* (Honolulu: University of Hawai'i Press, 1994), p. 165.

[61] Tej, *Provincial Administration*, pp. vi, 118.

[62] Ibid., p. 119.

He continues:

> Furthermore, the provincial nobility were also deprived of their
> traditional sources of livelihood, for they were forbidden to engage in
> tax-farms or in business. They were not allowed to have any other source
> of income besides their salaries.[63]

Resistance to the reforms and to central Siamese authority in general
arose in the northeastern region in various forms, notably as millennial
movements lead by *phu mi bun* ผู้มีบุญ, or "people having merit."[64] Such
movements have a history stretching back centuries, and their appearance
is foretold in prophecies.[65] One of the earliest (recorded) of these was
led by a Lao man named Bun Kwang in Korat in 1699; he was finally
lured to Saraburi and defeated, then taken to Ayuthaya to be executed.[66]
In 1901–1902, at least a hundred such figures appeared in Isan, in part a
response, according to Ishii, to "agricultural failure and … exploitative
local authorities."[67] It was believed that a *phu mi bun* "would someday
appear in this world in a miraculous way to establish a utopian [Buddhist]
rule."[68] Often this coming was heralded by traveling *mo' lam* singers and
in palm leaf manuscripts, the copying of which was believed to bring merit
to the faithful. Stories surrounding the acclaimed figures foretold of strange
occurrences, like the transformation of buffaloes into ogres and soil into
gold. Ong Man, a millennial leader who emerged in the Ubon area in 1902,
amassed a huge following and eventually commanded as many as 2,000
troops, who believed that his magic would render them invulnerable to
bullets, knives, and other harm.[69] Like other such leaders, he was in the end
defeated and his followers killed or dispersed. Although severely suppressed,
phu mi bun have continued to appear up until the present day. Even now,
there are a number of ordained and lay figures in Isan, Laos, and the Shan
States who claim, or whose followers claim, that they are Phra Sri An, the
Maitreya or Buddha of the future.

---

[63] Ibid.

[64] Pejoratively referred to by the authorities as ผีบุญ or "phantoms of merit."

[65] For an in-depth new study on prophetic literature in the Lao tradition, see Peter
Koret, *Lao Literature of Buddhist Prophecy* (Poughkeepise: Benefit of the Doubt
Press, forthcoming).

[66] Yoneo Ishii, "A Note on Buddhistic Millenarian Revolts in Northeastern Siam,"
in *Southeast Asia: Nature, Society, and Development*, ed. S. Ichimura (Honolulu:
University of Hawai'i Press, 1976), pp. 67–8.

[67] Ibid., p. 71.

[68] Ibid., p. 68.

[69] Ibid., pp. 68–9.

Another major way in which the central government exerted control over the northeast was through the Sangha. The Sangha Act of 1902 established the authority of senior Siamese monks over monks in the northeast, according to Keyes.

> Local monks were also compelled, by the same act, to adopt a religious curriculum prepared by Prince Patriarch Vajiranyana, a brother of King Chulalongkorn. Despite their subordination to the Siamese dominated sangha, most northeastern monks still continued, however, to perpetuate a Lao ritual tradition.[70]

Until late in the 20th century, as Fallon notes, support for temple construction in Isan villages was controlled by the Department of Religious Affairs of the Ministry of Education, which promulgated regulations concerning design and materials. Monetary donations were encouraged while in-kind contributions were reduced, resulting in fewer villagers' carvings and designs being incorporated into new temples. This produced a homogenization and sameness of appearance of newer temple buildings in line with the standards and dictates of officials in Bangkok.[71]

Central Thai political control has also been extended in the last century with the expansion of communications (telegraph) and transport lines, thereby making Bangkok the economic focal point of the region as well as the political center. According to Keyes, in 1895, messages from Bangkok to Korat (by horseback and boat) took eight or nine days, and to Nong Khai or Ubon 12 days; but by 1900 the train line to Korat was completed, reducing message time to one day. The Ubon line was finished in 1928, and Khon Kaen in 1933.[72]

Even more important, however, were the educational reforms instituted under King Vajiravudh. As Cohen points out, "the language of education was Thai rather than the local Lao [or Khmer, Kui, etc.] dialect, and civil rituals such as homage to the flag became an important component of the curriculum."[73] The use of local languages and scripts was discouraged and later prohibited, and as the state schools increasingly took over the role of education from local Buddhist temples, Lao literary knowledge and influence declined. In addition, the schools' curriculum was dictated by the central Ministry of Education, which was thereby able to ensure that only

---

[70] Keyes, "Hegemony," p. 159.
[71] Fallon, *Peasants of Isan*, p. 293.
[72] Keyes, *Isan*, pp. 18–9.
[73] Cohen, *Thai Society*, p. 73.

approved versions of history, politics, and culture were taught. As Koret explains,

> The teaching of the history or culture of ethnic groups other than the Thai has been restricted within Thailand due to the belief that it would encourage regional separatism. This has resulted in the fact that the people of northeastern Thailand have been taught to look down upon their own culture and have little awareness that they have any history separate from that of the Thai.[74]

In 1933 the new national parliament was opened, and the regions gained representation in the capital. As Keyes notes, "the four leading northeastern MP's [...] were closely associated with the 'liberal' faction in Parliament lead by Pridi Panomyong."[75] In the same year, however, the royalist Boworadet Rebellion, based in Korat, attempted to restore the absolute monarchy. After the rebellion was put down, a number of "anti-government" people, including northeasterners, were arrested and accused of being communists. This was "the first occurrence of suppression of northeastern political leaders by the central government for alleged left-wing activities."[76] Such allegations were to arise repeatedly over the next half-century.

During the Second World War, when the government of Field Marshal Plaek Phibulsongkhram[77] collaborated with the Japanese and allowed them to occupy Thailand, the Seri Thai movement opposing the Japanese "had its strongest bases in northeastern Thailand and here forged links with [...] the Lao Issara,"[78] a Laotian anti-colonial nationalist movement. According to Keyes, this marked the beginning of a Pan-Laoist movement. After the war, a number of Lao Issara leaders and supporters opposing the French re-takeover of Laos fled to Isan. However, in 1947, Plaek led a military coup and re-established an authoritarian government. Any kind of opposition deemed threatening was suppressed, including expressions of regional

---

[74] Koret, *Whispered*, p. 15.

[75] Keyes, "Hegemony," p. 160.

[76] Keyes, *Isan*, p. 23.

[77] Plaek Phibulsongkhram has somehow become the only Thai prime minister to be commonly referred to by a portion of his conferred title rather than by his first name. For the sake of consistency, I will refer to him as "Plaek," rather than "Phibul." At the time of his promotion to captain in the army, he was given the title *Luang*, and assumed the accompanying appellation, Phibulsongkhram. His real name was Plaek Kittasangka. See Judith Stowe, *Siam Becomes Thailand* (Honolulu: University of Hawai'i Press, 1991).

[78] Keyes, 1995, "Hegemony," p. 160.

culture, which might lead to separatism. Many Isan people supported Pridi and parliamentary rule and thus opposed Plaek, who they already disliked in part for conscripting their fellow northeasterners to build the road to Petchabun (where he wanted to move the capital).[79]

With Pridi in exile and blamed for the death of King Rama VIII, his northeastern supporters were denounced as anti-king, as threats to Thai autonomy, etc. Five Isan MP's were arrested and charged with plotting a separatist movement to join the northeast to Indochina in a communist Southeast Asian Union,[80] but were then released. After the pro-Pridi counter-coup attempt in 1949, a number of Seri Thai leaders were shot dead in their homes. Three of the MPs were re-arrested and then died of gunshot wounds, allegedly "while trying to escape," in the notorious Kilo 11 Incident.[81] At that time, the stereotype propounded by government radio broadcast was that the northeastern leaders were "rebellious," "enemies of democracy," and "spreaders of Communism."[82] Later in 1949, two more Isan MPs were arrested on charges of separatism, but later freed. One, Tiang Sirikham, was elected in 1949 while under indictment and then re-elected in 1952. Soon afterward he disappeared, claimed by a newspaper to have escaped after hatching a new plot with Communist conspirators. He is generally believed to have been killed by the hated and feared Police General Pao, who is thought to have been responsible for hundreds of killings over several years as part of his role keeping Plaek in power. Some northeasterners joined former Lao Issara members and fled to Laos, including Maha Sila Viravong, originally from Roi Et,[83] who later became probably the most renowned scholar and proponent of Lao literature and culture, and whose daughters carry on the tradition in Laos today.

Suppression of local culture under Plaek was carried out in other contexts as well. On August 2, 1939, a government announcement was made, as follows:

> As the Government is of the opinion that the names *by which the Thais* in some parts of the country have been called do not correspond to the name of the race and the preference of the people so called, and also that

---

[79] Keyes, 1967, *Isan*, p. 32.

[80] This is quite different from the Southeast Asia League, a kind of forerunner to ASEAN. See Christopher Goscha, *Thailand and the Southeast Asian Networks of the Vietnamese Revolution 1885–1954* (London: Routledge, 1998).

[81] They were shot to death while in police custody on an empty stretch of road outside the capital with no other witnesses.

[82] Ibid., pp. 32–4.

[83] Keyes, "Hegemony," p. 161.

the appellation of the Thai people by dividing them into many groups, such as the Northern Thais, the Northeastern Thais, the Southern Thais, Islamic Thais, is not appropriate for Thailand is one and indivisible.

It thereby, notifies that the State Preference is as follows:

1. Do not call the Thais in contradiction to the name of the race or those referred to.
2. Use the word 'Thai' for all of the Thais without any of the above-mentioned distinctions.[84]

The claim to be in line with "the preference of the people," and the claim that, in Diller's words, "one could eradicate a dialect [and ethnic group] by eradicating its name,"[85] might be seen, along with many of Plaek's cultural edicts, as absurd and even silly. However, they underlie a pattern of repressive, intimidating, and violent practices by the government. For example, the above decree was accompanied by "rigorous enforcement of Central Thai ... as the national medium of instruction," which included the burning of materials written in Lao and other regional scripts.[86]

In 1957, General Sarit took over the government, sending into exile Pao and Plaek, whose government was accused of rigging the recent national elections. Sarit's mother was a northeasterner from Mukdahan, and his father had spent many years in the northeast in the course of his duties as an army officer. Sarit himself lived in Mukdahan for four years, between the ages of three and seven, with his mother and her family.[87] He was thus probably the only prime minister in Thai history to have been brought up, if only partially, in Lao culture in the northeast; indeed it is extremely likely that he was fluent in Lao language during that period. However, this fact seems to have had little influence on his later behavior; a better indication of his attitudes and motivation is the fact that he served as Minister of Defense under Plaek, and his deputy for a time was Thanom Kittikachorn,[88] who later became a similarly notorious prime minister, known for suppressing and killing dissenters, including those of Isan origin. Thus, a certain continuity in how Isan was perceived and treated over several decades by successive governments is indicated by the direct line in military authoritarian regimes.

---

[84] Thak Chaloemtiarana, ed, *Thai Politics: Extracts and Documents 1932–1957* (Bangkok: Social Science Association of Thailand, 1978), pp. 246–7.

[85] Diller, "What Makes," p. 106.

[86] Ibid.

[87] Thak, *Thai Politics*, pp. 681–3.

[88] This rendering of his name in roman script, though unsatisfactory, is the most commonly used.

Sarit's medical treatment in the US and England soon after taking power led to a period of "considerable political freedom" from 1957 to 1958.[89] In 1958, all the northeastern MPs in the pro-government party presented an ultimatum to the government, stating that if their demands were not met, they would leave the party and form a separate Northeastern Party. Their demands were: 1) an urgent short project to relieve suffering and hunger in Isan; 2) longer-term projects such as hydro-electric development; 3) the establishment of heavy industry in Isan; and 4) an increase in educational facilities. While no resignations occurred when the demands were not met, there was a meeting of 21 MPs from 12 of the 15 northeastern provinces and representing leftist, pro-government, and independent parties, who approved in principle that "only through socialism can conditions in the northeast be improved."[90] It was at this point that references to a "Northeast problem" started to become frequent in both government and foreign development contexts.

When Sarit returned to Thailand in 1958, he led a coup against his own government and ended the relatively free conditions that had prevailed in his absence. Five Isan MPs were arrested for having made trips to China and the USSR, while two others took refuge in Laos. In fact, the civil war in Laos had begun to concern the Thai government, which increasingly viewed Isan as potentially dangerous to Thailand. There was a fear that underdevelopment in the region might engender support for regionalism, insurrection, and separatism, which would in turn attract support from Laotian, North Vietnamese, and Chinese Communists.[91]

A Committee on Development of the Northeast was set up in 1960 with Sarit as its chair, its stated goal being to improve the standard of living of the people and increase "future economic stability and progress," as well as to establish that Isan was "an integral and inseparable part of the Kingdom of Thailand" and its people "Thai nationals."[92] The real purpose, however, was to intensify central government influence and control over the region. As has been pointed out elsewhere, little benefit seemed to accrue to northeasterners, whose increased contact with central officials merely resulted in increased exploitation, ill treatment, and corruption.[93] Indeed, there was little change

---

[89] Keyes, *Isan*, p. 43.
[90] Quoted in Keyes, *Isan*, p. 49.
[91] Ibid., p. 51.
[92] Keyes, "Hegemony," p. 163.
[93] Ibid., and David Morell and Chai-anan Samudavanija, *Political Conflict in Thailand: Reform Reaction Revolution* (Cambridge, MA: Delgeschlager, Guna, and Hain, 1981).

from the past when Bangkok "dominated the northeast in a colonial manner: taxes were levied, natural resources and agricultural goods were extracted and local labor was mobilized for military service and public projects."[94] Thus instead of improving the livelihood of Isan people, the government ended up further alienating and antagonizing them.[95] Projects that did produce results, such as the establishment of Khon Kaen as the "capital" of the northeast, or the founding of Khon Kaen University, often had little relevance to villagers' needs; this is hardly surprising as the villagers were never consulted.

As tensions with, and bad feeling toward, Bangkok increased under Sarit, government control remained tight, and since there were no legitimate avenues for political dissent, all dissent was seen by the Thai government as part of a Communist conspiracy to overthrow it. In 1961, government raids resulted in the arrest of alleged Communist agents (over 100 in December alone) in northeastern towns including Sakon Nakorn, the pro-government MP of which had been executed earlier that year as a Communist organizer. The December raid marked the first "battle" between government forces and local "Communists," northeasterners whom the government claimed were trained and controlled by the Pathet Lao, as the Communists in Laos called themselves.

The perceived threat of Communism in Thailand and its relation to similar movements in Laos, Vietnam, and to a lesser extent Cambodia, attracted the attention of the U.S. government. Both Plaek's and Sarit's avowed anti-Communism qualified them for instant and unquestioned American government friendship and aid. Since Americans were willing and even eager to support all kinds of counter-insurgency activities, successive governments in Thailand were equally pleased to exaggerate the Communist threat in order to maximize the financial and military assistance they received.[96] Massive resources and American "expertise" were channeled into four main kinds of efforts: 1) infrastructure projects, particularly roads like the Friendship Highway from Bangkok to Korat; 2) rural development programs, especially agricultural projects; 3) propaganda drives to cement allegiance to the Thai nation and king; and 4) research, predominantly social science studies of the northeast, which until then was largely an unknown area academically.[97]

[94] Luther, "Regional Identity," p. 185.
[95] Keyes, "Hegemony," p. 164.
[96] Cohen, *Thai Society*, p. 79.
[97] Ibid., pp. 79–80.

Another major impact of American involvement resulted from the American military bases at Korat, Udorn, Ubon, and Nakorn Phanom. According to Cohen, a third of Isan's GDP between 1967 and 1972 was attributable to US military spending.[98] Thousands of northeasterners were employed directly or indirectly by the bases. While the economic benefits to the northeast were enormous, the social effects were more problematic. For most northeasterners, American GIs provided their first contact with Westerners. These soldiers were generally either on Rest and Recuperation leave, or were about to be sent into active duty in or over Laos or Vietnam, unsure if they would return alive. In either case, they were looking to have fun and often had money to spend. These and perhaps other qualities frequently endeared them to northeasterners, many of whom, three or four decades later, still express fond memories of Americans they knew.[99] On the other hand, prostitution and drug abuse flourished around the bases, and the toll on local town and village communities was undoubtedly high. When the bases closed in the early 1970s in response to Thai political pressure and declining American involvement in Indochina, the economy of the northeast suffered a tremendous blow with lasting consequences.[100]

The demonstrations of October 1973 ushered in a new era of political and intellectual freedom in Thailand, and one in which Isan played an important role. With Thanom and Praphas sent into exile, open discussion of ideas proliferated, and a vast range of books and pamphlets of all political types, particularly on the left, became available. However, reaction to these freedoms and to communist activities, both real and imagined, also increased, with frequent assassinations of labor and political leaders. Criticism of all kinds of government activity, including that of the Internal Security Operations Command (which was in charge of internal security), reached levels never before seen in Thailand. When the Isan village of Ban Na Sai, in Nong Khai Province, was burned to the ground by Border Patrol Police and village defense volunteers as an allegedly communist stronghold, the People for Democracy Group investigated and produced evidence (which included bringing Na Sai villagers to Bangkok) that contradicted the

---

[98] Ibid., p. 80.

[99] From time to time in Isan or Bangkok, I meet Northeasterners with experiences dating from this time; they are generally men in their fifties or older (who often speak unusually good English) and who express apparently strong and sincere positive feelings about American friends and co-workers from the period.

[100] Cohen, 1991, *Thai Society*, pp. 80–1.

government's claims and suggested instead that the village was destroyed without provocation and its residents badly treated.[101]

The rightist backlash reached a head in October 1976 with a massacre and crackdown on perceived liberals and leftists. According to Girling, about 1,500 students and other young intellectuals fled to the jungle and joined the communist movement in the next six months.[102] Thus, as a reactionary dictatorship gained power in the capital, the leftist insurgency grew in the hinterlands. By 1977, all but two of the northeast provinces were "Declared Infiltrated,"[103] and many of the communists' bases were located in Isan. Interestingly, government propaganda at the time, including songs played on state and military radio stations, portrayed communist insurgents in Thailand as un-Thai. Such characterization dates from the 1940s and 1950s, when communists in Thailand were seen as either Chinese, Vietnamese, or Lao.[104] The approximately 40,000 Vietnamese living in Thailand, many of whom settled in Isan in the 1950s, have periodically been denounced as "spies," "terrorists," and "communists," even though no reliable evidence for the claims has ever been produced.[105] Thus, when the Communist Party of Thailand collapsed and its followers emerged from the jungle under a government amnesty program in the early 1980s, they returned to a society that viewed them not only as belonging to a failed movement, but as fundamentally antithetical to Thai-ness. The Isan people who had been in the jungle had never been ethnically Thai to begin with, and so were even another level outside of the Thai center.

At the end of the 20th century, Isan's political role continued to change. Politicians in Bangkok recognized the size of Isan's population and its resulting significance as a potential voting block. General Chavalit Yongchaiyudh became prime minister when his New Aspiration Party came to power in the mid 1990s in part as a result of votes cast in Isan, to which he had claimed a relationship. His attempt to woo Isan voters dates back to the late 1980s and his *Isan Khiow* อีสานเขียว or Green Isan development plan, which he touted from his position as head of the army. Keyes notes that after a rival military faction took power in the coup of 1991, the Green Isan program was "first scaled back and then declared to have been

---

[101] Morell and Chai-anan, *Political Conflict*, pp. 169–70.

[102] Girling, *Thailand*, p. 274.

[103] Ibid., p. 261.

[104] Chai-anan Samudavanija. "State Identity Creation, State-Building and Civil Society," in *National Identity*, ed. C. Reynolds, p. 73.

[105] Girling, *Thailand*, p. 268.

completed."[106] In October 1998, a newspaper was launched called *Meuang Isan* เมืองอีสาน or *Isan Land*,[107] alluding, ironically enough, to the idea of Isan as a separate country. Supported entirely by funds from Chavalit's *Phak Khwam Wang Mai* พรรคความหวังใหม่, or New Aspiration Party (NAP), it "sings Chavalit's praises and tears Chuan Leekpai [the prime minister who replaced him] to pieces."[108] The editor, Thittikorn Thetsrimuang, claimed that:

> [T]he paper was born from the initiatives of northeastern journalists [... and] wants to make northeastern people proud of their region and help them come together to have more political bargaining power. Now, we're supporting NAP because we see it as the party with policies that would help the northeastern people.[109]

This would seem rather to indicate the aspirations of NAP: to help itself by binding Isan people into an electoral unit and thereby increasing the party's power.

Attitudes

While physical facts and historical events are important in distinguishing Isan as a region, prevailing attitudes in society are at least as significant, if not more so. The way Isan people see themselves and the rest of Thailand, and the way they are seen by Thais in Bangkok and other parts of the country, can give a strong indication of the reality of Isan and its relation to Thai society as a whole. Moreover, it is these attitudes, in combination with the more objective aspects of Isan regionality, that shape modern Isan literature and the role it plays in Thailand in general and in the Thai literary world in particular.

Bangkok has set the tone for Thai attitudes toward Isan. Central governments of the 20th century have all taken a paternalistic and condescending attitude toward northeasterners, reflecting a view first enunciated

---

[106] Keyes, "Hegemony," p. 171.

[107] Anon., "เมืองอีสาน" แห่งทุ่งทานตะวัน. เนชั่นสุดสัปดาห์ 7, 333 (22–28 ต.ค. 2541) (1998a): 4.

[108] Prakobpong Panapool, "Isan Paper Good News — For NAP," *The Nation* [Bangkok], October 19, 1998. p. 1.

[109] Ibid., p. 1. The newspaper was reported to have a cover price of 25 baht but to be offered free initially. However, on several occasions in 1998–1999 when I looked for it both in Bangkok and some provinces in Isan, I was unable to find it and no one knew anything about it.

under Rama V and Prince Damrong.[110] Such opinions later became common among ordinary citizens, magnified no doubt by simple urban-rural divisions as well. Isan people are regularly seen as poor, uneducated, country bumpkins who make convenient and deserving objects of ridicule. In television shows, they are depicted as "impoverished, un-beautiful, unintelligent and uneducated, but good workers."[111] Vatcharin sums up the standard Bangkok view of Isan in the recent past:

> As for the Northeast, that was definitely a closed book. Indeed everyone in Bangkok did their best to avoid going there. Isan [...] was a notorious punishment post for civil servants and soldiers, a strange forbidding place of droughts and floods, of famine and neglect. Its people were not Thai as we were, but Lao [...]. Of course, we knew what the Isan people were like, as thousands of them were obliged to migrate south in search of work [...]. [It was] a region where any food product was in short supply.[112]

Isan as a parched, infertile, forbidding, and backward place is a standard refrain in many accounts. Keyes describes a guide put out by the Thai Fine Arts Department stating that, "It is amazing that in a land famous for its barrenness there should be so much evidence of a rich cultural heritage everywhere."[113] A Chulalongkorn University publication on Thai worldview denies difference by referring to a "Siamese Great Tradition" that "includes the core features of all culture areas [of the country]," and goes on to state that "the world view described in this volume is generally applicable to Thai people everywhere in the Kingdom."[114] Another writer, describing a trip to Isan in 1998, refers to the region as "having customs and a sub-culture [or "minor culture" อนุวัฒนธรรม] and ancient artifacts a thousand years old."[115] This myth of Isan culture (as well as Lao culture in Laos) being a

---

[110] Keyes, "Hegemony," pp. 170–1.

[111] Annette Hamilton, "Rumours, Foul Calumnies, and the Safety of the State: Mass Media and National Identity in Thailand," in *National Identity*, ed. C. Reynolds, p. 367.

[112] Vatcharin Bhumichitr, *Vatch's Southeast Asian Cookbook* (London: Kyle Cathie, 1997), p. 25.

[113] Quoted in Keyes, "Hegemony," p. 170.

[114] Chulalongkorn University, *Traditional and Changing Thai World View* (Bangkok: Southeast Asian Studies Program and Chulalongkorn University Social Research Institute, 1985), pp. v–vi.

[115] โมน สวัสดิ์ศรี, "สัญจรพบ 'นักเขียนอีสาน' 5 จังหวัด (2)," เนชั่นสุดสัปดาห์ 8, 343 (31 ธ.ค. 2541–6 ม. ค. 2542): 48.

faded, older, lesser (though perhaps purer and more authentic) version of Thai culture is so pervasive that it even finds its way into the most popular Western guidebook to Thailand:

> In many ways, the north-eastern region of Thailand is the kingdom's heartland. The older Thai [*sic*] customs remain more intact here than elsewhere in the country. [...] the pace is slower, the people friendlier, and inflation less effective [...] than in Thailand's other main regions. [...] Many of the people living in this area speak Lao or a Thai dialect that is very close to Lao.[116]

A Bangkok newspaper report in 1999 described how Isan people eat the most *som tam* in Thailand, even though the papaya plant's need for "fertile soil and abundant water" make it "not suitable for Isan.[117] The implied disdain for Isan people, as if they cannot choose a proper diet for themselves, is further indicated by the article's title, "The Love of Isan." Not only Isan people, but also Laotian nationals are ridiculed in ways that other ethnic groups and neighboring countries are not. For example, *The Nation* [Bangkok] published an article in which the director of the ITV cable station apologized to Laotian athletes participating in the Asian Games sports competition after deeply offending the Laotian *sepak takraw* coach by suggesting that the Lao players had no intention of winning the competition and "seemed to have forgotten their mother tongue" when they were heard singing Thai songs.[118]

Slights to Isan people and culture do not, of course, pass unnoticed, and Isan people are well aware of the prejudices against them. Isan responses are expressed in a great variety of ways and contexts. A Lao proverb (in poetic form) collected in Isan by Phra Srithammasophon states, "The worst suffering is the death of one's child, the second is the death of one's wife, the third is to leave one's relatives and flee to a distant place, [and the] fourth is to [have to] go down to the Central Thai plains to trade."[119] Here Central Thailand is understood to be a separate place; traveling to it involves subjecting oneself to difficulty for necessary material gain, usually for the sake of one's family but probably somewhat in conflict with the Buddhist

---

[116] Joe Cummings, *Thailand: A Travel Survival Kit* (Hawthorn, Victoria: Lonely Planet, 1990), p. 265.

[117] Anon., "The Love of Isan," *The Nation* [Bangkok], June 10, 1999.

[118] Anon., "Network Gives Apology to Lao Athletes," *The Nation* [Bangkok], December 12, 1998.

[119] พระศรีธรรมโสภน, ภาษิตโบราณอีสาณ. อุบลฯ: ศิริธรรม, 2500, p. 5.

ideal against appetitive thought and deed. Thus such travel represents a last resort, associated with danger, uncertainty for the family left behind, and suffering for the departer.

Isan reactions and self-awareness are expressed in modern daily life as well. A researcher at Mahasarakham University reported having heard, in about 1996, a small boy in a village in Isan say in Lao, "I'm not Thai. I'm scared that Thais will eat my gall bladder."[120] Such a sentiment, the researcher stated, was the kind of comment frequently made 20 or 30 years earlier. I heard a similar (though milder) sense of oppression expressed in March 1999, when I boarded a bus in Surin to go to Buri Ram. The air-conditioned coach had started in a town farther east and was stopping briefly in Surin and Buri Ram on its way to Pattaya, its final destination. Several passengers got on in Surin, and the man in front of me, noticing that all the seats were already full, remarked half to me and half to no one in particular (he was traveling by himself), "Pattaya passengers sit, Buri Ram passengers stand" พัทยานั่ง บุรีรัมย์ยืน. In one sense, it was a humorous and friendly remark made to a fellow passenger sharing an inconvenience, but then he repeated it, speaking to all the passengers in general. It then became clearly a statement beyond a simple complaint and spoke rather to the overall status of Buri Ram versus Pattaya, Isan versus Central Thailand. It was both a criticism of the superior position commonly assumed by Central Thais as a matter of course, and a statement of solidarity with other Buri Ram people and perhaps northeasterners more generally.

A more dramatic expression of resistance took place onstage at Ubon Ratchathani University in January 1999. A short story with an Isan setting by Manote Phromsingh, a local writer (see Chapter 6), had been adapted as a short play and was being performed at night after a conference on Thai literature. At the conclusion of the drama, a Bangkok journalist originally from Roi Et named Sumali called all involved up onto the stage. Using a microphone, she acted as master of ceremonies, asking each participant, all of whom were Ubon U. students, to state their name, major, year of study, and part in the play. Periodically Sumali made comments such as, "Who would have thought Ubon U. could have put such a good show together," and, "It's amazing that they did such a good job." She even made the erroneous statement (later corrected) that, "Ubon U. has no Faculty of Arts." She then spoke to the male and female leads, saying that they were "not inferior to professionals" but then asking them if they were nervous, as if

---

[120] กูบ่แม่นไทย กูย้านว่าไทยกินบี้.

they had never acted before. Her behavior, speech, and tone of voice were exactly like those of a Bangkok television show host. Her superior attitude was so noticeable that I became uncertain as to whether she was being herself or imitating a Bangkok television personality for the amusement of the audience.

One of the students she briefly interviewed said he had played the role of a buffalo in the play, and although the entire proceedings were conducted in Thai, he used the Lao word for buffalo, *khuay*, which sounds very much like the common impolite Thai word for "penis." The audience laughed, and Sumali moved on through the line of students on stage. When she finished interviewing the last one, she returned to the student who had played the buffalo, berating him in an attempt to force him to make amends by saying the word "correctly," as she put it. He responded that, "We are in Ubon" (a Lao-speaking area), but she persisted, going so far as to say, half-jokingly, that if he did not correct himself, he would be kicked (literally) off the stage.[121] She even made him say, "We are Thai people; we are in Thailand." As she became more insistent in trying to compel him to change what he had said, he became more quiet and reluctant and the situation became increasingly awkward, but she would not or could not back down. Finally, he said he had played the "buffalo," using the English word, not the Thai. Everyone laughed, and she had to let it go. Whether or not she had meant her impersonation of a Bangkok show host as a parody, either way the situation created was the same: a Bangkok Thai using whatever means were available (in this case, her status and the threat of public humiliation) to try and assert authority over an Ubon Lao in order to limit his self-expression, but meeting with resistance in the form of an insistence on the validity of Lao culture and a refusal (even when pressed) to submit to Thai control.[122]

Bangkok Thais and, to a lesser extent, Thais from other areas, commonly denigrate Isan culture, which occupies the lowest position in the status hierarchy of the country's four regions. Paradoxically, however, certain aspects of Isan culture have been partially adopted and embraced by the center. For example, increasingly since the early 1990s, Isan

---

[121] Probably not a conscious allusion to the *yonbok* incident in which Jit Phumisak was thrown bodily from a stage at Chulalongkorn University in 1953, but an interesting parallel.

[122] In fact, he did offer a compromise by repeating her phrase about being Thais in Thailand, but she remained adamant and unsatisfied; such a scenario can be seen as an exemplar of relations between Isan and Bangkok.

restaurants have proliferated in Bangkok,[123] and many other restaurants that do not claim an Isan affiliation also serve dishes like *lab, nam tok,* and even sticky rice, which have gained wide popularity. This latter type of restaurant, however, often does not prepare the dishes completely in the Isan style, leaving out ingredients like the *maengda* beetle that might prove unappetizing to those unfamiliar with them. *Luk thung* or country music, always popular among rural folk, has in the same period enjoyed resurgence in Bangkok as a uniquely Thai idiom. However, the *mo' lam* origins of much *luk thung* music are rarely acknowledged by Central Thai commentators. A Bangkok radio program conducted in Lao and playing *mo' lam* music was broadcast only in the middle of the night, probably so as not to take up primetime slots, but perhaps also partly because many night jobs as guards, taxi drivers, and construction workers are filled by Isan people. Isan silks, both Lao and Khmer, have become very popular among Bangkok fashion designers and textile collectors. A typical condescending attitude, though, is expressed by Songphan in his book, *Thai Silk, Isan Patterns*, where, in the foreword, he states that he studies Isan weaving for the sake of others all over Thailand.[124] The implication is that Isan culture needs to be discovered and explained by outsiders. A similar viewpoint was conveyed in a show and sale of other Isan crafts at Bangkok's upmarket Thaniya Plaza on November 28, 1998. The exhibition was advertised in the newspaper as, "'The Extraordinary Crafts of Northeastern Thailand', a two-week event that unveils the hidden heritage of Northeastern Thailand."[125] The declared goal of the show, "to nurture and enhance" traditional crafts, suggested that Isan culture was something weak that required both care and improvement.

Isan has not only been misunderstood and condescended to, but also co-opted and used for the center's purposes. An example is the Pak Mun Dam in Ubon Province.[126] There is a perception that the benefits of the plan, in the form of electricity, were always intended to accrue to Bangkok to feed its enormous and growing demand for power. The extra-budgetary costs, meanwhile, in the form of displacement of villagers, inundation of land, and other social and environmental impact, were to be borne entirely by the local

---

[123] These are not the unpretentious street stalls that have been catering to Isan people for decades, but rather upscale establishments offering exotic Isan cuisine to well-to-do Bangkokians.

[124] ทรงพันธ์ วรรณมาศ, ผ้าไทย ลาย อีสาน. กรุงเทพฯ: โอเดียน โสตร์, 2534.

[125] *The Nation* [Bangkok] November 20, 1998.

[126] See Keyes, "Hegemony."

people. Nonetheless, the whole project was described early on by Central Thai officials as a development project for the northeast.

Isan cultural sites and traditions have also been used and modified to fit the needs and desires of the center. In December 1998, as part of the promotion of the Asian Games in Bangkok, a short segment was shown on Thai television of Isan music and dance (which included a *khaen* and men's *phakhama* of Ubon or Surin style), but the performance was labeled "Thai Culture" at the beginning of the program.[127] Similarly, the excavations at Ban Chiang are often described as showing ancient Thai civilization, older than others in the Southeast Asian region, even though at the time of its existence, distinctions now made between modern ethnic groups (to say nothing of nationalities) had no meaning, as they did not exist. The National Museum in Ubon repeatedly uses terms like "Thai-Lao Culture" and "Thai Art, Ubon Ratchathani Craftsmanship, 19th Century" in describing items on display, but still refers to "Lao cities of the Northeast" in the context of Rama V's reorganization of the administrative system.[128]

Likewise, Khmer monuments in Isan are commonly claimed as Thai, although they pre-date even Sukhothai. Thus Phanom Rung in Buri Ram, after being refurbished by the Fine Arts Department, was dedicated in a ceremony presided over by Princess Sirindhorn on May 21, 1988, a day designated as Thai Cultural Preservation Day.[129] During the same period, the US was repeatedly denounced in the Thai press for having a Khmer lintel "belonging" to Thailand. Interestingly, there was little popular interest in Khmer monuments in Thailand until they were perceived to be under threat from outsiders. According to Keyes, the Fine Arts Department published a report in 1960 stating that Phimai and Phanom Rung monuments were "not second in quality to monuments in Cambodia" and that if developed for tourism, they would be of profit to northeasterners and, moreover, "the knowledge of their ancient and civilized heritage would make [Isan people] more conscious of defending their country and its traditions."[130] The same principle played a role in the Thai Commercial Bank's publication of an encyclopedia for each of the four regions of Thailand. One of

---

[127] Thai Channel 5, December 4, 1998, 5:40pm.

[128] These observations were made on a visit to the Museum on November 15, 1998.

[129] Craig Reynolds, "Introduction: Thai National Identity and its Defenders," in *National Identity*, ed. C. Reynolds, p. 15.

[130] Charles Keyes, "The Case of the Purloined Lintel: The Politics of a Khmer Shrine as a Thai National Treasure," in *National Identity*, ed. C. Reynolds, p. 278.

the forewords to the Isan volume credits the bank with funding the project and thereby protecting the ancient original "Thai" culture from threats from the outside.[131]

The Tourist Authority of Thailand (TAT), another central Thai government organization, has been very active in using Isan festivals for its own ends. The Rocket Festival in Yasothorn, the Candle Festival in Ubon, the Elephant Round-Up in Surin, and even the Mask Festival in Loei have all been packaged and promoted. Posters and pamphlets advertising these events are displayed in TAT offices in Bangkok and the provinces.[132] By providing financial support for the festivals, the TAT is able to influence how they are presented, what they consist of, and even when they are held.

The Elephant Round-Up provides a good example. Promotional materials give the impression that for many, many years, hundreds of elephants and their mahouts would traditionally join together once annually in Surin. When I attended the Round-Up in 1986, the main events were an elephant soccer game (played with a giant ball) and a re-enactment of an ancient battle on elephant-back. The entire festival lasted one to one-and-a-half days. In 1998, the year designated by TAT as "Amazing Thailand," the festival began with a parade through town to the stadium. Participating in the parade were various floats, a procession of older Kui men wearing only *phakhama* around their waists and shoulders, and several school groups wearing uniforms and carrying signs with messages in English like, "Love Me, Love My Elephant." One group wore matching red athletic shirts with the name of a politician on them. Although the Kui were mentioned by the announcer (raising elephants is specifically a practice of the Kui in Surin), there was no use of the Kui language. Also prominent in the parade was Surin silk. At a separate fairground adjacent to the stadium, a great deal of merchandise was displayed for sale, including food, furniture, and even textiles from distant Nan province.

The festival was scheduled to last two days or more. A TAT poster advertising it read (in both Thai and English), "featuring [...] holy ceremonies on elephant catching, elephant banquet [...] Surin products and agricultural produces contest.[...] Organized by the Surin Provincial Authority with support of the Tourist Authority of Thailand." Such events,

---

[131] ประเสริฐ ณ นคร, "คำนำ," in มูลนิธิสารานุกรมวัฒนธรรมไทยธนาคารไทยพาณิชย์, สารานุกรมวัฒนธรรมไทย ภาคอีสาน. กรุงเทพฯ: ธนาคารไทยพาณิชย์, 2528.

[132] The TAT Office in Ubon also displays photos of sights in Ubon Province, and sells postcards and local crafts.

particularly "holy ceremonies" related to elephants, would have to have been introduced by central Thai officials; Kui ceremonies are not a public spectacle, and careful rules and taboos are observed when they are carried out. Later, in Bangkok, I saw an old poster, produced by the Elephant Village Foundation Fund, bearing a photograph of a group of elephants with mahouts and a caption saying, "First Elephant Round-Up, Surin." It was dated 1955.

To what extent these various local festivals have been influenced, modified, or outrightly manufactured by TAT and similar agencies is a question that would require another study to answer. A contemporary example of the creation of such a celebration is the Phu Thai Pha Phrae Wa Festival. The *pha phrae wa* ผ้าแพรวา is a traditional textile of the Phu Thai, a Lao ethnic group. Queen Sirikit promoted the revival of the *phrae wa* along with many other crafts in Thailand, and the TAT gave seed money for a festival, while the National Culture Commission provided funds for research, which they later published. Although the customary overall color of the *phrae wa* was red, the Queen introduced more "fashionable" colors. These textiles are now cut and made into suits by non-Phu Thai people, and the festival has become an annual event.[133]

Bangkok's neglect, ignorance, oppression, exploitation, and (attempts at) assimilation and development of Isan have until recently prompted mostly scattered and disconnected responses from Isan people. Historically, Isan was a fragmented region of more or less autonomous polities, and only in the past few decades has it taken on some semblance of unity. This unity has arisen largely in opposition to Bangkok and in parallel with a growing sense of identity. As Mischung points out, "ethnic self-identification is in many cases simply a matter of context," and, "sets of alternative or complementary identities seem to be the rule in all regions of Thailand."[134] Thus a man from Khamsaenrat Village in Warinchamrap District of Ubon Province, for example, is likely to identify himself as a resident of Khamsaenrat when encountering someone from another village in the same district, of Warinchamrap when meeting someone from a different district in Ubon, of Ubon when talking to someone from a different province in Isan, and

---

[133] See *Silk Magazine*, January 1999. In 1999, the festival was held from February 26 until March 5.

[134] Roland Mischung, "The Hill Tribes of Northern Thailand: Current Trends and Problems of their Integration into the Modern Thai Nation," in *Regions*, ed. V. Grabowsky, p. 102.

from Isan or even "up-country" when asked by someone from Bangkok or elsewhere outside Isan. At the same time, of course, he has identities based on language, ethnic group, religion, education, profession, family, and so on. Even identifying oneself as an Isan person can have different meanings. The word "Isan" in describing a person's language or origin is frequently understood to mean "Lao," and there is disagreement among academics as to whether Khmer people in Isan call themselves "Isan."[135] My experience is that, once again depending on the context, Khmer people in Isan do at times refer to themselves as "Isan people." On the other hand, "Isan language" always seems to mean Lao.

Many Isan people became aware of an Isan identity and their part in it through encounters with Central Thais, often when working in Bangkok. As television became ubiquitous in Thailand, it replaced the need for personal experience and transmitted a sense of Isan-ness (in contrast to Central Thai-ness or other regions' identities) to people without their having to encounter actual Thais from outside Isan. Kanala recounts Isan people's impressions in the 1960s of Central Thais as unfriendly and having a superior attitude.[136] Isan workers outside Isan tend to associate with other Isan people from nearby villages, districts, or provinces. In comparison to Central Thais, who are Thai nationals and mostly ethnic Thais as well, Isan people are Thai nationals but ethnically Lao, Khmer, etc. This does not mean that they identify strongly with Laotians or Cambodians across the border, who are sometimes looked down upon in turn as being poor and backward. In some circumstances Isan people are in a neither/nor situation, caught in the middle between being fully Lao (or Khmer) and fully Thai. As one Laotian woman in Luang Phabang put it, "When Isan people go to Bangkok, they're looked down on as Lao; but when they come to Laos, they're disliked for being Thai."

Conclusion

There are two important aspects of the fact of Isan being a region. The first is that differences between Isan and the rest of the country are multiple, varied, and deep-seated. Isan is distinct from the rest of Thailand, and especially from the center, in almost every conceivable way, from geography and

---

[135] See Keyes, "Hegemony," p. 157, who says they don't; and Grabowsky, "The Isan," p. 107, who says they do.
[136] Kanala, *Political Change*, p. 226.

climate to economics, history, language, culture, and social position. The other major aspect of Isan's regionality is the many attitudes and reactions that have arisen as part of the relationship between the Isan region and the Thai center. The central Thai side of that relationship has primarily consisted, by turns, of ignorance, contempt, suppression, exploitation, and neglect: from the forced migration of Lao people to Siam in the 19th century;[137] the official suppression of local learning in favor of a centralized education system under King Chulalongkorn; the crushing of Men with Merit millenarian movements in the early 1900s; the replacing of local lords and princes with outside administrators, and the imposition of Central Thai clerical overseers in the Isan Sangha throughout the 20th century; to the assassination of elected Isan Members of Parliament under Plaek; the destruction of whole villages (such as Ban Na Sai) by the Army in the 1970s for suspected communist sympathies; the ruinous development projects oblivious to local needs and interests; and the still-current popular images of Isan people as country bumpkins deserving to be treated as the butt of jokes and the object of contempt by Bangkok Thais (who meanwhile rely on Isan labor for the very existence of urban Bangkok and the functioning of its economy). Isan people, for their part, have at various times shown anger, resentment, resignation, feelings of inferiority, and regional pride in their dealings with the center. Their opposition to the central government's attempts to deny and obliterate their distinct identities has been expressed through, among other things, continuing to teach traditional literature and scripts (mostly in monasteries); periodically leading armed resistance movements; mounting agricultural and environmental protests that often reach Bangkok; and voicing their political desires and demands more and more in public. Isan people have increasingly felt common bonds and expressed pride in Isan identity (or more accurately, identities). The roles that these feelings, forces, and identities have played and continue to play in modern Isan literature are discussed in the remaining chapters of this book.

---

[137] The ironic modern counterpart to this was the Thai resistance to providing refuge to Laotian and Cambodian people fleeing repressive and dangerous conditions in their home countries in the 1970s and 1980s.

CHAPTER 2

Early Isan Writers

Modern Isan literature, i.e., writing in Thai by Isan writers, arose in the late 1950s. Writers from Isan who might have been active prior to that time would have been indistinguishable from central Thai writers. Fiction production in the first half of the 20th century was exclusively an urban activity, with urban subject matter aimed at urban readers. Furthermore, up until the late 1950s, writing was strongly restricted by government policy, and expressions of regionalist sentiment would have been suppressed. In late 1957, however, Plaek was forced out of government by Sarit's military takeover, and at the end of the year Sarit sought medical attention overseas. As a result, government controls on publication were allowed to relax.[1] It was at this time that Isan writing began to emerge. While Isan writers would not begin to identify themselves as such until a decade or so later, their work at this time began increasingly to take Isan as subject matter or backdrop. Rom Ratiwan was the earliest of these writers, followed closely by Lao Khamhawm and then Kanchana Nakkhanan.[2] All writers in this period were simply Thai writers; the practice of classifying authors by region (common in the 1990s) had not yet arisen; writers' origins were not yet given particular attention by editors, readers, or other writers. What is significant, however, is that this early generation of Isan writers was the first to write about Isan specifically from their own experience as Isan people.

---

[1] Charles Keyes, *Isan: Regionalism in Northeastern Thailand* (Ithaca, NY: Southeast Asia Program Data Paper #65, Cornell University, 1967).

[2] I do not include Pleuang Wannasri (born Surin 1922, died Kunming 1996) here because he was primarily a political activist and essayist (and sometime poet) rather than a fiction writer.

Rom Ratiwan

Rom Ratiwan รมย์ รติวัน was born Thawi Ketawandi ทวี เกตะวันดี in Loei
Province in 1932. His family came from a long line of rice farmers and
carried on the tradition. His father, however, received some education and
worked for the provincial treasury. Rom often accompanied him on his
official duties, passing through forests and foothills while visiting villages
on the way to Udorn.[3] Rom attended elementary school at a temple near
his home and then secondary school in Loei town, except for a year spent
with his older sister in Chiang Rai. After completing M. 5 (the fifth year
of secondary school) in Loei, he moved to Bangkok in 1948 and became
a temple boy while preparing to enter a program in railroad engineering. It
was around this time that he began writing fiction, and he published his first
story, *Lo'n Mi Kha Phiang Mai Hai Jup Pak* หล่อนมีค่าเพียงไม่ให้จูบปาก (*Her
Only Value is in Not Allowing a Kiss*), in the newspaper, *Nakorn Luang*
(date unknown).[4] Rom subsequently followed the pattern, common to most
fiction writers of the time, of making his living as a journalist. Thus, after
completing his engineering program, he studied journalism in evening
school at Chulalongkorn University. Starting out in lowly newspaper jobs,
he worked his way up through proofreader, jail reporter, and so on, taking
one position after another at many different newspapers, until he was writing
a regular column for the *Daily News*. Eventually he became president of the
Journalists' Association of Thailand, serving three successive terms from
1963 through 1965. He also wrote a number of screenplays for films directed
by Khunawut and others.[5]

In 1974, aged only 42, Rom died of an illness at Chulalongkorn
hospital, leaving behind his wife and two young children. His funeral was
attended by people from several spheres: writers, journalists, filmmakers and
stars, and politicians. An editor of *Thai Rath* newspaper dubbed him "Fighter
without a Medal" นักรบผู้ขาดเหรียญ. According to Somrom, "The thing we must
remember above all about him is that he was a journalist who held fast to
ideals and helped to build a clear code of ethics for emerging journalists."[6]

While "Rom Ratiwan" was Thawi's most commonly used pen name, he
also went by Roy Rithiron รอย ฤธิรณ, Butsaba Roengchai บุษบา เริงชัย, Khrieo

---

[3] สมรม สทิงพระ, เส้นทางนักเขียน. นนทบุรี: Writer, 1994, p. 97.
[4] Anon., "รมย์ รติวัน," in รมย์ รติวัน, เสียงแคนและเปียนโน. กรุงเทพฯ: ประพันธ์สาส์น, 1987,
pp. 6–7.
[5] Anon., "รมย์ รติวัน นักรบผู้ขาดเหรียญ," โลกหนังสือ 1, 8 (2521): 115–8.
[6] สมรม, เส้นทาง, 1994, p. 99.

Khonklangkheun เครียว คนกลางคืน, and Khaen แคน, the last most clearly identifying his connection to Isan. His books include the following:

1) *Kaptan Khrio* กัปตันเครียว (*Captain Khrio*), 1959, novel;
2) *Nai Phan Tai Din* นายพันใต้ดิน (*The Underground Colonel*), 1960, novel; also translated into Japanese;
3) *Pui Nun Kap Duang Dao* ปุยนุ่นกับดวงดาว (*Kapok Fluff and Stars*), 1965, a collection of short stories;
4) *Yat Yu Su Lok Phala* หยัดอยู่สู้โลกพาลา (*Steadily Resisting a Wicked World*), 1969, reprinted July 1976, short stories;
5) *Siang Khaen Lae Piano* เสียงแคนและเปียนโน (*Sound of the Khaen and the Piano*), 1972, reprinted 1987, a collection of columns from the newspaper, *Daily News*;
6) *Ko'n Tawan Ja Kheun* ก่อนตะวันจะขึ้น (*Before the Sun Rises*), 1976, short stories; and
7) *Thon Thewada Nak Su Jak Thi Rap Sung* โทน เทวดา นักสู้จากที่ราบสูง (*Thon Thewada, Fighter from the Plateau*), 1980, novel (published posthumously).

Rom's book, *Kapok Fluff and Stars*, is a collection of short stories, most of which were first published between 1957 and 1965 in periodicals such as *Piyamitr*, *Sakun Thai*, and *Saen Suk*. The earliest story in the collection is "*Phra Jao Kho'ng O'm*" พระเจ้าของอ้อม (Awm's God). Awm is a boy aged seven or eight who, while eating lunch one day with his carpenter father, watches wealthy children in fancy clothes laugh and play. When one of the children falls into the canal, Awm's father dives in and saves him. After carrying the boy safely to his frightened parents, Awm's father is at first virtually ignored but then called back by the wealthy boy's father, who takes out a wallet full of hundred baht notes but offers a mere 20 baht bill as a reward. Awm's father refuses the money, which annoys the rich man; meanwhile the mother loudly attributes her son's survival to God. Awm decides that his own father is God, since the mother proclaims that God saved the boy's life, but the carpenter replies that he has never had a God. The story ends with Awm musing that God is in people like his father, but not in rich people, who have to call out for his help.

The story is written in a straightforward style, and shows a clear contrast between the working class and the wealthy. The former are depicted as solid, honest, and dignified, while the latter are frivolous, snobbish, and petty. The poor naturally help others without thought of reward, while the rich feel a sense of entitlement, taking for granted that their needs will be served and thus making almost no effort to reasonably compensate or even thank those who help them. Although Awm is young, he is a thoughtful, sensible boy, and since we follow the story from his point of view, we also are made to consider his idea that God resides in people like the noble working-class carpenter. This condemnation of the rich, and glorification of the poor in their suffering and dignity, is a common thread in Rom's work.

The title piece of the collection, "Kapok Fluff and Stars," was written in 1964, a year before the book's publication. It takes the form of a letter from a young man in the city to his mother back home on the farm. The son speaks of his ambitions in the face of alienation, loneliness, and society's contempt for farmers. He compares himself to kapok fluff floating on the winds of his ancestors' farming traditions, winds that keep him from drifting down and being trampled in the mud. However, having recently received some public honor (which he does not name), the young man also fears that he might instead end up like the kapok fluff that floats up toward the stars but then falls back to the ground. He draws inspiration from his conviction that even though stars fall and people lose hope, there are always more stars in the sky and more hope in humanity. This is not a story *per se*, but an expression of resoluteness in the face of adversity. Since there is neither mention of Isan nor specific allusion to it, Rom may be seen to be making a statement about the perseverance of farmers and people of farming origins in general. However, one can also see an autobiographical element to the piece. Rom, from a long line of farmers, wrote this soon after becoming president of the Journalists Association, and, in using this letter form, could be speaking with his own voice. As such, it is the articulation of the feelings of a writer whose roots are in the Isan countryside but who makes his living in the urban center of Bangkok.

A telling contrast is provided by a comparable piece in Rom's second book of short stories, *Steadily Resisting a Wicked World*, published in 1969, five years before the author's death. "Story in a Book Distributed at a Funeral" (or "Story in a Cremation Volume") นิยายในหนังสือแจกงานศพ also takes the form of a letter, but this time from a father to his young son. The father uses the pronoun *jao* เจ้า for "you," thus identifying himself as a Lao speaker. He talks of growing up poor and struggling to get beyond poverty, and maintains that the poor do not go to nightclubs and brothels like rich members of high society. The father also states that work is what creates life and lends meaning to it, and is the only thing that gives rise to love and understanding among humanity. He describes how writing has been his work and has supported the family, but he encourages his son to seek the path that is right for himself. The father ends by exhorting his son never to take up weapons, as this would be a crime against the country. The parallels with Rom's own life are obvious, and the themes are familiar as well: the value and dignity of poverty, the righteousness of the poor, the evil of the rich, etc.

The socialist realist elements in Rom's work become increasingly noticeable as his writing develops. In the same volume, the story *"Khrap, Mae Phom Cheu Phraew Sopheni"* ครับ แม่ผมชื่อแพรว โสเภณี (Yes, My Mother's Name is Praew Prostitute), is a prime example. A teacher notices that one of his students has the last name of "Prostitute" and visits the student's home to find out about it. There he sees the boy living in a shack with an aunt whose meager income from making paper bags is threatened by the local Chinese merchant's cheap plastic bags. "So this is what poor people are like," the teacher says to himself. The aunt tells the story of the boy's life, criticizing F.M. Sarit by name for closing down brothels as part of his social clean-up program and thus depriving herself and the boy's mother of making a living. Finally, the teacher gives the boy a new last name, as if that would solve all his problems. The story describes the difficult lives of the poor, and shows how their suffering is multiplied by capitalists (the Chinese merchant) and those in power — a typical socialist realist tale.

When *Steadily Resisting a Wicked World* was published for the second time in July 1976, the publisher's foreword proclaimed the stories to be Literature for Life.[7] He went on:

> All of Rom Ratiwan's work exposes for the reader the exploitation and injustice of society. Every letter of his writing is a shout for fairness for people who are oppressed and persecuted. And even though his life has come to an end, the sound of those shouts still echoes loudly to this day.[8]

Rom's novel, *Thon Thewada, Fighter from the Plateau*, is another in the Literature for Life mold. Rom's statement about his writing, quoted in the foreword to the novel, is the clearest expression of his sentiments along these lines:

> My stories are barren, and not much refreshing liveliness is to be found in them. I admit that this is still the case. The reason that they have not changed is that the true stories of the lives of vast numbers of people tend to be always barren. Moist and refreshing belongs specifically to

---

[7] See Chapter 3 for discussion of Literature for Life and its relationship to Isan literature.

[8] สำนักพิมพ์ผ่านฟ้าพิทยา, "คำนำของสำนักพิมพ์," in รมย์ รติวัน, หยัดอยู่สู้โลกพาลา. กรุงเทพฯ: ผ่านฟ้าพิทยา, 2519b [1976], p. 7.

the wealthy only. I do not know how to write about them, nor have I ever wished to write about them either.[9]

The publisher goes on to state that *Thon Thewada* is "the story of the struggle of a young son of Isan" เด็กหนุ่มลูกอีสาน, thus alluding to the well-known award-winning novel, *Luk Isan* (*Son of Isan* or *Child of Isan*) by Khamphun Bunthawi (see Chapter 4), published in 1976. Using classic Literature for Life rhetoric, the publisher remarks that Thon Thewada "struggles fearlessly for justice" and that "even fetters cannot imprison his mind."[10] Finally, the novel is claimed to be of a quality equal to that of *Looking Ahead* by Sriburapha and *The Specter* by Seni Saowaphong, two of the most celebrated works in the Thai Literature for Life movement. All of this firmly establishes the political-literary credentials of *Thon Thewada*. However, these above statements, published in 1980, came somewhat late, as the whole Literature for Life movement and its ideological foundation in Thailand were about to collapse utterly (see Chapter 5).

Rom Ratiwan, then, might be considered the first Isan writer in the sense that he came from Isan, used Isan subject matter, and began writing from his own experience, which included a point of view about Isan. This, however, developed into an agenda, and he became increasingly socialist realist in his style and themes in the 1960s, subordinating the importance of Isan in his work. His writing fit well with the general mood of the mid-1970s, so that even after his death his popularity increased. His books were reprinted, and he was ranked, at least by some, with the heroes of the time: Sriburapha, Seni Saowaphong, and also Khamphun Bunthawi, the first Isan writer to win a major award for a book specifically about Isan. In the 1980s, though, Rom's popularity dropped along with that of Literature for Life in general. At least two of his books were reprinted in 1987, but with the change of mood and the widespread loss of interest in such writings, his work did not regain popularity and has gradually been forgotten. Due to Rom's early death in 1974, he never had the chance to develop beyond Literature for Life. Because his writing had become strongly associated with a particular time and movement, Rom Ratiwan was left behind when tastes changed and literature moved in new directions. Nonetheless, he played a role as one of the earliest Isan writers and the first to make Isan a significant presence in his work.

---

[9] สำนักพิมพ์โคมทอง, "คำนำ," in รมย์ รติวัน, โทน เทวดา นักสู้จากที่ราบสูง. กรุงเทพฯ: โคมทอง, 2523 (1980), p. 4.

[10] Ibid.

Kanchana Nakkhanan

Kanchana Nakkhanan กาญจนา นาคนันท์ is another early writer from Isan. Although Isan has never been the major concern of her work, nor has she apparently ever referred to or even thought of herself as specifically an Isan writer, she does play a role in the development of modern Isan writing. She was born a decade earlier than Rom and Khamsing, and the start of her writing career similarly predates theirs. Her body of work is much larger as well, and she continued to produce new works through the end of the 20th century. While Rom and Khamsing come from farming families and their work primarily reflects a regard for the daily lives and concerns of village people, Kanchana comes from an educated urban family, and her writing, when set in the countryside, tends to concentrate on urban people's encounters and relationships with it. In addition, whereas Rom was best known for his short stories and newspaper columns, and Khamsing is famous for his short stories and political activities, Kanchana is widely known for her novels and children's books. Among Isan writers, she is one of the very few women, and also is perhaps the most popular with the general reader. Furthermore, she is the only Isan writer to have won a truly international prize (from Unesco, see below).

Kanchana Nakkhanan was born Nongchanai Prinnyathawat in 1921 in the town of Chaiyaphum. From the age of three or four, she and her mother went to live with her grandmother in Thannyaburi, north of Bangkok. In 1929, at age eight, she returned to Chaiyaphum with her mother and enrolled in school there. After completing elementary school and one year of secondary school, she moved to Korat, where she completed her secondary education. She then went to study elementary school teaching at Suan Sunantha Teachers' College in Bangkok. Having completed the course in 1940, she continued in the secondary school teaching program and graduated two years later.[11] During the following two years, she taught elementary school in Chaiyaphum. When her request for a transfer was denied, she resigned and returned to Bangkok, where she enrolled at Thammasat University, receiving her BA in Law in 1950. She continued to teach school in Bangkok. In 1953 she married, and she and her husband had had two children by the time of his death in 1958. Afterward she

---

[11] Information on Kanchana's life comes from Anon., "กาญจนา นาคนันท์," in ทองเพียน, สารมาศ (เรียบเรียง), ประวัตินักเขียนไทย เล่ม 3. กรุงเทพฯ: กรมศิลปากร, 2539 [1996], pp. 5–9; and Anon., "ชีวประวัต กาญจนา นาคนันท์," in กาญจนา นาคนันท์. ผู้ใหญ่ลีกับนางมา. กรุงเทพฯ: บรรณกิจ, 2538 [1995], p. 9.

began a Masters' program at Thammasat, but in 1961 illness forced her to quit her studies as well as her teaching job. Her husband's pension proved insufficient for raising their two children, and it was at this time that she decided to make writing her main occupation. She has lived and written in Chanthaburi ever since.

Kanchana's first book was *Jutmai Plai Thang Kho'ng Kanda* จุดหมายปลายทางของกานดา (*Kanda's Final Goal*), written in Chaiyaphum and published in 1946 to great popularity. Unlike other novels of the time, which took place in Bangkok and tended to lecture the reader, *Kanda's Final Goal* was set in the countryside and had a more entertaining tone. Its serial publication began in *Nakhorn San* daily newspaper but was continued and concluded in the women's weekly magazine, *Satrisan*, where Kanchana continued to publish exclusively until 1969. Since then, her work has appeared in many publications, including *Lalana, Sakun Thai, Ying Thai*, and *Daily News* (Monday). By 1996, her work included some 30 novels, 40 short stories, nine children's books, and several television scripts, textbooks, and poems. Eight of her books were made into films, four into television movies, and almost all of her work has been broadcast as radio productions. In 1968, she received a Unesco prize for her children's story, *Wide World* โลกกว้าง, and subsequently she was awarded prizes by Bangkok Bank and the Ministry of Education for some of her other children's books and novels.

Among Kanchana's best-known works is *Phu Yai Li Kap Nang Ma* ผู้ใหญ่ลีกับนางมา (*Headman Li and Mrs. Ma*), published in 1965. The novel was praised by the renowned writer and critic M.L. Bunleua Thephayasuwan with these words: "We now have in the Thai literary world a novel of which we can boast according to the standards of the West, in the category of romantic-realism."[12] Soon after its publication, the novel was put on the extra-curricular reading list of Kasetsart University and has been on school reading lists ever since.[13] The book has been made into films and television series (broadcast as recently as September 1998) and is still in print. According to Bunleua, the book paints a clear and endearing picture of the countryside and engenders in the reader feelings of love for Thai people living there, who produce the food on which city people depend. Another critic, Kanmani, remarks that the novel shows all sides of life in the countryside, including people's character, traditions, and ways of life that are more full than lives

[12] ม.ล. บุญเหลือ เทพยสุวรรณ, 1968. "คำนำ," in กาญจนา, ผู้ใหญ่ลี, 2538 [1995], p. 4.
[13] Anon., "ชีวประวัติ," 2538 [1995], p. 10.

in the cities.[14] Readers enjoy scenes of farming, traditions of farmers on the edge of the capital city, and the funny occurrences between the city girl and the country boy.[15]

An important aspect of the novel, both for its creation and its subsequent popularity, is its relationship to a popular song called "*Phu Yai Li* ผู้ใหญ่ลี" (Headman Li). Around 1965 the song became a major hit, due largely to its catchy tune and humorous content, and it is still widely known today. Its subject is a village headman in Isan, who is portrayed as ignorant and stupid and thus becomes the butt of the song's humor. The words to the first two verses are as follows:

> In 1961 Headman Li beat the drum to call a meeting
> The villagers assembled at Headman Li's house
> Headman Li spoke of the purpose for calling the meeting
> An official directive has come through for villagers to raise ducks and swine[16]
> Old Man Shakey asked 'What are swine?'
> Headman Li stood up to answer:
> 'Swine? They're just common little dogs'
> Little dogs, common little dogs
>
> The sun was extremely hot
> Headman Li was riding his horse, Old Johnson
> In the hot hot[17] sun he wore dark glasses
> Headman Li feared a storm was brewing
> But when he took off his glasses
> The sky was clear and bright
> Clear and bright, clear and bright
> The sky was clear and bright[18]

The mocking tone of the song is unmistakable, as is the reference to Isan through the strategic use of Lao.

The novel, *Headman Li and Mrs. Ma*, concerns a young woman, Malinee (or Mrs. Ma), who moves to Rangsit (at that time a farming area outside of Bangkok) to take possession of land inherited from her

---

[14] กานต์มณี ศักดิ์เจริญ, "บทเสริมท้ายเรื่องผู้ใหญ่ลีกับนางมา," in กาญจนา, ผู้ใหญ่ลี, 2538, pp. 590–2.

[15] Anon., "ชีวประวัติ," 1995, p. 11.

[16] "สุกร" an elevated Central Thai term for "pig."

[17] "ฮ้อน" is recognizable to Central Thai listeners as the Lao word for "hot."

[18] พิพัฒน์ บริบูรณ์ (undated tape), รำวงมาตรฐานผู้ใหญ่ลี.

recently deceased grandmother. Malinee leaves behind her life in Bangkok, including her friends, her job as a secretary, and her suffocatingly inflexible boyfriend. In the village of Khlong Sip Et, where the land is located, she meets Linawat (Headman Li), a university graduate in agriculture who is determined to improve the lives of the villagers. The story follows Malinee as she comes to understand village life, becomes a part of the community, and eventually marries Linawat. As Ranjuan points out,[19] the hero and the heroine are depicted in a very positive light, but not to the extent of losing their humanity. Their strengths and weaknesses make them into whole, real characters, rather than the caricatures that are often encountered in popular fiction. Malinee is pretty, intelligent, open-minded, and self-reliant, having taken care of herself from an early age after losing her parents. However, she has shortcomings, too; she is unable to cook, even rice, and she is unsure of herself when visiting the monastery, as she lacks experience in appropriate speech and behavior when dealing with monks. Similarly, while Linawat is handsome, intelligent, generous, skilled, and principled, he is also not infallible. Overall, however, he represents a new kind of farmer in a new era, whom urbanites must accept and respect, and thus he also represents a new kind of character in fiction. He is educated in the latest agricultural methods, but he still engages in all levels of work himself, from that of the hired farm hand to the farm owner and the village head. In the story, Linawat is contrasted with Malinee's old boyfriend, who rejected his own farming roots in order to become successful in Bangkok. The reader thus sympathizes with Linawat and the other villagers, and with Malinee for joining them. Furthermore, according to Ranjuan, Kanchana uses scenes that make the urban reader accompany Malinee as she smells the buffalo, sees the sun rise, and eats *nam prik*. The reader plows the fields, threshes the rice, and hopes for rain along with the farmers, and thus sympathizes with them and understands how difficult their work is. While this may sound serious and dull, Kanchana is able to make it light and enjoyable.[20]

The role of Isan in this novel is small but significant. Many of the farm workers in the village, including those formerly employed by Malinee's grandmother, are seasonal workers from Isan, while some, like Nai Wow and Nai Bai, seem to have moved to Khlong Sip Et permanently. They are depicted, like the other characters, as real people with abilities

---

[19] รัญจวน อินทรกำแหง, วรรณกรรมวิจารณ์ ตอนที่ 1. กรุงเทพฯ: ดวงกมล, 2521a [1975], pp. 137–9.

[20] Ibid., pp. 139–43.

and weaknesses. There is also some implication, and the reader is free to suppose, that the ancestors of many of the villagers, including Linawat himself, may have come from Isan originally. The song "Headman Li" is mentioned in the first chapter, when Malinee reads the letter informing her of her inheritance and that the name of the village head in Khlong Sip Et is Li. Her friends wonder why he lives in the Central region but has an Isan name,[21] and they make jokes that he must be as laughable as the character in the song. Malinee then explains that there are at least 20 headmen named Li in Thailand. In Chapter 3, after Malinee has reached the village, the song is mentioned again, and she learns that both Linawat and the villagers like to sing it. However, it is made clear early on that this Headman Li is different. There is also a comment on the misunderstanding (in the song) of the word *suko'n* or "swine," namely that it is of little consequence because "people who live in different regions use different languages."[22]

It is noticeable that the author wishes to counteract the negative image of Isan, and of country people in general, that is perpetuated in the song. Indeed she says as much in an undated statement published in the 1995 edition, where she also explains the origins of both the song and her novel.[23] In 1943, Kanchana says, when she went back to teach in Chaiyaphum, she heard about a civil servant who, while visiting villages, encountered one that had an extremely high number of puppies everywhere. When he asked about it, he was told that the headman, named Li, had attended a meeting at the county seat at which the participants were told to encourage the villagers under their administration to breed *suko'n*. Returning to his village, Headman Li was asked what *suko'n* were. No one knew, but putting their heads together, they reasoned that since *sunak* apparently meant "large dog," *nak* meaning "large" or "much," *suko'n* must mean "small dog." Kanchana continues:

> Please don't think they were stupid. These people had spoken the local language since birth, and had received only a little bit of education, so it wasn't possible for them to understand every term. The story was considered humorous, but I saw it as an endearing indication of what good citizens they were. [...] I thought that Headman Li might live in Chaiyaphum because the Chaiyaphum people I had met were lovable and a bit slow, and should have been given more education.[24]

---

[21] กาญจนา, ผู้ใหญ่ลี, 2538 [1995], pp. 3–4.

[22] Ibid., p. 27.

[23] กาญจนา นาคนันทน์, undated. "ผู้ประพันธ์คุยกับผู้อ่าน," in กาญจนา, ผู้ใหญ่ลี, 2538 [1995], pp. 5–8.

[24] Ibid., p. 5.

Later, Kanchana relates, the song appeared and was widely discussed and analyzed, even in university circles. She suspected that the song may have even played a role in the founding, that very year, of Khon Kaen University. In addition, she states that the official order to raise pigs must have come out around the time she first heard the story in 1943, during the Second World War, when the Plaek government issued many edicts which it said would help win the war. Kanchana maintains that the real Headman Li was one of many citizens who contributed to the war effort and the subsequent "victory" (as she put it).

In describing her motivations for writing the novel, Kanchana states the following:

> During the time that the song 'Headman Li' was a big hit, people in Bangkok, whether they had a radio or not, heard the song I don't know how many times daily. Every time I heard it, I thought with sympathy of Headman Li and Isan people. Then I thought, why not create a new Headman Li whom no one could ridicule. The only way to do it was to have him be well-educated. Since I didn't have a good enough knowledge of farmers in Isan, I had to move Headman Li to the fields of Rangsit, an area I had known well since childhood. But I was not knowledgeable about farming; I had only my love of farm and field to use as a base. My writing this story thus depended on my mother for details. [...] My purpose in writing *Headman Li and Mrs. Ma* was nothing more than to make it a light novel[25] (after having written a heavy story and been attacked so strongly in a weekly publication that I barely survived).[26]

It appears, then, from the above, that Kanchana did not have much of any political agenda in her writing (unlike many other Isan writers), but she did wish to present Isan and Isan people positively. Evidently she did not even think of herself as a Chaiyaphum or Isan person, in spite of having been born in Chaiyaphum and having spent many years there studying as a child and later teaching as an adult. This is in part an indication of the extent to which Isan people were looked down on by other Thais, especially during the first several decades of her life.[27] Nonetheless, however Kanchana views herself and her origins, her novels are not merely stories of light

---

[25] เรื่องอ่านเบาสมอง.

[26] Ibid., pp. 6–7.

[27] It seems that her mother, and probably her father as well, were originally from Central Thailand, and this may also have contributed to her holding herself somewhat apart from Chaiyaphum and Isan.

entertainment. At least in the case of *Headman Li and Mrs. Ma*, she was motivated in her writing to counter negative stereotypes of the time and portray Isan people, and Thai farmers in general, as real multi-dimensional people worthy of sympathy and respect. She was one of the very first Thai writers to do so.

Lao Khamhawm

Lao Khamhawm ลาว คำหอม is often cited as the best short story writer in Thai literature. He is also one of the two main figures in modern Isan writing (the other being Khamphun Bunthawi; see Chapter 4). Lao Khamhawm's collection of short stories, *Fa Bo' Kan*,[28] is probably the most widely translated work of modern Thai literature and is known in many Western countries. The author himself, having reached a venerable age, plays the role of mentor and is an inspiration to many Thai writers of later generations, whether from Isan or other parts of the country. With a relatively small body of work amounting to about five different[29] books, Lao Khamhawm is known for his past political activities almost as much as for his written work. His writing career, or more accurately, his reputation as a writer, has undergone two major transformations. In the 1950s he was a Thai writer discussing issues of the countryside for the attention of an urban Thai audience, but by the 1990s he was being proclaimed specifically an Isan writer and spokesman. In addition, his political involvements led, in the 1970s, to his books being banned and his fleeing the country to live in exile for four years; now, however, his work is part of the national school curriculum, and he has been awarded the title of National Artist, receiving a testimonial from the hand of Princess Sirindhorn herself.

Lao Khamhawm was born Khamsing Srinawk in 1930 to a farming family in Bua Yai District of Nakhorn Ratchasima Province. The Lao language was spoken in the family home. Khamsing completed most of secondary school, with financial help from his brother, in Bua Yai town, and later passed a secondary school equivalency exam. Moving to Bangkok,

---

[28] "Fa Bo' Kan" (ฟ้าบ่กั้น) has been variously translated as "The Sky Does Not Protect Us," "The Sky Does Not Divide Us," "The Sky Is No Boundary," and even "The Sky's The Limit." The title of the English translation, by Domnern Garden, of this short story collection is *The Politician and Other Stories*.

[29] As discussed below, Lao Khamhawm's essays and short stories have been collected and reprinted in different combinations, thus making impossible a precise count of his books.

he began working as a journalist and applied to study journalism at Chulalongkorn University. He later said that his desire to become a journalist stemmed from seeing journalists' influence and ability to change society for the better.[30] Between 1950 and 1951, he published some short stories under the pen name "K.S.N."[31] in *Naew Na* daily newspaper, where he was a political news reporter. None of these stories appears to have survived,[32] nor has his poetry, published under the pseudonym Chayo Somphak ชโย สมภาค.[33] Khamsing was unable to finish his degree at Chulalongkorn due to illness, and in 1952 he left Bangkok to take a job as a civil servant with the Forestry Department in Lamphun. In 1956, he resigned and became a research assistant with Cornell University's research project in rural Central Thailand, where he became acquainted with Western academics, including Herbert Phillips.

In 1958, Khamsing began writing short stories under the pen name Lao Khamhawm, publishing them mainly in the weekly newspaper *Piyamitr*. That same year, he founded a publishing house called *Kwian Tho'ng* เกวียนทอง (Gold Oxcart) and collected seven of his stories in the volume *Fa Bo' Kan*. Before the year was out, however, Field Marshal Sarit had taken over the government, and in the repressive atmosphere that followed, most newspapers were closed.[34] Khamsing stopped writing, ceased distribution of his book, and returned to farming in Pak Chong, Korat. In 1960, he began to write short stories again. Between 1967 and 1968, he traveled to France, Germany, Israel, the US, and the Ivory Coast on literary and agricultural trips. In 1969, a new edition of *Fa Bo' Kan* was published, this time with six additional stories (making a total of 13). Between 1970 and 1976, Khamsing published regularly, particularly in *Sangkhomsat Parithat*[35] under the editorship first of Sulak Sivarak and then Suchart Sawatsri. Many of these stories were collected in Khamsing's second book, *The Wall*, published in 1973.

---

[30] Anon., "วัยเด็ก," 2537a [1994]; interview published in *Writer Magazine*, April 1993; reprinted in Anon., หอมคำ ... ลาว คำหอม (Bangkok: Manager Media Group, 2537b [1994]), pp. 23–31.

[31] ค. ส. น.

[32] วัชระ บัวสนธ์, 2533 [1990], "ข้อสังเกตของบรรณาธิการ," in ลาว คำหอม, 2535 [1992]. ฟ้าบ่กั้น. กรุงเทพฯ: กำแพง, p. 18.

[33] See Anon., หอมคำ, 1994b, p. 7.

[34] Anon., "วัยเด็ก," 2537a [1994], p. 24.

[35] สังคมศาสตร์ปริทัศน์ *Social Science Review*, an influential journal in the 1960s and 70s; see Chapter 3.

During this period, Khamsing began to serve as a mentor to younger writers, intellectuals, and students. According to Somkhit Singsong (see Chapter 3), Khamsing introduced Somkhit and his generation to the works of a number of older writers including Sriburapha and Jit Phumisak. The farm at Pak Chong, Somkhit explained, "was like another university for us, especially those who were determined to travel the road of literature."[36] As an example of Khamsing's influence, Somkhit comments that Surachai Janthi-mathorn (see Chapter 3) wrote the song "*Jit Phumisak*" after learning about Jit at Pak Chong. Toward the end of this period, in 1976, Khamsing wrote the screenplay for the film *Tho'ngpan* ทองปาน, which tells the story of attempts by activists to persuade farmers to make their voices heard in the planning stages of a large development project. The film was never widely screened in Thailand due to political events immediately following its completion.

In 1975, the Socialist Party of Thailand registered for national elections. Khamsing, who had been elected vice president of the party, ran unsuccess-fully for Parliament as representative from Korat. After the rightist mas-sacre and takeover of the government in October 1976, the Socialist Party was banned, along with many books on theories of economics, society, and politics, as well as certain literary works, including *Fa Bo'Kan*.[37] Khamsing fled to the jungle,[38] and then to Laos (where he met up with Somkhit and many others), and eventually joined his family in Sweden. During his years in exile, Khamsing became a member of the Swedish Writers' Association and also went on a lecture tour in the US. *Fa Bo'Kan* had been translated into English by Domnern Garden and published by Oxford University Press in 1973,[39] and was subsequently translated into Swedish, Danish, and other languages. Khamsing's reputation in international circles began at this time, and as a result grew in Thailand as well.

Khamsing returned to Thailand in 1980 and took up farming again in Pak Chong. His novel, *Maew* แมว (*The Cat*), about an old man living alone

---

[36] สมคิด สิงสง, undated, "ฟ้าบ่กั้น และ ลาว คำหอม ที่ผมรู้จัก," in Anon., หอมคำ, 2537b [1994], p. 118.

[37] Ibid., p. 120.

[38] According to Streckfuss, what concerned the government was not Khamsing's writings, but rather "reports that he agreed to serve as prime minister in a provisional Thai government to be set up in Laos." David Streckfuss, *Truth on Trial in Thai-land: Defamation, Treason, and Lèse Majesté* (London and New York: Routledge, 2011), p. 276.

[39] Khamsing Srinawk, *The Politician and Other Stories*, trans. D. Garden (Kuala Lumpur: Oxford University Press, 1973).

with his pet, appeared in 1984. In 1986, he published *Lom Laeng* ลมแล้ง (*Dry Wind*), a collection of short stories written during 1980 and 1981, followed by *Krateng Luk Liap Khua Lok* กระเตงลูก เลียบขั้วโลก (*Cradling the Kids Up to the Edge of the Pole*),[40] an account of his exile in Sweden, in 1988. In 1992, he was made a National Artist. A later book, *Praweni* ประเวณี (*Intercourse*), published in 1998, is a bilingual edition in Thai and English of a single short story.

There is frequently some confusion in keeping track of Lao Khamhawm's work, due to changes in different editions of his books. Short stories have been added or removed in various printings, or changed their order in the volume, or even had their names changed. Collections of stories have been reissued under new titles, and some stories have migrated from one collection to another. The English translation of *Fa Bo' Kan* does not contain all the same stories as any of the Thai editions. Because *Fa Bo' Kan* has, among all of Khamsing's books, the most complicated history, the most influential position, and the most significance for Isan literature, I will discuss it below, after his other books.

Kamphaeng กำแพง (*The Wall*) was first published in 1975, and its contents were separated into four sections, the first being "short stories" and the other three "written accounts" (ข้อเขียน) from 1971, 1972, and 1973 respectively. The three short stories from the first section and one of the "written accounts" were later included (as short stories) in the 1979 edition of *Fa Bo' Kan*. The remaining 13 "written accounts" were republished, with four additions, as *Kamphaeng Lom* กำแพงลม (*Wall of Wind*), in 1993. *The Wall* contained a short foreword from the publisher, noting that most of the pieces were written after *Fa Bo' Kan* and originally published in *Sangkhomsat Parithat*. There was no mention of the author being from Isan. *Wall of Wind*, however, has a secondary title, "Points of view on the city and countryside," and the publisher's foreword uses two Lao expressions. The first is used in thanking Suchart Sawatsri for writing an "appetizing" (แซบหลาย) foreword, while the second ends the foreword with "Be Well" (สบายดี). These are among the few Lao expressions that Bangkok Thais are likely to understand. The foreword by Suchart contains many references to Isan food and the restaurant where he and Khamsing regularly met while working for *Sangkhomsat Parithat*. Suchart explains that the book's title refers to the unseen wall between people which causes problems and which Khamsing wants to break down; it became the title of Khamsing's column

---

[40] English title according to Domnern Garden.

in *Sangkhomsat Parithat*. Thus, during the time between the publication of these two books (or two editions of the same book), *The Wall* and *Wall of Wind*, Khamsing's identity shifted from being a Thai writer in general to being an Isan writer in particular.

The film *Tho'ngpan* is probably the first attempt to represent Isan on film in a realistic and sympathetic way. Filmed in Bua Yai, Korat, in 1976, it is a notable product of the Art for the People movement (see Chapter 3). In addition to writing the screenplay, Khamsing also appeared in the film, along with Sulak Sivarak, Surachai Janthimathorn (the Isan writer and musician; see Chapter 3), and other Thai and Western academics and intellectuals. Originally the film was to be based on a short story by Khamsing, but the filmmakers later decided to depict real events instead.[41] Around the time that the author was to write the screenplay, a seminar was held to discuss the Pha Mong Dam project. Tho'ngpan was one of the villagers asked to join the seminar because they were to be affected by the dam. Khamsing shared a hotel room with him, and conditions of his life in the film are based on what he told Khamsing in the hotel room. Tho'ngpan had been worried about his sick wife, and after losing his last 20 baht, he left the seminar before its conclusion. When the seminar group went to visit the area that was to be flooded by the dam, they stopped at Tho'ngpan's house and found him drunk next to the body of his wife, who had died before his return. In discussing the film later, Khamsing noted that the poverty of the farmers is the country's biggest problem, but the powerful ignore it, "which is why more than half the people who made the film couldn't stay in their own country."[42] The film was not shown publicly until 1999, and even then only as part of an academic discussion with a small audience.[43]

The Cat, Khamsing's only novel, was published in 1984, but it was already more than half-written when he fled the country in 1976. In the foreword to the second printing, he explains how in Sweden, he became a member of the Swedish Writers' Association, from whom he received support. He decided then to continue work on the novel, but when he wrote home to ask that the manuscript be sent to him, he learned that it had been

---

[41] คำสิง ศรีนอก, undated. "บอกเล่าความเป็นมาของหนังเรื่องทองปาน," in Anon., หอมคำ, 2537b [1994], pp. 54–5.

[42] Ibid., p. 55.

[43] In 2006, however, it was made commercially available as an inclusion in a booklet about the film, published in conjunction with a seminar on development in the Mekong Basin: ชาญวิทย์ เกษตรศิริ, บ.ก, 2549. ทองปาน. กรุงเทพฯ: มูลนิธิโครงการตำราสังคมศาสตร์และมนุษยศาสตร์.

confiscated by the authorities along with many other personal belongings. Thus he had to begin again from scratch. Like his other books, *The Cat* has not enjoyed nearly the popularity of *Fa Bo' Kan*. While a few commentators have praised its use of language and evocation of the conditions of life for old people in the countryside, and one critic even called it his best work,[44] others consider it boring, and overall it has not been successful.

In 1986, Khamsing published a collection of short stories entitled *Nithan Chao Ban — Lom Laeng* นิทานชาวบ้าน — ลมแล้ง (*Folktales — Dry Wind*). Nearly all the stories had originally appeared in the periodical *Khao Jaturat* in 1981 and 1982. As with most of Khamsing's work, the settings are villages of which the unspecified locations are incidental to the stories' significance. When the book was reprinted in 1988, the title was shortened to *Lom Laeng* ลมแล้ง (*Dry Wind*), and several short commentaries on the book were included. One, a reprint of an article from the *Bangkok Post* by its literary editor, "Gap,"[45] stated:

> This is one of the most authentic of all short story collections I have ever read. [...] The folk tales in Lom Lang describe the timeless lifestyle of the Northeastern villager but in the setting of today. [...] The stories are true; and the events are real. [...] They're incidents which take place beyond the city, and therefore are exclusively the dilemmas of up-country people.[46]

Another commentator claimed:

> The stories in *Dry Wind* are able to reflect from many angles the lives of the poor in the countryside. These stories should be considered the best stories that have been written of the 'stories for life' variety.[47]

A third opinion made no mention of either Isan or socialist realist literature, noting simply that, "*Fa Bo' Kan* showed life in the countryside thirty years ago [while] the new book shows the conditions of the people in facing development and progress today."[48] Thus it seems that commentators see

---

[44] Somphong Thawi, interview, March 1, 1999, Bangkok.

[45] Kanchana Spindler.

[46] Gap, "'Lom Lang' (The Dry Season Wind) ... Timeless Lifestyle of Villagers," *Bangkok Post*, February 22, 1987. Reprinted in ลาว คำหอม, ลมแล้ง. กรุงเทพฯ: สุขภาพใจ, 2531 [1988]. p. 6.

[47] ภาค พิเรทร (untitled excerpt from ฟ้าเมืองไทย ฉบับที่ 968). Reprinted in ลาว, ลมแล้ง, 2531 [1988], p. 7.

[48] บัญชา เฉลิมชัยกิจ, "สำนักพิมพ์สุขภาพใจ," in ลาว, ลมแล้ง, 2531 [1988], p. 9.

in these stories what they want to see, be it authentic Isan tradition, leftist political message, or simply depiction of village transition.

Pronouncements on *Fa Bo' Kan* have been similarly varied and equally influenced by the preexisting notions of the pronouncer. The stories in *Fa Bo' Kan* have been praised as classics of Thai literature,[49] adopted for use in the secondary school curriculum,[50] banned as a threat to the security of the state,[51] claimed as Literature for Life,[52] applauded for excellence as Isan literature,[53] and cited as among the best stories in 100 years of the Thai short story.[54] Phaya Anuman Rajadhon is said to have prevented Khamsing from joining the Siam Society by alleging that *Fa Bo' Kan* was communist propaganda, without ever having read the book himself.[55]

As noted above, *Fa Bo' Kan* was first published in 1959 by Khamsing's own press and originally consisted of seven short stories,[56] but after a warning to Khamsing that he was under scrutiny, he stopped distribution. In the late 1960s, some of the stories were reprinted in the magazines of university literary clubs, along with notes from the editors indicating that they had tried unsuccessfully to contact the author. According to Khamsing, this meant that they did not know who he was.[57] In 1967, a group including Suwanee Sukhontha and Sulak visited Khamsing at his farm. Sulak was then the editor of *Sangkhomsat Parithat*, and Khamsing had been introduced to

---

[49] นพพร สุวรรณพานิช. Comment on back cover of ลาว คำหอม, ฟ้าบ่กั้น. พิมพ์ครั้งที่เก้า. กรุงเทพฯ: กำแพง. 2535 [1992].

[50] คำสิง ศรีนอก, interview with ไทยนิกร, "ทำไมผมออกจากป่า," undated. Reprinted in Anon., หอมคำ, 2537b [1994], p. 20.

[51] สมคิด, "ฟ้าบ่กั้น," undated, p. 119.

[52] วัลยา วิวัฒน์ศร, "เขียดขาคำ," in Anon, หอมคำ, 2537b [1994], p. 124.

[53] อัศศิริ ธรรมโชติ, quoted in Anon., "ฟ้าบ่กั้น สวรรณไม่แบ่ง อิสานฮักแพงสืบสานนานมา," ผู้จัดการ, 26 กันยายน 1994. Reprinted in Anon., หอมคำ, 2537b [1994], p. 143.

[54] สมาคมนักเขียนแห่งประเทศไทย, *100 ปี เรื่องสั้นไทย*. กรุงเทพฯ: ประพันธ์สาส์น, 2528.

[55] Herbert Phillips, pers. comm., September 1998. Another account describes Phaya Anuman as non-commital when asked by authorities and Malai Chuphinit as stating that the book was not Communist. In any case, Khamsing has never become a member of the Siam Society.

[56] "ไพร่ฟ้า," "คนพันธ์," "เขียดขาคำ," "หมอเถื่อน," "นักการเมือง," "คนอูฐ," and "ชาวไร่เบี้ย." The first five of these are translated in the English edition respectively as: "Dust Underfoot," "Breeding Stock," "Gold-Legged Frog," "Quack Doctor," and "The Politician." The last two stories have not been translated, but their titles mean "Camel Person" and "The Moneyed Farmer."

[57] Anon., "วัยเด็ก," 2537a [1994], p. 24.

him by a Western academic doing research on Thai intellectuals.[58] Suwanee noticed a copy of *Fa Bo' Kan* in a corner, wiped the dust off, and began to read. Khamsing supposed that, as an artist, she was attracted by the cover artwork. She liked what she read and asked who the author was. This led to the book's second printing. This second edition included the original seven stories (one with a new name)[59] plus six more.[60] In addition, the book was illustrated throughout with rural scenes by Thepsiri Suksopha, now a well-known artist. The order in which the stories were arranged was also changed, with "Dust Underfoot" moving from the beginning to the end of the book. One critic, Watchara, states that this was due to fear of the authorities, since the story's subject matter (improper behavior on the part of a Bangkok official) might be seen to be inflammatory.[61] However, this story is also recognizably based in the Northern region, and its position as the first story in the collection would thus contradict a probably still nascent image of the author as an Isan writer. *Fa Bo' Kan* was printed a third and fourth time in 1974. At its fifth printing in 1979 under the editorship of Suchart, four more stories, taken from *The Wall*, were added.[62] According to Watchara, these stories were added to increase the copyright revenues to the author, who was still living in exile in Sweden.[63] Since then, the book has been reprinted many more times.

Lao Khamhawm has been called an Isan writer, and his work Isan writing, so many times now, that the claim is never questioned. However, a close look at *Fa Bo' Kan*, his best-known work (some would say his only really successful or significant work), reveals that only a few of the stories

[58] Undoubtedly Herbert Phillips, who later published "The Culture of Siamese Intellectuals."

[59] "คนอูฐ," or "Camel Person," became "คนหมู," or "Pig Person."

[60] "ฟ้าโปรด," "กระดานไฟ," "สวรรยา," "ชาวนาและนายห้าง," "แขมคำ," and "อุบัติโหด." In the English edition, these are titled respectively: "Dunghill," "The Plank," "Owners of Paradise," "The Peasant and the White Man," "Dark Glasses," and "Clash."

[61] วัชระ, "ข้อสังเกต," 2533 [1990], p. 11. More specifically, the story and its title could be interpreted as alluding to a certain sensitive and exalted institution.

[62] "ยมทูต," "อีกไม่นานเธอจะรู้," "ป้าย," and "เป-โต." Only the first one of these appeared in the English edition, as "Sales Reps for the Underworld." The second was translated as "You'll Learn Soon Enough" by Benedict Anderson and Ruchira Mendiones (*In the Mirror* [Bangkok: D.K. Books, 1985]). The third was translated as "Nametag" by David Smyth and Manas Chitakasem (*The Sergeant's Garland and Other Stories* [London: Oxford University Press, 1998]). The fourth has not been translated.

[63] วัชระ, "ข้อสังเกต," 2533 [1990], p. 12.

have any recognizable connection to Isan.[64] Of these, only one ("Gold-Legged Frog") appeared in the original edition, and another ("Sales Reps for the Underworld") was not included until the fifth edition. A few of the rest of the stories in *Fa Bo' Kan* take place explicitly in places outside Isan.[65] In fact, the majority of the book's stories take place in a non-specific countryside, which could be anywhere in rural Thailand. Even the stories that do have some kind of link with Isan do not take the region as an integral part of their plot or message. Isan serves merely as a backdrop or context, and in most cases could be replaced by some other location without detriment to the story. The title, *Fa Bo' Kan*, while generally taken to be Isan Lao language (thus indicating a major affinity with Isan) could actually just as well be *Kam Muang* or "Northern Thai" language instead. Indeed if we look at Khamsing's life, we see that he spent the eight or ten years before the initial publication of *Fa Bo' Kan* living in the Central and Northern regions, not Isan. His close contact with villagers throughout those years came through his work with the Forestry Department in the North and the Cornell project in the Central region. It seems very likely that his work with the Cornell researchers suggested to him new ways of looking at villagers and observing in detail the conditions of their lives. The story, "The Peasant and the White Man," undoubtedly comes from that experience, with the Western character bearing a discernible resemblance to Herbert Phillips, one of the researchers on the project.

Indeed the West has played a significant role in Khamsing's work and career. His time with the Cornell project brought him into contact with western academics and their research methods and interests. These scholars also facilitated his acquaintance with other intellectuals, both Thai and foreign. *Fa Bo' Kan* was the first major work of modern Thai literature to be translated into English. This fact, along with its issuance by a respected British publisher and the subsequent attention it received in Western universities and other spheres, enhanced his reputation at home as well. His residence in Sweden, and trips in Europe and the US, increased his contacts with foreign intellectual and literary circles. The translation of *Fa Bo' Kan* into Swedish, Danish, and other languages further increased his international standing, and the Thai literary community took note of this as well. Indeed, Western commentary on Khamsing's work has been translated into Thai and

---

[64] These are "Gold-Legged Frog," "Dunghill," "Dark Glasses," and "Sales Reps for the Underworld."

[65] "Dust Underfoot" in the North, and "The Peasant and the White Man" in the Central region.

appears, for example, in *Wall of Wind*,[66] along with a Thai scholar's essay about such commentaries.[67] After Khamsing returned to Thailand in 1980, Western academics went on seeking him out, and they continue to do so to this day.

In an interview with the periodical *Putuchon*[68] (originally published in 1975, but undated when reprinted in a 1994 collection), Khamsing stated that he wrote *Fa Bo' Kan* in the countryside after spending time in the city. He felt that they were like two different countries, and he wanted people in the city to know how villagers lived and to understand the virtues of these fellow citizens in order to make life better. "I wrote the stories as a cry of suffering in the form of short stories, to show the bitter and pitiable conditions, while working in an artistic medium," he said.[69] Several years later, in an interview with *Writer Magazine*,[70] he expanded on this, describing how students in the early 1970s began to get involved in rural development projects and saw that the countryside resembled what he described in his stories.

> Some people began to write about the countryside. That was what I had hoped for originally. I never meant to write for farmers to read. I wanted people with power in the cities to understand and sympathize with people like Nai Nak Na-ngam [the main character in "Gold-Legged Frog"].[71]

Khamsing made a similar statement again in 1998 at a panel discussion on literature in Bangkok.[72] Thus it is clear that Khamsing began writing for the sake of villagers in general, not Isan people specifically, and that his subject was the countryside at large, rather than the Isan region in particular. Contrary to the claims of Wanlaya[73] and others, Khamsing's

---

[66] "'ฟันผมหาย' แผลลึก ของ ชีวิตไทย เรื่องสั้นของ ลาว คำหอม" (translated from Herbert Phillips, *Modern Thai Literature* [Honolulu: University of Hawai'i Press, 1987]), in ลาว คำหอม, กำแพงลม. กรุงเทพฯ: ใบบัว, 2533 [1990], pp. 7–9.

[67] สุเนตร ชุตินธรานนท์, "เมื่อฝรั่งมอง ลาว คำหอม," in ลาว, กำแพง, 2533 [1990], pp. 10–6.

[68] Anon., "สัมภาษณ์ คำสิง ศรีนอก," undated. Reprinted in Anon., หอมคำ, 2537b [1994], pp. 14–9.

[69] Ibid., p. 15.

[70] Anon., "วัยเด็ก," 2537a [1994], pp. 23–31.

[71] Ibid., p. 28.

[72] "เขียนหนังสืออย่างไรจึงได้เป็นมือรางวัล," Matichon Building, November 25, 1998. See also สัจภูมิ ละออ, 2541 [1998]. "ฝันของศิลปินแห่งชาติ ลาว คำหอม และ 2 ซีไรท์เรื่องสั้น." กรุงเทพธุรกิจ (12: 3728) 6 ธ.ค. 2541, p. 8.

[73] วัลยา, "เขียดขาคำ," 1994, pp. 121–4.

writing is not Literature for Life; he does not attempt to provide solutions for the problems he describes (one of the four tenets of that movement, see Chapter 3), but rather tries only to express these problems in an artistic way for the edification of city readers. According to Witthayakorn, Khamsing has expressed a lack of faith in Literature for Life but is nonetheless a progressive writer who reveals social evil and injustice and believes that literature must relate to life and society.[74]

Khamsing in the year 2000 was an elder statesman of Thai literature with credentials of political commitedness. Younger generations of writers were still coming to his farm to pay respects, perhaps receive words of encouragement, and possibly learn something about the craft of writing from a man whose work is a standard to which many aspire. On his birthday (December 25) in 1998, at least 16 writers went to his farm, including Chat Kobjitti, Wat Wanlayangkul, and four Isan writers: Yong Yasothorn (see Chapter 5), Phaiwarin Khaongam (see Chapter 6), Prachakhom Lunachai (see Chapter 6), and Siowjan Raemphrai (see Chapter 6).[75] Despite the fact that Khamsing did not consciously start out as an Isan writer, most people consider him to be one now. Hence, Phaithun Thanya (a well-known writer from the South) states that his first knowledge of Isan came from reading *Fa Bo' Kan* at teachers' college,[76] and Chatchawal Khotsongkhram (a rising young Isan writer, see Chapter 6) also speaks of the importance of the book as Isan literature.[77]

Khamsing has not tried to change the public perception of himself as an Isan writer. In 1994, he spoke at a seminar on Isan, local knowledge, and development, where he asked that people look more deeply at Isan and see more than just its poverty.[78] He also has publicized his cultural connections with Laos. For example, he wrote a foreword to the Thai edition of a book of short stories by the Lao writer, Uthin Bunnyavong. His purpose in doing so, said Khamsing, was to encourage communication between Laos and Thailand, and also to express his deep respect for Uthin's father-in-law,

---

[74] วิทยากร เชียงกูล, "คำนำเชิงวิจารณ์ จากฉบับพิมพ์ครั้งที่ 3 พ. ศ. 2517", 2517a [1974]. Reprinted in ลาว, ฟ้า, 2535 [1992], p. 236.

[75] วรรณฤกษ์, "ฐานวรรณกรรม," ฐานสัปดาห์วิจารณ์ (245) 2–8 ม.ค. 2542, p. 60.

[76] ไพฑูรย์ ธัญญา, "ความประทับใจจากการอ่าน ฟ้าบ่กั้น," in Anon., หอมคำ, 2537b [1994], pp. 137–9.

[77] ชัชวาลย์ โคตรสงคราม, "ฟ้าบ่กั้น ในความเก่าหลัง," in Anon., หอมคำ, 2537b [1994], pp. 140–1.

[78] Anon., "ฟ้าบ่กั้น," 2537c [1994], p. 143.

Mahasila Viravong.[79] In May 1999, Khamsing hosted a party at his house for the Lao ambassador to Thailand, evidently inviting the press as well. An article covering the event reported that Khamsing gave a speech in which he recalled the safe haven offered to him in Laos when he fled Thailand in 1976.[80] Afterward, there was a performance of Lao music, and Khamsing explained the origins of the Lao song "*Duang Champa*," which was made popular in Thailand by Surachai Janthimathorn and the band Caravan (see Chapter 3).

Khamsing was the first Thai writer to take the countryside as his primary subject and treat it with both artistry and realism. Michael Smithies, writing in 1972, gives the following perspective on Khamsing's accomplishments:

> Modern Thai literature is not dominated by realism or solicitous concern for the condition of society. It has tended to consist primarily of feminine novelettes describing situations of conflict arising from love affairs which run across class lines or family obligations; largely written by members of the aristocracy for its own distraction, it was and is oriented towards the capital and uninterested in the surrounding countryside. [...] Khamsing Srinawk occupies an unusual position in that he writes about the peasant world; he is of the peasant class himself.[81]

As Witthayakorn notes, "Because Lao Khamhawm comes from the country-side about which he writes, he makes the reader sympathetic to country people while also entertaining him/her."[82] Thus Khamsing's subject matter sets him apart, but what further distinguishes him is the quality of his writing, his keen observations, and his sense of humor, all of which, in the best stories, combine and lead to a conclusion that is at once telling, touching, humorous, and sarcastic.[83] Assiri Thammachot, another of Thailand's best-known short story writers, expressed his admiration for *Fa Bo' Kan* as follows:

> [*Fa Bo' Kan*] is a collection of short stories that might be considered the first to open the world of Isan to the world's gaze through literature.

---

[79] Anon., "วัยเด็ก," 2537a [1994], p. 28.

[80] Anon., "ดอกไม้มิตรภาพไทย-ลาว เบ่งบานรับลมฝนกลางเขาใหญ่," เนชั่นสุดสัปดาห์ 8, 362 (13–19 พ.ค. 2542) (1999): 4–5.

[81] Michael Smithies, "Introduction," in Khamsing, *The Politician and Other Stories*, trans. D. Garden (Kuala Lumpur: Oxford University Press, 1973), p. xiii.

[82] วิทยากร, "คำนำ," 2517a [1974], p. 233.

[83] An excellent example of this is the story, "คนพันธ์," or "Breeding Stock."

[… It is] regional literature that reaches the national level. It is the best
collection of short stories since short stories began.[84]

According to Witthayakorn,

[Khamsing's writing] broadens the horizons of city people who aren't
familiar with the countryside, and, having been translated, also broadens
the horizons of foreigners and increases their understanding of Thai
people. [For in the end], the heavens do not really separate people
from each other; it is only people who build various walls between
themselves.[85]

Conclusion

Modern Isan literature first emerged as a discernible current in modern Thai
literature in the late 1950s. Early Isan writing reflected the sense of injustice
felt by Isan people under the oppressive control of the central government,
and was able to appear on the literary scene only with the relaxation of that
control. Rom Ratiwan, Lao Khamhawm, and Kanchana Nakkhanan were
the first Isan writers (of fiction). Although they did not explicitly identify
themselves as Isan writers (with the exception of Lao Khamhawm, later in
his career), their work expressed Isan themes, subjects, and settings for the
first time in modern Thai literature. Rom's novel, *Thon Thewada, Fighter
from the Plateau*, was the first book of Thai literature to refer to Isan
specifically in the title. His shorter works also frequently articulate, often
with autobiographical allusions, the feelings of an Isan person surviving in a
Central Thai world. As his career progressed, his work became increasingly
socialist realist in tone and content, and largely for this reason is rarely read
today. Kanchana, though born and raised primarily in Isan, has never allied
herself with Isan writing. Nonetheless, one of her most successful novels,
Headman Li and Mrs. Ma, was written in part as a response to central Thai
negative views of Isan people, as epitomized in the popular song, "Phu Yai
Li". Her novel represents one of the first attempts in popular fiction to depict
Isan and other rural people in a sympathetic light.

Lao Khamhawm has become an important figure in Thai literature,
primarily as a result of one book, *Fa Bo' Kan*. This collection of short
stories was the first to take rural people as a legitimate subject of literature,
and also the first to use a regional language in its title. The clash between

---

[84] อัศศิริ, 1994, quoted in Anon., "ฟ้าบ่กั้น," 2537c [1994], p. 143.
[85] วิทยากร, "คำนำ," 2517a [1974], p. 237.

village ways of life and the forces of authority is a common theme in his work. Initially Khamsing was not considered to be specifically an Isan writer, even by himself, it seems, and most of his stories are not recognizably related to Isan, but rather to rural Thailand in general, including the north. However, through successive reprints of his work, especially *Fa Bo' Kan*, and perhaps his own self-presentation, he gained an unquestioned reputation as a major pillar of Isan writing and became a model and an inspiration for many aspiring writers, especially those from Isan. His literary and political endeavors also were in tune with certain currents in the 1960s and 1970s and influenced several of the principal Isan writers of that era, as will be shown in Chapter 3.

CHAPTER 3

Isan Comes to the Center

The year 1963 marked the beginning of a new era for Thai literature, and even though Bangkok remained the literary center of the country, Isan and Isan writers played a major role in this new era. FM Thanom Kittikachorn took power after Sarit's death, and the so-called "dark age" began to lift. Intellectual activity gradually came out into the open again as economic growth fueled an expansion of the education system.[1] Rapid social change and dislocation gave rise to new problems without easy or obvious solutions. Students and other young intellectuals questioned their society, and their own place in it,[2] as well as the world in general. They sought ways of understanding, and then improving, what they saw around them. This combination of conditions prevailed in a time that came to be known as *Yuk Sawaeng Ha*, the Era of Search.

Certain individuals, groups, and activities have become emblematic of the times. In 1963, Sulak Sivarak founded the journal *Sangkhomsat Parithat* (*Social Science Review*), and his wide-ranging commentary as well as his "defense of Thai political and cultural autonomy from excessive American influence won him a small, but increasingly influential, youthful intellectual following."[3] In addition, the journal's coverage of issues and ideas related to poverty, agriculture, and development contributed to an interest in conditions in the Thai countryside. As time went on, this interest focused increasingly on Isan, a region hitherto largely ignored in Bangkok.

---

[1] Benedict Anderson, "Introduction," in *In the Mirror*, ed. Benedict Anderson and Ruchira Mendiones (Bangkok: Duang Kamol, 1985).

[2] Manas Chitakasem, "The Development of Political and Social Consciousness in Thai Short Stories," in *The Short Story in South East Asia: Aspects of a Genre*, ed. J.H.C.S. Davidson and H. Cordell (London: SOAS, 1982), pp. 87–8.

[3] Anderson, "Introduction," p. 26.

The general intellectual appetite characteristic of the Era of Search was both expressed and influenced by two groups of intellectual artists and writers.[4] One of these, calling itself *Num Nao Sao Suay* (in Anderson's rendering, "The Young and the Beautiful"),[5] associated with Silapakorn University, was more artistically and culturally oriented and demonstrated a certain nationalistic, conservative, even radical conservative sensibility. As Anderson notes, the members of this group "strongly championed an *echt* 'Old Siamese' culture and literature."[6] Thus it is not surprising that no Isan writers were part of this group and that its relevance for Isan was minimal. However, the other well-known group, *Phra Jan Siow* (The Crescent Moon), was more eclectic in its interests and membership, and included at least three Isan writers: Surachai Janthimathorn, Prasert Jandam, and Tak Wongrath. Although Anderson describes the group as "young writers associated with Thammasat University" and "under the intellectual leadership of Suchart Sawatsi,"[7] in fact there was no real head *per se*, and not all those involved had a connection to Thammasat.[8]

Phra Jan Siow concerned itself with a wide range of international intellectual movements and their relevance to literature, including surrealism, existentialism, symbolism, realism, and Marxism and other leftist politics. At the same time, the group also criticized the notion that all good things came from the West, objecting to "the old attitude that only Farang can do things well."[9] Questioning authority and the relationship of people to their society were popular themes. According to Surachai, those involved in the group were friends and, although of different ages, did not call one another by the kin terms that Thais normally use to acknowledge elders.[10] A classic work of the period, written by Witthayakorn Chiengkun, one of the better-known members of the group, is *Chan Jeung Ma Ha Khwammai* (*Thus I Come to Look for Meaning*). This collection of poetry, short stories, and plays, many of which question the methods, purposes, and efficacy of the Thai university,

---

[4] For further discussion of these groups, see ภิญโญ กองทอง, "จาก 'พระจันทร์เสี้ยว,' 'หนุ่มเหน้าสาวสวย' ถึง วรรณกรรมเพื่อชีวิต," in กัณหา แสงรายา และ เจษฎา ทองรุ่งโรจน์, บ.ก. ปริทรรศน์วรรณกรรมไทยสมัยใหม่. กรุงเทพฯ: มูลนิธิสถาบันวิชาการ ๑๔ ตุลา, 2546.

[5] Anderson, "Introduction", p. 28.

[6] Ibid.

[7] Ibid.

[8] Surachai Janthimathorn, Interview, March 6, 2000, London.

[9] วิทยากร เชียงกูล, "บันทึกของผู้เขียนในการพิมพ์ครั้งแรก," in ฉันจึงมาหาความหมาย. นนทบุรี: พระจอมเกล้าวิทยาลัยเทคนิค, 2517, p. 39.

[10] Surachai Janthimathorn, Interview, May 14, 1999, Bangkok.

was shocking at the time but also expressed feelings that were widely held among young intellectuals.

This search for meaning and scrutiny of society and its institutions was for many initially a wide and unfocused pursuit. However, as time went on, there arose a particular concern with injustice in society, and in turn a growing attention to causes of and solutions to this widespread and widely perceived injustice. In other words, politics became more and more the major topic of interest among students and other progressive members of society. At first, the search for political knowledge resembled a reinvention of the wheel: the younger generation was not aware of the efforts by earlier generations to provide alternatives to the prevailing rightist establishment. However, as the political atmosphere in the early 1970s became more vocally expressed in demonstrations, articles, discussions, etc., some members of the older generation who were still available (i.e., not dead, imprisoned, or driven underground or into exile) became involved. Khamsing Srinawk, for example, spoke to young writers at his home, encouraging them and informing them about past writers like Sriburapha. Works that had appeared during past intervals of relative laxness on the part of the government, such as the 1957–1958 period, were rediscovered.[11] Books and articles on the purpose of art, the role of the writer, social class conflict, and so on, were republished and widely circulated. Such works included *Chiwit Kap Khwam Fai Fan* (*Life and Aspirations*) by Banjong Banjoetsin, *Phi Sat* (*The Specter*) by Seni Saowaphong, and *Rao Chana Laew Mae Ja* (*We have Won, Mother Dear*) by Nai Phi. Jit Phumisak's book, *Sinlapa Pheua Chiwit Sinlapa Pheua Prachachon* (*Art for Life, Art for the People*) was rediscovered and "reprinted in 1972 by a student group at Thammasat University."[12] This work was to have an enormous influence on Thai literature over the next decade and beyond.

Sinlapa Pheua Chiwit Sinlapa Pheua Prachachon was first published by Jit in 1957 under the pseudonym, "Thipakorn" ("One Who Lights the Way").[13] It is in effect a manifesto for the Art for Life movement, expressing its characteristics, criteria, and aims. The book begins by denouncing "art for

---

[11] Rachel Harrison, "Introduction," in *Sidoru'ang*: *A Drop of Glass and Other Stories*, ed. Sridaoru'ang, trans. R. Harrison (Bangkok: Duang Kamol, 1994), p. 23.

[12] Ibid., p. 24.

[13] Craig Reynolds, *Thai Radical Discourse: The Real Face of Thai Feudalism Today* (Ithaca, NY: Cornell University, 1987), p. 34.

its own sake," which serves only the bourgeoisie, and encouraging art "that serves the lives of the people."[14] Thus,

> The value of art can lie only in its value for the human masses. [...] Art that is useless to human life has so little value it is not even worth the discharge from a cat's eye.[15]

Jit exhorts the artist:

> Reflect reality creatively and use your art as a spear and a lantern, a spear that pierces, stabs, and skewers the enemies of the people. [...] Declare for everyone to see:
>
> 1. The bad conditions of life as it truly is
> 2. The origins of the baseness of life
> 3. Ways to improve and change the baseness of life to return to goodness and beauty
> 4. Forceful examples of the new goodness and beauty of the coming life.
>
> This is leading art to serve the lives of the people.[16]

Furthermore, "Artists must learn about the lives of farmers, workers, hopeless people, women, and youth in order to understand their true conditions, and then reflect those conditions in art."[17] Jit then goes on to describe what the nature of art should be, stating, "Art that is truly great must be something that ordinary people can understand and admire equally with high-level intellectuals, even though they look at art from different standpoints."[18] The goal of the movement is clear, as are its Marxist origins:

> Art for life and art for the people, which is a movement of the oppressed masses of the people, must be victorious over and eradicate art of the middle classes, that is, art for art's sake and pure art, through the complete, forceful, and unanimous struggle of the masses of workers and farmers.[19]

---

[14] ทีปกร, ศิลปะเพื่อชีวิต ศิลปะเพื่อประชาชน. กรุงเทพฯ: ต้นมะขาม, 2521, p. 77.

[15] Ibid., pp. 177–8.

[16] Ibid., pp. 77–8. There is a striking parallel here between the four elements of this prescription and the Four Noble Truths of Buddhism. The obvious difference, however, lies in Buddhism's promulgation of the Eightfold Path versus Jit's endorsement of Marxist revolution. Jit's apparent inspiration by Buddhist philosophy is particularly interesting given his criticism of Buddhism's goals and practices. See, for example, จิตร ภูมิศักดิ์, "ผีตองเหลือง," โลกหนังสือ 4, 12 (ก.ย. 2527) (1981): 40–2.

[17] ทีปกร, ศิลปะเพื่อชีวิต, 2521, p. 226.

[18] Ibid., p. 78.

[19] Ibid., p. 170.

After the uprising of October 14, 1973, and the collapse of the Thanom dictatorship, works like those of Jit, Seni, and Banjong became freely available as censorship all but disappeared. Not only literature, but music also blossomed under the relaxed conditions. Songs for Life bands with a folk-rock orientation, often influenced by American musicians like Bob Dylan and Joan Baez, expressed the social and political sentiments of the times. These included bands like *Khomchai* (Shining Lantern), *Kammachon* (Proletariat), and *Kharawan* (Caravan), the last of which has been the most long-lasting and influential. Caravan[20] comprised four musicians, all from Isan, the leader of whom was the writer Surachai Janthimathorn. These bands became extremely popular, but their importance for the period has not been fully recognized. Music, especially the kind played by these bands, is generally more compelling and accessible than literature, especially political writings. Sila Khomchai (a Songs for Life musician in the eponymous band and later SEAWrite Award winner) has pointed out that a great many young people in the 1970s were attracted to the music first, and as songs became part of the struggle, they listened to the lyrics and developed an interest in the underlying ideas and politics.[21] From there they began later to read books and become more politically active and aware. In fact, a whole generation was politicized by Songs for Life music, and these bands, with Caravan at the forefront, made a lasting and irreversible impact on Thai society.

In the early 1970s, a diversity of new ideas flourished in young intellectual circles. As Hong has noted:

> The student leaders who precipitated the 14 October uprising were in many ways intellectual pioneers who had no set of received theories. They explored ideas of Marxism, the New Left, existentialism, liberal democracy, and Buddhism in their opposition to the dictatorial regime.[22]

---

[20] Caravan still occasionally appears in concert, particularly commemorative shows, but for the most part the band is no longer active as a group; instead, the respective members continue to be involved with music to varying extents.

[21] Sila Khomchai, speaking on October 14, 1998 at Sanam Luang at the Commemoration of the 25th Anniversary of October 14, 1973. For an article covering his comments and the panel discussion at which he made them, see Anon., "วรรณกรรม-เพลงเพื่อชีวิต '25 ปี ไม่ใช่การเฉลิมฉลอง แต่เป็นการฟื้นฟูวัฒนธรรม'," เนชั่นสุดสัปดาห์ 7, 333 (2541): 56–7.

[22] Hong Lysa, "Warasan Sethasat Kanmu'ang," in *Thai Constructions of Knowledge*, ed. Manas C. and A. Turton (London: SOAS, 1991), p. 104.

As time went on, however, experimentation decreased and particular ideas gained credence and were supported, while others fell out of favor and were opposed. According to Sathien Janthimathorn, "The events of October 14, 1973 simply brought an end to the confused Era of Search."[23] After 1973, the new aesthetic that was demanded in books by Jit and others gained in popularity. "Literature for Life" became the watchwords among progressive writers (though the movement was roundly criticized by others for its single-mindedness, lack of traditional literary beauty, and overtly leftist political agenda). At the same time, rightist reaction became more and more vociferous. Laos, Cambodia, and Vietnam were all falling under the hammer and sickle, causing panic in some Thai circles. With mounting assassinations of labor and farm leaders, and a monk declaring that killing communists was not morally wrong,[24] Thai society was becoming increasingly polarized.

Students were going out into the country to learn about the lives of "the people" and to try (often rather naively) to improve rural conditions by implementing their own development and public works projects. Isan, as the poorest region of the country, naturally became a major object of interest, sympathy, and activity among these activists. In addition to Surachai, other Isan writers like Prasert Jandam, Somkhit Singsong, and Udorn Thongnoi, through their poems (including songs) and prose, focused attention toward Isan and provided authentic knowledge and insight into Isan life.[25] Indeed, the new political conditions that obtained in the early to mid-1970s were in many ways an inversion of the previous status quo. Those who had formerly

---

[23] เสถียร จันทิมาธร, "คำนำ," in อุดร ทองน้อย. อีสานกู. กรุงเทพฯ: ประพันธ์สาส์น, 2518, p. 9.

[24] Kittiwutto, a monk in Chonburi Province, gave encouragement to right-wing extremist groups by stating that killing communists was righteous and would not bring about karmic retribution. See John S. Girling, *Thailand: Society and Politics* (Ithaca, NY: Cornell University, 1981), pp. 156, 211–2.

[25] Other Isan writers expressed similar ideas and engaged in related activites to the four writers discussed in this chapter, but were less productive, accomplished, and influential. These include:

1) Somsak Wongrat (from Khon Kaen); member of *Phra Jan Sieow*; author of *Kan Klab Ma Kho'ng Khon Si Thao* (*The Return of the Grey Person*), 1987, a collection of short stories; now a film critic.

2) Tak Wongrat (brother of Somsak); author of *Nok Si Khao Lae Khon Phanejo'n* (*The White Bird and the Wanderer*), 1977, short stories; still occasionally publishing short stories in periodicals.

3) Wirasak Khukhanthin (from Srisaket); author of *Jeung Tawat "Ai Kae Noi!"* (*So He Snapped, "You Little Sheep!"*), 1984, a novel; also a musician in the Songs for Life band *So'ng Wai* (Two Ages).

been at the bottom of Thai society were now in a position at the top, in the sense that they had an unassailable validity or genuineness, a kind of native competence of underprivilege. Being from Isan had a legitimacy and a cachet that it had never had before. As an Isan person, one had a (reverse) status that a Bangkok person could never have. The idea of the new, inverted, social order is expressed in Caravan songs with such titles as "*Pla Noi Kin Pla Yai*" (Small Fish Eat Big Fish),[26] and "*Nam Thuam Fa Pla Kin Dao*" (Water Floods the Sky, Fish Eat the Stars).

In addition to Jit's manifesto on art, one other work in the Literature for Life vein had major influence on Isan writers of the time. This was Nai Phi's poem, "Isan." Although Nai Phi himself was not from Isan, he was greatly respected for his poetic skills, his political point of view, and his strong convictions (he had joined the CPT in the jungle and abroad, and remained with the party for decades). Even today, he is one of the few outsiders accepted by Isan writers as qualified to write about Isan.[27] The poem "Isan" became an anthem for the region and remains so to this day. Part of it was incorporated into a Caravan song, "Caravan." The poem expresses the suffering of the people and their oppression by the government, and uses a number of Lao words (Nai Phi spent many years in Laos with the Communist Party).[28] Like Nai Phi, Jit was not from Isan either, but spoke one of its languages (Khmer), having lived in Battambang, Cambodia. He was even "taunted by a teacher for being Cambodian" in high school in Bangkok[29] (much as Isan people are often ridiculed for being Khmer or Lao). In addition, Jit died in Isan, in Sakon Nakhorn Province (after being shot by a government official), giving him one final connection with Isan.

By 1976, Literature for Life had become the dominant mode for new writing in Thailand, and writers had adopted as their subjects factory workers, poor farmers, urban homeless, prostitutes, minorities, the disabled, the elderly, and other dispossessed members of society.[30] In

---

[26] This line is an expression from traditional Lao literature describing a time of social turmoil; Caravan uses it as a allegory of Marxist revolution. Peter Koret, pers. comm., May 14, 1999.

[27] Yong Yasothorn, Interview, October 23, 1998, Bangkok–Chachoengsao.

[28] See Appendix at the end of this chapter for an English translation of the poem.

[29] Reynolds, *Thai Radical Discourse*, 1987, p. 19.

[30] In the West, Literature for Life would generally be called "socialist realist." In Thailand, it has also been called *wannakam satho'n sangkhom* (literature that reflects society), *wannakam satjaniyom* (realist literature), *wannakam sangsan* (creative literature), and so on. See ดวงมน จิตร์จำนงค์, "สืบเนื่องจากคำถาม 'ทำไมวรรณกรรมสะท้อนสังคมจึงแก้ปัญหาสังคมไม่ได้'," เนชั่นสุดสัปดาห์ 8, 366 (10–16 มิ.ย. 2542): 44–5.

Anderson's view, writers of this period were "often imbued with the painful consciousness that the same forces made possible their own success and the degradation of the people and the environment with which they had grown up"; thus the embracing of Literature for Life "was felt as a way of atoning for a tainted privilege."[31] Phillips ascribes the movement's popularity in part to "a powerful didactic strain in Thai literary tradition."[32] However, he goes on to state that, "This movement ended abruptly with the coup of October 1976." In fact, though, Literature for Life continued quietly in the cities (despite censorship)[33] and more loudly in the CPT-controlled areas around Thailand, of which a large number were in Isan. Surachai, Prasert, Somkhit, and Udorn all fled to the jungle in 1976 (some before the coup), along with the rest of Caravan and many other writers. There they continued to produce Literature for Life (and Songs for Life), purposefully rejecting the standards and conventions of more established or traditional literature in favor of principles and practices of its own, generally in the service of the Party. Furthermore, after General Kriangsak Chomanan took over the government in 1978 and liberalized its policies, the political situation again relaxed somewhat, and debate on the role of art in society continued. That debate continues to this day, as does the influence of Literature for Life (see Chapters 5 and 6).

For modern Isan writers, their prominence, influence, and recognition had arisen in the early 1970s and reached a kind of golden age after 1973, when their work was widely read and they enjoyed a unique status as spokespeople for a region that was at the heart of a noble cause. This golden age of Isan writing was soon to reach its zenith.

Surachai Janthimathorn

Surachai Janthimathorn สุรชัย จันทิมาธร was born in the provincial capital of Surin in 1948. At the age of six, his father moved the family to Ratanaburi District, also in Surin Province. Surachai's mother and father were Khmer, and both spoke Khmer language; his mother could not read or write, but his father could read Khmer in addition to Thai.[34] However, Thai was spoken at

---

[31] Anderson, "Introduction," p. 43.

[32] Herbert Phillips, *Modern Thai Literature* (Honolulu: University of Hawai'i, 1987), p. 57.

[33] For a discussion of censored books during this and previous periods, see ธนาพล อิ๋วสกุล, "หนังสือต้องห้าม ความรู้ที่ถูกจองจำ." สารคดี 22, 260 (2549): 133–74.

[34] Surachai, Interview, 1999.

home with their seven children (of whom Surachai was the middle child),[35] while Lao was the predominant language of their village. As a child Surachai liked to go and listen to performances of different kinds of *mo' lam*, often staying all night until dawn.[36] After completing secondary school in Surin, Surachai went to Bangkok in 1965 to continue his education. He wanted to study at the Pho Chang arts school, but did not pass the entrance exam. He was disappointed because he wanted to be a painter, and eventually entered another school, but he was never a serious student, he says, and quit after a year.[37]

At this time (mid–late 1960s), Surachai turned his energies toward writing poetry, short stories, and cartoons (he had begun writing as a child back in Surin). Writing initially under the pen name Th. Sen Jenjad[38] ท. เสน เจนจัด (the "Th." standing for "Thao," the Lao equivalent of "Mr."), he became part of a group called "Poets' Universe under the Phut Bridge" กลุ่มจักรวาลกวีใต้สะพานพุทธ,[39] which included his older brother Sathien (later a well-known critic and journalist) and Prasert Jandam (see below).[40] Surachai's "birth" as a short story writer came in 1967,[41] when two of his stories were published in a single issue of *Siam Rath* weekly; these were "*Laeng Khen*" แล้งเข็ญ (Drought) (later reprinted as the eponymous story of Suchart Sawatsi's 1975 anthology), and "*Khon Lae Khon Ba*" คนและคนบ้า (People and Crazy People)[42] (both stories also later appeared in Surachai's first book, see below). No one had ever done this before, and it was like an announcement: he felt he had been accepted as a writer. After that, writing became a regular source of income for him. He even wrote ghost stories to make money, and once tried to write a smutty story but began laughing at himself after half a page and had to stop.[43]

---

[35] วาสนา ไชยรัตน์, "การวิเคราะห์เรื่องสั้นของสุรชัย จันทิมาธร." ปริญญานิพนธ์ มหาวิทยาลัยศรีนครินทร วิโรฒ ประสานมิตร, 2534, p. 4.

[36] Surachai, Interview, 1999.

[37] Ibid.

[38] See ดินสอสี, "'สุรชัย จันทิมาธร' วันนี้ยังมีบทกวีในเสียงเพลง," กรุงเทพธุรกิจ วันอาทิตย์ 12, 3742 (20 ธันวา 2541): 8.

[39] The Phut Bridge (*Saphan Phut*) crosses the Chao Phraya River, linking Thonburi with Bangkok proper.

[40] Anon., "ตามรอย...สุรชัย จันทิมาธร ในวันที่ไร้ 'ดวงตะวันสีแดง' ส่องทาง," เนชั่นสุดสัปดาห์ 8, 352 (4–10 มี.ค. 2542): 4. This article was later reprinted as ภาวิณี อินเทพ, "สุรชัย จันทิมาธร กับ 'ดวงตะวันสีแดง'," กรุงเทพธุรกิจ วันอาทิตย์ 12, 3832 (21 มี.ค. 2542): 3.

[41] สุรชัย จันทิมาธร, มาจากที่ราบสูง. กรุงเทพฯ: กำแพง, 2533, pp. 31, 42.

[42] Ibid.

[43] Anon., "ตามรอย," 2542, p. 4.

By 1967, Surachai had joined *Phra Jan Siow* (The Crescent Moon) and was also associated with other circles, such as *Num Nao Sao Suay* (The Young and the Beautiful) and *Na Phra Lan* (In Front of the Royal Field).[44] He learned from other writers and artists in these groups, including Suwanni Sukhontha, the influential writer and later editor of *Lalana* magazine. Through writing for *Siam Rath* newspaper, Surachai came to know Rong Wongsawan, a journalist and writer with a growing reputation for innovative style and subject matter, and helped gather material for Rong's books.[45] Other writers who influenced Surachai in this early period were Lao Khamhawm, particularly, and Manas Janyong, as well as Western writers like Hemingway and Steinbeck.[46]

Surachai describes his first four or five years in Bangkok as a difficult period:

> I didn't have much money, and there weren't really people who understood [my situation]. It was lonely. I relied on loneliness to write. Sometimes I didn't talk to anyone. I was talking to myself. I wasn't a singer [yet]. When a singer goes somewhere, people recognize him. But not a writer. I went here and there, on the bus, [...] I lived like that, poor, in Bangkok. [...] I had to support myself. I had to rely on loneliness, so it made me write a lot about Isan. And then when I wrote, someone would read it and so on. It was kind of a way out. I wrote in this way, showing the lives of Isan people in terms of loneliness that exists in the capital, too. My writings at first were all about Isan.[47]

Music was also becoming an important part of Surachai's life.[48] In the early 1970s, he was playing the guitar, sometimes joining informally with friends, and listening to folk and protest musicians from the West. With the dramatic changes that accompanied October 14, 1973, the political atmosphere in Thailand became much more conducive to open expression. Surachai began playing regularly and performing with Wirasak Sunthornsri, who had been born in Bangkok but grew up in Korat. Surachai also played with Prasert Jandam, an Isan writer from Srisaket (see below), and other like-minded musicians. It was Surachai's collaboration with Somkhit Singsong

---

[44] Another group of young writers from Thammasat and Sinlapakorn Universities.

[45] ดินสอสี, "สัพเพเหระเรื่องการเขียนกับ สุรชัย จันทิมาธร," กรุงเทพธุรกิจ วันอาทิตย์ 12, 3923 (20 มิ. ย. 2542):16.

[46] Surachai, Interview, 1999.

[47] Ibid.

[48] For a full-length discussion of Surachai's life in music, see ชูเกียรติ ฉาไธสง, กำเนิดในยาม พระเจ้าหลังไหล. กรุงเทพฯ: สามัญชน, 2548.

(see below), a native of Khon Kaen, that produced what became the anthem of the student movement of that era: "*Khon Kap Khwai*" คนกับควาย (People and Buffalo). At the time it was written (around the early part of 1974), Surachai, Somkhit, and Visa Khanthap, who was also involved in writing the song, were staying together in a flat in Lard Prao, Bangkok. During those days, Surachai (and other young writers) moved around frequently, often staying with friends, sometimes sleeping at the offices of *Sangkhomsat Parithat* by Chulalongkorn University, and generally living as a wanderer (*phuphanejo'n*) and a seeker (*phusawaengha*), experiencing life without a schedule or routine. These practices were an important part of the sensibility of the times, and had a major presence in literary and musical expression then.

In 1974, Surachai and Wirasak joined with Mongkol Utoke (from Roi Et) and Thongkran Thana (from Korat),[49] both of whom at the time were playing in a group called *Bangkalathet Baen* (Bangladesh Band), to form a new band, Caravan. The fact that all four of the band members were from Isan, Surachai has acknowledged, played a role in their successfully joining and working together.[50] The band and its music became increasingly well-known, especially among students and political activists, performing at rallies and demonstrations both in Bangkok and up-country. Caravan's songs, combining local tunes with influence from Western folk music (at times even borrowing Western melodies),[51] expressed and tapped into the widespread feelings of dissatisfaction, alienation, and injustice. As noted above, many students became politically conscious and involved after hearing performances and listening to cassette tapes of Caravan (and other Songs for Life bands).[52] Caravan was especially outspoken in opposing the Vietnam War and the American influence and military presence in Thailand. This is perhaps not surprising given that the greater part of the American military presence was based in Isan. Songs like "*Amerikan Anta-rai*" อเมริกัน อันตราย (Dangerous American), and "*Khorat Khap Sai Ai Kan*" โคราชขับไส่ไอ้กัน (Korat Kicks Out the Damn Yanks), eloquently denounced American power, arrogance, and misdeeds, as well as the collusion of

---

[49] Surachai, Interview, 1999.

[50] Ibid.

[51] For example, the song "*Tai Sip Koet Saen*" (Ten Die, A Hundred Thousand Rise Up) uses the tune of Bob Dylan's "Hard Rain"; "*Khang Thanon*" (By the Side of the Road) is based on The Doors' version of "Light My Fire"; "*San Saeng Tho'ng*" (Weave the Golden Light) uses the melody of "Find the Cost of Freedom" by Crosby, Stills, Nash, and Young. Anon., ตำนานชีวิตคาราวาน. กรุงเทพฯ: ดอกหญ้า, 2536a.

[52] Ibid.

Thai officials. The song "*Jit Phumisak*," the melody of which is based on a traditional Irish song popularized in the 1970s by the British band, Traffic, eulogized this increasingly famous hero of the left during the period that he was still being rediscovered. Part of Nai Phi's poem, "Isan," was incorporated into Caravan's own theme song, "Caravan," which summoned listeners to their cause.

Most of Caravan's songs were written by Surachai, and many used Isan themes and even Isan languages (mostly Lao, but at least one song used Khmer).[53] The band also used traditional Isan instruments, like the *phin*, the *so'*, and the *khaen* (described in Chapter 1), in additional to their standard guitars. Some songs were written by other members of the band, or by non-members, like Prasert Jandam. In 1974, Surachai participated in the making of the film *Tho'ngpan* (see Chapter 2), appearing in the film as a kind of troubadour playing the *khaen* (a common symbol of Isan, and of Lao culture in general) and singing Caravan songs; he is also credited as one of the directors.[54] During this time, other members of the band worked with a *mo'lam* from Isan[55] and wrote such songs as "*Soeng Isan*" เซิ้งอีสาน, a piece in the traditional Lao *soeng* form[56] that describes in Lao language the suffering and oppression of Isan people under American imperialists and their Thai lackeys. Its powerful lyrics end with the line, "With our feet and with clubs let's drive those mothers out."[57] Similarly, "*Lam Ploen Jaroen Jai Khap Lai Amerika*" ลำเพลินเจริญใจขับไล่อเมริกา (The Great *Lam Phloen* for Kicking Out America) is also in a *mo'lam* song form, the *lam phloen*. Mongkol was inspired to write it (in Lao) in 1975 after a hearing a *lam phloen* troupe perform in Thongkran's home village on the Korat-Khon Kaen border.[58] It begins with the traditional words, "When I open the curtain ...," and continues:

> I see the country full of Westerners. It's a vexing sight. Let's help each other chase them out [...] Good people of Isan, join together.

[53] The song, "*Khanyom*" (I), uses a Khmer first person pronoun in its title. The first line, sung by Surachai, states, "*Khanyom pen khon khamen*" (I am a Khmer person). See Caravan's album, *Khon Klai Ban* (*People Far from Home*), which also contains a national song of Laos and other Indochinese themes.

[54] ชาญวิทย์, บ.ก., ทองปาน, 2549.

[55] Mongkol Utoke, comment at concert, September 19, 1998, Bangkok.

[56] A call-and-response form sung as part of the *Bun Bang Fai* or Rocket Festival celebrations.

[57] See the album, อเมริกัน อันตราย. See also Anon., ตำนาน, 2536a, pp. 138–9.

[58] Anon., ตำนาน, 2536a, p. 154.

Oy, people, turn and see the huge big-noses, kick them out, they're
plundering the country.[59]

On October 6, 1976, Caravan was in Korat for a performance. They
received word of the atrocities committed by police and paramilitary groups
in Bangkok, and that same night decided to join the resistance movement
in the jungle. A friend with connections in the Communist Party told them
how to make contact. During the next several years in the jungle, Caravan as
a band ceased to exist. The members still had contact with one another, but
they received political and military training[60] and then were given different
duties. Eventually an art unit was established, in which those involved wrote
songs and read Mao Zedong's tract on art, the contents of which Surachai
strongly disagreed with. Sometimes the CPT superiors would change the
names of the songs written by members of the art unit to reflect a stronger
sense of struggle. Some songs were broadcast over CPT radio, *The Voice
of the People of Thailand*. Often theater performances with music were
arranged, but those by Surachai were strongly criticized by Party members.
Dissatisfaction with the situation began to grow among the musicians, a
number of whom, including Surachai, became withdrawn, spending time
hunting, fishing, or practicing by themselves.[61]

After a time, members of the art unit, including Surachai, were sent
to Laos, eventually reaching what was known as Post Number Three. There
they met many other intellectuals and artists, including Nai Phi. Surachai
later published an article in the literary magazine *Thanon Nangsue* in which
he described his encounters with, and impressions of, this influential poet.[62]
Nai Phi's song, "*Khit Theung Ban* คิดถึงบ้าน" (Missing Home), also known as
"*Deuan Phen*" เดือนเพ็ญ (Full Moon), later became one of the most popular
songs played by Caravan, crossing over to people of all political persuasions.
Surachai particularly liked the song because of its beautiful sound, as well
as the fact that Nai Phi had had experiences with it similar to what Surachai

---

[59] Ibid., pp. 154–5.

[60] It was during such training that Surachai wrote the song, "*Thang Thom Haeng
Raeng Fai*" (Surge Ahead and Mobilize Our Strength), a stirring call to arms, full
of Marxist terminology, and still popular today. Ironically, this song has become
a favorite among the younger male segment of Surachai's fans, few of whom are
likely to have any real understanding of its underlying ideology. Surachai, Interview,
1999.

[61] วีระศักดิ์ สุนทรศรี, คาราวาน: ตำนานทัพหน้าวงดนตรีเพื่อชีวิตของไทย. กรุงเทพฯ: กำแพง, 2536.

[62] See สุราชัย จันทิมาธร, "คิดถึงบ้าน คิดถึงนายผี ..อัศนี พลจันทร," ถนนหนังสือ 3, 4 (ต.ค. 2528):
16–9.

had with his own songs, that is, the CPT authorities did not approve of it.[63] During Surachai's time with the CPT, there was much discussion about the coming new society, and Caravan's songs were criticized by some as being too Western and "old society." There were also arguments about aesthetics, and accusations about Songs for Life being a movement of the capitalist class. Song lyrics were checked for appropriateness, and more arguments arose over the changes that were made. When Wirasak and others could not take seriously a Chinese socialist realist film they considered ridiculously slavish toward its hero, someone suggested their rations be reduced. Around this time, Khamsing Srinawk withdrew from the Party, criticizing it as lacking in freedom and following China too closely.[64]

According to Wirasak, Surachai's philosophy of doing what he wanted was especially at odds with the Party's thinking, i.e., that he should do what they told him. He would often say, "I won't follow the Party like cattle." He asked to go to the front, and soon afterward left Laos for Thailand. The other Caravan musicians went to Sipsongpanna in China to study music and dance. Although the food, language, and surroundings were similar to Thailand in some ways, they felt uncomfortable being away from their own country, studying instruments all day long. Then came Vietnam's announcement that it would no longer support the CPT, and the Kriangsak government's offer of amnesty to people in the jungle.[65] A year later, in 1980, Wirasak left the jungle and returned to the city. Mongkol did so as well some months later, having studied music for two years in China. Surachai traveled around, living with hill tribe people, collecting local songs, and playing music for the villagers. Eventually, in 1981, he and Thongkran also returned to Bangkok. After some time, they all agreed to get back together to perform at a concert for UNICEF, which was organized by Surachai's brother Sathien.[66] Since then, they have gone their separate ways, occasionally reconvening to perform on certain occasions, such as commemorations of October 14.

For Surachai, as for most of those who came out of the jungle, resuming life in Bangkok was a whole new struggle. His stories from that time (early to late 1980s), for example "*Khang Thanon*" (By the Side of the Road), show his disaffection, alienation, and disillusionment with both the movement he left behind and the society he rejoined. Gradually, however, he became

[63] Anon., ตำนาน, 2536a, p. 211.
[64] วีระศักดิ์, คาราวาน, 2536.
[65] Ibid.
[66] Anon., ตำนาน, 2536a.

more integrated, and he wrote less and less literature, other than songs. His earlier books, though, have been reprinted at least a dozen times, and a new book, *Tawan Si Daeng* (*The Red Sun*), appeared in 1999, consisting of old but previously unpublished material. Also in 1999, however, in *Siam Rath* weekly, he had a regular column, "*Phan Ta Phan Jai*" (Catching the Eye, Capturing the Heart), in which he talks about recent travels in Laos, mixing stories, poetry, and travel narrative.[67] In the early 21st century, Surachai was devoting his time to music, writing new songs, releasing new albums, and performing frequently with his own band.[68] In 2010, he was made a National Artist in Literature. Surachai is regularly referred to as *Ajan Yai Phleng Pheua Chiwit* (The Senior Professor of Songs for Life). Caravan has in fact inspired, and even taught, later generations of musicians in the Songs for Life mode; Surachai has performed with two of the most successful of these, Phongsit Khamphi and Chukiet Chathaisong, who are, like the members of Caravan, both from Isan (Nong Khai and Buri Ram, respectively). In 1999, Caravan gave a 25-year commemorative concert, at which they performed old favorites and rarely-heard classics, as well as new material concerning journalistic responsibility, the prime minister at the time (Chuan Leekpai), etc. Surachai spoke Lao at times during the concert, something he rarely did in the past (at least in Bangkok), and the stage was decorated with a set resembling the Angkor-era Khmer ruins at Phimai or Phanom Rung.[69]

The following is a complete list of Surachai Janthimathorn's published books as of 2000:[70]

1) *Ma Jak Thi Rap Sung* มาจากที่ราบสูง (*Coming from the High Plateau*), 1969, a collection of short stories written from 1966 to 1968;

2) *Doen Pai Su Hon Nai* เดินไปสู่หนไหน (*Which Path to Tread*), 1970, a collection of short stories written in 1969;

---

[67] See, for example, the issues of March 28–April 3 and June 13–19, 1999.

[68] He was also playing soccer with old friends on two different teams, which he referred to somewhat humorously as "Teams for Life." Surachai, Interview, 2000.

[69] This appears to be a manifestation of *tho'ngthin niyom* (regionlism/localism) (see Chapter 5). The concert was recorded and released on CD, the cover of which showed the stage set with its Angkor-style lintel bearing a central figure playing the *khaen*.

[70] The words to many of Caravan's better-known songs, as well as accounts of the band's experiences and the origins of the songs, were published in 1984 (and reprinted many times thereafter); see Anon., *Tamnan Chiwit Kharawan* (*Chronicle of the Life of Caravan*) (Bangkok: Do'k Ya, 1993), cited above as Anon., ตำนานชีวิตคาราวาน. กรุงเทพฯ: ดอกหญ้า, 2536a.

3) *Khwam Ba Ma Yeuan* ความบ้ามาเยือน (*Madness Comes to Visit*), 1974, a collection of short stories written from 1970 to 1972;

4) *Ko'n Thi Fa Ja Sang* ก่อนที่ฟ้าจะสาง (*Before Dawn*) (shortened to *Ko'n Fa Sang* ก่อนฟ้าสาง in later editions), 1981, a novel about Lawa people "resisting the power of the State";

5) *Ko'n Khleuan Kharawan* ก่อนเคลื่อนคาราวาน (*Before the Caravan Movement*), 1982, a reissue of short stories written from 1967 to 1974;

6) *Kheu Khon Lamkhen Dontri Kharawan* คือคนลำเค็ญ ดนตรีคาราวาน (*People of Hardship: Caravan's Music*), 1985, a collection of short memoirs concerning Caravan and their travels and performances in Japan, with illustrations by Mongkol Utoke;

7) *Khang Thanon* ข้างถนน (*By the Side of the Road*), 1987, a collection of short stories written from 1974 to 1987 (to 1988 in later editions);

8) *Tawan Si Daeng* ตะวันสีแดง (*Red Sun*), 1998, a collection of short stories, poems, memoirs, and interviews, ranging from 1975 to 1998 (with a few undated), but mostly from the early to mid-1980s; and

9) with Prasert Jandam: *Jareuk Bon Nang Seua* จารึกบนหนังเสือ (*Inscribed on Tiger Skin*), 1975, poetry, mostly by Prasert.

Surachai's first book, *Ma Jak Thi Rap Sung*, comprises stories written when he was only 18 to 20 years old. Even so, the stories show a high degree of skill and innovation. The lives and experiences of Isan people, whether in Isan or outside it, make up the predominant subject, and principal points of interest are the feelings of the characters toward themselves, their world, and one another. In the writer's preface from 1987,[71] Surachai talks about the practice of writing and the authors who influenced him, including Lu Xun; Hemingway and his method of advancing the story through dialogue; R. Janthaphimpha, a romantic writer; Manas Janyong; O'. Udakorn; Suwanni Sukhontha; and Lao Khamhawm, with his "strange name" and his declaration, "I am Isan."[72]

"*Laeng Khen*" แล้งเข็ญ (Drought), written in 1967, is one of Surachai's most important stories. Suchart Sawatsi credits it as one of the first stories to show its independence from the kind of lackadaisical tales with O. Henry-type surprise endings that held sway in the 1960s. The esteem with which Suchart viewed Surachai and his work is demonstrated by the fact that Suchart not only included "*Laeng Khen*" in his first anthology of contemporary Thai short stories of the time, but named the anthology after

---

[71] สุราชัย จันทิมาธร, "จากผู้เขียน," in มาจากที่ราบสูง. กรุงเทพฯ: กำแพง," 2533, pp. 11–4.
[72] Surachai, Interview, 1999.

it.[73] Ranjuan also praised the story *"Laeng Khen"* and its author, saying, "Surachai tends to write stories that show that conscience still exists."[74] In fact, Suchart's collection both reflected, and added impetus to, the interest and concern for poor and oppressed people living in disadvantaged areas, especially Isan. As Ranjuan notes:

> *Laeng Khen* is a collection of short stories that do not please and entertain, but rather produce a feeling of wilting and pity. Yet we should not be discouraged; on the contrary, they make us more understanding and sympathetic toward these lives of hardship … Perhaps they help us see a picture or a way to help improve these lives to have a better and more just existence, beyond studying the thoughts and characteristics of the writing of these writers of the present.[75]

Surachai's story, *"Laeng Khen,"* relates a minor but telling incident in the lives of a poor Isan family existing under extremely hot and dry conditions. All of the village youth have gone to Central Thailand to work, and those who remain spend their time searching for food (frogs, toads, crabs, honey, etc.). The father in the story takes his young son out and instructs him (and, simultaneously, the reader) in Isan ways of finding food. The father catches a frog, which they take home for the mother to cook. The boy's hunger drives him to eat part of the cooked frog secretly before meal time. The mother notices and scolds him, but then at dinner when the father asks who has eaten the missing part, she wants to take the blame yet is unable to lie. The father becomes angry and is on the verge of hitting his son, but stops himself. For a moment no one eats, until the father offers the leg, the best part of the frog, to the boy.

The story evokes an atmosphere of heat, aridity, barrenness, and hunger, of poverty and emotional stress, of quiet struggle to retain one's humanity in the face of adversity. The dialogue, consisting of succinct sentences in Lao, gives the story an authenticity in harmony with its stark imagery. It bears similarities with Lao Khamhawm's story, *"Fa Prot"* ("Dunghill" in English) (see Chapter 2), in which two children and an old man try to outsmart each other and take possession of newly discovered edible dung beetle larvae. However, while Khamsing concentrates on the plot and its denouement, Surachai emphasizes the ambience of the setting and the emotions of the characters. As Sila Khomchai has commented:

---

[73] สุชาติ สวัสดิ์ศรี, บ.ก, แล้งเข็ญ. กรุงเทพฯ: ดวงกมล, 2518.

[74] รัญจวน อินทรกำแหง, วรรณกรรมวิจารณ์, ตอนที่ 3. กรุงเทพฯ: ดวงกมล, 2521, p. 19.

[75] Ibid., p. 21.

> With Nga [Surachai] nothing is halfway ... His writing is exciting. While at first there was influence from Lao Khamhawm, after that he clearly had his own methods; they were clearly Surachai. In his work it is hard to get a story, but one gets a lot of feeling.[76]

Other stories in *Ma Jak Thi Rap Sung* show the same ability to create an atmosphere and depict the emotional interactions of the characters, in the process giving a clear impression of Isan society. For example, "*Bon Rot Fai Chan Sam*" บนรถไฟชั้นสาม (On the Third Class Train) describes the scene on a train from Ubon to Bangkok. The passengers, all from Isan, spend the time talking, drinking, sleeping, or thinking. The train car is like a discreet bit of Isan space moving down the tracks. Bonds form as the passengers talk, share their foods, and help one another. When the train reaches Bangkok, however, the temporary community disintegrates; people separate and disappear into the city. The camaraderie and apparent purity of the people on the train contrast sharply with the dirty, smelly, impersonal, corrupt, and corrupting world of Bangkok. This theme of the honesty and goodness of Isan (or other rural) people, compared to the selfish and unscrupulous world of Bangkok, becomes a common one in Isan (and other) writing.

"*Nok Phirap*" นกพิราบ (Pigeons), another story in the same collection, was cited by Sathien Janthimathorn as an example of a groundbreaking, new, experimental piece. Writers in the Era of Search of the late 1960s and early 1970s, he says, were tired not only of the O. Henry-style plot twists, but also with romance books, serialized stories in 100 parts, and action-driven plots with climactic endings. The new writers wrote with emphasis not on the story's outline, but rather on feelings and the journey of feelings of the characters.[77] In "*Nok Phirab*," the narrator visits a temple in Bangkok with friends and is reminded of his hometown, its administrative elevation to sub-district (*king-amphoe*), and the resulting "progress": more people, dust, theft, and alienation. The narrator tells of how, on his last visit home, a merchant friend who used to raise pigeons no longer had any: they had slowly disappeared as they were apparently caught and eaten by newcomers who had no knowledge of, or interest in, the birds' keeper. The story is like a fragment, a memory, very nostalgic and melancholy. Without any action and with no real plot, it tells of social change and sustains an atmosphere of loss

---

[76] Anon., "ทัศนะของเพื่อนมิตร ต่อ 'บทกวีในเสียงเพลง' ของ สุรชัย จันทิมาธร," กรุงเทพธุรกิจ วันอาทิตย์ 13, 3742 (20 ธ.ค. 2541): p. 8.

[77] เสถียร จันทิมาธร, "วรรณกรรมในยุค 'แสวงหา' ของหนุ่มสาวรุ่นใหม่," in สายธารวรรณกรรมเพื่อ ชีวิตของไทย. กรุงเทพฯ: เจ้าพระยา," 2527, pp. 375–414.

in the aging of a small town and its people. Although Isan is not mentioned explicitly here, the story seems to be autobiographical, told as a first person narrative by a man who moved to Bangkok after finishing secondary school up-country.

While *Ma Jak Thi Rap Sung* is essentially a book of Isan-related material, Surachai's second collection, *Doen Pai Su Hon Nai* (*Which Path to Tread*), is a book of search, as its title indicates. While still drawing on the author's Isan background, this latter collection embodies a quest for meaning and direction. Written when Surachai was still only 21, these stories are characterized by feelings of loneliness, alienation, and melancholy. "*Sunthari Kap Tho'ng Sen*" สุนทรีกับทองเสน (Sunthari and Tho'ng Sen), for example, is a story about a lonely and directionless young man from Surin. Nonetheless, many of the pieces contain images and symbols that became emblematic of the Era of Search and the Art for Life zeitgeist of the early to mid-1970s: the yellow bird and freedom, blooming flowers and the developing consciousness of youth, bridges and coming together, travel and life experience, etc. The title of the story, "*Nok Si Leuang*" นกสีเหลือง (Yellow Bird), became the title of a Song for Life that was later sung regularly in the jungle as a eulogy for those killed on October 6, 1976.

Surachai's third book, *Khwam Ba Ma Yeuan* (*Madness Comes to Visit*), contains stories written between 1970 and 1972, and was first published after October 14, 1973. It is full of alcohol, marijuana, and aimlessness, as is illustrated by "*Kham Kheun An Mon Mo'ng Lae Rai*" ค่ำคืนอันหม่นหมองและร้าย (A Dismal and Devilish Night). In this story, a young man wastes time drinking alone and having thoughts of punching out his quiet, hardworking co-worker, which he later regrets. However, another story, "*Lom Hai Jai Kho'ng Tho'ng Thung*" ลมหายใจของท้องทุ่ง (Breath of the Open Fields), is an exception. It consists entirely of descriptive imagery of nature, fields, and the creatures inhabiting them (buffalo, bird, snake, lizard, etc.), as well as the sound of local music: "The songs of the local *phin* do not have much variation, but the sounds are so sweet."[78] Perhaps because of its distinctiveness, this story was not included until later printings of the book. In the book's preface, Surachai talks about his using and abusing alcohol and marijuana and subsequently giving them up (years later).[79] Even so, the image of Surachai as a heavy drinker and drug user, reinforced during the

---

[78] สุรชัย จันทิมาธร, "ลมหายใจของท้องทุ่ง," in ความบ้ามาเยือน. กรุงเทพฯ: สามัญชน, 2541a, p. 63.

[79] สุรชัย จันทิมาธร, "จากผู้เขียน," in สุรชัย, ความบ้า, 2541c, pp. 9–14.

1970s and 80s, persists to this day, a reputation that he seems unable to shake off, or, perhaps more accurately, that Thai society is unable or unwilling to revise or give up.[80]

The late Rong Wongsawan's mid-1970s comment on Surachai, printed in the same collection, is instructive:

> Some people think he is a traveller without a destination. His free heart is a compass needle that points neither north nor another direction. With an old cotton bag hanging from his shoulder, a guitar, and long hair, he is ready to travel wherever his mood takes him, like a *tudong*[81] monk without a robe. Some of the songs he writes show the torment of [a part of] society that is taken advantage of in a way worthy of tears, and some political groups have taken a keen interest. His short stories have received fitting acceptance in society that has a tendency to listen to the ideas and opinions of the young [...] His poetry has its own particular personality, and even though it cannot yet be praised as successful, it is widely known in university circles. And it appears that success is not the prize he is after. This is his third collection, *Khwam Ba Ma Yeuan*. Certainly he has some things to tell his readers about the complex mechanisms of goodness and beauty.[82]

After 1972, when the last stories in *Khwam Ba Ma Yeuan* were written, Surachai wrote less literature as such and turned more toward music and songwriting (see below). In 1981, he published a short novel (his only one), *Ko'n Fa Sang* (*Before Dawn*), about a group of Lawa people (a hill tribe in Northern Thailand) and their struggles against state oppression.[83] Only in 1987 did a new collection of his stories appear, called *Khang Thanon* (*By the Side of the Road*). The material in this book was written between 1974 and 1986 (later editions include stories through 1988), although there is a gap from the years that Surachai was in the jungle. In the preface, Surachai describes leaving the jungle, abandoning his gun and uniform, and hitchhiking into the nearest town; he also talks about

---

[80] Thus, even in 2000, long after he had quit liquor and cigarettes, interviewers still regularly asked him how much he drank, or made insinuations that he was intoxicated.

[81] Wandering.

[82] รงค์ วงษ์สวรรค์, "รงค์ วงษ์สวรรค์ เขียนถึง สุรชัย จันทิมาธร," in สุรชัย, ความบ้า, 2541c, pp. 17–8.

[83] This book was published in Bangkok while Surachai was still in the jungle. Without Surachai's knowledge, an editor removed several pages from the manuscript, which are now lost.

the war and death he witnessed, and about reentering society, writing, and restarting Caravan.[84] Overall, as noted above, themes of disillusionment, alienation, and readjustment predominate, overshadowing what little Isan content is evident.

One story in the collection, "*Seua Tua Sutthai*" เสื้อตัวสุดท้าย (The Last Shirt), concerns an old man who has come to Bangkok after being evicted from his shack in a rural village by a *thao-kae*, or Chinese landowner. As the old man begs on the streets of the capital, he remembers his childhood in Isan catching frogs and crabs. When he has collected enough money in his begging cup, he tries to buy a shirt that caught his eye in a shop window, but the shop workers ridicule him and refuse to sell it. When he dies at the end, they give the shirt to the corpse-gatherers to put on his body before taking him away. The story once again sets up a contrast between the virtues of Isan people and the vices of others. The old man likes to sing and amuse people, speaks in a brief and straightforward style, and suffers silently; he faces the injustices of the greedy landowner, the mean shop-keepers, and the uncaring city people who pass him on the sidewalk. The shirt is a kind of grail that represents the old man's attempt to become part of the society of the city, but is denied him; only by dying does he reach his goal and gain the trappings of the community around him, but even then he remains separate.

The role of the shirt is similar to that of the telephone in the title story of the collection. The story is told from the point of view of a young man in the capital who is looking for work but encounters difficulties at every turn. These include the heat and pollution of the streets, a lack of money for the public phones, a feeling of inferiority toward the well-dressed and groomed people around him, and a shortage of help and sympathy from his friends. In the end, he gazes through a shop window at the fancy telephones on display, and muses on the vast gulf that separates these elegant luxury items from the common public phones that are an unpleasant and unavoidable part of his life.

Khang Thanon also contains a short story, "*Lakho'n Mai Mi Cheu*" ละครไม่มีชื่อ (Play without a Name), which describes an impromptu stage drama. Two women circle around each other, preparing to fight, while the director (a man) goads them on, until finally one of the women kills him. Initially the story resembles an allegory of the oppressed (women, the poor, etc.) rising up in revolution. However, the date of the work points to another

---

[84] สุรชัย จันทิมาธร, "จากผู้เขียน," in ข้างถนน. กรุงเทพฯ: สามัญชน, 2532, pp. 12–4.

interpretation as well: it was written in 1982, just after Surachai had quit the CPT's armed struggle and left the jungle. The rift between pro-Chinese and pro-Vietnamese (and Soviet) factions in the Party, in which the former eventually dominated, resulted in mass defections and the virtual destruction of the CPT.

Surachai's poetry and songs have similar qualities to his stories. "*Thanon Mitraphap*" ถนนมิตรภาพ (The Friendship Highway) uses visual imagery and poetic language in discussing an Isan-related subject while exposing hypocrisy and injustice. In this case, the target is the US government and its construction of the highway from Bangkok to Korat. As the song points out, this road was named (and is still called) the "Friendship Highway," even though it was built to transport bombs and other war materiel used to bring death and suffering to millions of people in Vietnam, Laos, and Cambodia. In the playing of the song, a guitar is used in a thrumming manner, imitating the sound of helicopters, as a line is sung about the Westerners' departure; the listener cannot help but think of the ignominious and panicked evacuation from the top of the American Embassy in Saigon in 1975. The song ends with the repeated word, "friendship, friendship, friendship ...," showing Surachai's talent for biting sarcasm as well as melodious phrasing.

The popular Thai song, "*Phu Yai Li*" (Headman Li) (see Chapter 2), also figures in Surachai's work. He stated that he considers the song important and funny, not insulting to Isan. Nevertheless, in at least two of his own songs, he makes clear reference to "*Phu Yai Li*" and seems to be, at least in part, trying to counteract its mocking attitude toward Isan people. The first of these is "*Ban Na Satheuan*" บ้านนาสะเทือน (Trembling Farm Hut), which he wrote in the jungle in 1981. At the time, he had just received a letter informing him of his mother's accidental death, but the letter had taken months to reach him, and the funeral was long past. Part of the song (translated below) deals with difficulties in Isan villages, but takes the point of view of the villagers themselves, as distinguished from the original "*Phu Yai Li*" song, which made fun of the villagers and made no attempt to see them as real people.

Ban Na Satheuan (Trembling Farm Hut)

In the year 2524 [1981], Headman Li beat the drum to call a meeting
The hot wind surrounded and stifled like a smoldering fire all over the parched land
In our village the old and the aged, every one of them, is depressed
Rice is expensive, things are expensive, Headman Li makes no argument

He has no energy even to tell the news of villagers who have gone to
work in the city
Abandoning their carrying poles and grain baskets
Changing out of their sarongs into jeans
Men sell their labor to live, women sell their bodies to eat
It's saddening to hear
While grandma, with her clouded eyes, and her granddaughter, hang
their heads and beg.[85]

The other song making reference to "*Phu Yai Li*" is called "*Phu Yai La*" ผู้ใหญ่ลา, and is on the album, *Rak Lae Wang* รักและหวัง (*Love and Hope*), released by Surachai (not Caravan) in 1993. In this song, Surachai repeats the line, "*ma no'i ma no'i thammada*" (little dogs, common little dogs), from the original song, but with a twist. While in the 1961 song, this line was the main punchline inviting people to laugh at the Isan headman (who misunderstood a Central Thai word for "pig"), in Surachai's version the same line is used to refer to corrupt and dishonest politicians from Central Thailand who take advantage of Isan villagers.

An important aspect of Surachai's work has been his associations and collaborations with other writers and musicians. These include members of groups like *Phra Jan Siow*, Isan writers like Somkhit Singsong and Prasert Jandam, the other members of Caravan, and local musicians from Isan and other regions of Thailand. The support, encouragement, inspiration, ideas, and attitudes that passed between them have at times been crucial to Surachai's creativity, and have produced lasting written and musical work. As one commentator has noted, "poems and friendship mixed to form the power of songs" in the early 1970s,[86] but in fact this is applicable to a much wider time period. In Thai society, where solitude is generally shunned and considered suspect, the life of a writer can at times be a particularly alienating and discouraging one. At the same time, gregariousness, group effort, and mutual assistance are often cited as characteristics of Isan culture. Thus, Surachai has drawn on his Isan background in ways that have affected his work psychologically, morally, and aesthetically.

The issue of Surachai's ideology is one that invites consideration. Having espoused revolutionary ideas and spent five years with the armed struggle of the Communist Party of Thailand, Surachai initially appears to be (or to have been) a confirmed Marxist. However, a close examination of his life and work shows he had a much looser and less regimented

---

[85] สุรชัย จันทิมาธร, "บ้านนาสะเทือน," in Anon., ตำนาน, 2536a [1993], pp. 218–9.

[86] พิมลราศ, "อะคูสติก สุรชัย จันทิมาธร 'เฉพาะกาล' ลานหญ้าหอศิลป์," ฐานสัปดาห์วิจารณ์ 4(5): 243(308) (19–25 ธ.ค. 2541): 40.

philosophy of life and politics. His disagreements and dissatisfaction with the CPT began almost as soon as he joined one of their jungle bases. He would not be told what to do or say, and indeed has never been willing or able to conform. It is his aversion to injustice and his feelings of solidarity with the disenfranchised, rather than advocacy of any particular political doctrine, that have lead him to express, with feeling and eloquence, anti-imperialist and anti-tyrannical views. His seeming anti-Americanism, most evident in a number of his songs, is not opposition to the US *per se*, but to the policies and actions of a misguided American government. His fondness for American music and his experience playing with American musicians demonstrate this. Furthermore, while Surachai has shown great admiration for Jit Phumisak and Nai Phi, writing and performing several songs based on their lives and works,[87] that admiration is based less on their political rhetoric than on their forceful, articulate, and poetic output.

Isan is the underlying foundation of Surachai's work, influencing both style and content, as is apparent in most of his work. In fact, though, Surachai's sensibility overall is characterized by openness and eclecticism. It is these attributes that have led him to make use of Southern Thai local melodies, Hmong traditional tunes, and American and Okinawan folk songs in his music. In the same way, he has taken inspiration in his writing from an equally diverse range of authors, as noted above. While he readily uses Lao[88] and sometimes Khmer language in his work, he also makes use of Northern Thai, Hmong, and even Japanese and English. His novel of a Lawa community is based on his experience living with Lawa people, and he spent many months gathering musical material from all over Thailand and Laos before leaving the jungle.

Recently, Isan has returned to prominence in Surachai's work, as he continues what he has always done: using Isan as his base and point of departure. During Caravan's 25-year commemorative concert in Bangkok in 1999, they played a number of Lao songs from their past, and Surachai

---

[87] These include "*KhitTheung Ban*" (Missing Home), a song by Nai Phi; "*Karawan*" (Caravan), which incorporates words from Nai Phi's poem, "*Isan!*"; "*Poep Khaw*" เปิบข้าว (Eat Rice), based on a poem by Jit Phumisak; and "*Jit Phumisak*," a song about Jit's life and legend. Surachai has also recited Nai Phi's poetry at concerts, including "*Taling Kho'ng So'ng Khang*" ตลิ่งของสองข้าง (Mekong Riverbanks), which refers to the river by its Lao name, "Kho'ng," not its Thai name, "Khong."

[88] In addition to the songs and stories noted above, see also those discussed in วาสนา, "การวิเคราะห์," 2534; and จิตกวี กระจ่างเมฆ, "ศึกษาวรรณกรรมเพลงเพื่อชีวิตของ สุรชัย จันทิมาธร," ปริญญานิพนธ์ มหาวิทยาลัยทักษิณ, 2541.

spoke Lao freely on stage several times between songs, telling stories and making jokes. In doing so, he seemed to be participating in the growing regionalism and regional pride that has become noticeable in Thailand (see Chapter 5), showing once again his continuing ability to develop and change with the times.

Surachai Janthimathorn is a writer and musician with an unmistakable Isan sensibility. His work is evocative and poetic, full of imagery and expressive language. At the same time, he can speak forcefully against injustice and the suffering it causes. His music played a major role in raising the political consciousness of a generation and galvanizing them into action. Although he is undoubtedly the best-known Isan writer in modern Thai history, his fame is due to his songs, not his prose. Hardly a week passes in Thailand today without a mention of, if not an entire article on, Surachai in the press. However, not only is he a well-known and gifted artist, but, perhaps more significantly, he is unusual in having developed through and participated in all the major progressive literary movements in Thailand from the 1960s to the present. Surachai grew up in the Dark Age of Thai literature, subsequently became a leading figure in the Era of Search and then the Art for Life movement, and went on to take up arms against the government. The disillusionment experienced by many writers after the collapse of that cause finds notable expression in his work of the 1980s. Since then, he has shared many of the goals and sentiments of the growing regionalism in Thai literature.

Prasert Jandam

Prasert Jandam ประเสริฐ จันดำ is one of the major figures among writers in the post-Dark Age period from the late 1960s to the late 1970s. His name is almost synonymous with Isan writing, political struggle, and Literature for Life of that era. During his lifetime, he published at least a dozen books of his own, plus several more in collaboration with other writers of the 1970s. Although best known for his poetry, he also produced many short stories, a novel, and a memoir. His life epitomized the habits, ideals, and convictions of a generation of writers and activists, from his rural roots, his peripatetic life in Bangkok, and his involvement with *Phra Jan Sieow*, to his fondness for alcohol, his efforts as champion of the cause of social justice and the interests of the poor, and his participation in the jungle insurgency. All of these factors have contributed to his increasingly legendary status in Thai writing circles, and especially among Isan writers, since his death in 1995.

Prasert Jandam was born in 1945 in Uthumphornphisai District of Srisaket Province. He began elementary school in his hometown, but then moved to Buri Ram, where he completed elementary school and continued with secondary school.[89] He later worked in Bangkok and attended Suan Kulab Academy, where his fellow students included Witthayakorn Chiengkun. However, Prasert had to repeat a year because he "liked reading books and writing more than studying."[90] He then attended teachers' college, but quit before completing the first year. He had always wanted to be a writer, he said,[91] and at this point he began to work for a newspaper. He also enrolled in the night school program in journalism at Thammasat University. By 1967 or 1968, he had joined *Phra Jan Siow*[92] and was writing poetry and short stories as his main work; he also wrote serialized novels under pen names in three different weeklies.[93] By 1969, he had completely given up studying and was spending all his time writing. In addition to the poetry and short stories that were his main interests, he also earned significant income from writing scary stories, racy romances, and action adventures for the popular press.[94]

After October 14, 1973, *Phra Jan Sieow* was rarely meeting, and its activities had decreased drastically. At this time, Prasert met Somkhit Singsong, who invited Prasert to join his project, farming and teaching in Sap Daeng Village, Khon Kaen.[95] To Somkhit's surprise, Prasert immediately agreed to join him, so by the end of the year (1973) they were in Sap Daeng, starting an unofficial school in which to teach village youth. Prasert's third book of poetry, *Ro'i Kro'ng Jak Sap Daeng* (*Verses from Sap Daeng*), came out of this experience. Prasert describes his friend:

> Somkhit is a good thinker, planner, and organizer. He left his university studies when he saw that the only way he could bring progress to the people of his village was to actually carry out his project.[96]

---

[89] Anon., "เกี่ยวกับผู้เขียน," in ประเสริฐ จันคำ, ดอกคูนเสียงแคน. กรุงเทพฯ: มิ่งมิตร, 2532b, p. 10.

[90] ประเสริฐ จันคำ. พลิกตำนานเพื่อชีวิต. กรุงเทพฯ: ดอกหญ้า, 2534, p. 10.

[91] Ibid., p. 72.

[92] Prasert says the name came from a group of poets in the past in China called "Cresecent Moon," ibid., p. 11.

[93] The specifics of these works are not recorded.

[94] ประเสริฐ, พลิกตำนาน, 2534.

[95] According to Prasert, *sap* is a kind of natural spring, and *daeng* here refers to species of tree with red wood that grew next to such a well in the village. However, people who were opposed to Somkhit's project interpreted the name as something like "red blot," in other words, a hive of communists. Ibid.

[96] Ibid., p. 72.

However, official support and funding for the project did not materialize, and even though the books used in the school were Ministry of Education texts, accusations were made (in the form of gossip and rumor) that "theoretical texts" (i.e., Marxist works) were being taught. Sap Daeng came under scrutiny, hostility grew, and threats of violence were made. Prasert, as an outsider, felt especially vulnerable, and eventually he left the village for good and returned to Bangkok in 1975. Later that year, an article appeared in the newspaper reporting that Somkhit had been shot (not fatally) in Khon Kaen.

For some time, Prasert felt extremely disillusioned and unsettled, and spent his time traveling, writing, and drinking with friends. He wrote a few songs, with Songs for Life musicians like Visa Khanthap and Surachai, which were performed and later recorded by Caravan, including "*Paen Oet Toet*"[97] แปนเอิดเติด (Flat and Featureless) and "*Jotmai Jak Chao Na*" จดหมายจากชาวนา (Letter from Farmers). Prasert also helped friends campaign for parliamentary elections, primarily in Ubon Province. It was there that he decided to join the armed struggle against the government. In April 1976, he traveled with three friends to a small village on the Ubon-Cambodia-Laos border, where they met CPT cadres. One of those three friends was Surasi Phatham, who later directed the film *Khru Ban No'k (Rural Teacher)*,[98] based on the book by Khamman Khonkhai (see Chapter 4). Prasert then disappeared from Thai society for nearly six years, although he did publish one book during this period, *Pakka Kap Krasun (The Pen and the Bullet)*, in 1978.

After coming out of the jungle, Prasert got involved in election politics, running for provincial assembly in Buri Ram under the slogan, *Kin Im No'n Un Leuak Prasert Jandam* (Eat Enough, Sleep Soundly: Vote for Prasert Jandam). After two failed attempts, he ran for the national parliament from Surin Province, but was again unsuccessful.[99] He then returned to Buri Ram and took up farming again. In the late 1980s, he converted to Christianity.[100] According to the writer and critic Phailin Rungrat, in the 1990s he changed in other ways as well, in his view of the world, his looking into himself, and his understanding of life.[101] His later work shows an increased love

---

[97] This title is in Lao, but the lyrics are mostly in Thai.

[98] Ibid., p. 116.

[99] นฤมิตร ประพันธ์, "ไปฟังเสวนา 'รำลึก ประเสริฐ จันดำ...' ณ ศูนย์สังคีตศิลป์ชั้น 4 ธนาคารกรุงเทพฯ ผ่านฟ้า," จดหมายข่าวสโมสรนักเขียนภาคอีสาน 2, 6 (2539): 11.

[100] ประเสริฐ จันดำ, "จากผู้เขียน," in ประเสริฐ, ดอกคูน, 2532b, pp. 8–9.

[101] ไพลิน รุ้งรัตน์, ลมหายใจสุดท้ายของ ประเสริฐ จันดำ. กรุงเทพฯ: ดอกหญ้า, 2539, pp. 6–16.

and concern for nature, and a calmness and peace, even in thoughts about death, that apparently came from a belief in God.[102] One thing that did not change, however, was his excessive alcohol consumption. After being twice hospitalized, he died in Buri Ram in November, 1995.[103]

Prasert's books include the following:

1) *Do'k Khun Siang Khaen* ดอกคูนเสียงแคน (*Khun Flowers and Khaen Sounds*), 1970, short stories;

2) *Ro'i Kro'ng Jak Sap Daeng* รอยกรองจากซับแดง (*Verses from Sap Daeng*), 1975, poetry;

3) *Pakka Kap Krasun* ปากกากับกระสุน (*The Pen and the Bullet*), 1978, short stories;

4) *Chao Na Laeng* ชาวนาแล้ง (*Farmers of Parched Fields*), 1981, novel;

5) *Daen Din Thi Dan Deuat* ดินแดนที่ดาลเดือด (*Land of Sweltering and Seething*), 1982, short stories and poetry;

6) *Mu Ban Hao*[104] หมู่บ้านเฮา (*Our Village*), 1984, short stories;

7) *Fo'i Fon Bon Man Fun* ฝอยฝนบนม่านฝุ่น (*Rivulets of Rain on a Curtain of Dust*), 1985, poetry;

8) *Nang Hai* นางไห้ (*She Wept*), 1987, short stories;

9) *Bot Phleng Haeng Reudu Kan* บทเพลงแห่งฤดูกาล (*Songs of the Times*), 1988, poetry;

10) *Phlik Tamnan Pheua Chiwit* พลิกตำนานเพื่อชีวิต (*Reworking the "For Life" Chronicle*), 1989, memoir;

11) *Kheu Kao*[105] คือเก่า (*Same as Before*), 1990, short stories;

12) *Malet Khao Kheun Ruang* เมล็ดข้าวคืนรวง (*Rice Seed Returned to the Stalk*), undated (1991?), poetry;

13) with Narong Janreuang: *Malai So'ng Chai* มาลัยสองชาย (*Two Men's Garland*), 1968; and

14) with Visa Khanthap: *Nam Thuam Fa Pla Kin Dao* น้ำท่วมฟ้า ปลากินดาว (*Water Floods the Sky, Fish Eat the Stars*), 1975.

Prasert is remembered and respected by many Isan writers today for his skill as a writer and his unfailing empathy for his compatriots, the downtrodden people of Isan. However, he did not simply write about the adverse conditions of life in Isan and the struggles and suffering of its

---

[102] Ibid., pp. 6–12.

[103] นฤมิตร, "ไปฟัง," 2539, p. 11.

[104] This title is in Lao.

[105] The title is in Lao.

people. Prasert was able to present a more complete portrait of Isan people as human beings, not just victims. A good example of this is the short story, "*Kheun Phayu*" คืนพายุ (Storm Night), in the collection, *Nang Hai* (*She Wept*). A man leaves his wife and baby in their hut as he hurries out to catch fish for their dinner. However, a major storm blows in, and by the time he has fought his way back to the hut, the entire structure has disappeared. He finds his wife and child safe, if frightened, under a tree nearby. In spite of their loss, they express joy and thankfulness at surviving and being together. Thus the author emphasizes their strength and caring for one another, rather than their disaster and loss, thereby avoiding reducing them to mere objects of pity.

The title story in the same collection, *Nang Hai*, shows Prasert's skill and creativity as well. First published in *Matichon Weekly* in October 1986, the piece is what the author calls *klo'n reuang san*,[106] "a short story in verse," that is, one that resembles standard prose on the page but is written entirely in verse, even the dialogues. The author thus goes beyond his stated goal, "presenting images of the lives of the poor, both in the city and the countryside,"[107] and gives multi-dimensional portraits with innovation and finesse.

His later work, though simpler, is no less concerned with Isan and the lives of its people. His collection from the early 1990s, *Malet Khao Kheun Ruang* (*Rice Seed Returned to the Stalk*), is subtitled, "only resembling poetry."[108] In the foreword, the author talks of being from a long line of rice farmers, and of his consequent ability to work the land. He describes the book as "raw and fresh, like a local or Lao curry with just two or three kinds of vegetables, and of course the indispensable *pla ra* [fermented fish], the basic food of us Isan people."[109] He compares himself to a grain of rice:

> As a farmer's son who strayed from the land, I'm like a grain of rice strayed from the stalk, fallen into various places, not sterile or rotten, but perhaps pierced and gnawed by weevils and insects, still in the state of being a rice-seed, not white and beautiful on a pretty-colored plate.[110]

The verses in this collection have a simplicity and a sweetness in place of the political aggressiveness of his earlier poetry. However, they still

---

[106] ประเสริฐ จันดำ, "ถ้อยคำจากผู้เขียน," in ประเสริฐ.. นางให้. กรุงเทพฯ: วลี, 2530 (no page numbers).

[107] Ibid.

[108] ประเสริฐ จันดำ, เมล็ดข้าวคืนรวง. กรุงเทพฯ: แสงดาว, (undated)a [2534?], cover.

[109] ประเสริฐ จันดำ, "จากเมล็ดข้าว — พลัดรวง," in ประเสริฐ, เมล็ดข้าว, (undated)a [2534?], p. 3.

[110] Ibid.

comment on the direction of Isan society and culture, as can be seen by the following two poems:

> *Kutji* (Dung Beetle)
> *It's a buffalo dung insect*
> *Its life continues when there is buffalo dung*
> *Burying itself in there peacefully*
> *Poking its head out*
> *When dug up with a shovel*
> *Take it to fry, sweet-smelling with salt*
> *That is food*
> *One day when no buffalo remain*
> *One day when there are no buffaloes*
> *Where will we find kutji?*[111]

> *Khwai* (Buffalo)
> *Look at the picture and you'll say they live with the plow*
> *Look again and you'll see they live with people*
> *Feeding the world up to the present*
> *Eating grass for strength*
> *For flesh, for skin*
> *Flesh buffalo*
> *Steel buffalo*
> *Which will rule the world of the future?*[112]

Narong Janreuang, with whom Prasert wrote his first book, described Prasert's writing as follows:

> Prasert Jandam is lucky to have had a great amount of life experience. He has travelled in every region, every province, and almost every district of Thailand … Furthermore, his stories are full of life. They are not stiff, dried up, and full of bookish expressions. Prasert's characters are ordinary people who we have seen, met, or talked to. They are not superlative to the point of being inhuman, or so evil as to be unrealistic. And the ordinariness of these characters impresses the reader, who could easily be an ordinary person.[113]

Prasert himself described the goal of his writing in *Fo'i Fon Bon Man Fun* (*Rivulets of Rain on a Curtain of Dust*): "It is my intention to write about events and reality on the ground of the plateau directly."[114]

---

[111] ประเสริฐ, เมล็ดข้าว, (undated)a [2534?], p. 9.

[112] Ibid., p. 45.

[113] ณรวค์ จันทร์เรือง, "จาก ณรวค์ จันทร์เรือง ถึง ประเสริฐ จันคำ," in ประเสริฐ, ดอกคูน, 2532b, pp. 8–9.

[114] ประเสริฐ จันคำ, ฝอยฝนบนม่านฝุ่น, กรุงเทพฯ: ก่อไผ่, 2528 (no page number).

After Prasert's death, he began to take on the qualities of a mythic character. In 1996, Phailin published *Lom Hai Jai Sutthai Kho'ng Prasert Jandam* (*Prasert Jandam's Last Breath*), in which she describes the "amazing, miraculous" sensation she felt from looking at his papers after his death.[115] She also chaired a seminar that year called *Ramleuk Prasert Jandam* (*Recollections of Prasert Jandam*).[116] Many people attended and described their memories of Prasert: that he was kind and well-liked, that the happiest time of his life was teaching in Sap Daeng, and so on. Several poets read work dedicated to him, including Naowarat Phongphaiboon, Wat Wanlayangkul, Phaiwarin Khao-ngam (see Chapter 6), and Seri Thatsanasin (also from Isan). Surachai sang three songs, including Prasert's "*Jotmai Jak Chao Na*" (Letter from Farmers). The participants also discussed Prasert's heavy drinking. Narong Janreuang recounted how, sometimes when Prasert was very drunk, his dedication to truth and justice would lead him to verbally attack policemen in uniform.[117] Prasert's drinking himself to death became a cautionary tale for many. The *Newsletter of the Isan Writers' Association* published an article in 1999 entitled, "Commemorating Five Years of the Departure of the Great Poet of the People, Prasert Jandam." The article included a photograph of a framed picture of Prasert, displayed at his funeral, in which he is pointing a finger at the viewer. The caption reads, "Picture adorning the front of Prasert Jandam's coffin, as if to say, 'Take a good look at my life'."[118]

The same publication earlier that year published a hagiographic account of Prasert's birth and life:

> In the midst of terrible aridity, in Khok Village, Uthumphornphisai District, Srisaket Province, on the 24th of November, 1945, a small, dark-skinned boy was born, opened his eyes, and saw the hardships of the people.
>
> [...] This rough-skinned farmer's son was Prasert Jandam, the solid, tough fighter-poet. The land of Isan must take note of his life and work in order to inform those who come after, that they may remember and study them.
>
> He was an intellectual who was branded a foe of the country. It is nearly unbelievable that during his 52 years of breath, his life was full of struggle. Thus it is not surprising that his life stood on the other side

---

[115] ไพลิน, บ.ก., ลมหายใจ, 2539, p. 5.

[116] See นฤมิตร, "ไปฟัง," 2539 (1996), pp. 11–5.

[117] Ibid., p. 14.

[118] Anon., "รำฦก วาระครบรอบ ๕ ปี กับการจากไปของมหากวีศรีปวงชน 'ประเสริฐ จันดำ'," จดหมายข่าวสโมสรนักเขียนภาคอีสาน 5, 21 (พ.ย. - ธ.ค. 2542): 13.

of contentedness. He ate and drank poverty instead of rice; he had liquor to cleanse his wounds; he had sad poems as consoling friends.[119]

This article was a follow-up to the presentation, at the Cho' Karaket Meeting in February 1999, concerning four Isan writers (including Prasert) whose importance was perceived as gradually being forgotten (another was Rom Ratiwan, see Chapter 2). The previous month, Suchart Sawatsi had republished a "rare" interview with Prasert from 1986, noting, "This is one of the best interviews showing the essence of Prasert."[120] Judging from the interview, that essence seems to consist of a stubbornness, idealism, and impatience with nonsense; an abiding concern for the welfare of the common people, especially those of Isan; an enduring criticism of government and society; and a vision of responsibility for improving the lives of others. Appreciation for his accomplishments continues to be expressed. In Caravan's concert commemorating their 25 years as a band, the first song they played was Prasert's "*Paen Oet Toet*." Also, a kind of homage has been paid to Prasert by a poet of apparently similar ideals who uses the pen name, "Prasert Jankham."[121]

What is it that has made Prasert Jandam into a legend? Certainly, it is in part his skill as a writer and his qualities as a person. However, his work was not widely read after his death. Although he published many books, most were in short print runs that soon disappeared, and only a few were reprinted, often not until many years later. In addition, as he himself noted in 1990, his writing expresses "old issues of Isan that don't change."[122] Furthermore, a writer who is no longer publishing, and no longer in the news, tends to be forgotten in Thailand. On the other hand, if much of a writer's work is unavailable, this can contribute to the mystique. Perhaps Prasert shares some similarities here with Jit Phumisak, who died young and whose body of work was only partially obtainable as his reputation grew in the 1970s. Undoubtedly Prasert's early death is a factor in his mythic status, especially as it was caused by alcohol, an element in the lives of nearly all

---

[119] เจริญ กุลสุวรรณ, "ลำนำรำลึก นักเขียนอีสานผู้ล่วงลับ การแสดงที่หลายคนยังติดตาม และถามถึง," จดหมายข่าวสโมสรนักเขียนภาคอีสาน 4, 18 (มี.ค. - เม.ย. 2542): 13.

[120] สุชาติ สวัสดิ์ศรี, บ.ก, "กูคือประเสริฐ จันคำ," เนชั่นสุดสัปดาห์ 8, 346 (21–27 ม.ค. 2542): 46.

[121] See ประเสริฐ จันคำ, "สิ่งที่เราเรียกร้อง," เนชั่นสุดสัปดาห์ 8, 354 (18–24 มี.ค. 2542): 52, and ประเสริฐ จันคำ, "แด่พระองค์ผู้ล่วงลับ," เนชั่นสุดสัปดาห์ 7, 336 (12–18 พ.ย. 2541): 52.

[122] ประเสริฐ จันคำ, "ครั้งสุดท้ายระหว่างคนเขียนรูปกับคนเขียนเรื่อง," in คือเก่า. กรุงเทพฯ: ดอกหญ้า, 2533, pp. 5–6.

Thai writers, not least those of Isan. Probably most of all, however, he has become a legend for what he is seen to represent: a writer who participated in, and to a considerable extent was responsible for, the golden age of Isan writing in the 1970s, when Isan and its concerns held a critical importance on the national stage, and its writers enjoyed a status and a role in political and literary events on an equal footing with Central Thais.

Somkhit Singsong

Somkhit Singsong สมคิด สิงสง is another writer whose name is permanently associated with the artistic and political developments of the 1970s. His close circle of friends at the time included Surachai and Prasert. Somkhit has published several books, including poetry, short stories, and novels, but by far his most popular and famous work, though not everyone knows he is its main author, is "*Khon Kap Khwai*" คนกับควาย (People and Buffalo). This song was made famous by Caravan and became the *de facto* anthem of the protest movements of the 1970s. Beyond this, however, Somkhit is best known as the creator of the development project in his home village of Sap Daeng in Khon Kaen Province in the mid-1970s. This project attempted to improve the lives and raise the consciousness of the villagers, but was branded as communist and forcefully ended during the events surrounding October 6, 1976. After several years with the jungle-based armed struggle, Somkhit returned to Sap Daeng, where he has lived ever since, continuing his efforts for his fellow Isan people and occasionally publishing his writings.

Somkhit Singsong was born in 1948 in Sap Daeng Village, Manjakhiri District, Khon Khaen Province.[123] He attended elementary school in his home province before moving to Bangkok and finishing secondary school while working in journalism. He enrolled as a student of journalism and communications at Thammasat University in 1969, and began organizing his fellow students to participate in development activities in Sap Daeng. In 1973, he wrote the words to the song, "*Khon Kap Khwai*," along with Visa Khanthap, as well as another song, "*Khao La Lan*" ข้าวลาลาน (Rice Departs from the Fields), which was also performed and recorded by Caravan. At this time, Somkhit's first book appeared, *Mahori Haeng Chiwit Itsara* (*Songs of a Life of Freedom*), a collection of poetry and plays published "to raise funds to carry out extra-curricular projects for country youths."[124] Notably, it was

---

[123] วิวัฒน์ โรจนาวรรณ, บ.ก, นักเขียนอีสาน. บุรีรัมย์: สโมสรนักเขียนภาคอีสาน, 2542a.

[124] สมคิด สิงสง, มโหรีแห่งชีวิตอิสระ. ขอนแก่น: รุ่งเกียรติ, 2515, back cover.

published in Khon Kaen, making it one of the few books by a contemporary Isan writer (in a modern genre) to be published outside Bangkok.[125]

Somkhit was in his fourth year at the university when the events of October 14, 1973, occurred, after which he quit the university and returned to Sap Daeng to implement his development project full-time. He was joined by Prasert Jandam and for a time by others, including Wirasak Sunthornsri (of Caravan). He started a school for the children of farmers, worked to improve local roads, and did whatever else seemed useful. During this period, he was active in politics and became a member of the central committee of the Socialist Party of Thailand.[126] As time went on, right-wing hostility to people like Somkhit increased. Journalists had labeled Sap Daeng as "Sickle and Star Village."[127] In mid-1975, Prasert left Sap Daeng under threat; some months later, Somkhit was shot by unknown assailants.[128] According to Somkhit:

> Sap Daeng Village was like a school of politics for many progressives. [...] Around the time of October 6, 1976, it was surrounded and suppressed. So I fled into the jungle.[129]

The Socialist Party had been outlawed, and Somkhit, traveling to Laos, met all the rest of the central committee, including Khamsing Srinawk.[130] Ironically, threats and accusations had forced Somkhit (and many others) into joining the communists when otherwise he would not have.

Somkhit wrote prolifically while in the jungle. Two of these books found their way to publication in Bangkok: *Khao Khiow* (*Green Rice*), and *La Ko'n Na Wang Lek* (*Farewell to the Wang Lek Fields*). Many other works, however, were only ever printed by CPT printing presses and did not circulate outside CPT areas.[131] One of these was a story called, "*Bak*

---

[125] Two other Isan writers who have had books published in Isan rather than Bangkok are Fon Fafang and Manote Phromsingh (both discussed in Chapter 6).

[126] สุมาลี โพธิ์พยัคฆ์, "สามแพร่งชีวิต — สมคิด สิงสง," จดหมายข่าวสโมสรนักเขียนภาคอีสาน 3, 8 (ม.ค. - ก.พ. 2540): 4–9.

[127] Ibid., p. 5.

[128] ประเสริฐ, พลิกตำนาน, 2534, p. 107.

[129] อิสรีอิน, "'คนกับควาย' สมคิด สิงสง และหมู่บ้านซับแดง ยุคขี้ข้าฝรั่ง," เนชั่นสุดสัปดาห์ 8, 361 (6–12 พ.ค. 2542): 62.

[130] สุมาลี, "สามแพร่ง," 2540, p. 6.

[131] As Surachai notes, some of these may have touched on the three forbidden topics of Nation, King, and Country, since areas under CPT control were not subject to the laws of the Kingdom of Thailand. สุรชัย จันทิมาธร, "จากผู้เขียน," in ก่อนฟ้าสาง. กรุงเทพฯ: กำแพง, 2531, pp. 9–16.

Yan[132] บักย่าน (Scaredy-Cat), which was singled out for special praise by Pleuang Wannasri in a communiqué from Kunming, China.[133]

By 1982, Somkhit had come out of the jungle and returned to Sap Daeng, where he formed the Mun River Writers' Group with other writers from Isan (see Chapter 5). He served as village headman, and twice stood for election to the national parliament.[134] He was one of the founders, in 1989, of the Isan Writers' Association (see Chapter 5), which had developed out of the Mun River group, and served for seven years as its first president. Thereafter, he continued to initiate agricultural activities, addressing issues of farmers' debts, water, etc., and was reportedly "determined to start a Foundation for Water and Quality of Life to tackle issues like these in detail."[135] He also established a publishing house at Sap Daeng (see below).

Somkhit's published books include the following:

1) *Mahori Haeng Chiwit Itsara* มโหรีแห่งชีวิตอิสระ (*Songs of a Life of Freedom*), 1972, poetry and drama;

2) *La Ko'n Na Wang Lek* ลาก่อนนาวังเหล็ก (*Farewell to the Wang Lek Fields*), 1979, novel;

3) *Tamnan Haeng Mu Ban* ตำนานแห่งหมู่บ้าน (*Chronicles of a Village*), 1981, short stories;

4) *Khao Khiow* ข้าวเขียว (*Green Rice*), 1981, novel;

5) *Ai Phloi* ไอ้พลอย (the title refers to the name of the main character), 1982, novel (rewritten version of *La Ko'n Na Wang Lek*);[136]

6) *Dae Phaen Din Isan* แด่แผ่นดินอีสาน (*To the Land of Isan*), 1989, opinions (serialized in *Khao Phiset* magazine);

7) *Khon Bon Mo'* คนบนมอ (*People on the Hill*), 1990, short stories;

8) *Phu Ruk Ran* ผู้รุกราน (*The Invader*), date unknown, novel.

Somkhit wrote the words to the song, "*Khon Kap Khwai*" (People and Buffalo), during one of his trips to Bangkok from Sap Daeng. Visa Khanthap helped him finish it, and Surachai wrote the music. This song has been discussed by Herbert Phillips in his book on modern Thai literature, but the account contains several errors. For example, Phillips claims that

---

[132] The title is in Lao.

[133] แคน สาริกา, "ฝนแรกของวรรณกรรมภูพาน," ถนนหนังสือ 4, 4 (2529): 19.

[134] Anon., "สมคิด สิงสง," *Writer Magazine* 1, 7 (เม.ย. 2536) (1993): 69.

[135] อิสรีอิน, "คนกับควาย'," 2542, p. 62.

[136] แคน สาริกา, "ฝนแรก," 2529, p. 20; ทวีศักดิ์ ปินทอง, นวนิยายกับการเมืองไทย ก่อนและหลังเหตุการณ์ 14 ตุลาคม 2516 (พ.ศ. 2507–2522), กรุงเทพฯ: รักอักษร, 2546.

the words were "based on a poem by Chitr Phoumisak" and "arranged as lyrics by Surachai" for "the Caravan Singers."[137] In fact, Caravan did not yet exist (and was never called "the Caravan Singers"), and Surachai has stated clearly that the words were written by Somkhit with Visa.[138] What is more significant is Phillips' rather inaccurate translation of those words, in a way that would appear to misrepresent the original text. Phillips uses phrases like, "carry guns," "our manhood broken," and "the oppressors will die," that simply do not exist in the original Thai. Furthermore, he includes a line about the bourgeoisie "elevating themselves into a superior class" and devouring "the excess value of our labor," and then criticizes the song based on this (in fact non-existent) so-called "howler" of a "Marxist lyric."[139] While it is true that the song expresses strong, leftist-influenced sentiment and is intended to rouse the listener into political action, Phillips' treatment of it is unfortunate both for the readers of his book and for the composers of the song (see the Appendix below for the original Thai and my translation).

Laeng Khen (*Drought*), the 1975 anthology of short stories edited by Suchart, included a piece by Somkhit entitled, *"Rao Yang Mai Chana Do'k Reu Pho"* เรายังไม่ชนะดอกหรือ พ่อ (Haven't We Won Yet, Father?), an unmistakable reference to Nai Phi's work (discussed in Chapter 3 above), *Rao Chana Laew Mae Ja* (*We Have Won, Mother Dear*). Somkhit's story begins with an old man walking barefoot down the hot road that leads back to his village, unable to get a ride because he does not have enough money for the bus fare. He is returning from a rally in town at which his son addressed the crowd with these words:

> The farmers of every area are talking about poverty, talking about feeling inferior, talking about being taken advantage of by commercial middle-men, talking about the callousness of the money-lenders, talking about the low-down evil officials who connive with the money-lenders to make contracts in order to buy and sell our houses and land.[140]

Later, the son returns home and tells his father that the rally was successful in forcing the government to accept their demands. However, his father shows him the legal document that has just arrived, evicting them from the house and giving ownership to a money-lender. Ironically, part of the original loan taken out by the father was used for the son's education in Bangkok,

[137] Herbert Phillips, *Modern Thai Literature*, 1987, pp. 328–9.

[138] สุรชัย จันทิมาธร, "คนกับควาย," in Anon., ตำนาน, 2536a [1993], pp. 100–2.

[139] Phillips, *Modern Thai Literature*, 1987, p. 329.

[140] สมคิด สิงสง, "เรายังไม่ชนะดอกหรือ พ่อ," in สุชาติ, บ.ก., แล้งเข็ญ, 2518, p. 304.

it is implied. The title of the story also appears as its last line, when the young man realizes that true victory, or even significant improvement in the situation in Isan, is still far off.

If we were to take the quotation from the young man's speech above and change the second word from "farmers" to "writers," we would get a fairly accurate summary of the themes and topics of Isan literature (and much of Thai literature in general) in the 1970s. Heat and aridity, and the influence of foreign "imperialists," also referred to in the above story, were the other principal topics of interest for Isan writers in this period. These common concerns, and the increasingly aggressive Literature for Life responses to them, were features of Somkhit's later novels as well. In the foreword to *La Ko'n Na Wang Lek* (*Farewell to the Wang Lek Fields*), the publisher describes the book as a novel of Isan and an example of "Literature for Life, a life of struggle against injustice."[141] Furthermore, the author "understands the life and realities of being a villager; his characters thus have lives that are as real as the people in the region."[142] Finally, the publishers

> hope readers will not just become aware of problems and then ignore them, but will solve and ameliorate the problems in order to bring about a better existence for these country people, because they share a common destiny with us.[143]

Even in the writer's foreword to the second printing of *Khao Khiow* (*Green Rice*) in 1993, Somkhit still uses typical Literature for Life rhetoric:

> Pages of the history of our land record the events of unrest and the flood of blood between October 14 and 18, 1973, when students and the people numbering in the thousands and millions joined together in a peaceful way on Ratchadamnoen Avenue to demand democracy, but were suppressed through the force of weapons of war and fell injured and dead like falling leaves.[144]

Indeed, by the late 1970s, even sympathetic critics were tiring of the sameness of Literature for Life themes and styles. In an article about *La Ko'n Na Wang Lek* in the magazine, *Lok Nangseu*, Roi Rawiwan praised Somkhit's authentic portrayals of "the locations, the daily lives, and the

---

[141] Anon., "คำนำ," in สมคิด สิงสง. ลาก่อนนาวังเหล็ก. กรุงเทพฯ: ปิยะสาส์น, 2522 (no page numbers).

[142] Ibid.

[143] Ibid.

[144] สมคิด สิงสง, "คำนำผู้เขียน," in ข้าวเขียว. กรุงเทพฯ: ดอกหญ้า, 2536, p. 5.

culture of villagers," but criticized the novel as lacking pacing, realistic events, and ability to sustain the reader's interest.[145] Roi summarizes this view in a passage that could apply equally to many other *Pheua Chiwit* (Literature "for Life") writers:

> *La Ko'n Na Wang Lek* can be considered a *pheua chiwit* novel that reflects the poverty and bitterness of Isan people as a result of facing dangers from nature and from individuals in uniform, so that characters like Phloi don't have many choices. Nonetheless, while the content is rather good, the form is still somewhat lacking, for example in the use of theory in dialogues, using words that are not compatible and harmonious. This is something that young writers should think about. Otherwise their work will not be convincing, or will be strident, and thus become too formulaic.[146]

Sap Daeng Village remains at the center of Somkhit's life, work, and inspiration. His experiences growing up and living there formed the foundation for his early writing, including the song "*Khon Kap Khwai.*" *Khao Khiow* is essentially an autobiographical novel describing the life of an Isan boy who goes to Bangkok to study, organizes development projects for his home village, quits school to bring his projects to fruition, and then sees them destroyed by hostile members of a corrupt establishment. After several years in the jungle, Somkhit again established himself and his projects in Sap Daeng. He continued to use both literature and songs to spread his message and drive the Sap Daeng movement, establishing *Kratho'm Laiseu* (Hut of Letters) in Sap Daeng to publish and distribute writings. During the last decade of the 20th century, the Hut issued a book of Somkhit's poetry, *Saithan Haeng Kan — Phak Kawiniphon* สายธารแห่งกาล — ภาคกวีนิพนธ์ (*The Course of Time — Poetry Section*), which "records the thoughts and circumstances of his life during his forties," as well as *Yak Hai Do'k Mai Ban Nai Wan Phrung Ni* อยากให้ดอกไม้บานในวันพรุ่งนี้ (*I Want the Flowers to Bloom Tomorrow*), a collection of "short stories that relay circumstances, thoughts, and consciousness."[147] Sap Daeng's publishing house also began to produce a monthly periodical, *Rapsung — Riw Khabuan Khwam Khit Jitsamneuk Lae Phumipanya* ราบสูง — ริ้วขบวนความคิดจิตสำนึกและภูมิปัญญา (*Plateau — A Procession of Thoughts, Consciousness, and Local Knowledge*). Topics in the first

---

[145] ร้อย รวีวรรณ, "เราจะเริ่มต้นกันใหม่ ... บทวิเคราะห์ 'นักเขียนรุ่นใหม่' หลังเหตุการณ์ 6 ตุลา," โลกหนังสือ 3, 1 (ต.ค. 2522): 47.

[146] Ibid., p. 48.

[147] อิสรีอิน, "'คนกับควาย' ," 2542 (1999), p. 62.

issue included "Water and the Quality of Life" and "Water — An Everlasting Permanent Problem."[148] Somkhit described the purpose behind the journal:

> It's creating an atmosphere. We're not hoping to have readers by the tens or hundreds of thousands. [...] We want it to be like *Sangkhomsat Parithat* was. [...] They are not distributed in shops, but must be ordered. Rather than printing piles and having them sit around, they can be printed as needed, according to the number of orders. Back issues as well. Creative communication from the plateau is a declaration from people making books who do not kowtow to publishers in the capital.[149]

Thus Somkhit is a man of ideas, of letters, and of deeds, who continues to work in the interests of his fellow villagers, and whose identity and existence are inseparable from Isan.

Udorn Thongnoi

Udorn Thongnoi อุดร ทองน้อย is another Isan writer who was a strong proponent of Literature for Life in the 1970s. In all of his books of the period, he discusses the suffering and injustices of life in Isan, pledges to struggle for the good of the people, and encourages the reader to join that struggle. Like some other Isan writers, Udorn also became involved in conventional politics, but he was more successful than many, becoming elected to the position of MP from Yasothorn. After the collapse of the CPT, Udorn's writing output diminished, and his political stance softened. His later work attempts to explain Isan life to the non-Isan reader.

Udorn Thongnoi was born in Kudchum District of Yasothorn Province, studied in Bangkok for a time, and finally graduated from secondary school in Srisaket Province.[150] He then studied law at Thammasat University and was on the executive committee of the National Students' Center of Thailand.[151] After graduating, he worked as a journalist for *Thai Rath* and other newspapers. In 1975, he published his first book, *Isan Ku (My Isan)*, a collection of poetry, plays, and short stories. At about the same time, he was elected to parliament from Yasothorn as a member of the Socialist Party of Thailand. He was the youngest representative in the national assembly.[152]

---

[148] Ibid.

[149] Ibid., p. 63.

[150] ถนนหนังสือ 2, 10 (เม.ย. 2528): 65.

[151] เสถียร, "คำนำ," 2518, p. 9.

[152] Anon., "จากสำนักพิมพ์," in อุดร ทองน้อย. หมาเน่า อีแร้ง และแมลงวัน. กรุงเทพฯ: แสงดาว, undated (2533?), p. 3.

However, his term was short as the parliament was dissolved that same year. At the end of 1975, he traveled with a delegation of the Socialist Party to China, after which he published a book, *Tawan Si Daeng So'ng Thang* (*The Red Sun Lights the Way*), describing the trip and his realization that socialism in Thailand was still in its infancy. Within a few months, he published another book containing poetry and an essay on Isan and the need to join the armed struggle. That year, 1976, he went into the jungle, where he continued to write and taught journalism in CPT schools.[153] In 1980, he published two more books, evidently written in the jungle and taken to Bangkok. After quitting the insurgency, he did not publish another book until a decade later. At the end of the 20th century, he was living with his family in Bangkok and rarely publishing.

Udorn's published works include the following books:

1) *Isan Ku* อีสานกู (*My Isan*), 1975, poetry, plays, and short stories;

2) *Sai Leuat Nang Neua Lae Kraduk Kho'ng Khon Yak Rai* สายเลือด หนังเนื้อ และ กระดูกของคนยากไร้ (*Blood, Flesh, and Bones of the Underprivileged*), 1976, poems and an essay;

3) *Tawan Si Daeng So'ng Thang* ตะวันสีแดงส่องทาง (*The Red Sun Lights the Way*), 1976, account of a trip to China by the Socialist Party of Thailand;

4) *To'ng Mi Sak Wan* ต้องมีสักวัน (*There Must Come a Day*), 1980, short stories;

5) *Wan Thi Daet Pen Si Leuat* วันที่แดดเป็นสีเลือด (*The Day the Sun Shone the Color of Blood*), 1980, novel; and

6) *Ma Nao I Raeng Lae Malaeng Wan* หมาเน่า อีแร้ง และแมลงวัน (*The Rotting Dog, the Vulture, and the Fly*), undated (1990?), short stories.

Udorn's first work, *Isan Ku* (*My Isan*), is an aggressive, even militant, book full of the rhetoric of the Literature for Life movement. The title itself, using the impolite[154] pronoun *ku* for the first person, proclaims the author to be a forceful, proud, and belligerent native of Isan. Although published when Udorn had recently been elected to parliament,[155] the book's cover shows him holding an assault rifle. The poems, plays, and stories in the book have titles like, "*Ban Thuk Tho'raman*" บ้านทุกข์ (House of Torment), "*Ya*

---

[153] แคน สาริกา, "ฝนแรก," 2529 (1986), p. 21.

[154] Impolite in Bangkok, but commonly used in many rural areas.

[155] It is probably the only book published by an MP in which he refers to himself as *ku*.

Tho'" อย่าท้อ (Don't Be Discouraged), *"Chan Pen Muanchon"* ฉันเป็นมวลชน (I am the Masses), *"Nak Patiwat"* นักปฏิวัติ (Revolutionary), *"Khon Hap Luk Raboet"* คนหาบลูกระเบิด (People Carrying Bombs), and *"Wan Neung Phom Ja Kha Khon Thang Lok"* วันหนึ่งผมจะฆ่าคนทั้งโลก (One Day I'll Kill the Whole World). The author is described in the foreword by Sathien Janthimathorn: "One noteworthy point about Udorn is the sincerity of this person from the countryside who, although he has come to live in the capital, is able to see and reflect the lives of Isan people vividly."[156]

Udorn's next book, *Sai Leuat Nang Neua Lae Kraduk Kho'ng Khon Yak Rai* (*Blood, Flesh, and Bones of the Underprivileged*), was published less than a year later, yet shows an even more radicalized point of view. In the foreword, after reaffirming his identity, and in effect, his credentials, by stating, "I am a child of Isan region farmers,"[157] the author presents his new stance and indicates the means he will adopt to reach his goal:

> Some of these poems were written abroad, especially in China, Vietnam, and Laos […] I publish this work on the occasion of having to leave the national assembly. But I will stand firm and continue the revolution of society. Definitely I will join the blood, flesh, and bones of the under-privileged as I cease to use shrewd words and excited discussion.[158]

The reader is given the impression that Udorn has taken up the Marxist cause, an impression that is reinforced by the poems in this book, including *"Chon Chan Phu Yak Rai"* ชนชั้นผู้ยากไร้ (The Underprivileged Class), *"Prawattisat Kho'ng Prachachon"* ประวัติศาสตร์ของประชาชน (The People's History), and *"Kao Pai Khang Na Bon Hon Thang Kho'ng Phu Yak Rai"* ก้าวไปข้างหน้าบนหนทางของผู้ยากไร้ (Stride Ahead on the Road of the Underprivileged). In the poem, *"Pheuan Phu Su Nai Pa"* เพื่อนผู้สู้ในป่า (Friends Who Struggle in the Jungle), Udorn expresses his disillusionment in working within established political institutions, after which he gives an unmistakable alternative:

> *Those in parliament can only argue in raised voices*
> *And then must destroy and sell their honor*
> *Like a den of gangsters, a house of prostitutes*
> *All they do is sell out the people.*[159]

---

[156] เสถียร, "คำนำ," 2518 (1975), p. 13.

[157] อุคร ทองน้อย, "คำนำ," in สายเลือด หนังเนื้อ และ กระดูกของคนยากไร้. กรุงเทพฯ: สัญญาน, 2519, p. 1.

[158] Ibid., p. 2.

[159] อุคร ทองน้อย, "เพื่อนผู้สู้ในป่า," in สายเลือด, 2519, p. 10.

The second half of this short book is taken up by an essay called, "*Kheun Pai Ha Pheuan Bon Phu Khao!*" ขึ้นไปหาเพื่อนบนภูเขา (Go Up and Join Friends in the Mountains!), exhorting Isan people to join the armed struggle in order to liberate and transform Isan and Thailand.

Udorn's later work, by contrast, is different from his Literature for Life writings in two major ways. The first is one of theme and tone. Not surprisingly, he no longer takes Marxist ideas and inspiration as the basis for his writing. What takes their place is a sense of humor, a rare element in Isan writing up to this time and one that is entirely lacking in *Pheua Chiwit* writing of the 1970s and earlier. The second significant change in Udorn's work is his intended audience. His earlier books are primarily aimed at other Isan people. Although he does not use much Lao in those writings, he does consistently present himself as a fellow Isan person with a continuing commitment to Isan concerns. This perhaps reflects both his convictions and his interest in politics at that time. These earlier poetry and prose pieces tend to speak directly to Isan people, encouraging them to rise up and improve the conditions of their lives. Later on, however, his stories are written for Thai people in general, especially those not from Isan. These tales depict and explain the thoughts and behavior of Isan people for an audience unfamiliar with them.

Both of these changed characteristics of Udorn's latter work are seen in the title story of his collection, "*Ma Nao I Raeng Lae Malaeng Wan*" (The Rotting Dog, the Vulture, and the Fly), the first sentence of which sets its tone of irony and humor: "Adults tend to argue endlessly about whether, when a dog dies, the vulture or the fly will smell it first ..."[160] The story is told from the point of view of a child explaining to an outsider the follies of adults and often making humorous parenthetical remarks about Isan village life. Although there is no direct reference to politics at all, a reader knowing Udorn's background cannot help but see the story at one level as social criticism, and wonder if the vulture and the fly might be taken for more than they appear. The humorous and at times sarcastic tone of this and other stories in this collection remind the reader of some of Lao Khamhawm's work. However, all of these stories by Udorn are about Isan people, places, and events, and are presented as such by a statement on the book's cover: "*Ruam Reuang San Thi Rap Sung*" (Collected Plateau Stories).

Udorn Thongnoi was less prolific and less well-known than either Sura-chai, Prasert, or Somkhit, and he eventually largely faded from the literary

---

[160] อุดร ทองน้อย, "หมาเน่า อีแร้ง และแมลงวัน," in หมาเน่า, undated (2533?/1990?), p. 69.

scene of both Isan and Thailand in general. He did, however, play a significant role in expressing, as well as stimulating, concern with Isan, opposing
injustice, and improving society, all of which were notable characteristics of
the literary, political, and social movements of the 1970s. His literary change
of direction, from at first trying to speak to Isan people and incite them to
action, to later describing their culture to outsiders in entertaining ways, has
perhaps not had much impact on Isan writing overall. This is probably due
to his relatively low level of literary production and his lack of involvement
with other Isan writers from the 1980s onward. In fact, his name did not
even appear in the booklet of Isan writers published in 1999 by the Isan
Writers' Association, except on the page listing "Isan writers about whom
information can still not be found."[161] Nevertheless, the direction of Udorn's
development as a writer in some ways mirrors that of many post-1970s Isan
writers, and of Isan writing in general (see Chapter 5).

Conclusion

The 1960s and 1970s in Thailand were a time of momentous and lasting
change in literature no less than in politics. The Era of Search, which began
after Sarit's death, was characterized by discovery and experimentation with
a wide variety of different philosophies, political ideologies, and writing
styles. By the mid-1970s, the Art for Life movement had gained ascendancy
as the most prominent among these, and Isan served as the ideal source for
artistic material based on conditions of suffering and injustice. Socialist
realist art, music, and writing became the dominant mode of expression in
progressive creative circles. Surachai Janthimathorn and Prasert Jandam
participated in the Era of Search and evolved along with the times, becoming
major exponents of Art for Life. Surachai's band, Caravan, consisting
entirely of musicians from Isan (and at times using Isan instruments and song
forms), played a major role in attracting young audiences, first to Songs for
Life, and then to the leftist politics behind those songs. Surachai's innovative
and evocative style marks both his music and his writing, but he is better
known by far for his songs, which he continues to write and perform, while
his prose is less widely read and appreciated.

Prasert became an icon both of Literature for Life and of Isan writing,
perhaps even more so after his death. Readers seemed to respond to his
commitment to Isan people and his celebration of their lives in his work. His

---

[161] วิวัฒน์, นักเขียนอีสาน, 2542a, p. 3.

legend has grown as people have rediscovered his writing and associated him somewhat nostalgically with the golden age of Isan political activism and literary presence on the national stage. Somkhit Singsong also participated in that golden age in many ways, writing the words to *"Khon Kap Khwai,"* the anthem of the student movement in the 1970s; promoting self-reliance and social justice through development projects in his home village of Sap Daeng in Khon Kaen; and producing a widely read novel of the times, *Khao Khiow*. In a similar vein, Udorn Thongnoi was an increasingly vociferous supporter of leftist social change, serving briefly as a member of parliament and producing several Literature for Life books.

All four of these Isan writers fled to the jungle in 1976 and emerged in the early 1980s. With the collapse of the left, the Literature for Life movement also lost popularity, although the movement's influence is still discernible in much Isan writing thereafter (sometimes to the distaste of readers and critics). In its place, a new sensibility began to take shape in the late 1980s and grew in the 1990s. This sensibility, based less on politics and more on regional language, culture, and identity, is explored in Chapter 5. In the meantime, two other Isan writers without strong political affiliation produced work in the 1970s and 1980s that rose to national prominence by winning literary awards, being made into films, and becoming part of the national school curriculum. These writers and their work are the subject of Chapter 4.

APPENDIX

Isan![162]
by Nai Phi

In the sky there's no water
Your tears falling in lines
The sun strikes your head
Your chest heaves and moans
The great lake is Nong Han
Allowing life like the Chi River
Look around in amazement
Thinking in your heart
Dear brothers and sisters
Standing motionless
They claim that we're stupid
Love you lastingly
They call honesty foolish
And clever as the representatives
Oppressing and harrassing us
Travelling all over
Intensifying our bitterness
We endure self-sacrifice
In the sky there's no water
Yours tears falling in rows
Our two hands are strong
Pity Isan to the end
The storm gathers strength
Isan's many millions

In the soil only sand
Dissipate and disappear
The land cracks and splits
Shifting apart year – round
The Mun River passes like a ghost
Penetrating and waiting
So, Isan is like this
Things aren't so good, are they?
Where is sympathy?
What do you wish for?
These, our friends, you see
So why do they seem lacking ...
Who is so virtuous
With their brave cheating ways
Who are they? Let it be revealed
Coming to torment and trouble
Like a plague of death
Though it comes not easily
In the soil only sand
Are shed as blood! soothing the soil
There are those who hear our protests
Don't fall back, resist with both arms
Around the jungle and plains
Is there anyone to defeat us?

---

[162] นายผี, "อีศาน," in วิมล พลจันทร. รำลึกถึงนายผี จากป้าลม. กรุงเทพฯ: ดอกหญ้า, 2533, pp. 6–7.

People and Buffalo[163]

by Somkhit Singsong
and Visa Khanthap

People farm the rice fields in the manner of people
People and buffalo farm in the manner of buffalo
People and buffalo have profound meaning
Profound from farming the fields through the ages
Working energetically through the ages
Happy and contented down to the present

Go, Let us go
Shoulder the plow and go work the fields
Impoverished and melancholy for ages
For ages our tears have fallen inside
With bitter and hard hearts
However agitated we will not be intimidated

It is a song of death
Our humanity swiftly disintegrates
The bourgeoisie use us and divide the classes
The farming class thus sinks down
Farmers are maligned as uncivilized
What is significant and certain is death

---

[163] Translation based on song lyrics (in Thai) taken from Anon., ตำนาน, 2536a, p. 103.

คนกับควาย[164]
สมคิด สิงสง, วิสา คัญทัพ

คนก็คนทำนาประสาคน
คนกับควายความหมายมันลึกล้ำ
แขงขันการงานมาเนิ่นนาน

ไปเถิดไปพวกเราไปเถิดไป
ยากจนหม่นหมองมานานนัก
ยากแค้นลำเค็ญในหัวใจ

เป็นบทเพลงเสียงเพลงแห่งความตาย
กฎุมพีกินแรงแบ่งชนชั้น
เหยียดหยามชาวนาว่าป่าดง

คนกับควายทำนาประสาควาย
ลึกล้ำทำนามาเนิ่นนาน
สำราญเรื่อยมาพอสุขใจ

ไปเถิดไปแบกไถไปทำนา
นานนักน้ำตามันตกใน
ร้อนรุ่มเพียงใดไม่หวั่นเกรง

ความเป็นคนสลายลงไปพลัน
ชนชั้นชาวนาจึงต่ำลง
สำคัญมั่นคงคือความตาย

---

[164] Ibid.

CHAPTER 4

Isan Writing
Enters the Mainstream

Of all the many Isan writers active in the 1970s, two in particular stood out, gaining recognition from official institutions of Thai literature: Khamphun Bunthawi and Khamman Khonkhai. Khamman's fame was largely the result of the film that was made of one of his books, *Khru Ban No'k* (meaning "Rural Teacher," but published in an English translation under the unfortunate title, *The Teachers of Mad Dog Swamp*). Khamphun's work, too, has been made into films and television series, which have contributed to his prominence as well. However, his winning of important literary awards has probably been the major factor in his renown. Khamphun won the SEAWrite Award in 1979, the first year it was given, for his novel, *Luk Isan* ("Child of Isan", called *A Child of the Northeast* in its English translation), and thereafter became a literary celebrity in Thailand.

Khamphun Bunthawi

Among Isan writers (excepting Kanchana Nakkhanan, who does not identify herself as an Isan writer), Khamphun Bunthawi คำพูน บุญทวี is the most prolific, the most famous, and the most popular. In addition, he is different from other Isan writers in another important way: he is entirely outside the Literature for Life stream that has so dominated Isan writing since both the movement and the regional literature began to gain visibility in the 1950s. Other Isan writers in the 1970s (as previously shown) were overwhelmingly involved with Literature for Life, and the vast majority of Isan writers before and since were at least influenced by it. This is true even of Khamman, whose work was more popular and well-known, outside the primarily young and intellectual circles which Literature for Life dominated, than that of other Isan writers of the time (late 1970s).[1] Khamphun, by contrast, shows no connection at all to the movement, whether in style, subject, or goals. Indeed, politics are absent from nearly all of his work. Instead, Khamphun seems concerned primarily with telling a good story and, along the way, relating the customs and traditions of Isan people.

Khamphun Bunthawi was born Khun[2] Bunthawi in 1928 in a Lao-speaking village in Sai Mun District of what is now Yasothorn Province (but at the time was part of Ubon Province). His father was from Isan and his mother from Savannakhet, Laos. After finishing the fourth year of elementary school in his village, he continued his studies in Yasothorn town. While in secondary school, he had his name changed to Khamphun by his father. According to his own account, he was a poor student; his weakest and most hated subjects were Thai language, drawing, and grammar.[3] After completing school, he moved to Bangkok to make a living. As Khamphun describes it:

> I had to go to Bangkok because Bangkok was the great city of progress. You don't have to dip up the water in Bangkok, just turn on the tap, they said, and it flows out. You don't have to light lanterns. There were boats. You could see iron float on water, which was naval ships. The only thing I wanted to do was go to Bangkok.[4]

He worked in many different jobs, pedaling a *samlo'*, doing day labor, milking cows, loading ships, etc. At one point, he returned to Yasothorn briefly to start a *ramwong* troupe. Among the songs they performed was *Phu Yai Li*. After the troupe broke up, he returned to Bangkok, and then eventually moved down south to join a friend in Satul, where Khamphun became a rural elementary teacher.

Khamphun taught school for four years, and married a woman from the South, with whom he had several children. After repeated requests to be transferred to a teaching post in Yasothorn were all turned down, he quit teaching. He then worked in Bangkok again for two years, after which he returned to the South and was hired as a prison guard in Patthalung. Over the next several years, he worked at several prisons, mostly in the South. At this

---

[1] Excluding Surachai, whose fame was due to his songs rather than his stories, as noted previously.

[2] คูน meaning "lucky, beneficent, precious" in Lao.

[3] ประเสริฐ ไสววรรณ, "วิเคราะห์นวนิยาย และเรื่องสั้น ที่สะท้อนชีวิตชาวชนบทอีสานของ คำพูน บุญทวี". ปริญญานิพนธ์ มหาวิทยาลัยศรีนครินทรวิโรฒ ประสานมิตร, 2532.

[4] Khamphun Bunthawi, Interview, June 25, 1999, Bangkok.

time (late 1960s), however, his wife became seriously ill. Financial pressures related to her medical bills put severe strain on the family, and Khamphun went into debt. He began reading books in the library. One that particularly impressed him was the novel *Papillon*, about a prisoner who escaped from a French penal island. The novel was made into a successful film starring Steve McQueen. Khamphun decided to become a writer:

> I read *Papillon*, and lots of books, and decided, I'm going to become a writer. So I can take care of my wife, who has breast cancer. In order to sell as a film, maybe. Back then they bought [scripts] for films for ten thousand [baht] or more.[5]

Khamphun continued working as a prison guard, but also began writing stories. Ajin Banjaphan played a decisive role in encouraging Khamphun's writing by publishing his first stories in 1970, including his first serialized novel, *Nithan Luk Thung* (*Country Tales*), in the weekly *Fa Muang Thai*.

> I sent my first story to *Fa Muang Thai*. [...] Ajin sent me a letter telling me to keep writing. He wrote letters to me twice. I was so happy. I pictured him as an important person. A famous person was encouraging me. I was very happy, so I really started writing, mostly about Isan people's lives.[6]

Khamphun was also influenced by other writers, including Suwanni Sukhontha and Manas Janyong.

> I liked Manas Janyong's short stories. He was a true country boy, he wrote just like we talked ... He wrote about music groups, *phin phat* music, and so on, and it was just like we were sitting there listening to it. [...] He could describe a scene and you'd see it clearly. It was easy to understand. Manas Janyong was considered the king of the short story. I liked him the best. I'm a country boy, too. Describing a scene riding in a car, getting out of a car, I couldn't write about that, because I'd never ridden in a car. Riding a buffalo, going out into the fields, this I could write.[7]

Khamphun wrote different kinds of stories, including some about southern ghosts, and Isan ghosts, and, in 1975, a serialized novel, *Manut Ro'i Khuk*

---

[5] Ibid.

[6] Anon., "ผมจะเขียน 'ทุ่งกุลาร้องไห้ ...' สัมภาษณ์ คำพูน บุญทวี ผู้เขียน 'ลูกอีสาน'," โลกหนังสือ 1, 4 (ม.ค. 2521): 40–52.

[7] Khamphun, Interview, 1999.

(*Human Beings of 100 Prisons*), which was made into a film.[8] He wrote quickly, he said, drawing on his experiences, and his main motivation was to earn money, in order to take care of his wife and send his children to school.

> I had a lot of experiences, but I didn't have imagination. When you're indigent you lack imagination. So mostly I took from real life, 80% from real life. Whatever I saw, in the South, in the North, in Isan, wherever, saw someone hit his friend, saw people catching a python, hunters in the fields, the forests, these stuck and became short stories. Stories that come out of my imagination, there are very few. Because I don't read much. I read few novels.[9]

Khamphun continued writing in this manner. For awhile, he was not very successful in his attempts to write longer works, and turned again to Ajin for advice. Ajin suggested he read the Thai translation of *Little House on the Prairie*. After reading only two chapters, he became inspired and determined to write the true story of his own life.[10] He sent the first few chapters to Ajin, who told him, "You have truly good things in you, and yet you are not aware of it."[11] This was the origin of his best-known work. In 1975–1976, this novel, *Luk Isan*, was published serially in *Fa Muang Thai* to great popularity, judging by readers' letters.[12] The novel was published as a book (actually in three volumes) at the end of 1976, and in 1977 was awarded the prize for Best Novel by the Thai National Book Association. According to Jacqueline de Fels, Khamphun was disappointed to discover, on asking the amount of his prize money, that he would receive only a simple plaque; he became even more unhappy when informed that he would have to borrow a suit to receive the award, and, furthermore, would have to pay for his own round trip ticket to Bangkok from Phatthalung.[13]

In 1977, the year of his wife's death, Khamphun published, in *Plaek* weekly, another serialized novel called *Nai Ho'i Thamin* (*The Brutal Buffalo Wrangler*). It was collected in a single volume later that year and won

---

[8] สมรม สทิงพระ, "คำพูน บุญทวี," in บนถนนนนักเขียน. กรุงเทพฯ: ไรเตอร์, 2536, pp. 99–102.

[9] Khamphun, Interview, 1999.

[10] สมรม, "คำพูน," 2536, p. 101.

[11] ประเสริฐ ไสววรรณ, "วิเคราะห์," 2532, p. 212.

[12] สำนักพิมพ์บรรณกิจ, "จากสำนักพิมพ์," in คำพูน บุญทวี. ลูกอีสาน. กรุงเทพฯ: บรรณกิจ, 2540 (no page number).

[13] Jacqueline de Fels, *Promotion de le Litterature en Thailande: vers les Prix Litteraires 1882–1982* (Paris: INALCO, 1993), p. 621.

honorable mention from the Book Publishing and Distribution Association of Thailand. The biggest boost to Khamphun's writing career, though, came in 1979, when the Southeast Asian Writers' Award was established.[14] *Luk Isan* won the award, competing against 17 other Thai novels written over the previous five years, including *Nai Ho'i Thamin* and Khamman Khonkhai's *Bantheuk Kho'ng Khru Prachaban* (*Notes of a Rural Elementary School Teacher*).[15] As part of the award, Khamphun was flown to Singapore to meet the winners from other ASEAN countries, and also traveled to Germany. He chronicled his experiences on these trips in *Luk Isan Khi Reua Bin* (*Child of Isan Rides an Airplane*), published in 1980.

Thereafter, Khamphun's fame grew enormously. *Luk Isan* now is read in secondary schools, and was made into a film by the well-known director Khunawut. Until his death, Khamphun was honored as the senior figure in Isan writing. He published at least two dozen books between 1980 and 2000, including novels, short story collections, humorous memoirs, and non-fiction works on Isan history and culture. In 1999, he received the annual Award of Honor at the Cho' Karaket annual meeting, held in Buri Ram. In early 2000, Khamphun began writing a column for *Siam Rath* weekly, in which he discussed topics of contemporary interest, usually related to Isan. He and his wife, Kim Lan, a Vietnamese-Thai woman from Isan who is also a writer, started their own publishing house, Poey Sien, based in their home in Nonthaburi, and continued to publish Khamphun's work, both new and old, offering over 30 titles.[16] In 2001, Khamphun was made a National Artist in Literature. He died in 2003, and his cremation was presided over by Princess Sirindhorn.[17]

Khamphun Bunthawi published over 30 books between 1976 and 2000. The following is a partial list:

1) *Manut 100 Khuk* มนุษย์ 100 คุก (*Human Beings of 100 Prisons*), 1975, novel;

2) *Luk Isan* ลูกอีสาน (*Child of Isan*), 1976, novel;[18]

---

[14] For concise information on the SEAWrite Award and its Thai winners, see สัจภูมิ ละออ, *25 ปี ซีไรต์*. กรุงเทพฯ: สยามอินเตอร์บุ๊คส์, 2546.

[15] นรินติ เศรษฐบุตร, "10 ปี ซีไรท์ คำให้การเรื่องรางวัลวรรณกรรมสร้างสรรค์แห่งอาเซียน ปี 2522–2531," in ประเสริฐ, วิเคราะห์, 2532, pp. 221–4.

[16] They also published two books by Kim Lan.

[17] ลันนา เจริญสิทธิชัย, "ปราชญ์อีสาน," *คำพูน บุญทวี*. นนทบุรี: โปัยเซียน, 2546.

[18] The English translation, by Susan Fulop Kepner, is called *A Child of the Northeast*.

3)   *Nai Ho'i Thamin* นายฮ้อยทมิฬ (*The Brutal Buffalo Wrangler*), 1977, novel;

4)   *Yai Ko' Tai Mai Yai Ko' Tai* ใหญ่ก็ตาย ไม่ใหญ่ก็ตาย (*The Important Die, the Unimportant Die As Well*), 1977, novella and four short stories;

5)   *Seuak Koet Ma Ruai* เสือกเกิดมารวย (*Seuak was Born Rich*), 1977, short stories;

6)   *Mon Rak Sao Isan* มนต์รักสาวอีสาน (*An Isan Girl's Love Spells*), 1978, novel;

7)   *Wiraburut Muang Tai* วีรบุรุษเมืองใต้ (*Hero of the South*), 1978, novel;

8)   *Sip Ha Hua Ro'* สิบห้าหัวเราะ (*Fifteen Laughs*), 1978, short stories;

9)   *Luk Thung Khao Krung* ลูกทุ่งเข้ากรุง (*Country Boys in the City*), 1979, novel;

10) *Lab Hua Ro'* ลาบหัวเราะ (*Laughing Lab*), 1979, short stories;

11) *Sat Phut Dai* สัตว์พูดได้ (*Talking Animals*), 1980, short stories for youth;

12) *Lam Duan* ลำดวน (name of main character), 1990, novella for youth;

13) *Luk Lam Nam Khong* ลูกลำน้ำโขง (*Child of the Mekong River*), 1990, novel;

14) *Phaen Plon Meuang Isan* แผนปล้นเมืองอีสาน (*Plan to Plunder Isan*), 1992, novel;

15) *Sao Jin Luk Isan* สาวจีนลูกอีสาน (*Chinese Girl, Child of Isan*), 1993, novel;

16) *Nai Na Maengda A-ko Sopheni Dek* นายนา แมงดา อโก โสเภณีเด็ก (*Broker, Pimp, Dancer, Child Prostitute*), 1993, novel;

17) *Nak Leng Tra Khwai* นักเลงตราควาย (*Homegrown Hoodlum*), 1994, novel;

18) *La Khru Pai Kho' Mia* ลาครูไปขอเมีย (*Leaving School to Take a Wife*), 1994, novel;

19) *Kham Hai Kan Kho'ng Khon Khuk* คำให้การของคนคุก (*Statements of Prison People*), 1994, non-fiction; and

20) *Kret Prawatsat Isan Phi Ba Phi Bun* เกร็ดประวัติศาสตร์อีสาน ผีบ้าผีบุญ (*Isan Historical Fragments: Millenialist Figures*), 1998 (reprinted), non-fiction.

Luk Isan is by far Khamphun's best-known work. Having won Thailand's foremost literary prize the first time it was awarded, this novel was assured lasting fame. Equally important is the book's unique characteristics: it tells in simple, straightforward fashion the everyday experiences of a young boy in Isan during the 1930s. The fact that the author himself grew up in Isan during the 1930s gives the novel an authenticity that is reinforced by its unpretentiousness. One anonymous critic attributed the book's popularity (as well as that of *Nai Ho'i Thamin* and Khamman's *Bantheuk Kho'ng Khru Prachaban*) to readers' being "bored with stories about the capital" and "turning instead to characters who are unimportant, regular people rather than Thais studying abroad, as has been the case."[19] Keyes suggested that "nostalgia for a more traditional way of life" was felt "among readers who regretted the loss of the way of life that had been obliterated in the rush to development in Bangkok."[20] Although there may be some truth in this, most of the book's readers were Bangkok residents who had never lived in the countryside and certainly would not feel any connection to the culturally and linguistically distinct Northeast. One commentator, writing in *Lok Nangseu* in 1977 noted that *Luk Isan* was different from other books of the times, which were primarily concerned with romance, adventure, or sex. In addition, while other books about the Thai countryside generally described a city person's experience there, Khamphun's book presented the countryside from the point of view of the country people themselves, thus informing the reader about Isan life.[21]

At the start of the novel, the main character, Khun, is a boy about eight years old. We see his world through his eyes, and learn the customs and practices of his family and his village as he does, experiencing life alongside him in the company of his parents, siblings, friends, neighbors, the abbot who teaches at the temple school, etc. The quotidian events of Khun's life make up the substance of the novel: talking to his father, arguing with a friend, attending school, thinking about food, searching for food, preparing food, eating food. Indeed, what strikes most readers more than anything else about the novel is its constant attention to food: gathering, preparing, eating, sharing, discussing. Minute details related to food are recounted throughout the narrative. This of course is part of its realism: getting enough food (and water) was the never-ending concern of people in that unforgiving and unpredictable environment and era. Many Thai readers find this a fascinating aspect of the book; others feel that it contributes to the book's failure to hold their interest. In the absence of a prominent storyline or major events, the reader must be satisfied with the minor details and slow pace of the novel.

---

[19] Anon., "อภิปรายเรื่องนิยายชนะการประกวดใครใครก็ชอบนายฮ้อยทมิฬ," โลกหนังสือ 1, 12 (ก.ย. 2521): 13.

[20] Charles Keyes, "Hegemony and Resistance in Northeastern Thailand," in *Regions and National Integration in Thailand 1892–1992*, ed. V. Grabowsky. (Weisbaden: Harrassowitz, 1995), p. 167.

[21] Anon., "วิจารณ์หนังสือ ลูกอีสาน," โลกหนังสือ 1, 1 (ต.ค. 2520): 76–9.

Naraniti Sethabut, former president of the Language and Book Society of Thailand (Thai PEN Club) and frequent member of the SEAWrite Committee, describes some of the reasons for *Luk Isan* winning the first SEAWrite Award:

> *Luk Isan* has a special quality [...] It has harmony and unity [...] [It] shows the characteristics of Isan people which few can write about persuasively, and makes people interested in what Isan is like. Previously we have talked about the frustration of lacking food, but this writer makes the reader feel that this is the life of most Thai people in this region.[22]

Ranjuan agrees, noting that, "Among the 36 chapters, there almost isn't one that doesn't talk about the topic of eating. We feel both pity and the desire to snatch the food away and eat it ourselves because it seems so delicious."[23]

Khamphun's style of writing distinguishes him from other writers, as several critics have pointed out. Somrom notes that, "every story he has written is charming in its simplicity; he tells the story directly, and he is the only person who can write like this. [...] He writes without rules and without theory, which gives his writing its own style."[24] The anonymous commentator in *Lok Nangseu* (mentioned above) states that Khamphun writes "with simple, honest language as if coming from the heart of the boy, Khun."[25] However, criticism has also been made that anachronisms appear in the narrative; for example, cream and handshakes did not exist in Isan in the 1930s, according to the same commentator.[26]

Ranjuan describes the importance of language in the novel:

> It can be said that [...] *Luk Isan* has exceptional meaning in its use of language: not the language of the city, nor of the countryside, but an easy, natural language. It sounds innocent and has charm hidden within.[27]

For her, "the thing that invites interest in [Khamphun's book] is the language and expressions he uses,"[28] including expressive words for sounds, Lao

---

[22] นรินติ, "10 ปี ซีไรต์," 2532, p. 223.

[23] รัญจวน อินทรกำแหง, วรรณกรรมวิจารณ์ ตอนที่ 3. กรุงเทพฯ: ดวงกมล. "ลูกอีสาน," 2521c, p. 117.

[24] สมรม, "คำพูน," 2536, pp. 99–101.

[25] Anon., "วิจารณ์," 2520, p. 78.

[26] Ibid., p. 79.

[27] รัญจวน, วรรณกรรม, 2521, p. 120.

[28] Ibid., p. 119.

turns of phrase, and terms for local customs. This regional language use is also discussed by Prasert Sawaiwan in his Masters' thesis on Khamphun, in which he comments on the author's choice of nouns and pronouns, and use of Isan/Lao proverbs and regional wisdom, or *phaya*.[29] However, in practice, the author's technique is generally to use a Lao word or expression once, give the Thai equivalent in parentheses, and then use only the Thai term from then on. This gives the book the flavor of Lao language without requiring the reader to actually understand or learn any Lao words.

Chai-anan Samudhavanija describes *Luk Isan* as a jewel of Isan and a record of social history.[30] Ranjuan, by contrast, states that even though the book tells about a time several decades ago, it is also a novel of Isan today. The only difference, she says, is that Isan people back then would never leave their land, while today many go to Bangkok and elsewhere (even as some Bangkok people try to return to the land).[31] This issue of whether or not to leave the land is one of major significance, and a key to understanding the novel, as Nopphorn Prachakul discusses in an insightful article on *Luk Isan*.[32] Nopphorn believes that the non-fiction qualities of the book are stronger and draw the reader in more than its novelistic qualities. The great amount of detail serves to record reality more than to move the narrative along. The story is told through the character of Khun, who learns by listening and seeing and, in the manner of children, enlarges everything in importance (for example, when told he will be starting school, he jumps up and down with anticipation, but the news is unlikely to bring similar excitement to the reader).

As we follow Khun through daily life, we perceive the two major themes of the novel: 1) that of human struggle in the face of difficulty; and 2) that of attachment to birthplace (even though it is the very source of that difficulty). There are few dramatic events in the story. Instead, dramatic tension is created by the conflict between these two core values: staying alive versus staying put. As fellow villagers pack up and move, and others pass through on their way elsewhere, while the heat intensifies and food is scarce, the temptation to move increases.[33] The prohibition against moving

---

[29] ประเสริฐ ไสววรรณ, วิเคราะห์, 2532.

[30] ลูกข้าวนึ่ง, "ชัยอนันต์ สมุทวนิช มองลอดแว่น. มีอะไรใน 'ลูกอีสาน'," เนชั่น (online) 12 เม.ย. 2000 (2543) (no page numbers).

[31] รัญจวน, วรรณกรรม, 2521.

[32] นพพร ประชากุล, "มีอะไรในลูกอีสาน," เนชั่น (online) 19 เม.ย. 2543 (no page numbers).

[33] Ibid.

comes from Khun's grandfather and those before him, and is so strong that when Khun's family can hold out no longer, they still vow to leave only temporarily, in order to find provisions so that they can then return home.

Luk Isan is a book about life overall, not events. In Nopphorn's words:

> *Luk Isan* in fact is thus a presentation of the process of learning life and the world (in the context of Isan culture) in the form of a story. [...] The world of *Luk Isan* is composed of sky and earth. The sky stimulates people to test their own dignity. That is the meaning of Isan-ness.[34]

According to the *Lok Nangseu* commentator, the book is better than a research report in informing us about Isan. In addition, it serves to counteract negative stereotypes about Isan people by showing their dignity and resourcefulness in struggling to survive in an often hostile environment. Khun's father is shown as a hard worker with many skills, especially related to finding food, be it catching frogs, fish, or birds, training the dogs to help in hunting, etc. Khun's mother is equally skilled in her many tasks, including pounding rice, preparing food, tying grass to repair the roof, and so on, which she carries out diligently instead of "sitting and beautifying herself at home while her husband works, as many women in the city do."[35] As Wenk has noted,

> Khuun's family are law abiding and exhibit common decency in adverse situations, especially of material need. [...] Malice and greed are associated with those who are not Thai nationals, i.e., the Chinese and Vietnamese who are mainly traders.[36]

Even so, the Isan people in the novel are not idealized. Khun, for example, is not especially brave, intelligent, or good in school.[37] Various characters and their shortcomings are presented against the background of honest Isan folk; without such characters, "the image of humanity would be too perfect,"[38] and the novel would suffer.

Not all critics, however, have been satisfied with Khamphun's characterizations. Cho'petch Manidaeng, writing in *Lok Nangseu*, stated that Khamphun aimed primarily to entertain, and that his book thus lacked depth

---

[34] Ibid.

[35] Anon., "วิจารณ์," 2520, p. 77.

[36] Klaus Wenk, *Thai Literature: An Introduction*, trans. E. Reinhold (Bangkok: White Lotus, 1995), p. 82.

[37] ช่อเพชร มณีแดง, "คำพูน บุญทวี เขาจะเลือกเส้นทางสายไหน," โลกหนังสือ 1, 4 (ม.ค. 2521): 49–52.

[38] รัญจวน, วรรณกรรม, 2521, p. 118.

and detail. Since the author wrote without opinion or feeling toward the characters, she claims, they lack weight and life, and remain strangers to the reader. Cho'petch attributes these weaknesses to Khamphun's depending largely on relating his experiences to drive the story, and thereby failing to provide a satisfying richness or complexity.[39] Khamphun has stated that 80 percent of the story did in fact come from his own experience.[40] Cho'petch, though, contradicts herself later in the same article:

> But Khamphun's detailed memory and ability to write with subtlety, and the true liveliness and feeling of the Isan people in his work, [...] make the reader better able to understand the lives, thoughts, and sentiments of Isan people; and to understand why they have always been so poor. Sometimes they must spend an entire day catching only a few small animals to prepare as food. Their lives cannot be rushed. They must wait for nature, wait for opportunities, wait ... and keep waiting.[41]

Luk Isan was made into a film in 1982 by the well-known director Wichit Khunawut (Vichit Kunavudhi).[42] Khamphun acted as advisor for the film and also helped find the locations.[43] According to de Fels, the director's concern for veracity prompted him to film the story with the actors speaking Lao.[44] The final version featured subtitles in Central Thai. This caused controversy in Thailand, where making a major film entirely in Lao was unheard of at the time. Keyes states that, "many Central Thai were offended by the dialogue being in a Lao dialect."[45] In addition, Khamphun reports that:

> Some of the new generation of Isan people were not interested. They didn't want to have Isan language [in the film]. They were ashamed. [...] [But Lao refugees] wrote and asked to see the movie, in the U.S., in Germany.[46]

Thus the film was not very popular in Thailand. Nonetheless, de Fels reports that it received "numerous distinctions, both in Thailand and abroad."[47]

---

[39] ช่อเพชร, "คำพูน," 2521.

[40] Khamphun, Interview, 1999.

[41] ช่อเพชร, "คำพูน," 2521, p. 50.

[42] โดม สุขวงศ์, ประวัติภาพยนตร์ไทย, กรุงเทพฯ: องค์การค้าของคุรุสภา, 2533.

[43] Khamphun, Interview, 1999.

[44] de Fels, *Promotion.*

[45] Keyes, "Hegemony," 1995, p. 167.

[46] Khamphun, Interview, 1999.

[47] de Fels, *Promotion*, p. 620.

In 1988, Susan Fulop Kepner's English translation of *Luk Isan*, entitled *A Child of the Northeast*, was published in Bangkok.[48] A French translation, *Fils de l'Isan*, appeared in France in 1991.[49] Kepner's translation brought *Luk Isan* to a Western audience for the first time. It was then one of only a half-dozen Thai novels to have been translated into English, and thus became a significant representative of Thai literature for English language readers. Unfortunately, Kepner's translation is not a faithful rendering of Khamphun's original work. First of all, as is apparent from the "Translator's Introduction," when she began the task of translating this veritable documentary of Isan life, she had very little knowledge or experience of the Isan region, language, or culture depicted so painstakingly in the book. Moreover, her tendency to make embellishments and additions unwarranted by the source text quickly becomes evident if one compares her version to the original. In Chapter 8, for example, Khun's father refers to *nai ho'i*,[50] a kind of Isan cowboy who trades in buffalo. Kepner, however, transforms this term into *nai ro'i*,[51] which would be its Central Thai equivalent, except that the concept does not exist in Central Thai.[52] Thus, perhaps unconsciously mirroring Central Thai prejudice, she negates Lao or Isan aspects of the novel, the very characteristics that make it unique and provide the purpose for which it was written. More damaging, though, is her insertion of her own values and mores into her translation. In Chapter 1 of the Thai book, Khun's father, in a single sentence, encourages the boy to be a good student.[53] In the English version, Kepner follows that original line with a few sentences that she invents herself: "Koon frowned. 'How can that [being a good student] help?' 'Good things come to those who work hard.'"[54] The fact that Kepner inserts material that clearly does not exist in the source text is itself problematic.[55] However, what is truly troubling is the content behind her additions. The idea that "good things come to those who work hard" expresses (and reveals) the sensibilities of a Protestant work ethic. It is not

---

[48] By Duang Kamol.

[49] By Fayard, นพพร, "มีอะไร," 2543.

[50] คำพูน บุญทวี, ลูกอีสาน. กรุงเทพฯ: บรรณกิจเทรดดิ้ง, 2540, p. 65.

[51] Kampoon Boonthawi, *A Child of the Northeast*, trans. S.F. Kepner (Bangkok: Duang Kamol, 1991), p. 118.

[52] The word "*nai ro'i*" นายร้อย in Thai means junior officer, something totally different from *nai ho'i*.

[53] คำพูน, ลูกอีสาน, 2540, p. 4.

[54] Kampoon, *Child*, p. 26.

[55] The addition cannot be considered an explanatory note, because it violates, rather than supports, the sense of the original work.

part of an Isan Buddhist worldview. The culture of Isan as portrayed in the novel becomes misrepresented in the English translation, making Kepner's version somewhat inaccurate and misleading.

The success of *Luk Isan* has been bolstered by the awards it received, the film that was made from it, and the translations of it into Western languages. In several subsequent books, Khamphun used the words "*Luk Isan*" as part of their titles, sometimes even to refer to himself, as in *Luk Isan Khi Reua Bin*. Many of his books bear the label, "Thailand's First SEAWrite Writer," on their covers. This has made Khamphun vulnerable to the charge of opportunism, that he was capitalizing on fame merely to sell books and make money. Cho'petch implicates editors, publishers, readers, and Thai society generally in this commercialization of Isan culture, but also blames Khamphun for spending money beyond his means and thus having to write indiscriminately, producing quantity without quality for the sake of financial remuneration.[56] Given that Khamphun published dozens of books after *Luk Isan*, and very few have attained critical acclaim or even much popularity, combined with the fact that in interviews he often showed concern about the income potential from writing (see below), such criticism may have some merit.

One book that has met with considerable success, however, is *Nai Ho'i Thamin* (*The Brutal Buffalo Wrangler*). This novel won honorable mention from the Book Publishing and Distribution Association of Thailand, and is Khamphun's second most acclaimed work. Thai television's Channel 7 purchased rights to the film version and produced a 20-part series,[57] with the film script adaptation written by SEAWrite Award-winning writer Assiri Thammachote.[58] The issue of whether to use Lao or Thai language in the film was difficult to resolve, since producers wished to use Thai in order to try to avoid the controversy that accompanied the film of *Luk Isan*.[59] When *Nai Ho'i Thamin* was finally shown on Channel 7 at the end of 2000, the result was something of a disaster, with Central Thai actors playing the main roles and sounding preposterous speaking an oddly accented Thai in an attempt to simultaneously convey a Lao flavor while still being comprehensible to a Central Thai audience.

---

[56] ช่อเพชร, "คำพูน," 2521.

[57] Assiri Thammachote, pers. comm., June 5, 2000, London.

[58] While Assiri is not from Isan, he stated that he felt able to adapt the script due to his having lived in Isan, his being married to an Isan woman, and his consulting with Khamphun and also discussing the project with other Isan writers. Pers. comm., October 10, 1998, Bangkok.

[59] Khamphun, Interview, 1999.

Nai Ho'i Thamin is essentially a true story, based on the life of a man named "Khen" (as he is also called in the novel) whom Khamphun knew in Yasothorn.[60] In the foreword, Khamphun describes the meaning and cultural origins of the term *"nai ho'i."* Though related to the Thai term for "captain," *nai ho'i* is a Lao term referring to a man who (in a past era) accepted buffalo on behalf of Isan villagers to herd down to central Thailand to sell. Such a man had to be brave, decisive, experienced, and knowledgeable. He had to know where to find water and take shortcuts, how to avoid bandits and disease, what to do about problems arising en route, etc. The *nai ho'i* was often a legendary figure whom, it was said, even poisonous snakes were afraid to approach; he could dispatch evil spirits and knew how to cure sick buffalo using tree bark, herbal remedies, or spells and incantations.[61] Making the trip to Central Thailand was referred to in Isan as "going to the land below" or "going to Thai" (ไปไทย).[62] Such a trip was difficult and dangerous enough that Isan people have proverbs about it, such as, "Whoever wants to suffer, let him go and sell buffalo in the land below; if he wants to be happy and far away, let him ordain at the temple."[63]

Nai Ho'i Thamin was originally published serially in the weekly magazine, *Plaek*, in 1977, and by the end of that year it was republished as a single volume. In 1978, it was discussed in a seminar at the National Library in Bangkok. One of the participants described it as a book that ought to be read "because it is a subject that we never knew about [...] that made me realize that, yes, Thailand has cowboys, too."[64] Another noted that the novel "contains humor and knowledge about the occupations of Isan people which no longer exist, because trains and cars have taken their place."[65] One critic, though, felt that the characters lacked flesh and feeling, that the reader could not understand their behavior and motivation, and that the events and the story as a whole did not tie together.[66]

Such criticisms may be valid when the book is set alongside other novels and judged as an imaginative work of fiction. However, *Nai Ho'i Thamin*, and Khamphun's work in general, is better understood as a story

---

[60] คำพูน บุญทวี, "คำนำของผู้ประพันธ์ในการพิมพ์ครั้งที่ 4," in นายฮ้อยทมิฬ. กรุงเทพฯ: โป๊ยเซียน, 2541a, pp. 4–6.

[61] Ibid.

[62] Khamphun, Interview, 1999.

[63] คำพูน , "คำนำ ... 4," 2541a, p. 5.

[64] Anon., "อภิปราย," 2521f, p. 12.

[65] Ibid., p. 13.

[66] Anon., "นายฮ้อยทมิฬ," โลกหนังสือ 1, 12 (ก.ย. 2521): 136–7.

told from experience, an oral tale committed to paper. In such a context, the value of the book lies in the details and the events, while its goal is to inform as well as to generate interest and entertainment. A standard or conventional novel typically is created specifically as a written document and need not pass through initial stages of actual occurrence and then retelling; it is generally expected to have certain characteristics, such as well-rounded characters, character development, and a plot structure that builds gradually to a climax. However, these are not standard or required elements of a story that is primarily recounted, i.e., told, rather than written, especially in Isan. Viewing Khamphun's book as a story that he relates to an audience, rather than a novel that he has written for a readership, makes its appreciation more accessible.

The fact that the vast majority of Khamphun's books are based on his own experiences, or to a lesser extent experiences described to him by others, supports the idea that his books are essentially oral tales. His "novel," *Luk Thung Khao Krung* (*Country Boys in the City*), relates the comical adventures of two unsophisticated Isan friends, one clever and one slow, in Bangkok. None of the characters could be described as "fully realized," nor do they develop through the course of the book, and the plot has no particular trajectory. Instead, the people encountered by the pair are stock characters, even stereotypes, the two protagonists remain the same from start to finish, and the story line is merely a chain of silly, slapstick, humorous episodes. As a novel, this book would not be considered successful by the usual criteria. However, as a humorous narrative of well-observed vignettes based on real events, poking good-natured fun at newcomers to the capital, it passes the time agreeably. This is one reason that (oral) stories are told, sufficient in itself.

Luk Thung Khao Krung raises another important issue: that of intended audience. The book is easily, and perhaps primarily, appreciated by Isan people, especially those who have moved to Bangkok and can relate to the main characters. The language they use, the circumstances they encounter, and the reactions they have are likely to appeal immediately to Isan people with similar experiences. Indeed, like many comic books, but unlike almost any other novel, *Luk Thung Khao Krung* was for sale in the 1980s at Mo' Chit Bus Station,[67] one of the two main arrival and departure points for travelers between Bangkok and Isan.[68] In fact, Khamphun is one of the few,

---

[67] Peter Koret, pers. comm., December 1997.
[68] The other is Hualamphong train station.

possibly even the only, Isan author who writes with the expectation that Isan people will make up a significant, if not predominant, portion of his audience. As he has stated,

> I write for bookworms to read, and for Isan people to read, especially. [...] Most of my stories take place in Isan. I bring their lives into my writing. [...] In a hundred years, two hundred years, Isan could be a factory making nuclear material, or else a big factory making cloth ... or it could be blown up by a nuclear bomb. So Isan people who are still alive will be able to read about what their lives, their parents' lives, were like; to know what struggling in an arid land is like.[69]

In the foreword to *Luk Thung Khao Krung*, written 20 years before he made the above comment, Khamphun made a similar statement, noting that he wrote the book not to look down on Isan people's simplicity, but rather for merriment, because everyone has a lack of sophistication; another reason was so that Isan people in 50 or 100 years could see how Isan had been previously.[70] With *Nai Ho'i Thamin*, too, his purpose was, at least in part, to create an account that would preserve an aspect of Isan culture that had disappeared in his lifetime.[71]

While chronicling and disseminating Isan culture and traditions were clearly important to Khamphun, another goal seems equally important to him: making money. He recounted how his primary purpose for writing initially was to raise money to provide for his wife's medical care and his children's livelihood.[72] In interviews, he commonly discussed how much he was paid for different stories, what film rights are worth, how publishers took advantage of and swindled him, etc.[73] He took over the job of publishing his books himself, mainly, it seems, in the hope of increasing his income from them. In an interview in 1999, he described himself as one of the few writers in Thailand who made a living as a writer, and suggested that most writers are able to survive because they come from wealthy families, except for Isan writers, who "are all poor" and "have to work, become teachers, and so on."[74] He also described how difficult it was to get a serialized story

---

[69] Khamphun, Interview, 1999.

[70] คำพูน บุญทวี, "คำนำของผู้เขียน," in ลูกทุ่งเข้ากรุง. กรุงเทพฯ: บงกด, 2522a, pp. 3–4.

[71] คำพูน บุญทวี, "คำนำของผู้ประพันธ์ในการพิมพ์ครั้งที่ 5," in นายฮ้อยทมิฬ. กรุงเทพฯ: โป๊ยเซียน, 2541b, p. 3.

[72] Khamphun, Interview, 1999.

[73] See, for example, ช่อเพชร, "คำพูน," 2521, and สมรม, "คำพูน," 2536.

[74] Khamphun, Interview, 1999.

published in a weekly magazine, especially after the start of the economic crisis in the late 1990s, and he joked that writers who already have such contracts try to extend their stories to a thousand parts in order to continue collecting the paycheck as long as possible.[75]

Khamphun's most popular and acclaimed books were written in the 1970s, during the height of the Literature for Life movement. Superficially, his work might appear to be a part of that movement, taking as it does the lives of poor people in Isan as its subject matter. As Nopporn has pointed out, Khamphun used the same kind of raw material as Literature for Life writers but in a different way, and thus his writing was separate from that movement: "In *Luk Isan*, for example, Isan-ness means learning to live with hardship, being able to resist it with dignity, and not requiring sympathy from others, because sympathy tends to be deeply tied to contempt."[76] At least one student from Isan disliked *Luk Isan* for exactly this reason: she felt the book caused readers to pity Isan people, thus perpetuating the disdain that other Thais have for Isan.[77] In any case, Khamphun's writing cannot be considered Literature for Life because he did not share the movement's goals or political point of view. He did not expect any results from his writing in terms of social change or improvement, he said,[78] nor did he believe such an outcome was possible:

> In my understanding, writing can't change things. If people with influence read, they merely become informed. But for them to use it in their political endeavors, for the mouths and stomachs of the people somehow, I think it's impossible.[79]

In Lok Nangseu's 1978 interview, Khamphun asked the interviewer, "Can you tell me something? They analyze my work and say it's Literature for Life. What is this Literature for Life anyway?"[80]

Not only does Khamphun exist apart from Literature for Life, he is outside of modern Thai literary movements in general. As he himself stated in 1978,

> I don't mix much with anyone. But I'd like to read different types of criticism. It would be another way for me, because my basic knowledge

---

[75] Ibid.

[76] นพพร, "มือะไร," 2543 (no page numbers).

[77] แหม่ม, pers. comm., March 1998.

[78] ช่อเพชร, "คำพูน," 2521.

[79] Anon., "ผมจะเขียน," 2521e, p. 45.

[80] Ibid., p. 49.

is limited. I didn't study to a high level, only the sixth year of second-ary school.[81]

Many years after making this statement, though, he mentioned Hemingway, Steinbeck, Marquez, and French and other Western writers in conversation, yet his later books remained largely the same as his early ones in terms of style and subject matter. The only real change was that in the late 1990s he wrote some non-fiction books based on aspects of Isan history. This perhaps was a reflection of the trend of regionalism among Isan and other authors in Thailand, in which they have consciously taken their own region and its historical past as subject matter for their writing (see Chapter 5).

In general, though, Khamphun's work is principally autobiographical, based on real experience. This includes his books about the South, like *Rak Amata Thi Ko' Narok Tarutao* (*Eternal Love on Tarutao, Island of Hell*), which are gleaned from his life and the stories he heard there. His books about prisons, such as *Manut Ro'i Khuk* (*Human Beings of 100 Prisons*), recount events he witnessed or heard about while working as a guard in several prisons. Even his historical work, including *Kret Prawatsat Isan* (*Isan Historical Fragments*) and *Phaen Plon Meuang Isan* (*The Plan to Plunder Isan*), are apparently based primarily on oral history and word-of-mouth accounts. Khamphun began writing a regular column in *Siam Rath* weekly in 2000, covering whatever subject interested him, usually related to Isan, such as politics, education, children's future, etc. These columns were written off the top of his head in his usual chatty, humorous style, and thus bear the same qualities of spoken tales, anecdotes, and opinions that characterize his writing overall. In fact, Khamphun's work is mainly memoir, an extension of the stories one tells to friends. Thus he was, in a sense, the modern literary inheritor of the Isan oral tradition. He told stories in an oral style, the same way he talked: using humor, repetition, and reduplicative expressions in a non-linear, non-goal-oriented recounting of life experiences. These characteristics (excepting the factual basis, perhaps) are also the hallmark of traditional Isan oral arts. His books are, in effect, spoken tales set down in print.

Khamman Khonkhai

Khamman Khonkhai คำหมาน คนไค is the other Isan writer, after Khamphun, whose work became popular and well-known in the late 1970s among

---

[81] Ibid., p. 47.

Thai readers generally. While Isan plays a major role in his work, both as background and subject matter, Khamman's primary interest, and the central topic of the majority of his writing, is education and teaching. Like Witthayakorn Chiengkul, Khamman's concern with the state of education in Thailand began in the 1960s, but rather than focusing on university issues in the capital, Khamman has concentrated his attentions on primary and secondary education in the provinces. Like Khamphun, most of Khamman's writing is based on real events, and much of it is in the form of letters describing incidents at schools in Isan. His two best-known books, *Khru Ban No'k* (*Country Teacher*)[82] and *Kha Ratchakan Khru* (*Destroying the Teachers' Civil Service*),[83] are novels but are based on true stories. Unlike Khamphun's, Khamman's work has been influenced by the Literature for Life movement, or at least motivated by the same idealism that gave rise to it. Khamman's written output decreased markedly in the last decade of the 20th century, and his primary vocation continued to be that of an education official in the Thai government.

Khamman Khonkhai is the pen name of Somphong Phalasun. He was born in 1937 in what was then Amnat Jaroen District[84] of Ubon Province, and completed primary and secondary school there.[85] After receiving the highest score in Ubon on the post-secondary school qualifying exams, he was awarded a higher education scholarship by the provincial government.[86] He then studied at teachers' college and was in the first group of students in Thailand to earn a diploma in education. Subsequently, he studied at Prasanmitr University, graduating with a bachelor's degree in education. Sathien Janthimathorn was a fellow student of Khamman's at Prasanmitr (where they met in the library) and recalls Khamman's early enjoyment of writing and interest in "things not taught in the classroom."[87] After graduating, Khamman returned to Ubon province, where he taught school and wrote a column for *Siam Niko'n* weekly. Eventually, he was forbidden to continue the column by the Ubon Provincial Education Officer. He then

---

[82] Published in English translation as *The Teachers of Mad Dog Swamp*.

[83] Published in English translation as *Teacher Marisa*; see below for comment on the double meaning of its Thai title.

[84] Now Amnat Jaroen Province.

[85] วิวัฒน์ โรจนาวรรณ, นักเขียนอีสาน. บุรีรัมย์: สโมสรนักเขียนภาคอีสาน, 2542, p. 27.

[86] เสถียร จันทิมาธร, "ก่อนจะเป็น ครูคำหมาน คนไค," in คำหมาน คนไค. จดหมายจากครูคำหมานคนไค. กรุงเทพฯ: บรรณกิจ, 2518a (no page numbers).

[87] Ibid.

won a fellowship in 1968 from USAID to study for a master's degree in Colorado, where he remained for two years before returning to Ubon.[88]

Khamman began his career in education as an elementary school teacher in the rural village of No'ng Ma Wo' in Ubon, then became a supervisor of education, and later the provincial head of education.[89] Working his way up in the Ministry of Education, he moved to Bangkok, and eventually became the Deputy Secretary-General of the Teachers' Council of Thailand.[90]

Khamman has published the following books:

1) *Jotmai Jak Khru Khamman Khonkhai* จดหมายจากครูคำหมานคนไค (*Letters from Teacher Khamman Khonkhai*), 1975, letters;

2) *Bantheuk Kho'ng Khru Prachaban* บันทึกของครูประชาบาล (*Notes of a Rural Elementary Teacher*), 1976, non-fiction;

3) *Khru Ban No'k* ครูบ้านนอก (*Country Teacher*), 1978, novel;

4) *Bak Si Doe*[91] บักสีเดือ (*Country Hick*), 1978, novel;

5) *Jotmai Jak Khru Ban No'k* จดหมายจากครูบ้านนอก (*Letters from a Country Teacher*), 1978, letters;

6) *Jotmai Jak No'ng Ma Wo'* จดหมายจากหนองหมาว้อ (*Letters from Mad Dog Swamp*), 1979, letters;

7) *Prasa Khon Ban No'k* ประสาคนบ้านนอก (*In the Manner of Country Folk*), 1980, novel;

8) *Kha Ratchakan Khru* ฆ่าราชการครู (*Destruction of the Teachers' Civil Service*), 1980/1981, novel;

9) *Yim...Khon Krung* ยิ้ม...คนกรุง (*Smile...Urbanites*), 1986, short stories;

10) *Mai Banthat Khot* ไม้บรรทัดคด (*The Crooked Yardstick*), 1991, short stories;

11) *Phaya Phumipanya Isan* ผญา ภูมิปัญญาอีสาน (*Proverbs: Isan Folk Wisdom*), 1996, collected proverbs; and

12) *Kham Khong Pai Lao* ข้ามโขงไปลาว (*Crossing the Mekong to Laos*), 1997, non-fiction.

Khamman's literary career started in 1967 when he began writing about educational issues in columns for newspapers and periodicals, including

---

[88] Ibid.

[89] Anon., "รู้จักกับนักเขียน," in คำหมาน คนไค, จดหมาย, 2518, back cover.

[90] Gehan Wijeyewardene, "Translator's Introduction," in Khammaan Khonkhai, *The Teachers of Mad Dog Swamp*, trans. G. Wijeyewardene (Chiang Mai: Silkworm, 1992), p. xiv.

[91] This title is in Lao.

Pheuan Khru Ubon, Chao Nam Dam, Siam Niko'n, and *Witthayasan*. Some of his columns in *Siam Niko'n*, which were written in the form of letters from where he taught in Ubon to fellow teachers and friends, were collected in his first book, *Jotmai Jak Khru Khamman Khonkhai* (*Letters from Teacher Khamman Khonkhai*), published in 1975. According to Sathien,

> It was not only teachers in Isan who read and saw his clarity and vividness. His fellow teachers in the North, South, and East also shared these bitter experiences, and it was like the collective feeling of the whole lower-level civil service.[92]

Sathien further noted that Khamman's letters also appealed to those outside of teaching circles who sent their children to school and heard similar stories to the ones Khamman described. Finally, Sathien made a prediction:

> For someone who writes with the liveliness of Khamman Khonkhai, the limits to his writing are certainly not restricted to letters only. When he makes the attempt, I am certain that he will progress far beyond this, with nothing to stop him.[93]

This prediction proved correct. In 1976, Khamman published *Bantheuk Kho'ng Khru Prachaban* (*Notes of a Rural Elementary Teacher*), another non-fiction work, which received an award from the annual National Book Contest.[94] His biggest success as a writer was soon to follow. In Khamman's own words,

> Around 1977, Surasi Phatham, a young son of Isan, came to me in Ubon and said he wanted to make a film about the life of a rural teacher, based on my [second] book, *Bantheuk Kho'ng Khru Prachaban* [*Notes of a Rural Elementary Teacher*].[95]

Khamman persuaded the director that there was much else to say beyond what was in the book mentioned, and thus proposed to write a new book showing the true picture of the life of a rural elementary school teacher and the lives of villagers in Isan between 1976 and 1977. Thereafter, Khamman and others in the film project's writing unit set down the whole outline of the book, including the names of the characters. This was the origin of *Khru Ban No'k*.[96] Khamman states his goals in writing the book as follows:

---

[92] เสถียร, "ก่อนจะเป็น," 2518a (no page numbers).

[93] Ibid.

[94] วิวัฒน์, ed., นักเขียน, 2542a.

[95] คำหมาน คนไค, "จากผู้เขียน," in ครูบ้านนอก. กรุงเทพฯ: การเวก, 2521c p. (5).

[96] Ibid.

> It must be a true story, i.e., based on true stories of a rural elementary
> teacher; the body of the story must show the lives of rural villagers and
> Isan customs and culture as much as possible; and finally, I would try
> to present teaching methods related to being an elementary teacher that
> were in keeping with the intentions of the new curriculum announced in
> the teaching year 2521 [1978] as much as the story would allow.[97]

Khamman dedicated the book to the teacher on whose life it was based,
and expressed appreciation to the teachers who taught him to write. He
also included the following disclaimer, in which he attempts to counter in
advance the standard criticisms from the right, thus giving an indication of
the divisiveness of Thai society at the time:

> The opinions and sympathies about education and the country are made
> with a pure heart and goodwill toward the country, in the capacity of a
> Thai who is aware of the need to help develop the country for progress
> and security. I have no other bias hidden within at all.[98]

The novel, *Khru Ban No'k*, was published in 1978, soon after the film
was released. It seems likely that Khamman had read and was influenced by
Khamphun's book, *Luk Isan*, perhaps desiring to emulate that book's success.
As quoted above, Khamman refers to Surasi, the director, as a young "*luk
Isan*," and expresses a desire to "show the lives of rural villagers and Isan
customs and culture as much as possible." The book contains many scenes
of gathering, preparing, and consuming local foods in Ubon. One could
argue that this is merely coincidence, or that it reflects an abiding concern
of Isan people generally, but with *Khru Ban No'k* being written so soon
after Khamphun's book garnered prizes and fame (though before it won the
SEAWrite Award), one cannot help but infer a connection. Whatever the
case, Khamman's book as well as the film were very successful in Thailand.
The novel has been translated into English and Japanese and, like the film,
has been used in university programs in both Australia and Japan.[99]

Khru Ban No'k has been strongly praised for two principal reasons. The
first is its striking depiction of school and life in rural Isan. According to a
critic writing in *Lok Nangseu* under the pseudonym Mai Rakmu,

> The outstanding thing about this novel is its reflection of the impover-
> ished existence of villagers in the countryside, the failure to carry out

---

[97] Ibid., p. (6).
[98] Ibid.
[99] Anon., "...โรงเรียนคือแดนหฤโหด.. คำหมาน คนไค กล่าว". โลกหนังสือ 2, 10 (1979) (ก.ค.
2522): 21–5.

rural education (which might represent other levels as well, including even the university level) by the state which is based in urban society and travels into the countryside along with what is called progress.[100]

The same critic also states that Khamman captures the atmosphere of scarcity in the rural schools and is able to represent traditional customs and their origins in a harmonious fashion. Furthermore,

> If we compare [*Khru Ban No'k*] with *Luk Isan* by Khamphun Bunthawi [...] we see that in reflecting such images [of Isan] (which these two books share as a goal), *Luk Isan* is filled with various information presented directly, making the story rather more like non-fiction than a novel, while *Khru Ban No'k* tries to reflect these things in a timely way by blending them harmoniously with the advancing of the story.[101]

The other main reason that *Khru Ban No'k* has been widely praised is its clear expression of the author's ideals. As Mai notes, "This work by Khamman Khonkhai gives us hope that there are still writers who are concerned with social problems."[102] Thus, the value of the book lies in its emphasis on the strong principles of the main character, Piya, who, unlike his fellow graduates of teachers' college, decides to return to Isan to teach. He "is the representative of the new generation of teachers whose ideal is to work for the good of the whole, rather than thinking of their own survival."[103] Piya's upright life and righteous desire to deal honestly with everyone make him a model both for his students and for the book's readers. His struggle to expose the illegal logging and collusion of government officials around his village are depicted in a heroic light. The issue of logging and corruption in the countryside has remained relevant to Thai society.[104]

The primary weaknesses of the novel involve the rendering of its characters. The villagers tend to be simple, honest, and innocent, while the main villain is a Chinese businessman named "*Mangko'n*" (Dragon). In addition to these stereotypes, the characters' motivations are sometimes in doubt or unclear. Mai Rakmu considers the characters, especially Dragon, to be unrealistic and weak in their behavior and the reasons given for it; as an

---

[100] ใหม่ รักหมู่, "ครูบ้านนอก," โลกหนังสือ 1, 10 (1978) (ก.ค. 2521): 109.

[101] Ibid., pp. 109–10.

[102] Ibid., p. 115.

[103] Ibid., p. 110.

[104] See, for example, coverage of another logging scandal involving Thai government officials in กองบรรณาธิการ, "คุ้ย 3 คดีดังสาละวิน 'นึ๊กปาไม้' ใครร่วมงานป่า," ฐานสัปดาห์วิจารณ์ 5(6): 246(311) (1999) (9–15 ม.ค. 2542): 18–9.

example, he cites Dragon's decision not to kill a villager who accidentally discovers the illegal logging operation. "At times we cannot help but feel that Khamman has been impatient in bringing the story to a close in order to make it fit the length of a film," Mai notes.[105] In addition, the flow of the narrative is sometimes dragged down by the bureaucratic language used to identify the various education officials, such as "the Provincial Supervisor," "the assistant to the Section Head," and "the Deputy District Officer of the Provincial Capital," all of whom, along with several others, appear in Chapter 2, and are referred to by these titles.

In Thai (including Isan) society, the teacher occupies a very important and influential position as a figure of knowledge and authority worthy of respect.[106] Gehan Wijeyewardene has noted the Thai government's recognition of "the potential of rural schoolteachers for shaping attitudes and changing values,"[107] and further states,

> The standardization of language, and certain aspects of culture, has been part of the policy of modern Thai regimes. The system of primary schools with a bureaucratic teaching staff has up to now been its main instrument.[108]

In fact, as discussed in Chapter 1 above, the central Thai government has attempted since the early 1900s to absorb Isan and erase Isan culture where it differed from that of Central Thailand. The two main ways in which such a policy has been instituted are through central government administration (and force of arms) and the national education system. Khamman's work is thus subversive not just in its depiction of the corruption of government officials, but more fundamentally in its indictment of the government education system (both primary and secondary), one of the key tools by which regional identity is suppressed and (Central) Thai-ness inculcated. By revealing the fundamental and widespread flaws in the system, Khamman brings the entire bureaucratic educational endeavor into question.

In a talk given in 1979 at the Language and Book Society of Thailand (PEN International Thailand Center), Khamman stated that the incident at Ban Na Sai in 1975 (discussed in Chapter 3 above), with the many

---

[105] ใหม่, "ครู," 1978, p. 113.

[106] Niels Mulder compares the social position of teachers to that of mothers; see นีลส์ มุลเดอร์, "การสื่อแสดงความหมายทางวัฒนธรรมของแก่นเรื่องที่เด่นๆ ในวรรณกรรมสมัยใหม่ของไทย และชวา," โลกหนังสือ 4, 2 (1980) (พ.ย. 2523): 70–87.

[107] Wijeyewardene, "Translator's," 1992, p. xv.

[108] Ibid., p. xlix.

conflicting accounts of it, inspired him in his writing.[109] That incident was a milestone in citizens' efforts to call the Thai government to account for its actions when its own version of events differed from that of ordinary people. In response, Khamman advocated "revolutionizing" the education system so that students no longer simply absorb and believe everything they are told by their teachers (who are frequently Central Thai authority figures):

> Revolutionize it completely. We will have the students decide for themselves what is wrong, what is right. We will teach people to think and reason, and most important, we will teach everyone to search for knowledge and depend on themselves.[110]

He went on to describe the Thai education system as one of prohibitions, of negatives:

> Don't cut across the grass; don't throw paper; don't litter; don't make noise"; and so on. [...] And people in university circles are the same way. Those in senior positions are the same way [...] But they never say what students can do.[111]

In contrast to many of his contemporaries, both Isan writers and others, however, Khamman advocated revolution from within as the way to solve problems in the education system, and in Thai society in general. When asked, by Witthayakorn Chiengkul, whether his work (as a civil servant) or his writing did more for improving society, Khamman answered without hesitation, "My work."[112]

In the three years following the publication of *Khru Ban No'k*, Khamman published five more books, of which three continued to address the topic of education (the other two were novels concerned with rural-urban issues more generally). One of these, *Jotmai Jak Khru Ban No'k* (*Letters from a Country Teacher*), appeared only six months after *Khru Ban No'k* and received a National Book Week Award. More well-known, perhaps, is a novel Khamman published serially in 1980 and collected into a single volume in 1981, entitled, *Kha Ratchakan Khru*. The title means "Destroying the Teachers' Civil Service," but its pronunciation in Thai is identical to that of the common term for "civil service teacher" or "government teacher" ข้าราชการครู. As this play on words is probably "impossible to

---

[109] See Anon., 2522a, "โรงเรียน".

[110] Ibid., p. 23.

[111] Ibid., p. 25.

[112] Ibid., p. 24.

render in English,"[113] the book's translator, Wijeyewardene, has given to the English version the title, *Teacher Marisa*, after the heroine. According to Wijeyewardene, "The Thai title is particularly appropriate, for the ambiguity of the title suggests that this is both novel and sociopolitical critique."[114] The book serves as a kind of counterpart to *Khru Ban No'k*, depicting problems and struggles in a provincial town's secondary school, whereas the earlier book took place at and around a village primary school.

In 1986, Khamman published a collection of short stories called, *Yim... Khon Krung* (*Smile...Urbanites*). The author states in the foreword that the stories are his complaints about Bangkok, a city to which, as an Ubon person, he could never quite adjust. He also notes that the stories were originally published in his column, *Khon Ba Nai Muang Krung* (*Mad Person/People in Bangkok*), in *No'n Yim* monthly magazine, and that the column's title refers to himself, i.e., that he is the "mad person."[115] However, one suspects that by criticizing himself, Khamman really means to expose and parody certain aspects of the capital. This view is supported later in the same foreword when he states that the book is intended "for country people who don't understand Bangkok people, and for Bangkok people who don't understand themselves."[116]

Over the following 15 years, Khamman published only three books. The first was *Mai Banthat Khot* (*The Crooked Yardstick*), a collection of short stories on environmental themes. The second, published in 1996, was *Phaya Phumipanya Isan* (*Proverbs: Isan Folk Wisdom*), a collection of *phaya*, or philosophical and proverbial sayings in Lao. Khamman states that the purpose of the book is to inform both Isan and other Thais about *phaya*, and he expresses his hopes for the book: that folk wisdom will last a long time, that Isan and other people will understand Isan in new ways, and especially that the new generation of Isan people will understand themselves more widely and deeply.[117] Finally, *Kham Khong Pai Lao* (*Crossing the Mekong River to Laos*), is a non-fiction work on contemporary Laos. Published in 1997, it was inspired by two short trips (totaling three nights) that Khamman took to Laos in 1993 and 1994. He wrote the book for the following reason:

---

[113] Gehan Wijeyewardene,"Translator's Introduction," in Khammaan Khonkhai, *Teacher Marisa*, trans. G. Wijeyewardene (Bangkok: Pandora, 1984), p. 3

[114] Ibid.

[115] คำหมาน คนไค, "คำนำของผู้เขียน," in ยิ้ม...คนกรุง. กรุงเทพฯ: พลพันธ์, 2329a (no page numbers).

[116] Ibid.

[117] คำหมาน คนไค, "คำนำ," in ผญา ภูมิปัญญาอีสาน. กรุงเทพฯ: ไทยวัฒนาพานิช, 2539a, p. 3.

> I have no intention of guiding people to visit [Laos]. But I wish to lead readers to better know and understand Laos, Lao people, including Lao culture in some aspects, in order to build a good understanding between them."[118]

He does not state his reason for doing so, but presumably it is related to his desire to present Isan culture in a favorable light to the general Thai reader. Lao culture, whether in Isan or Laos, is maligned and misunderstood in Thailand. However, there appears to be another, more personal reason for Khamman's writing this book, related to Lao/Isan identity. Khamman has stated more than once that he is a rural person from Ubon and will always remain so, no matter where he lives or what position he holds,[119] and that he is not ashamed of it.[120] The last chapter in *Kham Khong Pai Lao* is an explanation of the Lao writing system, including the numerals and names of letters, and a discussion of the spoken language, with its linguistic iconicity and series of expressive terms. Such attention to the Lao nation, proverbs, language, and script shows Khamman's participation (whether consciously or not) in *tho'ng thin niyom* (regionalism or localism), a phenomenon that is manifested in the work of a number of Isan writers in the 1990s, as will be discussed in Chapter 5 below.

Khamman Khonkhai's writing in the 1970s and early 1980s was clearly influenced by, yet remained somewhat apart from, the predominant literary movement of the time, Literature for Life. Rather than committing himself to the wholesale dismantling and remaking of Thai society, Khamman concentrated primarily on the single issue of greatest importance to him (and, arguably, to the country): education. While much of his writing shows a socialist realist bent in its portrayal of the disenfranchised and the injustices they face, he does not provide solutions to the issues he raises. As he states in the seventh printing of *Khru Ban No'k*,

> [*Khru Ban No'k*] is a novel, but it is a novel reflecting the truth. I have only tried to set out those conditions which create problems in our society so that the members of society may recognize and understand them. I have no answers to these problems. It is the duty of all of

---

[118] คำหมาน คนไค, "คำนำผู้เขียน," in ข้ามโขงไปปลาว. กรุงเทพฯ: ต้นอ้อ แกรมมี่, 2540a (no page numbers).

[119] คำหมาน คนไค, "คำนำของผู้เขียน," in จดหมายจากครูบ้านนอก. กรุงเทพฯ: บรรณกิจ, 2521a (no page numbers).

[120] คำหมาน คนไค, "คำนำของผู้เขียน," in บักสีเคื่อ. กรุงเทพฯ: บรรณกิจ, 2521b (no page numbers).

us to find ways of alleviating these problems through mutual effort, contributing whatever we can to their solution. We do not have to await the birth of a second, or a third, Khru Piya to do this.[121]

Apart from the subject of education, Khamman is also concerned with the realities of life in Isan and the dilution of its identity. In Wijeyewardene's view, *Khru Ban No'k* "may be looked at as the author's confrontation of different ways of life," and shows Khamman's regard for "a category of people the author clearly sees as in danger of growing apart from its own origins."[122] Wijeyewardene, though, believes that this "category of people" means Central Thais:

> The vignettes of Thai life are for the benefit of the urban reader, perhaps prototypically the Bangkok student. The sophistication of metropolitan life, Western films and foreign philosophies divorce these people from the life of the village, even the life of the district centres. [...] It is no accident that the novel begins in a ballroom. This is a symbol of the life Piya rejects, but to which the author addresses his novel. It is a long bus ride between that ballroom and the schoolhouse of [No'ng Ma Wo' Village] but, Khammaan Khonkhai seems to be saying, it is a ride the reader must take if Thai identity is to be understood, if it is to survive.[123]

However, Wijeyewardene here makes a mistake in conflating Isan identity and Thai identity. To believe that Central Thais would, to any meaningful extent, look to Isan culture to reinforce their own identity is misguided. The difference in language and culture, and, more significantly, the perceived gap in status and sophistication, ensure that Bangkok Thais (the "urban reader" to which Wijeyewardene refers) continue to see Isan as an essentially separate, different, and inferior place, not as some kind of ancestral one.

Wijeyewardene goes on to state,

> The novel is in part a plea for the right of the language and culture to a continuing existence, a plea for the preservation of cultural integrity. Equipping the rural young for a better life in their native Thailand does not, and must not, involve the suppression of their own folk culture.[124]

This statement may be true, but not in the way that Wijeyewardene intends it to be, which is through his contention that Khamman's novel is a plea for

---

[121] Khamman, "From the Author," 1989, p. xiii.
[122] Wijeyewardene, "Translator's," 1992, p. xxxvi.
[123] Ibid., p. xl.
[124] Ibid., p. xlviii.

Central Thai youth to get in touch with their (alleged) roots. Rather, *Khru Ban No'k* represents an attempt by its author to enhance understanding, acceptance, and, hopefully, respect for Isan, its culture, and its people, among Thais in general (including Isan people themselves). Khamman's concern is for Isan and its well-being, not for Central Thais' use of Isan as a reminder of their (mythic) past. This is clearly demonstrated by Khamman's comment in the seventh printing of *Khru Ban No'k*:

> When we compare the essence of way of life of people and teachers of the rural northeast before 2519 [1976] with this year of 2531 [1988], there is not much that has changed. Some superficial changes have occurred such as the increase in the availability of material goods. Thus roads have improved and communications are more convenient, electricity and electrical goods such as television sets and refrigerators, vehicles such as saloon cars are more available. But people are poor, lack many necessities, are oppressed and exploited, and have no power to defend themselves whether in economic, political, or social life. The condition of the poor and exploited in the northeast has not changed between 2519 and 2531 — it may even have become worse.[125]

Khamman obviously cares about Isan for its own sake, largely as a consequence of his personal connection to it. This bond with Isan is the basis for a sensibility that is found throughout Khamman's work, and in much writing by other Isan authors as well. That sensibility, and the *tho'ng thin niyom* phenomenon it gave rise to, will be further investigated in the following chapters.

Conclusion

In the 1970s, Khamphun Bunthawi and Khamman Khonkhai produced work that transcended political affiliation and gained national attention. Each produced two novels that were particularly successful, winning national awards and being made into films. For Khamman, education has been the abiding concern in both his professional life and his writing career. While his books show some sympathy with prevailing progressive politics of the time, featuring protagonists who heroically oppose corruption and injustice, he avoids the simplistic and formulaic patterns that came to characterize, and eventually limit the popularity of, much politically committed literature of that era. Khamman has worked for the improvement of Isan and rural

---

[125] Khamman, "From the Author," 1989, pp. xii–xiii.

education there by informing the public about conditions, through his books, and by carrying out his responsibilities within the system.

Khamphun Bunthawi would have to be considered the most successful of Isan writers in terms of fame, awards received, size of readership, and number of books published. He was accorded great respect among other writers, both Isan and Thai generally, not least for becoming the country's first SEAWrite laureate, for his novel, *Luk Isan*. His writing is chiefly autobiographical, and his storytelling style, with its humorous, reduplicative, non-linear characteristics, recalls the techniques of Isan/Lao oral arts. It is ironic that he was firmly established in the Thai literary mainstream while at the same time being completely outside the main current that has dominated modern Isan writing since its emergence in the 1950s and continued to exert strong, some would say excessive, influence on Isan literature: the Literature for Life movement. Only after 1990 or so did a significant alternative to that movement begin to gain prominence. That alternative, *tho'ng thin niyom*, or regionalism, as it applies to Isan literature, will be the subject of Chapter 5.

CHAPTER 5

The Rise of Regionalism

Though the Literature for Life movement flourished in the mid-1970s, those blossoms were soon to yield bitter fruit. The events of October 6, 1976 forced a polarization in which politically active students and intellectuals had to decide where their loyalties lay. Those who fled to the jungle either strongly supported the Communist Party of Thailand (CPT) and the armed struggle, or felt their lives endangered to the point that they had no choice. While the Literature for Life movement held sway in the jungle in the service of the Party, in the rest of the country it faced increasing skepticism and experienced a marked decline in popularity. By 1982, it had lost the vitality of its youthful supporters and devolved into an ignored and moribund state. Such a complete reversal in prominence of this major literary movement was a result of a lethal combination of rejection by its consumers, the reading public, and repudiation by its producers, the writers of the Left.

As noted in Chapter 3 above, the political stridency and artistic simplicity (or simple-mindedness) that characterized Literature for Life could not hold the attention of readers. Formulaic plots, stock characters, and repetitive themes had made the literature predictable and dull. Fewer and fewer people were interested in reading stories of relentless sameness, in which, as Suchart Sawatsri has humorously noted, the same events seemed always to occur: "Father is ill, mother's in pain, the child's dead, and the buffalo's gone."[1] Cholthira Kladyu's criticism of Literature for Life was that it "could only pass on but not develop and improve" what had been framed by Banjong, Seni, and Jit;[2] in other words, it was stagnant.

---

[1] Suchart Sawatsri, Simmons Memorial Lecture, November 28, 1997, SOAS, London.

[2] Quoted in เสถียร จันทิมาธร, "วรรณกรรมยุค 14 ตุลาคม 2516," สายธารวรรณกรรม เพื่อชีวิตของไทย. กรุงเทพฯ: เจ้าพระยา, 2527b, pp. 459–60.

Literature for Life writers put emphasis on content and ignored form. In Cholthira's analogy,

> It's like food. If you just prepare it so that it's nutritional, without caring about the taste, no one will want to eat it. If there's no flavor, no beauty, then there's no art, and its usefulness is empty because no one likes to read it.[3]

Lawan Sangkhaphanthanon, in the final sentence of her MA thesis on socially reflective literature, covering 90 stories published between 1978 and 1982, determined simply that, "It should, then, be concluded that these short stories were not enough worthwhile to put interest in."[4] As a comment on Literature for Life in general, this sentiment would be widely shared.

While readers' experience with Literature for Life became one of boredom, writers' experiences were more profound and traumatic. By the early 1980s, the political movement underlying the literary one had collapsed due to both internal and external pressures. The widening rift between China and the Soviet Union gained new relevance in the region when Vietnam invaded Kampuchea and China responded by attacking the Vietnamese border. A parallel split occurred between factions of the CPT, already weakened by dissatisfaction among members who objected to what they considered the overly Chinese character of the CPT leadership.[5] At the same time, the offer of amnesty first conceived under Prime Minister Kriangsak Chomanan and then enthusiastically supported by Prime Minister Prem Tinsulanonda encouraged mass defections and finally the disintegration of the Party. The literary movement could no longer stand without its political foundation, especially as the literature was seen to be associated with failed (and thus illegitimate) political action.

By 1982, the CPT was effectively dead, and the promise and enthusiasm of the 1970s had turned to disillusionment and bitterness. Writers who came out of the jungle found a changed society characterized by economic rather than political struggle. Their experiences with politics and ideals belonged to a reality that no longer existed, and they were suddenly surrounded by people concerned primarily with themselves: private issues, personal problems, and economic interests.[6] Now these émigrés from the

---

[3] Ibid., p. 459.

[4] ลาวัณย์ สังพันธานนท์, "ภาพสะท้อนสังคมไทยจากเรื่องสั้นร่วมสมัย". ปริญญานิพนธ์ มหาวิทยาลัย ศรีนครินทรวิโรฒ พิษณุโลก, 2529, p. 175.

[5] วีระศักดิ์ สุนทรศรี, คาราวาน: ตำนานทัพหน้าวงดนตรีเพื่อชีวิตของไทย. กรุงเทพฯ: กำแพง, 2536.

[6] Suchart Sawatsri, Simmons Memorial Lecture, 1997.

jungle had to find a way to rejoin society, and the transformation demanded was enormous. They had come from a situation of belonging to a movement with others of like mind, making sacrifices, sharing hardship, dedicating themselves to a common goal, and witnessing the death of their comrades. What they had suffered was the total disintegration of that overarching organizational force in their lives and the loss of the very principles that sustained it. Furthermore, they were now surrounded at every turn by society's repudiation of those principles: cars, high-rise buildings, expanding wealth, a fast-growth economy. The experience of walking around day and night, wondering what to do with themselves, where to go, how to live, how (or whether) to fit back into society, etc., was depicted by Surachai (see Chapter 3) and other writers. Such feelings and questions found parallels in a literary experience of anomie or outside-ness, and a search for what to write about, from what point of view, for what audience, with what goals, etc.

The goals and concerns of the Literature for Life movement have not simply disappeared, of course. Many writers have moved in new directions but retained influence from the movement (see below). In addition, fundamental issues of Art for Life are periodically revisited in articles, seminars, and panel discussions. In 1998, for example, during a period of commemoration of October 14, 1973 after 25 years, an article appeared in *Sarakhadi* (the non-fiction feature monthly) entitled, "Why is Socially Reflective Literature Unable to Solve Society's Problems?"[7] The article was immediately reprinted in the literary journal *Cho'Karaket*, with a note stating that, "The occasion of October 14, 1973, will have greater meaning if individuals in literary circles join together to reassess sincerely the role and development of Literature for Life."[8] The article elicited an essay in response in the *Nation Weekend* entitled, "Consequences of the Question: 'Why is Socially Reflective Literature Unable to Solve Society's Problems',", which concluded that,

> Instead of saying that literature reflects society, we should say that it reflects the point of view toward society of individuals or groups (whether the creator, the publisher, or the audience). The quality of raising or building consciousness depends on the quality of thought of people.[9]

---

[7] นพพร ประชากุล, "ทำไมวรรณกรรมสะท้อนสังคมจึงแก้ปัญหาสังคมไม่ได้," สารคดี 162 (ส.ค. 2541).

[8] ช่อการะเกด 39 (ก.ย.–ต.ค. 2541), pp. 197–201.

[9] ดวงมน จิตร์จำนงค์, "สืบเนื่องจากคำถาม 'ทำไมวรรณกรรมสะท้อนสังคมจึงแก้ปัญหาสังคมไม่ได้'." เนชั่นสุดสัปดาห์ 8, 366 (10–16 มิ.ย. 2542): 44–5.

What is interesting about the article and the response to it is perhaps less what is said than the fact that the issues were still seriously debated (and considered worthy of debate). Other 1998 events and publications related to the subject included a panel discussion at Sanam Luang as part of the commemoration on the 25th anniversary of October 14, 1973;[10] a panel discussion at the Sirikit Center;[11] a concert, "Three Generations of Songs for Life," with the three most famous singers of the genre performing with the Bangkok Symphony Orchestra;[12] and a book of essays on Literature for Life by two prominent critics.[13] While all of these were rather major events in Bangkok, there were similar activities in the provinces, including a discussion at a small school in Surat Thani at which the question was asked, "Is literature useful to society or to individuals, or is it just a pretext for writers?"[14]

In addition to the unpopularity of the movement and the collapse of its political base, there was another reason that writers stopped producing Literature for Life: it did not work. No matter how much was written about social problems, the need for struggle, and the way to the ideal, the problems were not solved; society was not healed. In fact, the impoverished classes did not even read the literature; it had no impact on them. Writers since then have commonly admitted that although they may have written about Isan (or other) villagers, those villagers never saw the work; this is a realization gained in hindsight. Surachai stated it clearly during Caravan's 25-year anniversary concert:

> At that time [post-1973] we tried to write and sing songs for farmers and laborers. To speak truly, the work didn't reach the hearts of those classes much. The farmers didn't understand it at all. Mostly it was students, intellectuals, protesters. When we really sang for farmers, they were confused.[15]

---

[10] See Anon., "วรรณกรรม-เพลงเพื่อชีวิต '25 ปี ไม่ใช่การเฉลิมฉลอง แต่เป็นการฟื้นฟูวัฒนธรรม'," เนชั่นสุดสัปดาห์ 7, 333 (22–26 ต.ค. 2541): 56–7.

[11] "อดีต ปัจจุบัน และอนาคต วรรณกรรมเพื่อชีวิต," October 23, 1998.

[12] At the Sirikit Center, September 26, 1998.

[13] รื่นฤทัย สัจจพันธุ์, ไพลิน รุ้งรัตน์, หนังสือฝ่ายวรรณกรรม รำลึก *25 ปี 14 ตุลา พ.ศ, 2516–2541,* กรุงเทพฯ: ชนนิยม, 2541.

[14] น้ำพุ แสนสวย, "'ทำไมวรรณกรรมสะท้อนสังคมจึงแก้ปัญหาสังคมไม่ได้'." เนชั่นสุดสัปดาห์ 7, 329 (13–19 พ.ค. 2542): 44–5.

[15] Surachai Janthimathorn, "25 Years of Caravan" Concert, Sala Chalermkrung, Bangkok, April 25, 1999.

As writers began to accept the new political and economic realities in the early to mid-1980s, with many making the transition from *pa* (jungle) to *meuang* (town), they started to come to terms with questions about what to do and how to proceed. Some writers continued to produce formulaic work expressing loss, or so-called "wounded literature."[16] In time, though, many turned away from recent experiences and national and international struggle, and began to look closer to home: to their cultural roots and their region of origin. Perhaps there was also nostalgia for what seemed like a simpler, less painful time and place. Many Isan writers felt a renewed interest in Isan, not from a political point of view, but in terms of culture and tradition. Rapid economic change, with its increased central control (through road construction, corporate growth, etc.) meant that traditional culture was being eroded under the influence of the national culture, dominated by Bangkok. Here was a new cause that one could be concerned with, but that could be joined on one's own terms, with scaled-down expectations. One could act locally in one's own district or province, without having to be associated with or submit to a formal national or international movement. The region began to be taken as a source of inspiration, a place of meaning, where culture replaced politics and the focus of opposition was cultural imperialism, ignorance, and dilution.

This new sensibility, of turning to the region for creative impetus, did not of course arise out of nowhere. In some ways, it was a return to a pre-1970 sense of one's own culture in the face of Central influence, in the Era of Search before politics became the dominant, virtually the only, paradigm among progressive writers. Such regional sentiment was expressed (as noted in Chapter 3) in Prasert's work, Surachai's early work, and at times in the work of other *Phra Jan Siow* writers of the time. Even in the mid- to late 1970s, when Literature for Life was dominant, publications appeared looking at traditional literary arts of Isan. Some of these were no doubt printed because they also supported a political agenda, for example *Pheun Wieng* by Prathip Chumpol,[17] an investigation of a suppressed Lao historical chronicle, and *Isan, Land of Blood and Tears*, by Suchart Phumiborirak,[18] a

---

[16] เจน อักษราพิจารณ์, "วรรณกรรมลำน้ำมูลสู่สโมสรนักเขียนภาคอีสาน," กรุงเทพธุรกิจ วันอาทิตย์ 31 ม.ค. 2542, p. 3.

[17] ประทีป ชุมพล, พื้นเวียง. กรุงเทพฯ: อดีต, 2525.

[18] สุชาติ ภูมิบริรักษ์, อีสาน ดินแดนแห่งเลือดและน้ำตา. กรุงเทพฯ: ชมรมหนังสือเปลวไฟ, 2514. This book was number 90 on a list of 96 books that were banned by the Minister of the Interior in an announcement made on June 1, 1980. The ban required that all the books be turned in to the authorities within 30 days. Enforcement of the ban was later allowed to lapse.

discussion of Isan's problems and prospects in relation to its culture. From 1978 to 1983, however, *Lok Nangseu* published several articles on traditional Isan (Lao) literature;[19] Isan music and history;[20] regional culture;[21] Khmer folk music;[22] and Isan folk performers.[23] Readers responded with letters to the editor, such as one in 1982 stating that people of the younger generation were interested in folk traditions, and asking for more coverage from the magazine.[24] Another article presented an interview with Phra Ariyanuwat,[25] a monk in Mahasarakham province whose extensive work with traditional Isan/Lao literature, and leadership of the Center for the Preservation of Northeastern Classical Literature, made him a major figure in Isan Studies later on (see below).

In Isan, the growing interest in local culture led to an awareness among individual writers that they were not alone in their pursuits. Informal groupings emerged among like-minded friends and acquaintances, often arising out of activities and arts clubs in schools. Many of the instrumental figures in organizing these groups were teachers in provincial institutions. Some of these smaller groups joined together with other writers to form the Mun River Literary Group (MRLG), which began modestly but grew to become a fairly large and influential organization. Fon Fafang, a writer from Srisaket, describes his recollections of its beginnings:

> At first I didn't know anyone, but as a person who likes to read books, I had to search for friends who had similar habits. I met Sorawut Sripetch in a bookstore and we had a chance to talk. And we had the idea to start a literary group in Isan. We also gained inspiration from a seminar of the literary unit at the musical arts center of Bangkok Bank, organized by Yip Phanjan on October 29, 1982. [...] The MRLG was set up on January 3, 1983, by unanimous agreement of the members of the group, including Akhom Thapsaeng, Yiem Thongnoi, Pramote Naijit; and also Thongkhram Phudetkla (Siowjan Raemphrai) was also in the group at first. I admit that our group was founded according to the pressures of literary circles which included both determination and conflict. Before

---

[19] Anon., "ฟังเขาคุยเรื่อง วรรณคดีอีสาน," โลกหนังสือ 2, 2 (พ.ค. 2521a): 6–11.

[20] Anon., "หนังสือชุด 'มรดกอีสาน'," โลกหนังสือ 2, 2 (พ.ค. 2521b): 130–1.

[21] Anon., "วัฒนธรรมพื้นบ้านสะท้อนเอกลักษณ์ของแต่ละท้องถิ่นเท่านั้นหรือ," โลกหนังสือ 2, 4 (ม.ค. 2522b): 131–2.

[22] สุกัญญา ภัทราชัย, "ตาโบ นักเจรียง," โลกหนังสือ 6, 4 (ม.ค. 2526): 12–3.

[23] มนัส พูลผล, "คนเพลงพื้นบ้าน กับงานวันเชิดชูเกียรติ," โลกหนังสือ 6, 6 (มี.ค. 2526): 12–5.

[24] คนอุบลฯ, "คนรุ่นใหม่สนใจ 'พื้นบ้าน'," โลกหนังสือ 6, 3 (ธ.ค. 2525): 6–7.

[25] Anon., "พระอริยานุวัตร หัวหน้าศูนย์อนุรักษ์วรรณคดีภาคตะวันออกเฉียงเหนือ," โลกหนังสือ 3, 5 (ก.พ. 2523): 74–7.

we took our last breaths, we wished to choose our own way. On the day we announced the funding [for the group], we cut our own forefingers as a declaration of our spirit, that we would have determination in our writing from then on.[26]

Pramote recalls a more political origin of the group:

The MRLG was born as a result of political trends after October 14 [1973]. It was continuous and mixed up with politics, the whole Thai national development group that came out of the jungle, and the writers' and intellectuals' groups. And also the political trend of how are we going to live our lives, what is a good way. I think it existed in every region.[27]

For most writers, though, the main value of the group was the mutual support and common interests, not politics. As Wongdeuan Thongjiow has noted,

Each person's aim in joining the group was not the same. I joined later. When the group started I was still studying in Bangkok. But I followed the news of Isan writers all the time. I felt that forming a group of Isan people wouldn't last. They would come together mostly just on an *ad hoc* basis. But the joining together of the Literary Group happened naturally with people who were determined. The joining together of the MRLG during the 17 years that have passed has been a cohesive literary joining. I think if we join together with awareness and feeling, it lasts. Like various *mo' lam* troupes that are still famous up to the present. Writing can be done without joining a group, but if you get together with people who have the same kinds of likes, basis of feeling, writing atmosphere, if friends with the same tastes join together, even though sometimes there are arguments, when we're apart we converse through letters, giving us motivation. If we didn't join together as a group, we might not write literature anymore.[28]

During the early period of the group's formation, in 1982–1983, those involved included Fon, Pramote, Somkhit, Wongdeuan (see Chapter 6), Siowjan Raemphrai (see Chapter 6), Jaroen Kulasuwan, Seri Thatsanasilp, Thirayut Daojantheuk, and other lesser-known writers, all over Isan. They agreed that, "if they sent work to be published in magazines, they would always use the name of the MRLG followed by the name of their own province."[29] This reinforced their feeling of solidarity and announced the

---

[26] เจน, "วรรณกรรม," 2542, p. 3.

[27] Ibid.

[28] Ibid.

[29] Anon., "การก่อเกิดของสโมสรนักเขียนภาคอีสาน," จดหมายข่าวสโมสรนักเขียนภาคอีสาน 4, 17 (ม.ค.–ก.พ. 2542b): 15.

existence of the group to the public. In April 1983, they arranged a seminar for the first time to exchange ideas among the members, to be held at a school in Buri Ram. A literary arts club was organized at the school, but after that the MRLG's activities gradually decreased.[30]

However, the leading core of the group was still active in Srisaket, with Fon, and in Yasothorn, with Pramote, Wongdeuan, Yiem, and Jaroen. They decided to start a movement, calling on their friends to continue their activities, by issuing a periodical for the group. Pramote, who volunteered to act as editor, suggested the name, "*Kheut Ho̒i*" (คึดฮอด),[31] and they began to find funding from private organizations to produce the magazine, which would publish the work of, and communicate among, members of the group. In mid-1984, the first issue appeared, commemorating the MRLG's second anniversary.[32] The cover illustration, painted by Pramote, showed several sets of footprints approaching a bridge, with some crossing but others turning back, and was accompanied by a *phaya*, or Lao poetic proverb:

> Travel the path unendingly
> Don't turn back and let them trample you
> If we die let us die ahead
> That they will praise our courage.[33]

For a time, the MRLG grew in size and expanded its activities, including organizing traveling literary projects in secondary schools, which were particularly successful in 1985–1986.[34] However, these outreach activities were not without incident. For example, in August 1986, the MRLG arranged a "traveling literary project"[35] for a secondary school and a village in Srisaket province. The project involved a day-long presentation, at each location, of literary reading, traditional music, and panel discussions on literature. The MRLG members participating in the project included Fon, Yiem, Seri, Phaiwarin Khaongam (see Chapter 6), and several others. They arrived in Srisaket the evening before the first presentation, where they were warned by a teacher from the school, "You are absolutely forbidden

---

[30] Ibid.

[31] Lao for "to think about, to miss," often used in the context of longing for one's friends, family, or home village.

[32] Anon., "การก่อเกิด," 2542b.

[33] Ibid.

[34] เจน, "วรรณกรรม," 2542.

[35] สัญญลักษณ์ ดอนศรี, "กลุ่มวรรณกรรมลำน้ำมูล เป้าหมายใหม่ของ กอ. รมน. อีสาน?" ถนนหนังสือ 4, 3 (ก.ย. 2529): 18–20.

to speak about politics tomorrow." Soon afterward, while they were eating at a restaurant, their car was vandalized: it had been urinated on, the tires were slashed, and both sides of the car were etched with an epithet meaning, "Mun River Bastards." The next day, the panel discussions, "How Does One Begin to Write?" and "What is Literature's Role in Society?" were presented, but local police arrived and the event was halted before its scheduled completion.[36]

In spite of such harassment by authorities, however, the MRLG continued to grow. More writers joined, including Manote Phromsingh (see Chapter 6), a close friend of Yiem's, and Sangkhom Phesachmala (see Chapter 6), a close friend of Wongdeuan's. Phongsit Khamphi (mentioned in Chapter 3), a young pop singer from Nong Khai in the Songs for Life tradition (later to become phenomenally popular), came to perform at some events.[37] Nonetheless, the group began to weaken again. *Kheut Ho't*, which rotated its editorship by province for each issue, lacked consistency, and its production failed to meet the stipulations of its funding. After funding ceased, the periodical was discontinued. Everyone decreased their roles in activities in 1987–1988. The leading core discussed whether the group had become too weak and should disband.[38]

Instead, they once again stepped up activities. *Kheut Ho't* was resuscitated, but on a small scale: produced by photocopy, it sometimes ran to only 20 copies, which were distributed among a narrow group. In Yasothorn, Apichet Thongnoi started the Pho'k Tree — Din Mountain Literary Group (PTDMLG) in order to hold a youth short story contest and run youth camps for writing. Other core members met with Khamsing Srinawk, who had joined the board of the Writers' Association of Thailand. He encouraged them with information about funding that was available[39] for literary activities.[40] A conference was organized, to take place in Chaiyaphum, by Sangkhom, who lived there, and Pramote. Chaiyaphum was chosen for its attractive mountainous landscape and because it is the source of the Chi River, the longest river in Isan.

With the backing of Chaiyaphum's governor, the planned literature seminar and meeting of the Writers' Association of Thailand took place on

---

[36] Ibid.

[37] Anon., "การก่อเกิด," 2542b.

[38] Ibid.

[39] Probably part of Prime Minster Chatchai Choonhavan's initiative for the regions. Ibid.

[40] Ibid.

September 14–17, 1989 at Thung Kamang. Leading MRLG members from Srisaket and Yasothorn felt that the MRLG had become weak, and that part of the reason could be the organization's name, which might cause anyone who did not live in the Mun River valley to feel excluded. Thus, one of the goals of the Chaiyaphum meeting was to set up an organization of writers, thinkers, and literary people for all of Isan.[41] The result was the Isan Writers' Association[42] (IWA), founded September 16, 1989 in Chaiyaphum. The purposes of the IWA were announced as follows:

1)   To be an organization to work together with thinkers, writers, and those who work in the literary arts in Isan to have a role in promoting creativity and disseminating their work more widely to the public;

2)   To be a place to exchange points of view and experiences with each other for the improvement of artistic literature;

3)   To promote more animation and liveliness in the atmosphere of artistic literature, and to encourage the rise of the new generation of thinkers and writers;

4)   To build diversity in personal and artistic literary work to serve as joint wealth for coming generations of the citizenry.[43]

The IWA adopted a symbol called the *khaen pak kai*, or *khaen* quill, a pen nib formed by two *khaen* placed alongside each other; the organization's seal contains this symbol surrounded by two grain-laden rice stalks.

Somkhit Singsong was made the first president of the IWA, serving from 1989 to 1996. One of his first priorities was to revive the periodical, *Kheut Ho't*. It was thus resurrected with the March 15–April 15, 1990 issue designated as Year 1, Number 1. The Lao title was retained, and immediately above it was written, "Love Isan, Read [followed by the title]." The cover also announced the birth of the IWA, and listed the price of the magazine, 22 baht.[44] The inside cover featured a photograph of Khamsing and others planting a tree sapling. Opposite was a letter from Somkhit as president, expressing New Year's wishes and noting the official founding of the IWA under the auspices of the Writers' Association of Thailand. The letter also listed the IWA's four goals (quoted above), and reported that the managing committee met at the Isan Art and Culture Institute of Srinakharinwirot

---

[41] Ibid.

[42] สโมสรนักเขียนภาคอีสาน, translated in the organization's documents as, "Esan Writer Club."

[43] Anon., "การก่อเกิด," 2542b, p. 16.

[44] It was available for purchase, as well as by subscription.

University, Mahasarakham. Finally, Somkhit's letter ended with the admonition, in Lao,[45] "Love Isan, Read '*Kheut Ho't*'," and, "Be Proud of Isan, Support '*Kheut Ho't*'."

The contents of this first issue demonstrate the aims, interests, and attitudes of the organization and its members. Page Four lists the words to the song, "*Rao Kheu Lam Nam Mun*" (We are the Mun River),[46] written by Jaroen. The rest of the magazine contains four short stories and eight poems, each by a different Isan writer; an essay on seeking folk knowledge and social change; three articles about the meeting in Chaiyaphum; and several columns on such subjects as the goals of the IWA, its connection to the MRLG, a report on youth from the Pho'k Tree — Din Mountain group, humorous stories, etc. There is also an "Isan Studies" column discussing ancient inscriptions found in Isan, including a full abstract in English of the MA thesis on which the article was based. This indicates that, while the group exists for the sake of Isan writers and is defined by its concern with Isan literature and culture, there is nonetheless a conviction that that concern has relevance not just for Thailand, but in the international arena.

Before long, *Kheut Ho't* again began to suffer from a decline in funding and enthusiasm. While the first issue was a 96-page, ostensibly monthly publication, with color photographs on its covers, by 1994 it had become a (roughly) bimonthly[47] magazine of less than half that length. The name had been changed to จดหมายข่าวสโมสรนักเขียนภาคอีสาน (*Newsletter of the Isan Writers' Association*),[48] and the covers consisted of black-and-white images (usually line drawings) reproduced on colored paper. The *Newsletter* was not consistently produced, either in time or in quality. From issue to issue, its masthead varied, its length fluctuated, and it was at times dated only by year and volume, reflecting the fact that it did not always appear during the months expected. Nonetheless, its mission remained largely unchanged, as did its content.

In late 1998, the *Newsletter* received a new infusion of enthusiasm, if not funds, under its new editor, Chaiya Wannasri (see Chapter 6). He recruited new contributors to reinvigorate its subject matter, as well as new

---

[45] Written in Thai script.

[46] Apparently inspired by the internationally known pop song, "We Are the World."

[47] Fon referred to it during this period as a *nang seu rai saduak*, or magazine published according to convenience rather than schedule.

[48] Or, "The Letter from the Esan Writer Club," as its English subtitle appears on the cover.

members of the Association to replenish its coffers. Records of membership expiration dates and dues paid had not been maintained, and Chaiya made an effort to get old members to renew their commitments and continue to pay dues (in 1999 amounting to 200 baht annually, increased from 150 in 1996). The *Newsletter* moved to Surin, Chaiya's hometown, took on a standard format and length (32 typeset pages), and included pieces by or about a whole range of writers, from the young and unknown to the giants of modern Isan literature, like Khamphun and Prasert.

In 1998 and 1999, the *Newsletter*'s goals, often listed in the publication, were carried forward from 1996:

1) To be the central source for reports on developments of the Association and its members;
2) To be a literary field for which the Association works continuously;
3) To be the source for the collection and documentation of members' written work published in various publications.[49]

Each issue normally contained a feature article on a particular Isan writer (such as Fon, Somkhit, Manote, etc.), usually with an interview; letters to the editor; a short story and a few poems by other Isan writers; an essay or account of a literary event; sometimes an article on a foreign writer (e.g., Franz Kafka, Kamal Ahmad Bamadhaj of East Timor, or a translation of, or commentary on, a work by a Lao writer); a discussion of Isan archaeology, music, or other cultural form; and news on Isan writers' activities and publications, both in periodicals and as whole books. Now and then, a self-reflective essay appeared, assessing a decade of the IWA,[50] exhorting writers to be motivated and creative, or asking questions like, "Have Isan writers really not gone beyond the deep sea of *Fa Bo' Kan* and *Luk Isan*?"[51]

The article, "A Decade of the 'Isan Writers' Association'," served as the cover story for the issue in which it was printed (September–October 2542/1999), and consisted of statements by seven Isan writers giving their views on the value of and changes in the IWA. Fon reckoned that the group was fine and that, "we do what we can."[52] Yiem decried the trend he observed of everyone growing apart, while Watthana Thammakul criticized

---

[49] จดหมายข่าวสโมสรนักเขียนภาคอีสาน 2, 5 (2539): 1.

[50] Anon., "1 ทศวรรษ 'สโมสรนักเขียนภาคอีสาน'," จดหมายข่าวสโมสรนักเขียนภาคอีสาน 5, 20 (ก.ย.–ต.ค. 2542): 8–13.

[51] สีพลอย มณีรัตน์, "เรื่องสั้นประเวณี," จดหมายข่าวสโมสรนักเขียนภาคอีสาน 3, 9 (มี.ค.–เม.ย. 2540): 24.

[52] Anon., "1 ทศวรรษ," 2542f, p. 9.

what he saw as Isan people's envy of others' success. Prida Khaobo', a writer and editor from Udorn who was active in the 1970s, described the weak thoughts and feelings of his group of friends after emerging from the jungle, and he noted that in joining the IWA their goals were to raise the quality of life in Isan, to have pride in their ethnicity, and to be respected by other ethnic groups. Sumali Phophayak, one of the writers often described as having grown up with the IWA, expressed her belief that Isan writers should get beyond story content about poverty and drought, even though such conditions continue to affect life in Isan.[53]

In the same issue of the *Newsletter*, Wiwat Rotchanawan, the president of the IWA, gave his thoughts on Isan writing and the Association in an article entitled, "'The Isan Writers' Association': Entering Its Second Decade, Reaching the Roots of the Countryside."[54] He stated:

> I believe that private work and work for the public must go together. What good is it to produce excellent work if people in society, especially youth, aren't molded to have the habit of loving reading and writing? Therefore members of the IWA must still go out and support activities of educational institutions of various levels. [...] Aside from creating written work, writers must create readers as well.[55]

In doing so, he said, they must respond to the criticisms that poetry is dead, the short story is dead, Literature for Life is dead. Thus, Wiwat acknowledged the view that much of Isan writing remained overly influenced by, or had failed to go beyond, the Literature for Life movement. He also mentioned criticisms (made by Nidhi Aeowsiwongse in *Matichon Weekly*) that Songs for Life lacked sincerity, that singers and songwriters did not believe in what they were writing about and did not investigate social problems. Wiwat felt that Isan writers do in fact understand the people and issues they write about, such as the Pak Mun Dam, the Forum for the Poor, etc. Poverty, crime, the disappearance of natural resources, and the like, are raw materials for writing, he noted. At the same time, however, he suggested that Isan writers must make progress and advance past the old Literature for Life approach in order to produce work that speaks to contemporary readers. In other words, he recognized the influence and validity of the Literature for Life tradition in Isan writing, but also exhorted writers to move ahead

---

[53] Ibid.
[54] วิวัฒน์ โรจนาวรรณ, "'สโมสรนักเขียนภาคอีสาน' สู่ทศวรรษที่ 2 สู่ชนบทอย่างถึงรากถึงโคน," จดหมายข่าวสโมสรนักเขียนภาคอีสาน 5, 20 (ก.ค.–ต.ค. 2542): 8–13.
[55] Ibid.

creatively. In so doing, Wiwat pointed out the direction that Isan literature would be likely to take in the future.

The phenomenon of regionalism, or *tho'ngthin niyom*,[56] that led to the formation of regional writers' groups in Isan (and elsewhere) also gave rise to another offshoot: the discipline of Isan Studies. Isan Studies had no single moment of beginning, but developed out of preexisting activities of traditional Isan scholars. Indeed, Isan Studies is a much closer descendant of Isan classical literary arts than modern Isan literature is. Early articles in the 1970s in *Lok Nangseu* and other publications of Central Thailand merely brought the attention of the general reader to the ancient cultural traditions (mostly of Lao origin, although Khmer and other groups' customary arts were sometimes also discussed) existing in Isan. However, scholars like Phra Ariyanuwat and Pricha Phinthong were already passing middle age in the 1970s and for many years had been practicing what came to be considered "Isan Studies." Significant formal or institutional attention, though, turned to Isan only in the 1980s. Just as Isan had previously attracted political attention, academics now focused a scholarly interest on the region, investigating folk traditions in literature, music, medicine, agriculture, etc.

One of the most notable developments of this academic regional interest was the establishment of Isan Studies centers at several higher educational institutions in the Northeast. One of the earliest of these was the Arts and Culture Center at the Rajabhat Institute (now Rajabhat University) in the provincial capital of Mahasarakham. It produced dozens of publications, by roneo and photocopy, on various aspects of Isan culture; many of these were still available for sale in 1999 from the shelves of its campus office. The Center also boasted a museum of Isan culture, consisting of two small rooms containing textiles, pottery, wood carvings, palm leaf manuscripts, and monks' pulpits from temples. There was also a wooden trunk from Laos, with a tag stating that, "it's the same as Thai Isan," thus reflecting an earlier Central Thai bias that negates Lao cultural identity in Isan and attempts to label it "Thai." The Center evidently suffered from a lack of funding, as it appeared that little had happened there in the last several years of the 20th century, and almost no information was available on the Center itself.

---

[56] Anthony Diller is probably more accurate when he states that ท้องถิ่นนิยม is "perhaps to be translated 'localism' (with a touch of 'local pride')"; see his article, "What Makes Central Thai a National Language?" in *National Identity and Its Defenders: Thailand 1939–1989*, ed. C. Reynolds, Monash University Papers in SEA No. 25, 1991, pp. 87–132.

Nearby, however, at Mahasarakham University (then recently up-graded to independent university status from its former position as a Srinakharinwirot University branch), the contrast could not be more striking. The University is home to the Isan Arts and Culture Research Institute, housed in its own, new, 42 million baht building. According to the 35-page booklet it publishes,[57] the Institute is under the patronage of Princess Sirindhorn, and at the time (1999) employed 25 administrators, researchers, and other personnel. It also maintains a separate building next door, housing its Palm Leaf Manuscript Information Center. The Institute grew out of a small information center founded in 1970 as the Northeastern Arts and Cultural Center, which was transformed by royal decree in 1986 into the Institute in its current form. Its objectives are listed as:

1)   To find, collect, and save information on the culture and all branches of the arts of Isan, whether documents, objects, behavior, or data;

2)   To study, investigate, and research Isan arts and culture so that it is of a quality that can constructively benefit society;

3)   To preserve, enhance, support, and disseminate Isan culture so that it is widely known and long-lasting.[58]

The Institute supports educational, cultural, and research activities related to all the provinces of Isan. In 1999, its publications included a pamphlet on the origins, goals, and activities of the Institute; a booklet covering the same subjects, and including an article on Isan history and a discussion of the 12-month cycle of customs in (specifically Lao) Isan tradition; and various research papers by its staff. It also sold books by other scholars at the University, including one called *Regional Works of Art*, and another entitled *Isan World View*. However, no list of publications was available.

Isan Studies in general, and the Institute in particular, have been prone to a number of problems.[59] Isan Studies centers exist in every Northeastern province, including some secondary schools, according to government policy. However, perhaps not surprisingly, substance has not always measured up to appearance. A feeling has existed that many of the people involved are not really interested in culture, including administrators, who therefore often do not get along with the researchers. A number of people

---

[57] "สถาบันวิจัยศิลปะและวัฒนธรรมอีสาน," มหาวิทยาลัยมหาสารคาม, (undated).

[58] Ibid., p. 10.

[59] The information and views in this paragraph are drawn from an interview with an employee of the Institute on June 9, 1999 in Mahasarakham.

who have researched and written about Isan are actually from Bangkok, and thus, in the eyes of some, the pursuit of Isan Studies often appears to be a career move more than a result of deep-seated feelings for Isan *per se*. In the words of one researcher, "When people talk about the importance of Isan culture and so on, we have to look at whether it comes from their soul, or if they have reasons of personal interest in saying such things." In addition, outside interest in the Institute and in Isan Studies overall has declined from its peak in about 1987. While the Institute has attracted some visits by researchers from Bangkok and from foreign countries who wish to use its resources, most of the local students who have visited have done so on impulse while passing by, rather than out of a real desire to study. Very few people have bought the Institute's publications. Furthermore, of all the employees at the Institute in 1999, for example, only two actually wrote articles. In view of this, it is difficult to escape the conclusion that Isan Studies has existed mainly due to the energies of a small number of enthusiasts, and that its practical importance in academics and society has been relatively minor.

For some scholars, Isan Studies is not simply an academic discipline, but a personal crusade. One such person is Wajuppa Tossa, an administrator at Mahasarakham University. In the 1990s, she published English translations of two "Isan folk epics" (i.e., classical Lao tales): *Pha Daeng Nang Ai* and *Phaya Khan Khaak*. Interestingly, the versions she used as the basis for her translations had been transliterated into Thai and compiled by Phra Ariyanuwat; she does not read the original Lao. Nonetheless, she still makes the comment that,

> Isan culture and customs are fading. [...] That I am a native of Isan, but could not fully understand the background of my own culture, is both embarrassing and disturbing.[60]

She also expresses her strong desire for a rediscovery of Isan culture:

> One of my profound objectives of translating these ancient texts has been to bring out as many translations as possible for the Thai people to see the significance of their own rich and valuable literature. Once Thai people, especially those from Isan, become more interested, they may want to read and retell these stories to their children. The language might then be preserved, along with its embedded culture.[61]

---

[60] Wajuppa Tossa, *Phaya Khan Khaak, the Toad King* (Lewisburg: Bucknell University Press, 1996), p. 21.

[61] Ibid.

This notion of saving something that is disappearing, and the regionalist sentiment underlying that notion, are frequently expressed among Isan scholars and writers. However, Wajuppa's entreaty goes a step further, taking on a normative, almost moralistic tone. Curiously, though, she refuses to use the word "Lao" to describe the language and literature she so champions. Instead, she uses terms like "Isan language," and invents misleading expressions, such as "Isan script" (to refer to traditional Lao writing systems, which are not specific to Isan), and "the original modern Thai text" (to refer to a modern Thai transcription of a classical Lao tale).[62] After these convolutions, she notes:

> The Isan people have been deprived of their own written language and literature since the reign of King Chulalongkorn (Rama V, 1868–1910) ... It is important now that Thai children from all over Thailand learn to read, write, and speak their local languages so that they can begin to recognize and appreciate the richness and complexity of their indigenous literature and culture.[63]

Finally, she insists:

> Parents should encourage children to speak Isan at home. Isan language and literature should be made available for students to learn. Isan children should be encouraged to learn to read and write Isan scripts, for they represent the spoken language of Isan.[64]

Not only is she apparently unaware that the Lao scripts to which she refers existed for centuries before there was such a political construct as "Isan," but she ignores the fact that so-called "Isan" (i.e., Lao) language is spoken by only part of the population of Isan, and that others speak Khmer, Kui, Mon, etc., and are not Lao at all. It might seem a challenge for "the younger generation of Isan"[65] to develop an interest and appreciation for their cultural heritage when its true origins and diversity are obscured in this manner.

Another manifestation of *tho'ngthin niyom* at Mahasarakham University is the Sirindhorn Isan Information Center in the central library. The Center, which acts as a repository of information related to Isan, seems dedicated to a celebration of Isan culture. The first thing a visitor encountered on arriving at the Center in 1999, though, was an assemblage of

---

[62] Ibid., p. 28.
[63] Ibid., p. 22.
[64] Ibid., p. 29.
[65] Ibid.

pictures of and books about the King, as if to reassure the visitor that, while Isan's cultural uniqueness was to be extolled, its unity with (or loyalty to) the rest of Thailand was not to be questioned. Thereafter, a bulletin board presented "Isan news, essays, and reports," including: a list of the (then) 19 provinces of Isan and their populations; a report citing Ubon and Amnat Jaroen as having the highest quality of life in Isan; a discussion of traditional knowledge and handicrafts in Sakon Nakhorn; an essay about the U.S. returning the notorious missing lintel to Phanom Rung; an article from *Siam Rath* on the Center itself; and a copy of the poem, "Isan," by Nai Phi. There were shelves shaped like, and named after, various Isan objects of daily use, some hugely enlarged, such as a rice pot, a bucket, a loom, a *khaen*, etc. One section contained dozens of MA theses on "Isan Literature," all of which were concerned with traditional and folk literature. The impression given (aside from a kind of theme park treatment) was that Isan literature and culture were a thing of the past, something to be remembered and enshrined, lacking continuity with life in the present.

At the Rajabhat Institute (now University) in Buri Ram, the Southern Isan Cultural Center, which opened in 1994, also uses Isan motifs in its design. As the Center here focuses on the local "Southern Isan" culture, the building housing it borrows architectural design elements from the ancient Khmer *prasat* ("castles") found throughout the southern provinces of Isan (Korat, Buri Ram, Surin, Srisaket, and Ubon), and employs them in its roof construction, windows, and even the signs that differentiate its men's and women's bathrooms. The Center maintains a Local Cultural Information Center, a small library with a large wall map showing "Ancient *Kho'm* [Khmer] Sites in Isan." The main Center also produces and distributes a large number of publications in Thai, including *Thai Kui Culture, Southern Isan Treasures, Buri Ram Regional Works of Art, Introduction to the Southern Isan Cultural Center, The Ancient Phanom Rung — Muang Tam Route, The Selling of Cultural and Spiritual Heritage, Phaya*,[66] and *Isan Heritage Handbook*, as well as a pamphlet about the Center in both Thai and English. The Center also runs a gift shop selling a variety of local and Central Thai items: books on local religion and traditional literature, children's books, miniature *khaen*, medallions bearing the King's likeness, clocks with Bangkok motifs (such as the ogres at Wat Phra Keo), and local products, including cloth, baskets, bags, shirts, and Isan pillows.

Thus the Southern Isan Cultural Center appears to promote Isan as a subject of both scholarly and touristic interest, purveying keepsakes as well

---

[66] Lao philosophical sayings in poetic form.

as knowledge. Isan culture is divided into easily consumable units, perhaps for urban and Central Thais who might otherwise not experience it at all. The Isan Cultural Centers, funded by the Central Government, become in some ways an extension of the Tourism Authority of Thailand's program of reducing Isan to individual elements that are quickly and comfortably recognized, enjoyed, and digested. Phimai, Phanom Rung, and the other "castles" become emblems for the glorification of a modern Thailand, in a way that completely obscures essential reality: that these monuments, the civilizations that produced them, and indeed the very cultures and peoples of Isan, are as different and separate from Central Thailand historically as they are geographically. Instead of embracing and appreciating these differences, Central authorities trivialize and shrink them to the level of souvenir trinkets, or a sound and light show[67] for the idle curiosity of the day visitor from Bangkok. Often this is carried out with the participation of Isan people themselves, who, consciously or not, perhaps feel that such attention, however misinformed, is better than none at all. The result, however, rather than teaching about Isan history and culture, perpetuates the legacy of Bangkok's aggression, exploitation, and condescension toward the northeast.

Yong Yasothorn

Yong Yasothorn ยงค์ ยโสธร is the pen name of Prayong Mulsan. He was born in 1948 in Kudchum District of what is now Yasothorn Province (previously part of Ubon).[68] After studying political science at Ramkhamhaeng University in Bangkok, he graduated from Sukhothai Thammathirat University with a degree in law. Yong worked as a teacher in the early 1970s, then as a journalist for a daily newspaper in 1973–1974, and served as a Member of Parliament in 1975. In 1976, he went into the jungle, where he stayed until 1981.[69] Thereafter, he made a living farming in Rayong, his wife's home province, dividing his time between Rayong and Yasothorn, and remained active in Isan literary circles. He also maintained an interest in politics. In 1998, he became head of the Eastern Region Writers' Association, a small writers' group he founded which, among other endeavors, was involved in

---

[67] For example, a Phimai Festival, featuring a sound and light show at the ruins, was organized by the Tourism Authority of Thailand and held November 13–15, 1998.

[68] ยงค์ ยโสธร, คำอ้าย. กรุงเทพฯ: มิ่งมิตร, 2539, p. 6.

[69] ถนนหนังสือ 2, 5 (ธ.ค. 2527): 71.

refurbishing the Sunthorn Phu monument[70] and otherwise commemorating this poet.

Yong has written poetry, a novel, and a number of short stories, and his work has appeared in various periodicals. He published his first book in 1988, a novel called, *Kham Ai* คำอ้าย (the name of the main character), which remains his major work. It won the Bua Luang Annual Literary Award in 1989, as well as the Award for Excellent Book for Libraries; it also received a commendation from the Department of Curriculum and Instruction Development of the Ministry of Education. In 1991, Yong published *Ro'i Wela* รอยเวลา (*Traces of Time*), a collection of poetry. At the turn of the millennium, he was working on a series of short stories to be published as a compilation.

Like many writers of his generation and background, especially Isan writers, Yong Yasothorn has strong political views. Indeed, he is particularly energetic in his rejection of the status quo, criticism of society, and denunciation of those in power.[71] He thus continued to be a vocal supporter of Literature for Life, even two decades after its decline, as well as a staunch Isan regionalist, in the sense of proudly proclaiming the unique characteristics of Isan. In an interview in 1998 in the *Nation Weekend*, he made the following statements:

> There are lots of Isan writers who write Literature for Life, starting with the era of Lao Khamhawm, an era which included Rom Ratiwan, who wrote Literature for Life stories specifically. But sometimes it isn't just Isan people who write about Isan people. There are many writers from other regions who borrow Isan to reflect Literature for Life writing. It's because Isan people have rather high thoughts, dreams, and truth, because Isan people have seriousness, sincerity. Whenever anyone passes by we welcome them; we accept visitors easily; we don't need many levels [of politeness]. And Isan people show friendliness in everything.
>
> I'm a bit lazy so I don't have as much work out as some people. People from other regions who come to Isan all create *pheua chiwit* [for Life] work, like Sanan Chusakul and Phaithun Thanya, who are Southerners. Today, whatever they say is Isan. I think Isan has a lot of inspiration for creative thinking. Whoever comes to Isan gets many kinds of inspiration and the ability to write. And the work usually reflects being oneself and struggling in life.

---

[70] เสมอ กลิ่นหอม. "ห้องสุนธรภู่ ฝันที่ใกล้จะเป็นจริง," ฐานสัปดาห์วิจารณ์ 5 (6): 245(310) (2–8 ม.ค. 2542): 65.

[71] See สนั่น ชูสกุล, "'บ้านเมืองจะไม่ฉิบหายได้ยังไง ... อย่างนี้ดีกว่า...'," จดหมายข่าว สโมสรนักเขียนภาคอีสาน (พ.ย.–ธ.ค. 2541), pp. 20–1.

Presently there are many Isan writers who write *pheua chiwit* work. Among poets, one has to respect Phaiwarin Khaongam. For short stories, Manote Phromsingh and Phisit Phusri, who are progressing. But as for novels, I don't see much. The issue of Literature for Life has been brought up again, pushed by important political events. It has been receiving a great deal of interest, but has been threatened by the economic tide, causing Literature for Life to not sell so much. There is only one group who can accept it. Even in art, it took 100 years before the world accepted Van Gogh. It's a question of human spirit. Literature for Life doesn't sell well because society has characteristics of a crowd: without substance, but wanting fame. Some people's writing is awful, laughable, but people accept it. Because in a way, Thai people are controlled and give up on themselves. Thai people don't have the quality of awakening themselves to the current situation. Hence literature that doesn't sell. Because our ability to expand our ideas is still narrow.

It's not that Literature for Life doesn't sell well. But it depends on many things: the power of the state, the mass media. Altogether it depends on the sentiments of the day. If they have good ideas to impart, then they will be easily accepted: ideas that allow people to depend on themselves. It's about having people think. We don't have to have 100 novels[72] creating a fashion. Maybe it's because government leaders don't like these issues. Our education system teaches us to believe, it doesn't teach us to think. It teaches people to believe what textbooks say. It's a consequence of bad karma. When there's a problem and you have to think, you can't come up with anything.

Many people still misinterpret the meaning of *pheua chiwit*. But for me, 'For Life' is for society collectively, for people of every group. Therefore, in every era, Literature for Life doesn't die, as long as the condition of our society remains like this, that is, as long as Thais still suffer in poverty, Isan is still desolate, and there is still social inequality. Even more so in this IMF era, the real *pheua chiwit* is returning to natural agriculture, agricultural breeding, truly for the lives of people. This is the true crux of the word *pheua chiwit* that is most complete.[73]

The term, *pheua chiwit*, or "For Life," as in Literature for Life and Art for Life, thus becomes for Yong an inclusive term for any social consciousness and progressive issue, including opposition to genetically engineered crops. In this view, Art for Life is reconstituted as a living political stance with contemporary social relevance, even involving health issues, where previously it was conceived more narrowly in mainly political-economic

---

[72] This is a reference to Witthayakorn Chiengkul's list of 100 important books.

[73] มาลี ร้อยสีพันใบ, "อีสานคือต้นแบบวรรณกรรมเพื่อชีวิต," เนชั่นสุดสัปดาห์ 7, 332 (15–21 ต.ค. 2541): 49.

terms. Few other writers in Thailand would claim that the "For Life" movement continues to play a robust role in Thai society to this extent.

While Yong is among the most politically-oriented of Isan writers (already a particularly political bunch, as discussed previously), his writing is surprisingly literary, rather than overtly political. His novel, *Kham Ai*, carries little of the ideological baggage of most other Literature for Life, and thus does not suffer from the strident tones, simplistic views, and formulaic construction characteristic of much work by followers of the movement. This is not to say that the novel is devoid of social consciousness or attention to the lives of the disadvantaged. The main character, a small boy in a poor Isan family, experiences one of the most exciting moments of his life when, as described in Chapter 1, he is given a new pair of shorts. The novel's project is to recount the dangers and difficulties, but also the joys and successes, of life in a small village. As in Khamphun's *Child of Isan*, the reader learns about Isan traditions and daily life alongside the young boy referred to by the novel's title. However, unlike Khamphun, Yong employs a finely crafted literary (written) style characterized by smooth transitions and subtle presentation. While Yong uses Lao words, he does not pander to the non-Isan reader by giving definitions for them, but instead conveys their meaning through context and then continues to use them in a natural way throughout the book. As the story moves along, we realize that this is not a simple Literature for Life tale of suffering and hardship. While injustice is depicted, it is not the primary focus of the narrative, but merely one element among many others, both positive and negative, in the reality of life in an Isan village.

Overall, *Kham Ai* has been very highly acclaimed (and reprinted at least three times), with many of those who have read it preferring it to *Child of Isan*. Perhaps the reason Yong's book has not been widely read (in Thailand)[74] is that it did not win the high-profile SEAWrite Award, or possibly the public felt that reading one novel about the life of a young boy in Isan was sufficient. Whatever the case, *Kham Ai* is, in the words of Duangmon Jitjamnong,

> a novel of captivating beauty, not through deep philosophical meaning, or a bitingly sarcastic view of life; rather, the beauty of a simple, modest, humble life, but with a solid, undaunted strength and a subtly graceful, enduring happiness.[75]

---

[74] It has not been translated.

[75] ดวงมน จิตรจำนงค์, quoted in ยงค์ ยโสธร, คำอ้าย, 2539 (back cover).

Kanchana Spindler, writing as "Gap," also gives the novel high praise:

> This is really an excellent novel. For once you don't feel like the author
> is trying to put ideas into your head. Things just happen the way they do
> in real life, with the author at the helm plotting it the way a fine novel
> should be plotted. The dialogue which definitely puts you back in Isan
> with its local dialect, is another brilliant part of the novel. The children
> in the village, the games they play, the way of life or love, both paternal
> and carnal, are pure and simple.
>   All our policy makers should read this book.[76]

Thus, while Yong Yasothorn continues to speak in favor of the
Literature for Life movement and its values, he avoids a strict adherence
to its prescriptions that would compromise his own work. Evidently he has
benefited from the passage of time and the criticisms of the movement, and
used his innate skills to produce a balanced, nuanced literary work with a
social conscience.

Pramote Naijit

Pramote Naijit ปราโมทย์ ในจิต was born in Yasothorn (then Ubon Province)
in 1954. He grew up speaking Lao at home, and considered himself Lao.[77]
After completing primary school in his home village, he attended secondary
school in the town of Yasothorn, and then studied at Ubon Teachers' College,
where he received a degree in Mathematics. He taught in Ubon, then Khon
Kaen, and finally returned to Yasothorn where, while continuing to teach,
he obtained a bachelor's degree from Sukhothai Thammathirat University.
He became interested in literature in 1977, when he began to read Ajin
Banjaphan's periodical, *Fa Muang Thai*. As a student, Pramote had written
love poetry, but he had not continued writing due to his feelings of dislike
for the Thai language. However, *Fa Muang Thai* sparked his interest,
especially its column, "They Started Here," which encouraged new writers.
At that time, he says, he was young, trying to understand life, and looking
for meaning. Reading deepened his understanding of the world. He began to
write, using mathematical principles to create short stories, which he saw as
mathematical proofs, ending with a kind of QED.[78] He entered a short story
contest sponsored by *Sakun Thai* magazine and won honorable mention in

---

[76] Gap, quoted in ibid.
[77] Pramote Naijit, Interview, Yasothorn Province March 29, 1999.
[78] Ibid.

1978 for his story, "*Sin Kap Chiwit*" ศีลกับชีวิต (Morality and Life), about a rural schoolteacher's struggles with ideals of morality and privations of daily life. Receiving this recognition was instrumental in propelling his continuing involvement with literature. He began to enjoy books, started reading *Lok Nangseu* magazine, and expanded his knowledge of literature. *Lok Nangseu* especially helped him to identify topics to write about.[79]

In 1982, Pramote became one of the founders of the Mun River Literary Group and became editor of its magazine. He continued to publish poetry and short stories under the pen name Pramot Pramote ปราโมช ปราโมทย์ in many different periodicals, including *Sakun Thai*, *Matichon Weekend*, *Siam Rath Weekly Review*, *Lalana*, *Cho' Karaket*, etc. In 1988, he began to translate modern short stories by Laotian writers into Thai, publishing them in a variety of magazines. His first book, *Thin Theuan* ถิ่นเถื่อน (*Savage Territory*), a collection of his own short stories (some new and some previously published), appeared in 1990. The following year he published *Kraduk Amerikan* กระดูกอเมริกัน (*American Bones*), a selection of his translations of short stories by the Laotian writer, Bounthanong Somsaiphon. Pramote used a pen name, Jintrai จินตรัย, for both this and the subsequent volume of his Laotian translations: *Khwai Doysan* ควายโดยสาร (*Passenger Buffalo*), a 1992 compilation of stories by Saisuwan Phaengphon. In 1999, Pramote was working on a group of his own short stories, for which he was gathering factual material locally, concerning the lives of people on opposite banks of the Mekong River.

Among the many stories that Pramote has written, two in particular illustrate the kinds of themes and issues that interest him. The first, "*Reu Kheu Bun Bang Fai*" หรือคือบุญบั้งไฟ (This Is the Rocket Festival?), appeared in his book, *Thin Theuan*, but was originally published in *Siam Rath Weekly Review* in 1990. The story is concerned with the destruction of Isan culture by Bangkok power, money, and influence, and the effects on village people and their customs, beliefs, morals, etc. The author establishes the location of the story as being in Isan by his descriptions of the different scenes and his use of Lao words in several parts of the story, including the title.[80] The story is narrated in the first person by a young man who travels during the Songkran holiday to visit a friend in a nearby village, which is in a state of deep anxiety and disgruntlement. The narrator is alarmed to witness preparations for the Rocket Festival, preparations that are out of season and

---

[79] Pramote, Interview, 1999.
[80] As noted in Chapter 1 above, Lao: *bangfai* = Thai: *bo'ngfai*.

thus against customary practice. He is told that the village is being forced to defy tradition in order to entertain Bangkok visitors who will be making a donation to the village temple. The narrator laments,

> The Rocket Festival of the people of Isan is turned into a toy, like children playing at shop-keeping. All that's left is a spectacle for tourists. Where have the original spirit and faith gone?[81]

In a state of fear, disgust, and confusion, the narrator rushes back to his village. The impact of the story is heightened by the use of symbolism and foreshadowing: the narrator travels on an old but faithful motorcycle; on the way to his friend's village, instead of being doused with water by fun-loving girls celebrating Songkhran, he is drenched by an unseasonable rain on a deserted road; toward the end, he gets lost in the chaos of the village he visits, but eventually finds his trusty motorcycle and flees, back to the stability of his (still traditional) home village.

The second story of Pramote's that illustrates his interests and concerns is "*Kraro'k Pheuak*" กระรอกเผือก (The White Squirrel), published in *Krungthep Thurakit* in 1994. Pramote innovatively brings a classical Lao tale to contemporary relevance by using it as inspiration for this short story. In Pramote's piece, which reads like a fable, or even a parable, a grandmother relates the traditional tale of *Pha Daeng Nang Ai* while the village around her suffers an analogous fate to the one she recounts. The villagers have overused their natural salt deposits, leading outsiders to exploit them and causing excessive salination of their farmland. This poisoning of the land by salt mining is a direct parallel to events in the classical tale, in which the white offspring of a Naga lord is caught, and all the villagers who eat it die. The old legend manifests itself in contemporary life in the village, just as the old tale is adopted by the modern short story. In invoking the classical tale and its moral lesson while criticizing capitalist greed and the abuse of natural resources, the author achieves a creative combination of traditional fable and social criticism that transcends either one.

Pramote's involvement with the modern literature of Laos illustrates another aspect of the *tho'ngthin niyom* phenomenon: looking at one's ethnicity (in this case Lao, but for others, Khmer, Kui, etc.) and investigating it in part as a transnational or supra-national phenomenon, something that is not delimited by state boundaries or defined by official administration. Interestingly, Pramote did not initially intend to translate the Laotian

---

[81] ปราโมช ปราโมทย์, "หรือคือบุญบั้งไฟ," in ถิ่นเถื่อน. กรุงเทพฯ: บางหลวง, 2533, p. 103.

literature himself. Khaen Sarika,[82] at the time a reporter with *Phujatkan*, had acquired some books in Laos in 1987 from a group of writers there and brought the books to Pramote. Pramote at first encouraged a friend to translate them into Thai, finally deciding to do it himself only after hearing nothing from the friend for nearly a year. Pramote had learned to read Lao (both the *Thai No'i*[83] and *Tham*[84] scripts) as a child, while he was ordained as a novice.[85] With practice, he was able to renew his skills, and when he got stuck, asked for help from his father, who had learned Lao while earning money as a *samlo'* pedaler in Viengjan under the old regime.[86]

In the beginning, while working on Laotian short stories, Pramote felt that translating them into Thai was not, and should not be, necessary, but that to adapt, interpret, or paraphrase them was sufficient. He felt that since Thai and Lao are close languages, he would not try to translate too much, and would keep the Lao expressions; "Thai people ought to learn Lao," he thought.[87] Thus in the first few years of publication of Thai versions of the stories, Jintrai (Pramote) was listed as the person who "*tho'tkhwam*" (interpreted, paraphrased) rather than "*plae*" (translated). Later, however, he came to feel that translation is an art and that the stories needed to be translated properly. He was determined that Thai people read the stories, although at first no one seemed interested and the books did not sell well. He attributes this to "the nationalism of Thai people" and their "tendency to look down on Laos."[88] Part of his reason for translating Laotian literature was that he wanted Thai people in general, not just in Isan, to learn about and better understand Lao people ("*khon chat Lao*," people of Lao race/nationality); he hoped to reduce Thai people's prejudice "so that they would see that Lao people are intelligent and modern."[89]

Eventually, many different magazines accepted Laotian stories for publication, including the three major weeklies, *Siam Rath*, *Nation*, and

---

[82] Khaen Sarika, though not from Isan originally, is fluent in Lao from his years with the CPT in Isan and Laos, and is on friendly terms with a number of writers in Laos. Pramote, Interview, 1999.

[83] Vernacular Lao alphabet.

[84] A Lao writing system used primarily in religious texts.

[85] Pramote is now a practicing Christian, a fact that only rarely finds expression in his work. Pramote, Interview, 1999.

[86] Pramote, Interview, 1999.

[87] Ibid.

[88] Ibid.

[89] Ibid.

Matichon, and the women's magazines, *Sakun Thai*, *Praew*, and *Na Kha*. Pramote also translated essays, including one by noted scholar Mahasila Viravong, which was published in *Sinlapawatthanatham* and featured on the magazine's cover. Pramote traveled to Laos twice, in 1991 and 1994, and met with several writers there. Later, however, he decreased his activities in this area, translating the work of one writer only, Saisuwan Phaengphong, with whom he developed a close friendship (though Saisuwan moved to Salt Lake City, Utah). Pramote feels that the main difference between Isan and Laotian writers is that the former have been influenced by broad popular trends both in Thailand and abroad, while the latter draw on their backgrounds and retain more characteristics of traditional literature in their writing. It is interesting to note that Pramote, having turned to concentrate more on his own writing and less on translating, feels equally close to Central Thai writers as he does to Laotian writers.[90] Perhaps this indicates a new stage, a maturity, in which he knows and coexists with both groups, but follows a path somewhere between them, finding his primary concerns closer to home, in or near Yasothorn Province. This may also partly explain why he considers himself a local writer (*nakkhien tho'ngthin*)[91] rather than an Isan or Thai writer: his inspiration is at a local level, rather than a regional or national one, even though his literary involvement is in a national and international context as well.

Fon Fafang

Fon Fafang ฟอน ฝ้าฟาง is the pen name of Wira Sudsang วีระ สุดสังข์, born in 1958 in Khun Han District of Srisaket Province. He attended elementary school in his home village and secondary school in the district seat, and then enrolled in the two-year program at Surin Teachers' College (later the Rajabhat Institute, now Rajabhat University). After graduating, he returned to his home village to teach. Wira's father was Kui, and his mother half Kui and half Khmer. At home and in the village at large, they spoke mostly Kui, and some Khmer (especially with his mother's relatives on her father's side). Wira learned to speak Lao when he was in secondary school, because Lao was the common language of the district seat. Thai, of course, was the language of the classroom, but was not used in daily life. Everyone spoke the local language outside the classroom, even Wira's teacher. As he commented,

---

[90] Ibid.
[91] Ibid.

"When we came out, we spoke Kui, we spoke Khmer; but when we entered the classroom, we students stood up straight: '*Sawatdi khrap, Khun Khru!*'"[92] Later, Wira married a Lao Isan woman and went to live with her family, in her Lao-speaking village. He now speaks all four languages fluently, and he is accepted, he says, as a native speaker by each of the communities.[93] At home, with his own wife and children, he speaks Lao. He also reads Lao, and subscribes to the Laotian periodical, *Vannasin*, an arts and culture magazine published in Viengjan.

Wira's writing began with songs. He enjoyed listening to *luk thung* (country music) and *kan treum* (Khmer folk music), and in about 1972 started to write song lyrics. In secondary school, he learned to write poetry, essays, and short stories, all of which he continued practicing at teachers' college. An important element in the development of his writing was his diligence in keeping a daily journal, writing in it every day over a period of several years. He also read a great deal. During secondary school, he had no money to buy food in the lunchroom, so he spent time in the library reading books instead. However, there was no one to encourage his interest in literature; on the contrary, he was often scolded for wasting his time filling pages and pages with his handwriting instead of preparing for exams. He did gain inspiration, though, from the work of some published writers:

> At the time I was in secondary school, I read work by Nimit Phum-
> thaworn, who wrote about teachers' stories in rural schools. I liked them
> a lot. I liked the atmosphere of the stories, the descriptions of the fields,
> of nature, the folksy-ness, the country-ness, the up-country atmosphere.
> It made me want to write like that.[94]

He began to read monthly magazines, and continued to do so through teachers' college and beyond, paying for them by skipping meals and eating only twice daily.

> I saved money to buy Ajin Banjaphan's *Fa Muang Thai*, because Teacher
> Nimit Phumthaworn wrote in there. Khamphun Bunthawi wrote in there
> at that time. I read *Fa Muang Thai* from '16 [1973] on. In '16 I was in
> secondary school. In '19 [1976] I went to teachers' college. And when
> I graduated, I wrote [for a subscription] again, and got *Fa Muang Thai*,

---

[92] Wira Sudsang, Interview, March 28, 1999, Srisaket. For more of this interview, see Martin Platt, "Interview with Fon Fafang, A Kui-Khmer Writer in Thailand," *Udaya* 2 (2001): 81–96.

[93] Ibid.

[94] Ibid.

Fa Muang Tho'ng, *Fa Achip*, *Fa Nari*, all of them magazines in Ajin Banjaphan's group.[95] I read them and then I tried and tried to write.[96]

Wira began to use the pen name, Yo'd Do'kya ยอด ดอกหญ้า.

At first, Wira's ideas about literature were molded by the magazines he read, which were full of action and adventure stories. He began to marvel at the kind of power that writers commanded, in their ability to create and destroy according to their own whims:

> I felt, 'Hey, writers are like gods: I pronounce you the hero, and have you fight ten villains and win, I'll make you win. Or I'll make you lose. Or I'll make you unlucky, I'll make you poor, I'll make you rich.' As if the writer were a god who could determine the characters' lives. As if the writer were something supernaturally powerful. That was my idea at the time. And I felt that writers were people who were respected, people who were magical, who could create and recount their own creations to other people.[97]

However, his views began to change in 1980, through contact with a friend whose literary interests were more political. Wira read Jit Phumisak's *Art*

---

[95] These four magazines were all published by Ajin Banjaphan but with somewhat varied content, readership, and dates of publication. ฟ้าเมืองไทย was the only weekly of the four (the others were all monthlies) and also lasted the longest, commencing publication in 1969 and ceasing in 1988 after 1,023 issues. Each issue included two or three short stories, installments of three or four serialized novels, and columns on literature, film, and music. The column, "They Started Here," presented the work of new writers. ฟ้าเมืองทอง was published from 1975 to 1986 and emphasized short stories, with eight to ten in every issue. Like ฟ้าเมืองไทย, its primary purpose was as a literary magazine; both publications also included some non-fiction articles on historical, biographical, and other subjects. ฟ้านารี lasted only from 1977 to 1982, and, as its title suggests, consisted of articles about women, particularly working women. It included short stories and various regular columns, and was aimed mainly at a lower-middle-class audience. ฟ้าอาชีพ, which was published from 1977 to 1987, was primarily a non-fiction magazine concentrating on vocational subjects. It was aimed at lower-middle-class readers in the countryside. According to Suchart, these four publications were characterized overall by an optimistic, traditional point of view and tended to appeal to rural more than urban readers. As their founder and editor, Ajin often encouraged young or emerging writers in the countryside (including some Isan writers, such as Khamphun, as noted in Chapter 4) and provided opportunities for them to publish their work. Suchart Sawatsri, pers. comm., July 9, 2001. See ถนนหนังสือ 2, 2 (ส.ค. 2527): 9–39; also ประทีป เหมือนนิล, 100 นักประพันธ์ไทย. กรุงเทพฯ: สุวีริยาสาส์น, 2542, pp. 441–9.

[96] Wira, Interview, 1999.

[97] Ibid.

for Life, Art for the People, and Seni Saowaphong's *The Specter*, both of which strongly influenced him, as well as works by Russian writers like Tolstoy, Chinese writers like Lu Xun, and Thai Literature for Life writers at the time like Suwat Woradilok, Wat Wanlayangkul, and Visa Khanthap. During the period of 1973–1976, Wira had not followed the news much nor paid attention to politics, but in the early 1980s he made up for this with particular enthusiasm for literary ideas of the Left. He was made aware, he says, of social issues, and felt, "Things have to be improved; I can't sit around and do nothing anymore."[98] He states:

> Since then, writers [for me] have been ordinary people who have to keep watch over society, keep watch over change. Also, writers have to serve the poor, have to reflect the lives of the poor for other parts of the society who don't know, take note of how poor people live, how they eat, how they sleep, how their lives are. And reflect these images for society to acknowledge, in order to subsequently alleviate them. [...] Those new ideas are still with me today, that we have to keep watch over society and always understand the way out, and learn and solve and serve.[99]

In 1981, Wira took the pen name, Fon Fafang, reflecting his dark view of society and its fragmentation,[100] and published his first piece, a poem called "*Kham Sang Pho*'" คำสั่งพ่อ (Father's Order), in *Matichon Weekend*. Having had 30 or 40 pieces rejected, the publication of this poem gave him renewed energy in writing. The following year, he began to meet with Sorawut Sripetch, a teacher who also lived far out in the countryside. They would meet in the town of Srisaket, buy books, and discuss them. After talking about the various literary groups in other regions, they decided one day (while meeting at the Srisaket train station) that they should start an Isan group. This was the beginning of the Mun River Literary Group.[101]

Thereafter, Wira wrote and published a wide range of work: short stories, poetry, essays, and non-fiction. He had a regular column in *Matichon Weekend* from 1995 to 1997 in which he discussed the customs and traditions of Isan villagers, and the changes that were occurring in those practices due to the new ideas and technology reaching the villages. He continued to teach at a village school in Srisaket, where he was part of a teachers' self-improvement group, *Cho'k Si Ngoen* (Silver Chalk). He has written

---

[98] Ibid.
[99] Ibid.
[100] *Fon* means to cut down to pieces; *fafang* means overcast, gloomy.
[101] Wira, Interview, 1999.

several supplementary curriculum books on Srisaket and Isan ethnic groups, history, and traditions. Students at the school speak Kui or Lao as their first language; the teachers, 90% of whom are from Srisaket, speak Lao amongst themselves outside the classroom. Wira was also involved in setting up a permanent exhibition at a temple outside the provincial capital, in which the cultures of four principal ethnic groups of the province are presented: Lao, Khmer, Kui, and Yoe (a group related to the Kui). He was a member of the provincial culture committee, and was in charge of a festival in December 1998 promoting cultural answers to economic problems. In 1997, he released an album of *kan treum* songs (Khmer folk music), with the Khmer title, "*Neung Toe Yang Na*" (What to Do?), on which he sings in Khmer, Kui, Lao, and Thai.

Wira's first five books are:

1) *1986 Het Kan Thi Tha Chang* 1986 เหตุการณ์ที่ท่าช้าง (*1986 Events at Tha Chang*), 1987, a collection of short stories;

2) *Chiphajo'n Haeng Tho'ng Thung* ชีพจรแห่งท้องทุ่ง (*Pulse of the Fields*), 1995, a collection of non-fiction articles from his column in *Matichon Weekly*;

3) *Fa Klai Ja Tai Fa* ฟ้าไกลจะไต่ฟ้า (*The Sky is Far Yet I Will Climb It*), 1996, poetry;

4) *Ban Thung Hai Thek* บ้านทุ่งไฮเทค (*High-Tech Village in the Fields*), 1997, a second collection of his non-fiction columns from *Matichon Weekly*; and

5) *Khwam Mai Ao Nai Kho'ng Khon Mai Ao Nai* ความไม่เอาไหนของคนไม่เอาไหน (*The Ineptness of the Inept*), 1999, a collection of short stories.

One of Wira's early short stories, published in 1984 in *Thanon Nangseu* (and later collected in *1986 Events at Tha Chang*), is called "*Kan Jan Jek Wab*" กันจัญเจกวับ. The title is not Thai, but Khmer, taken from a Khmer lullaby, and meaning, "O Tree Frog." The story's main character is a Khmer mother who, with two small children and a newborn baby, is abandoned in poverty by her Khmer husband; she expresses her tremendous sadness and her memories of getting to know and marrying her husband. What is remarkable about the story, however, is its extensive use of Khmer language (written in Thai script). The mother hears the lullaby being sung nearby, and the entire song is quoted in the story in Khmer, followed by a Thai translation. All the dialogue in the story (which takes the form of recollections by the mother in her thoughts about her husband) is presented in Khmer as well, and then also in Thai translation. The author provides footnotes explaining that the language is Khmer, and that the song is a

Khmer folk tune sung in Surin and Buri Ram. The story begins and ends with the Khmer words to the song, which is a lament (to a frog) by a woman who is unable to raise her children. Wira discussed in an interview why he used Khmer language:

> I wanted to have the atmosphere of Khmer-ness. Because when the song comes up, the sound carries in the fields and farms. If the dialogue had been in Thai, sweet and spectacularly beautiful, it would have clashed with the atmosphere of the scene. But the problem was that people who didn't understand the language didn't like to read it, except for those who were really interested.[102]

Perhaps not surprisingly, the story was not very well-received. While Wira felt that he succeeded in expressing the feelings of the Khmer protagonist and the Khmer song, few readers were able to appreciate it. Nonetheless, the writing of the story represented a unique and bold gesture, a declaration that Thailand is not exclusively Thai, nor Isan exclusively Lao, and that Khmer people's lives, too, are worth knowing about.

Another noteworthy story by Wira is "*1986 Het Kan Thi Tha Chang*" (1986 Events at Tha Chang), first published in *Kheut Ho't* in 1987 and then republished that same year in the collection named after it. The story takes place at a well-known river pier in Bangkok, where a woman waits at night for a ferry to take her home. She is at first mildly disgusted by a vagrant sleeping on the bench opposite her, but moves over to sit next to him when a young man comes onto the pier and frightens her by trying, out of loneliness, to talk to her. She fans mosquitoes away from the vagrant in order to give the impression to the young man that she and the vagrant are a couple. Eventually, the boat comes and the woman gets up to board. The young man asks, "What about your boyfriend?" and she replies, "Take care of him for me," as she leaves.

The story is deftly observed and increasingly suspenseful, evoking the setting and tense atmosphere in a very convincing manner. It has a socially relevant aspect as well, evincing but not belaboring the socioeconomic gap between the woman and the vagrant, and ironically commenting on their brief yet complex interaction, one that the sleeping vagrant himself is completely unaware of. Like much of Wira's work, this piece shows a distinct Literature for Life influence, but with attention to quality in form as well as content, possessing insightful observation, nuance, and psychological interest. In his later work, Wira continued to support Literature for Life

---

[102] Wira, Interview, 1999; see Platt, "Interview," 2001.

and its ideals. In 1997, he conducted an exchange, even a feud, with Wanit Jarungkitanan in the pages of *Matichon Weekend* for a period of many weeks; Wira argued for social conscience in literature, while Wanit attempted to dismiss him with rude and irrelevant remarks.[103] In the foreword to Wira's work, *The Ineptness of the Inept*, Wira notes that the book is a collection of "stories that reflect images of life of rural people, but ways of life that are half rural and half urban," and then states:

> If we talk about people exploiting each other in past decades, we see that the privileged committed acts against the underprivileged. But now we see that the underprivileged commit acts against each other, merely to allow themselves to be able to live.
>
> I hope this collection of short stories will be a large window allowing us to see more clearly the complexity of problems of half rural half urban ways of life, and will be a supporting factor in helping us see a way out for society.[104]

Wira clearly still held Literature for Life ideals, but he avoided the trap of formulaic stories and oversimplification of issues.

There are indications, however, of Wira's writing and interests developing in other ways as well. In 1998, he published a short story entitled "*Li Ju Sae Eung: Sao Kae Khang Ban Kho'ng Chao Kui*" ลี่จู แซ่อึ้ง สาวแก่ค้างบ้านของชาวกวย (Li-Ju Sae-Eung: An Old Maid Stuck in a Kui Village). The piece is about the life of Chinese woman, as narrated by the Kui man who grew up with and secretly loved her. As the daughter of the only Chinese family in an otherwise all-Kui village, Li-Ju has a complicated personal identity. She never marries, and it is implied that since her family would never permit her to marry anyone but a Chinese, she chooses not to marry at all. Kui village life provides the setting for an examination of the situation of a Chinese family in Isan, presented without the rancor or didacticism common to much Isan writing on the subject. The author deals with complexities of ethnic issues, rendering a sympathetic portrait

---

[103] See for example, วานิช จรุงกิจอนันต์. "กฤษณาสอนน้อง (2)," มติชนสุดสัปดาห์ 20 พ.ค. 2540, pp. 70–1; and ฟอน ฟ้าฟาง, "รำฟ้อนย้อนกฤษณาเป็นตายากหัว (1)," มติชนสุดสัปดาห์ 17 ม.ย. 2540, p. 69. Note that in their exchange, both writers express the age-old antagonism between Bangkok and Isan (as reflected even in the titles of their essays), with Wanich taking the patronizing Central position as the more knowledgeable older brother and Wira deflating that arrogance with his response in Lao.

[104] วีระ สุดสังข์, "คำนำ," in ความไม่เอาไหนของคนไม่เอาไหน. กรุงเทพฯ: ชมรมเด็ก, 2442, pp. 3–4.

of members of two ethnic groups that, though generally occupying opposite ends of the economic spectrum, have both frequently been denigrated in Isan. The author's accomplishment is that he has created a balanced story of Chinese-Kui subject matter in an Isan work of Thai literature.

Beyond just this single story, it appears that Wira feels increasingly allied with Kui identity. He narrates the above story in the first person, as the Kui friend of the protagonist. Moreover, one of his projects in 1999 was compiling a Kui-Thai-English dictionary. In an interview, he comments:

> I tend to be rather resentful about being ethnically Kui, that we don't have a written language, and I regret that the language is disappearing. I am a real Kui who has to speak Lao, has to speak Thai, has to speak Khmer, or, in the future I might have to speak English. My Kui language, people don't speak it. The new generation of kids, they don't want to speak Kui anymore. My Kui language is dying. [...] They still speak it, but in a hundred years I think it will have completely disappeared. Because in Srisaket in 1907, 92 years ago, you could say that the whole province, almost a hundred percent, was Kui. There are not even half of the Kui that there were. So in another hundred years, Kui language will probably be gone, will have disappeared entirely from memory. Because of that I'm doing a dictionary, so that people know that this ethnic group once existed. [...] Kui people have a cultural inferiority complex. People who have an inferiority complex feel ashamed. So when they live near Khmer people, they adopt Khmer culture to make them feel like Khmers. They have to speak Khmer. When they live near Lao people, they have to adopt Lao culture in order to make themselves similar to Lao.[105]

Wira also criticizes the government's failure to include any aspect of Kui history or culture in the national school curriculum. Surprisingly, though, he minimizes the importance of regionalism in writing and denies that there is such a thing as modern Isan literature. Instead, he emphasizes the universal quality of literature by Isan writers, and balks at allowing himself to be called a regional or Isan writer.[106] This concentration on local issues and communities while simultaneously making a claim to universality might at first appear contradictory. However, perhaps it can more usefully be seen as an attempt to bring greater attention to ignored groups, and to claim for them a status and recognition equal to that of other people of Thailand, particularly Central Thais.

---

[105] Wira Sudsang, Interview, 1999.
[106] Ibid.

Pira Sudham

Pira Sudham is the pen name of Pira Khaneungsathayatham. He was born in 1942 in Na Pho village in Buri Ram Province. The village was made up of Lao-speaking farming families, including his own; his father was also a *mo' lam* teacher. Pira attended school at a temple in the district seat where his parents had sent him to be a temple boy. He later moved to Bangkok, where he continued as a temple boy and student, eventually matriculating at Chulalongkorn University in 1960.[107] Two years later, he won a Colombo Plan Scholarship from the government of New Zealand and went to study English language and literature at Victoria University in Wellington. He subsequently spent three years in Australia, from 1969 to 1971, and then lived in Europe, primarily England, from 1975 to 1978. After returning to Thailand, he worked for several years in Bangkok as a public relations consultant for some European airlines,[108] an oil company, and a hotel chain,[109] and was also the president of the Siam Wine Society. He began to spend more and more time in his village, Na Pho, where he set up a number of projects, including a school and a foundation, to benefit poor families in the area. From the 1990s onward, he divided his time between his homes in Na Pho and Bangkok in Thailand, and Sussex, England.

Pira first discovered literature while in secondary school at a temple in Bangkok, where one of his duties was to sleep in the library as a guard. He first encountered Westerners when they came as tourists to the temple (Wat Benjamabophit, the renowned "Marble Temple"), and claims that until then he had no idea that the whole world did not speak Thai.[110] He made an effort to learn English, speaking with tourists and using a dictionary to read books. At age 19 he started to write fiction in English, although it took years, he says, before he felt he had reached a comfortable fluency.[111] Nevertheless, he continued to write in English only, and to this day, all of his work is in English. He explained why in an interview:

> Thai is a foreign language for me. Now English has become my second language [after Lao]. I think in English. When I speak Thai, it's translated in my mind. English has discipline of language and reasoning,

---

[107] วิวัฒน์ โรจนาวรรณ, ed., นักเขียนอีสาน. บุรีรัมย์: สโมสรนักเขียนภาคอีสาน, 2542a.

[108] David Myers, "Pira Sudham and the Rape of the Esarn People of Northeastern Thailand," *Asian Studies Review* 18, 2 (November 1994): 77–87.

[109] วิวัฒน์, ed., "นักเขียน," 2542a.

[110] คนเดียว,"จากนาโพธิ์ถึงโนเบล," สารคดี 148 (มิ.ย. 2540).

[111] Pira Sudham, Interview, December 3, 1998, Bangkok.

which is more suitable to me. It's not as rigid as French or German. I am allowed to maneuver in English, like Joyce. Thai enslaves the mind. Thais don't learn how to reason. The way parents answer children's questions is not logical. It's sloppy. In English you can't be sloppy. In Thai, you can have sentences without nouns, subjects. Sometimes you don't have to use tenses.[112]

He has often spoken about the damage allegedly done by Thai language and education. For example,

[In the West] I had a wonderful chance to learn, not by rote, but by thinking, discussing, and asking questions. I wondered why, as a child and a student in Thailand, I had to be quiet and blindly obedient … I grew up mentally in foreign countries, and I am grateful for that. However, parts of my mind had already been crippled, maimed for life, during the formative years in Thailand.[113]

Pira published all his work himself, without an editor, and felt that his writing "must be faultless."[114] He also distributed the books himself, eliminating any middleman; they could be found not only in Thailand, but in bookstores and libraries throughout the West (sometimes with a little insert saying, "With Compliments of the Author"). Together, by 1999, his first three books had sold over a million copies, including the French, Italian, and Japanese editions. Pira was opposed to having his work translated into Thai, saying that if Thais want to read it, they should read the English and escape the bondage of Thai language. Similarly, the few Thai writers Pira has read have been in English translation: Khamsing's *The Politician*, and Botan's *Letters from Thailand*; he read the former, he says, "in order not to duplicate him," and the latter in order to "see the point of view of the Chinese, since I write about the Chinese, too."[115] In addition to publishing and distributing his books himself, he also promoted them. The cover of each is emblazoned with the announcement, "Nominated for the Nobel Prize for Literature"; apparently he was nominated in 1990 by "a prominent Bangkok professor."[116] In an advertisement, Pira has also referred to his novel, *Monsoon Country*, as "the *Dr. Zhivago* of Thailand."[117]

---

[112] Ibid.

[113] Pira Sudham, "Voice from the Grass Roots," *Asia Magazine*, April 10–12, 1992, p. 50.

[114] Pira, Interview, 1998.

[115] Ibid.

[116] Myers, "Pira," p. 81.

[117] ถนนหนังสือ 1, 4 (ก.ย. 2526): 1.

Pira has produced three principal works, keeping them all in print, but as he published them himself, he has had a tendency to repackage and reissue them, adding, removing, and editing material. His first book was *Siamese Drama*, a collection of short stories first published in 1983. In 1991 it was transformed into *Pira Sudham's Best: Siamese Drama and Other Stories from Thailand*, including an excerpt from his novel, *Monsoon Country*, which originally appeared in 1988. In 1994, his third book, *People of Esarn*, appeared; it consists of a number of disparate parts, including: an autobiographical piece; several non-fiction vignettes concerning political killings, deforestation, and child prostitution; reprinted news articles; short descriptions (which are also included in *Pira Sudham's Best*) about the people aided by the Pira Sudham Estate; a statement of Pira's views on democracy, press freedom, human rights, and other popular topics likely to appeal to Western readers; and a one-page item, enclosed in a border, called "Small Wonder," which extols Pira himself. There is a section entitled, "An Esarn Notebook," which refers several times to the well-publicized killing of the activist Nid Chaiwana; in fact, however, Nid was killed in the North, and had nothing to do with Isan. Another short piece, "Remembering the Massacres," discusses the events of October 14, 1973, October 6, 1976, and May 1992. As far as can be determined, though, Pira had no involvement with any of these events, despite giving the impression of having participated; during at least one of the incidents cited (October 6, 1976), he was not even in Thailand. For these reasons, *People of Esarn* opens itself up to charges of sensationalization, misrepresentation, self-promotion, and commercialization of Isan. Early editions contained advertisements for expensive tours of the region for Westerners. The book might be considered more of a scrapbook than a work of literature.

Pira's novel, *Monsoon Country*, appears to be the work he is most proud of. It is the semi-autobiographical story of Prem Surin, a young boy from a poor farming family in Buri Ram who studies in Bangkok and then travels to England on a scholarship. After rejecting opportunities to lead a life of luxury and privilege in England and Germany, he returns to his home village and ordains as a monk. Many readers find the book to be rather peculiar in its apparently random plot, lack of character motivation, and uneven and anomalous style. The third person narration occasionally slips into first person, and photos throughout the text bear no obvious relationship to the story. At one point, Prem, while still a child, delivers an analytical monologue detailing his observations on the difficult situation his family is facing. Immediately afterward, his mother, who has barely been mentioned or had opportunity to speak in the 130 pages of the novel up to that point, presents a three-and-a-half-page soliloquy to her family on the same topic. Some readers, however, have reacted positively to the presence of issues of gender and sexuality in the book.

There is an important parallel between Prem the character and Pira the writer: both are extremely careful in controlling the image of themselves that they allow others to see. Prem rarely revels anything about himself to anyone around him; Pira takes this a step further by crafting and promoting a picture of himself and his work, a picture that seems designed to appeal to Westerners with a rudimentary knowledge and experience of Thailand. There are four main themes that appear repeatedly in Pira's portrayal of himself, his work, and his region: 1) the Thai education system's crippling effect on youth; 2) the poverty, ignorance, and suffering of villagers in a harsh, arid environment; 3) the social ills of corruption, exploitation, prostitution, environmental degradation, etc.; and 4) his own artistic ability, philanthropy, and service to village and community. The subjects he chooses to present seem calculated to provoke outrage and sympathy at the conditions in Isan while imparting a sense of the exotic, and then, ultimately, to advance Pira himself as a righteous crusader.

Evidently many have been convinced. All of his books in the late 1990s contained quotations or whole articles by Westerners praising his literary skills and good works, and he distributed complimentary articles about himself and his work to interested parties. Examples include the following, a statement by David Myers, a professor at Central Queensland University:

> In his fictional exposure of criminal and ruthless capitalist development in Thailand, and his championing of the poor and the commercially exploited, Pira Sudham is in his own modest way a Southeast Asian equivalent of Charles Dickens, exposing the cruelty of industrial capitalism in nineteenth-century England. He has the same inclination to pathos and sentimentality and the same depth of attachment to his people.[118]

Noel Rowe, of the University of Sydney, refers to "the helplessness and ignorance that characterize the Isan experience," and then makes the following assertion:

> Pira Sudham has not written any work in Thai. Writing in English, he aims not only to give the English reader insights into Thai life, but also to give significance to the lives of the rural poor in Thailand so

---

[118] Myers, "Pira," p. 81.

that 'they do not come into this world to merely exist, suffer, and die in vain.'[119]

The embedded quotation comes from Pira himself, and the piece from which the above passage is taken is, similarly, published by Pira himself, in his own book. Apparently, Pira felt that the poor led a meaningless existence, and that he had the power to save them from it.

Myers does make a useful point, however, when he notes that, "Pira Sudham has become the international voice of these forgotten people."[120] This is somewhat problematic, since many foreigners see Thailand largely through Pira's work. Their understanding of Thailand, and of Thai literature, is based on what they read in books like *People of Esarn* and *Pira Sudham's Best*. After all, he has been nominated for the Nobel Prize, they are told. Even in guidebooks he is cited as the authority to consult. In Lonely Planet's bible for travelers to Thailand, Joe Cummings shares his own dubious expertise through the following comment in his introduction to Isan:

> Travellers who want to know more about north-eastern Thailand should read the works by Pira Sudham, a Thai author born in Buri Ram. His autobiographical *People of Esarn (Isaan)* is especially recommended.[121]

Another guidebook, the *Thailand Traveller's Companion*, provides a list of places to visit in Isan (each with an accompanying descriptive paragraph): "Phimai, Udorn, Ban Chiang, Nong Khai, Loei, Wat That Phanom and Surin," and then, "Monsoon Country."[122] The entry describes Pira, his books, and the weekend trips he was organizing: "These private tours offer an excellent insight into northeastern village life. For further details, contact the author at ...," followed by phone and fax numbers and a post office box address, all in Bangkok.[123]

Pira seems to have charmed many of the foreigners who write about him, yet his pronouncements often come across as disingenuous. Myers quotes him as saying,

---

[119] Noel Rowe, "Foreword," in Pira Sudham. *People of Esarn* (Bangkok: Shire, 1994), pp. 8–10.

[120] Myers, "Pira," p. 77.

[121] Joe Cummings, *Thailand: A Travel Survival Kit* (Victoria: Lonely Planet, 1990), p. 265.

[122] Bradley Winterton, *Thailand Traveller's Companion* (Switzerland: Kümmerly & Frey, 1998), p. 214.

[123] Ibid.

When I wrote in *Monsoon Country* that "there are too many thieves in low and high places, making use of their power, their positions, their cunning, shamelessly, without conscience but with great capacity for avarice, to work only for their own advantage, and for their families, their own power bases, without caring for the good of all," I hoped that at least one or two of these broad home-truths would make some Thai readers think. When I talk of the lack of conscience, I aim to make them ask themselves whether it is justifiable to say that conscience is what most of us in our society don't have.[124]

We cannot help but wonder who the Thais whom he expects to read his work are. When we read on the back cover of *Monsoon Country*, an unattributed statement describing the novel as "covering two decades of socio-economic and political changes occurring in Thailand," our skepticism increases. In fact, much of the story takes place in Europe, and there are very few references to, let alone depictions of, change in Thailand. In his comments accompanying *Monsoon Country*, Pira deplores change, declaring that "words like 'strike', 'protest', and 'exploitation', once unheard in villages … creep into our minds, like dark agents of change."[125] Elsewhere, though, he claims that these "new words create awareness in the mind," and thus lead to "positive changes" and "positive progress."[126] Eventually, his statements work against each other, and his intentions become suspect. In the end, we are left to wonder whether Pira does not use Isan and the dramatized portrait he paints of it primarily for his own purposes, an act which places him dangerously close to the same category as those he purports to be dedicating his life to opposing.

Conclusion

The regionalistic sentiment of the *tho'ngthin niyom* phenomenon emerged forcefully in the early 1980s after the collapse of the political left and its associated Literature for Life movement. *Tho'ngthin niyom* has been for some Isan writers an extension of that movement, for others an alternative to it. Many writers in Isan turned to their cultural roots as a source of pride and inspiration. Academics, for their part, responded with the recognition and development, though not the actual establishment, of the discipline of Isan Studies. Finding commonality, writers joined together with like-minded

---

[124] Myers, "Pira," p. 86.
[125] Pira Sudham, *Monsoon Country* (Bangkok: Shire, 1988) (inside back cover).
[126] Pira, Interview, 1998.

comrades for friendship and support, establishing organizations like the Mun River Literary Group, which evolved (ironically with help from Central Thai institutions) into the Isan Writers' Association in 1992. Both Wira Sudsang (Fon Fafang) and Pramote Naijit were primary figures in both bodies, providing essential inspiration and energy. Members have been committed to raising the quality of Isan writing and bringing a culture of reading and writing to students in schools throughout Isan. Pramote has been primarily concerned with Lao culture and traditions, including Laotian writing across the Mekong in Laos itself. Wira has often concentrated on his Kui and Khmer roots while holding on to the ideals of Literature for Life. He never rejected or became disillusioned with that movement, perhaps because he was a latecomer to it and did not experience the same sense of personal loss or betrayal that many of those who were in the jungle did. Yong Yasothorn, among the most political of Isan writers, having served as an MP and then spent several years in the jungle, notably avoids many of the pitfalls of Literature for Life in his well-executed and critically acclaimed novel. Pira Sudham is an entirely distinct figure, writing in English and separating himself completely from Thai language, literature, and writers. He plays to a Western audience, confirming their expectations while capitalizing on their urge for fairness, their appetite for the exotic, and their desire to know the "real" Thailand.

These four writers come from Isan, write about it, and spend much or all of their time there, yet they differ in their feelings about the role that Isan plays in their work and the extent to which they consider that work to be of local versus universal relevance. One quality, though, that they may have in common is the fact that each has been, in different ways and for different reasons, an outsider in society. Wira grew up as a member of two disparaged ethnic minorities, learning Thai only as a fourth language. Pramote has for many years been a practicing Christian in a definitively Buddhist region and culture. Yong took up arms against the state and lived for years beyond the reach of its institutions. Finally, Pira spent many years abroad, writes only in English, has turned his back on his country's national language, and is a wealthy man from Thailand's poorest province. Such outsider status has evidently had little direct expression in Yong and Pramote's writing, but has been of major significance in Wira's work, and has completely defined Pira's life and books.

CHAPTER 6

Isan Writing at the
End of the 20th Century

Isan literary culture at the end of the 20th century was a complex agglomeration of people, publications, and events. While the outside observer might tend to think of literature in terms of books on a shelf, or perhaps short pieces in a magazine, and thus might be tempted to focus on texts, a more complete picture of the subject can be gained by expanding one's observations to encompass writers, readers, and the activities they engage in. As others have noted, writing is a solitary endeavor, and when a book is published in Thailand, it typically has a print run of 2,000 copies, reflecting a rather small reading public. The more successful books are reprinted, in special cases several times, but many effectively disappear after six months or a year. Judged by this situation alone, national literary life, and the Isan component of it, might appear moribund. However, the activities of writers, readers, publishers, critics, and others involved with literature combine to form a dynamic literary culture surrounding the comparatively static (or fading) existence of books. This larger context encompassing written materials often seems to get more attention than the materials themselves. In 1999, a variety of events occurred every week (primarily in Bangkok, but some in the provinces as well) with literature at their center, whether formal or informal, public or private, commercial, academic, or artistic, and many of them were discussed in the press. An understanding of Isan writing requires an examination of this literary culture.

On a day-to-day basis, the most obvious and omnipresent elements of literary culture are magazines and journals. In 1999, there were five principal weeklies (all published in Bangkok) with significant literary content: the news magazines, *Matichon*, *Siam Rath*, *Nation*,[1] and *Than Sethakit*;[2] and the Sunday edition of *Krungthep Thurakit* newspaper, which contains a section devoted entirely to literature.[3] These periodicals regularly publish poetry, serialized novels, and short stories (including foreign pieces translated into Thai), as well as reviews, interviews, and accounts of literary events, usually in the form of regular columns but sometimes as occasional or one-time features by freelance contributors.[4] Gossip, rumor, and innuendo about particular famous literary figures are often included as well. Now and then, one or another of the publications will have a running debate (or feud) in its pages, in the form of letters or columns, between advocates of certain points of view (such as the disagreement between Fon and Wanich described in Chapter 5). All of these kinds of articles commonly cover a variety of writers and literature, including those of Isan, and many are penned by Isan writers themselves. Until the end of the 1990s, there were also two major literary magazines in Thailand, both of which frequently featured materials by or about Isan writers. *Writer* magazine, a monthly, commenced publication in 1992 and closed in 1998. *Cho' Karaket*, which was founded in the late 1980s by veteran editor Suchart Sawatsri, ceased its quarterly publication in 1999, not long after a fire destroyed its offices.[5] Other national periodicals with some literary content include the monthly, *Sinlapawatthanatham* (*Arts and Culture*), university journals from Thammasat and Chulalongkorn

---

[1] This weekly Thai-language publication, เนชั่นสุดสัปดาห์, is not to be confused with the English-language daily of the same name; both are owned by the parent company, the Nation Group. The *Nation Weekend* contains a weekly literature and culture column by Suchart Sawatsri (using the pen name, Sing Sanamluang); in 1999 it was thus the only remaining periodical with regular input from Suchart.

[2] Of these, *Matichon*, *Siam Rath*, and the *Nation* weeklies are considered socially conscious and of better quality; they cover international and domestic news, politics, popular culture, literature, science, and sports.

[3] *Krungthep Thurakit* became a kind of replacement for the defunct *Writer* and *Cho' Karaket* magazines (see below), but is generally considered a weak substitute. (*Cho'karaket* has since been resurrected.)

[4] Some prominent writers were on the staff of these weeklies, e.g., Wat Wanlayangkul at *Siam Rath* and Wanich Jarungkitanan at *Matichon*.

[5] Both these publications labored under financial strain and insufficient subscriptions. For example, *Cho' Karaket* at its peak had less than 1,500 subscribers. Suchart Sawatsri, Interview, June 23, 1999, Bangkok.

Universities, and monthly magazines, aimed largely at women, like *Lalana*,[6] *Sakun Thai*,[7] *Satrisan*,[8] and *Phraew*.[9]

Literary groups and associations, which organize a variety of activities, are another important element of literary culture. Prominent examples include the Writers Association of Thailand and the Language and Book Society of Thailand (P.E.N. International Thailand Center). These groups conduct regular meetings, lectures, and seminars on literary topics, for example, "The Thai Short Story: Past, Present, and Future," held on September 26, 1998, at the Bangkok headquarters of the Language and Book Society; they produce their own publications, either periodically, such as the Society's journal, *Phasa lae Nangseu* ภาษาและหนังสือ (*Language and Books*), or occasionally, such as *Ramleuk 25 Pi 14 Tula* รำลึก 25 ปี 14 ตุลา (*Commemorating 25 Years of October 14*) by Reunreuthai Satjaphan and Phailin Rungrat, published in 1998; and they present annual national literary awards, such as the PEN Club Awards for outstanding short stories and novels.

National awards play a major role in Thailand's literary culture. Great attention surrounds the awarding of a prize, especially when a ceremony is held and the prize is presented by an august figure, such as a member of the royal family. The weeks or months leading up the announcement of the winner of the Southeast Asian Writers' (SEAWrite) Award, for example, are full of discussion, prediction, and rumor, both oral and in print, concerning which writers' work has been submitted, who has made the first cut, who is on the short list, what factors might come to play in the committee's decision-making process, etc. Moreover, a national award can transform a writer into a celebrity and their book into a bestseller with many reprints. As the critic Somphong Thawi has pointed out, Thai society tends to follow the tastes and opinions of a few people with high status, so an award gives

---

[6] In literary and artistic circles, *Lalana* has been the most widely respected of the women's magazines, due in large measure to the stature of its founding editor, Suwanni Sukhontha, who died in 1984.

[7] *Sakun Thai* is aimed at women of upper class families, including those of civil servants and military officers; its royalist, traditionalist point of view casts status in terms of both established Thai family lineage and elements of Western culture.

[8] *Satrisan* is similar to *Sakun Thai* in content, point of view, and intended audience.

[9] *Phraew* in the late 20th century gained a reputation as a women's magazine with regular literary content; it sponsored an annual literary contest and also published books by younger writers like Phaiwarin Khaongam and Chatchawal Khotsongkhram, as well as anthologies of short stories that previously appeared in the magazine.

the winner a legitimacy that readers might not have the self-confidence to bestow on their own.[10]

The SEAWrite Award receives the most attention of any literary prize in Thailand.[11] From its inception in 1979 until 1999, it was presented to Isan writers only twice: to Khamphun in 1979 for his novel, *Luk Isan*, and to Phaiwarin Khaongam (see below) in 1995 for his collection of poetry, *Ma Kan Kluay* (*Banana Branch Horse*). Another prestigious literary honor is the designation, National Artist in Literary Arts, given by the National Arts Commission and, like the SEAWrite, presented to the recipient by a member of the royal family. Lao Khamhawm was named a National Artist in 1992; Khamphun Bunthawi in 2001; Surachai Janthimathorn in 2010.[12] The *Cho' Karaket* editorial committee, led by Suchart Sawatsri, also gave respected awards to short story writers annually. In 1999 (after which there was a hiatus for some years), there were four categories: the Honorary Award for a senior writer (presented to Khamphun); the Committee's Choice and the Readers' Choice (one each); and Commendations (given to four writers). With the exception of the Honorary Award, all the prizes have been given to writers who published in the *Cho' Karaket* quarterly journal during the previous year. Other important awards include those given by the National Book Week Fair, the Book Publishers and Distributors Association, and Bangkok Bank.

Book fairs are held regularly to generate interest among the reading public. The National Book Week Fair is an annual Bangkok event where publishers set up stalls and sell current and back stock at prices generally discounted 10 to 20 percent (or more for some older books). Often the publication of new books is timed to coincide with the Fair, so that attending readers are the first to be able to acquire them, and at a discount as well, a double opportunity that strongly appeals to Thai consumers. The Fair is

---

[10] Somphong Thawi, Interview, March 1, 1999, Bangkok.

[11] The Award is presented annually to a writer from each of the Southeast Asian countries, for either a novel, a book of poetry, or a collection of short stories (alternating each year). For a discussion of the award for novels and its Thai winners, as well as other awards such as the National Book Award, see อิงอร สุพันธุ์วณิช, นวนิยายนิทัศน์. กรุงเทพฯ: ภาควิชวภาษาไทย, คณะอักษรศาสตร์, จุฬาลงกรณ์มหาวิทยาลัย, 2548. For a concise discussion of each Thai SEAWrite winner (book and author) for the first 30 years of the prize, 2522–2551 (1979–2008), see สัจภูมิ ละออ, ซีไรท์ไดอารี่. กรุงเทพฯ: สุขภาพใจ, 2551.

[12] In 1999, the honor was bestowed on Prayom Songthong who, though a native of Isan, has never identified himself as an Isan writer. Somphong, Interview, 1999.

frequented by writers, editors, publishers, critics, and other readers, and provides an enjoyable and stimulating place to collect books, eat and drink, and meet and socialize with friends and acquaintances. In October 1998, another book fair was held at the Sirikit Center in Bangkok as part of the effort to encourage reading during the economic downturn. Dozens of stalls were set up by publishers, bookstores, and independent dealers selling new, used, and rare publications. In addition, there were musical performances, poetry readings, lectures, and panel discussions, including one on the "Past, Present, and Future of Literature for Life."[13]

Seminars and panel discussions are another common aspect of literary culture. They can be sponsored by literary associations, as noted above, as well as publishers, schools, and universities. On November 25, 1998, the publisher of *Matichon* and *Sinlapawatthanatham* held a panel discussion in Bangkok entitled, "How Did You Become an Award-Winning Writer?" featuring Lao Khamhawm and two SEAWrite winners. Ubon Ratchathani University organized a conference called "Thai Literature in an Era Without Boundaries," which took place on the campus on January 15, 1999. The event consisted of dramatic poetry readings; a presentation by contemporary writers (including Phaiwarin) entitled "The New Generation, Literature, and Reading"; and a panel discussion, "From the Mun River Literary Group to the Isan Writers' Association," with Fon Fafang, Pramote Naijit, Wongdeuan Thongjiow (see below), Neramit Praphan (see Chapter 7), and others. Literary presentations were also made at schools throughout Isan under the aegis of *Cho' Karaket* during the months leading up to the organization's annual meeting in February 1999 in Buri Ram.

Other cultural events involve literature to varying extents. Caravan gives a concert every year or so, often in commemoration of a political event, such as October 14 or Black May, and individual members of the band perform more frequently throughout the year. In April 1999, they performed in celebration of their founding 25 years earlier; outside the concert, books (as well as recordings and T shirts) were sold, primarily Literature for Life works of the 1970s by Prasert Jandam and others. The 25th anniversary of October 14 was the occasion for a week of commemorative events in October 1998 at Sanam Luang. In addition to a Caravan concert, there were poetry readings, panel discussions (including one in which Lao Khamhawm was the senior figure), NGO presentations, art installations, and book stalls set up by publishers and independent dealers selling new and used books,

---

[13] Held on October 23, 1998.

including works from the October 14 era. A similar event on a much smaller scale was held at Chachoengsao Teachers' College later that month, with presentations made by writers and musicians from Bangkok and elsewhere, including Yong Yasothorn.

Book-launching parties are another feature of the literary landscape. In November 1998, Chukiet Chathaisong, a musician and *Nation* columnist from Buri Ram, celebrated the release of his book, *Chronicles of People, Chronicles of Songs*, a collection of his columns on writers and musicians in the Art for Life movement. The party was held at a small Bangkok restaurant and was attended by writers, musicians, and artists. Another book-launch was held at the same restaurant in May 1999. Sponsored by Dok Ya publishing house, the party marked the occasion of the publication of new books by six different authors, including Phisit Phusri (from Udorn, see below) and Win Liowwarin (whose book won the SEAWrite Award two months later). Dok Ya's managing editor, Raks Mananya (see below), arranged the party. He also put together a short play, performed on the spot as part of the festivities, that combined elements of all six books and gave onlookers a taste of the books' contents. A set of the six books was given to each of the invited guests (approximately 70 people).

Finally, informal social gatherings also play a substantial role in literary culture. In some instances, a circle of friends will meet at a particular spot on a regular basis. For example, Chukiet and a number of his musician and writer compatriots used to get together every Friday night at a certain Bangkok restaurant to eat, drink, and talk about anything on their minds, including literature. Some people showed up dependably every week, while others appeared only now and then. At times, new friends were invited along as well. However, in 1998, these gatherings decreased markedly in frequency due to the economic situation and the fact that many in the group were not regularly employed.

Other gatherings occur irregularly, sometimes in conjunction with a public event or a visit by a literary figure from out of town. On several evenings in October 1998, after various events at Sanam Luang for the October 14 commemoration, a dozen or so mutually acquainted writers, including Chukiet and Lao Khamhawm, met at a favorite restaurant nearby. Over food and the ever-present alcohol, they discussed books, people, their own projects, the events of the day, and so on. At one point, a poem, written by an unnamed outsider, was passed around the group. Several people present commented on it, mostly along the lines of what had already been said by Naowarat Phongphaibun (the senior person present), namely that the writer showed skill but what he expressed was faulty. Thus, these social gatherings, in addition to bringing friends together, can also act as a forum at which opinions are voiced, shared values are reinforced, and group bonds maintained.

A few nights later, the same restaurant was the scene of another get-together involving some of the same people and several others as well. As more people arrived, they moved around among three adjacent tables, talking and drinking. At one point, a young man arrived and sat by himself at a nearby empty table, facing the other guests at an angle. He ordered a beer and showed interest in the gathering next to him, but no one talked to or acknowledged him. After a time, he moved to a seat with its back to the group, and eventually he left. I was informed that the would-be comrade was "strange" and "aberrant', and that he knew the group and tried to insinuate himself into it, but that they were familiar with him and did not want him in their circle, and thus kept him out. In this way, literary social groupings maintain a sense of cohesiveness while expressing an exclusivity toward those they deem unfit, undesirable, or at odds with the group's standards.

Another, more substantial, social gathering occurred in the evening after the panel discussion on Literature for Life at the Sirikit Center during the October 1998 book fair. The party was held at a large restaurant in Nonthaburi and was attended by several dozen writers, many of whom had been present at the panel discussion. While eating, drinking, and talking to friends, the participants were asked to speak (into a microphone, because the group was so large) on the subject of Literature for Life. There was a recounting of the substance and opinions from the panel discussion, and at the same time a reiteration of alliances, divisions, and identities among those present. There did not seem to be much surprise at what was expressed, no startling opinions or new insights. Instead, it appeared that people mostly said what was expected, confirming one or another established point of view and clarifying their own place in relation to it.

The overall literary culture, briefly described above in its many aspects, is the context in which Thai (including Isan) writers and their work exist. For Isan writers, especially those of the new generation, the issue of what it meant to be an Isan writer was just one of the many questions and choices in the national literary scene. The 11 writers discussed in this chapter are noted Isan authors whose lasting contribution to Isan and Thai literature has yet to be determined. Though their ages vary by over two decades, they were all active in 1999 and have done most or all of their writing since 1990. Their opinions and actions, and the style and content of their works, show a greater range and variety than was characteristic of their predecessors, as will be seen below. This heterogeneity underlines the vast diversity of meaning of the term, "Isan writer" on the contemporary literary stage. In the following discussion, rather than attempting a recital of the contents of dozens of books and hundreds of short stories, I will highlight particular works that illustrate different writers' characteristics and accomplishments in relation to contemporary Isan literature.

Phaiwarin Khaongam

Phaiwarin Khaongam ไพวรินทร์ ขาวงาม is the best-known among the later generation of Isan writers, for two principal reasons. The first is his winning the SEAWrite Award in 1995, which made him an instant literary celebrity and brought wide recognition to his exceptional skills. The other is his energy and productivity. By 1999, he was publishing poems every week, producing a book every year or two, and frequently speaking at schools, particularly in Isan, in order to encourage reading and writing among young students.

Phaiwarin was born Phairat Khaongam in 1961, the third of nine children of a farming family in Roi Et Province, bordering Surin Province. His father is of Khmer origin in Surin, his mother of Lao descent from Roi Et. Phaiwarin grew up speaking Khmer at home as his first language, and then Lao, the language of many of his family's friends and neighbors. He learned Thai in school, finishing fourth grade in his village and completing the remainder of his elementary education nearby.[14] He graduated from secondary school at a monastery in Ayuthaya, having been ordained in Surin in 1974. After teaching at the monastery school for several years, he left the monkhood (and eight years in robes) and moved to Chiang Mai to work as a journalist. Two years later, he moved to Bangkok, in spite of an aversion to the city that he had developed while visiting it as a novice, and in 1999, was still living there.[15] Over time, he has supported himself working variously as an ice-cream seller, proofreader, and editor, and now makes a living as an independent writer.[16]

Phaiwarin's involvement with literature began at the monastery in Ayuthaya. There was a monk there who liked to write, and when Phaiwarin sought him out, they found they got along. The monk fostered his interests, encouraging him to read *Fa Meuang Thai* and write short stories. Books

---

[14] Phaiwarin Khaongam, Interview, June 22, 1999, Bangkok.

[15] Ibid.

[16] วิวัฒน์ โรจนาวรรณ, ed., นักเขียนอีสาน. บุรีรัมย์: สโมสรนกเขียนภาคอีสาน, 2542a.

he recalls reading at the time include Akatdamkoeng's *The Circus of Life*, Suwanni's *His Name was Kan*, and the Thai translation of Marie Corelli's *Vendetta*. Phaiwarin also read Khamsing's *Fa Bo' Kan*, which greatly impressed him, he says,

> especially the story called '*Fa Prot*' ['Dunghill' in Domnern's English translation], in which Isan kids fight over insects in buffalo dung. I thought, Oh, this writer can tell stories that are close to me. [...] When I read it, I felt, Wow, I've been like this. [...] I liked it. After that I wanted to write short stories and so on.[17]

Phaiwarin marks his beginning as a writer with the 1975 publication of one of his short stories in the periodical *Chaiyapreuk*, which at that time was edited by Witthayakorn Chiengkul. Phaiwarin's Thai teacher submitted the story without telling him, and then surprised the teenager by showing him the latest issue, with the story in it. Seeing his work in a recognized publication, and receiving the 70 baht payment from the magazine, Phaiwarin was inspired to continue. Soon afterward, he published, in the same periodical, an essay on the subject of farmers, which became his first publication to gain a significant level of attention from the reading public. From then on, Phaiwarin published more and more material, culminating in his first book, *Lam Nam Wanejo'n* ลำนำวะเนจร (*Songs of Forest Wandering*), in 1985. The following year, he published a collection of his earlier pieces entitled *Kham Dai Ja Oey Dai Dang Jai* คำใดจะเอ่ยได้ดังใจ (*Which Words Can Express My Heart's Utterings*). Four more books appeared over the next six years: *Mai Chai Kawiniphon Jak Chai Pa Arayatham*[18] ไม่ใช่กวีนิพนธ์ จากชายป่าอารยธรรม (*Not a Work of Poetry, From the Edge of the Civilized Jungle*) in 1987; *Reudi Kan* ฤดีกาล (*Time of Gladness*) in 1989; *Kheu Raeng Jai Lae Fai Fan* คือแรงใจและไฟฝัน (*Strength of Heart and Power of Dreams*) in 1991, which received the 1992 annual Award for Outstanding Book of Poetry from the

---

[17] Phaiwarin, Interview, 1999.

[18] This book is subtitled ที่พักของถ้อยคำ (*Resting Place of Words*). It is a collection of writings from 1984–1987 inspired by Phaiwarin's travels throughout Thailand. Each piece combines poetry and prose to express Phaiwarin's sensibility and mindfulness, including his complex feelings for the breadth and variety of the world along with his attachment to his village, a favorite theme. He takes common phrases from public signboards, such as หยุดตรวจ (Stop for Checkpoint), รับสมัครด่วน (Help Wanted Urgently), and โปรดเงียบ (Silence Please), and uses them as points of departure for meditations on friendship, self-expression, and the ways individuals function in society.

Ministry of Education; and *Thanon Nak Fan* ถนนนักฝัน (*Dreamer's Road*) in 1992. In 1995, Phaiwarin published *Ma Kan Kluay* ม้าก้านกล้วย (*Banana Branch Horse*), for which he won the 1995 SEAWrite Award. *Jao Nok Kawi* เจ้านกกวี (*The Poet Bird*) appeared in 1998, and *Tho'd Yo'd* ทอดยอด (*Sprout Out*) in 1999. His poems continue to be published nearly every week in *Siam Rath Weekly Review*.

Phaiwarin's most prominent work is certainly *Ma Kan Kluay*. Published in May 1995, it received the SEAWrite Award two months later, with the committee's citation reading, in part:

> *Ma Kan Kluay* is a collection of contemporary Thai poetry that shows the power of life and spirit of rural people who have entered the city with ambition and hope for a better life and have become an important creative force in society.[19]

During the following month, the book was reprinted six times, and by the end of 1998 (when the book had been in existence less than four years), it was in its 16th printing, a rare feat for any work of contemporary Thai literature. By contrast, Khamsing's *Fa Bo'Kan* was only in its 12th printing at the time, over four decades after its initial publication. An English translation of Phaiwarin's book, *Banana Tree Horse and Other Poems*, was published by B. Kasemsri (M.L. Birabhongse Kasemsri) in 1995.[20]

Why has *Ma Kan Kluay* been so popular? According to Naowarat Phongphaibun, SEAWrite Award-winning poet and SEAWrite Committee judge the year Phaiwarin's book was selected,

> Phaiwarin works constantly, making the quality of his work unquestionable. His *Ma Kan Kluay* particularly has a greater unity than his other books, that is, his way of thinking, direction, and presentation are arranged in stages, harmonious and compatible in substance, and he is able to use versification to serve content as he requires, which few people are able to do at this level.[21]

Phaiwarin is a highly skilled poet, in command of a myriad of Thai poetic forms, including *khlong*, *chan*, *kab*, *klo'n*, and *rai*.[22] However, his appeal

---

[19] กุหลาบ *et al.*, "คำประกาศของคณะกรรมการตัดสินรางวัลซีไรท์ประจำพุทธศักราช 2538," 2538, p. 6, in ไพวรินทร์ ขาวงาม, ม้าก้านกล้วย. กรุงเทพฯ: แพรว, 2540, pp. 6–7.

[20] The English translation tends to favor rhyme over faithfulness to tone and content. See Phaiwarin Khao-Ngam, *Banana Tree Horse and Other Poems*, trans. B. Kasemsri (Bangkok: Amarin, 1995).

[21] เนาวรัตน์ พงษ์ไพบูลย์, quoted in ไพวรินทร์, ม้า, 2540 (back cover).

[22] แพรวสำนักพิมพ์, "คำนำสำนักพิมพ์," in ไพวรินทร์, ม้า, 2540, pp. 14–5.

goes beyond mere ability. Chotchuang Nado'n, translator and *Siam Rath* editor, notes:

> After reading Phaiwarin's work, I feel that in *Ma Kan Kluay* Phaiwarin has grown (in thought) a great deal and, moreover, he represents in writing the feelings of people in society more widely. Thus, more people have come to like his poetry.[23]

Ma Kan Kluay consists of 45 poems written between 1991 and 1995, a period of unparalleled economic expansion and social change in Thailand. In a trend repeated (and magnified) from previous decades, the capital swelled with immigrants from the countryside while its skyline changed and grew almost daily.[24] Destruction, dislocation, and dissatisfaction were the inevitable accompaniments, and once again a sense of nostalgia arose among urbanites for some (mythic) pure and innocent existence in a village past. *Ma Kan Kluay* expressed these sentiments and, intentionally or not, tapped into them. Thai literature is read primarily by educated urbanites, some of whom have themselves migrated from the provinces or are the children of such migrants. Thus, *Ma Kan Kluay* struck a romanticist chord that was amplified by Phaiwarin's adept use of traditional poetic forms.

The term, *ma kan kluay*, refers to a children's toy that is ridden like a horse and made from the leaf blade of a banana tree, with part of the tree trunk as the horse's head and part of the leaf as its tail. It is a toy rarely seen anymore, certainly not in the city, yet it would be recognized or remembered by most Thais, other than perhaps the most urbanized members of the upper class. Phaiwarin's poem begins with a *ma kan kluay* made by the narrator's father, who, in the four-part opening section, represents tradition, honor,

---

[23] โชติช่วง นาดอน, quoted in ไพวรินทร์, ม้า, 2540 (inside front cover).

[24] For an extensive consideration of the theme of migration in modern Thai literature, see Ellen Boccuzzi, "Becoming Urban: Thai Literature about Rural-Urban Migration and a Society in Transition," PhD diss., University of California at Berkeley, 2007. I disagree, however, with at least two of her assertions, both of which she seems perhaps to ascribe, in part, to my own earlier work. First, she states that "much [...] 'Isan literature' was actually portraying people leaving Isan for Bangkok" (pp. 37–8); second, she claims that many Isan writers sought to represent issues of Thai villagers generally, not Isan specifically. However, as I hope this book (and my 2001 PhD thesis, on which she draws) demonstrate, the majority of Isan writers have, on the contrary, been at pains to draw attention to concerns of Isan people specifically, and to assert, and portray, the particularities of Isan in contradistinction to the rest of the country.

and steadfastness. The remainder of the poem consists of three sections. The first, "Realm of Fields," contains poems that evoke traditions of the countryside, such as rice farming and silk weaving, and the modern threats to those traditions. One piece, "*Jao Sao Bai To'ng*" เจ้าสาวใบตอง (Banana Leaf Maiden), describes the replacement of banana leaves by plastic bags for wrapping food, and wittily compares this to the supplanting of a virtuous country girl by an urban sophisticate in the affections of a fickle young man. The second section, "Realm of the City," describes the inhumanity of the city and the experience of country migrants in it. Poems in this portion speak of the loneliness and alienation of country folk (including children) living among crowds of strangers, tall buildings, traffic noise, smoke-filled air. One such piece, "*Khao Ro'ng Phleng Luk Thung Hai Meuang Fang*" เขาร้องเพลง ลูกทุ่งให้เมืองฟัง (He Sings Country Tunes to the City), incorporates the lyrics of popular country songs while playing on the Thai expression, "singing to buffalo" (*ro'ng phleng hai khwai fang*), underlining the uselessness and loneliness of singing to an unresponsive presence and living in an uncaring metropolis. In this section, as Kasien Techaphira[25] has pointed out, the city is not the opposite of the jungle; the city is the jungle.[26] Finally, the third part of *Ma Kan Kluay*, called "Any Realm," explores the human predicament in more general terms, touching on hunger, friendship, betrayal, love, pride, narrow-mindedness, etc. "*Narok Kho'ng Rao*" นรกของเรา (Our Hell) is an ironic treatment of the human tendency to rationalize and make the best of a bad situation.

Ma Kan Kluay, like much of Phaiwarin's work, is concerned with the human side of displacement and the country-city nexus. Isan plays a significant but secondary role in his writing. Some of what he talks about alludes specifically to Isan, as in his paean to silk weaving, or his use of Lao language in "*Ro'i Rai Ram Kho'ng Khao Kham Lae Phak Waen*" รอยร่ายรำ ของข้าวคำและผักแว่น (Rice Rhyme and Vegetable Verse) in Part One of *Ma Kan Kluay*. Overall, though, his words have a national resonance. His voice is in opposition to consumerism, commercialism, and materialism, providing a critique of social change without suggesting that there are necessarily any answers. Unlike many of his earlier compatriots, he appeals to sentiment and nostalgic evocation but does not necessarily demand attention to injustice and political action. Instead, themes of loss, loneliness, and alienation

---

[25] Kasien, the political scientist, social critic, and "public intellectual," frequently writes for the *Nation Weekend* on political, economic, and cultural issues.

[26] เกษียร เตชะพีระ,"จารึกร่วมสมัย," in ไพวรินทร์ ขาวงาม, 2540, pp. 137–76.

accompany his concern with the experience of those who live divided lives, part rural and part urban. Phaiwarin himself is one of them, having spent his childhood entirely in the Isan countryside but having lived thereafter primarily in cities. As he has stated, he is neither completely content with, nor completely free to ignore, either one:

> I am an Isan person who has come to live in the city and looks back at Isan ... I try to keep links, as if I were a reporter for the two worlds, the world of the village and the world of the city. When I go to the countryside, I take stories from the countryside and tell them to city people. [And] I tell stories of the city to rural people. [...] Now I feel that I am a person of many worlds, many moods. [...] Every world is distant from the others. How to link them?[27]

In Kasien's view, Phaiwarin has changed Thai poetry forever:

> *Ma Kan Kluay* has brought the Lao accent and accompanying issues, ideas, experiences, and life of Isan people into Thai poetry, changing Thai language and inscribing poetry with a mixture of Thai and Lao accents and issues, and leaving them as a monument in Thai language.[28]

Certainly Phaiwarin is not the first to introduce these things to Thai poetry, since others, like Surachai and Prasert, filled their poems with Isan words, images, and feelings 20 years before *Ma Kan Kluay*. However, Phaiwarin is perhaps the first to have such a command of the classical Thai poetic forms and use them to express experiences and concerns of Isan (and other rural) people. In his prolificness and his national and international status (at least in Southeast Asia), he brings these elements, both of Isan and of the Thai countryside generally, to prominence in the national literature.

Prachakhom Lunachai

Prachakhom Lunachai ประชาคม ลุนาชัย is perhaps the second most distinguished Isan writer of the later generation. By 1999, he had won virtually all the major Thai literary awards except the SEAWrite, for which he was a finalist twice, and his work is highly regarded by critics and other writers.

Prachakhom Lunachai (a pen name) was born in 1959 in Sai Mun District of Yasothorn Province. He finished fourth grade at the village elementary school and fifth grade in the nearby town. Thereafter, his family

---

[27] Phaiwarin, Interview, 1999.
[28] เกษียร, "จารึก," 2540, pp. 170–1.

moved to Nong Khai Province, where he completed elementary school, and then Bangkok, where he studied through the third year of secondary school. When limited resources prevented him from furthering his studies, he decided not to dwell on the disappointment, but to educate himself.[29] He worked at a wide range of jobs in the city, first in restaurants, then in factories making shoes, bread, and fish sauce.[30] At the same time, he read widely, he says, both Thai and foreign literature:

> The short stories and novels of progressive [Thai] writers, I read every one. Translations from English, from Russian, from German, or from India, from China, I bought and read every one. I liked John Steinbeck, Ernest Hemingway, like other people. I liked Lu Xun, Maxim Gorky, Anton Chekov, Fyodor Dostoyevsky. A lot of writing from India was translated into Thai. And I liked it [...] I still remember, I remember almost every book I read.[31]

Prachakhom worked on his writing constantly between 1976 and 1979, and had his first piece published in 1980,[32] a poem entitled, "*Sai Fon*" สายฝน (Falling Rain), in the women's magazine, *Satrisan*.[33] After several more poems appeared in various journals, his first short story, "*Bot Sutthai Haeng Tamnan Khon Yak*" บทสุดท้ายแห่งตำนานคนยาก (The Last Chapter of the Chronicle of the Unfortunate), was published in *Num Sao* magazine in 1982.[34] The payment for the story was 600 baht, but Prachakhom was unable to collect it because at the time he did not have a national identity card.[35] Over the next 11 years, he published a few stories in *Fa Meuang Tho'ng*; a page from one, "*Luk Reua*" ลูกเรือ (Crewman), he later discovered made into a paper bag containing sweets while he was working on one of many fishing boats that had hired him after he left Bangkok in 1983. After eight years of such work, he returned to Bangkok, and the following year, 1992, he stopped working in order to devote himself entirely to writing. Between 1993 and 1999, he published continuously, with over a hundred stories[36] appearing in

---

[29] Prachakhom Lunachai, Interview, June 24, 1999, Bangkok.

[30] ประชาคม ลุนาชัย, ฝั่งแสงจันทร์. กรุงเทพฯ: สหการคนวรรณกรรม, 2540 (inside back cover).

[31] Prachakhom, Interview, 1999.

[32] Ibid.

[33] ประชาคม ลุนาชัย, ตัวละครตกสมัย. กรุงเทพฯ: สหการคนวรรณกรรม, 2541 (inside back cover).

[34] Ibid.

[35] Ibid.

[36] Prachakhom has stated in an interview that he ceased writing poetry because it is no longer a suitable medium for what he wants to express: "My feelings aren't in poetry anymore. I think about characters, about people's behavior, which can't be communicated in the form of poetry." Prachakhom, Interview, 1999.

print, in addition to his four books: *Luk Kaew Samro'ng* ลูกแก้วสำรอง (*The Spare Glass Globe*), 1996, a collection of short stories; *Fang Saeng Jan* ฝั่งแสงจันทร์ (*The Moonlit Shore*), 1997, a novel; *Tua Lakho'n Tok Samai* ตัวละครตกสมัย (*A Character Out of Time*), 1998, a collection of short stories; and *Nattakam Haeng Chiwit* นาฏกรรมแห่งชีวิต (*The Drama of Life*), 1999, also a collection of short stories.

Prachakhom's numerous awards include the following: two awards in magazine contests for outstanding short story, one from *Lak Thai* in 1994, the other from *Chiwit To'ng Su* in 1995; three short story commendations from the Language and Book Society of Thailand (PEN International Thailand Center) in 1995, 1996, and 1997; the award for best short story in 1996, from *Cho' Karaket*; and two awards from the National Book Development Committee, for outstanding short story collection in 1997 and for outstanding novel in 1998. While Prachakhom had not yet won the SEAWrite Award by the end of the 20th century, *Fang Saeng Jan* was one of two finalists in 1997, and *Nattakam Haeng Chiwit* was on the short list of five in 1999.

Little of Prachakhom's work is explicitly about Isan. Instead, his writing reflects his wide experience in southern and central Thailand (including Bangkok), where he has spent most of his life. A notable exception to this is the short story, "*Phan Pheun Thin*" พันธุ์พื้นถิ่น (Local Breed), which appeared in his collection *Tua Lakho'n Tok Samai*. In the story, a town recognizably located in Isan (there are references to Khmer and Lao musical forms) plans a festival to attract tourists, to be held during Songkran. On the night of the staged celebration, which features Western music, many of the townspeople stay home for lack of interest, and three of the older ones spontaneously begin to play the songs that made them locally famous decades previously. Gradually, the Western tourists, bored with the lack of traditional culture being displayed in the official program, all leave the temple where the planned festival is being held and gather around the old musicians. Other villagers also gravitate toward the group. The local school teacher begins to feel pleased that his neighbors, young and old, are showing a renewed interest in their old customs, but then one of his students shatters his reverie by informing him that they are all just following after the foreigners.

The story is clearly influenced by Lao Khamhawm. The title is an allusion to "*Khon Phan*" คนพันธุ์ (called "Breeding Stock" in Domnern's translation), a story in *Fa Bo' Kan*. Several elements are common to both stories: social change, a desire for progress, villagers and their foibles, and silly decisions by those in power. The role of the Westerners is also similar in both pieces: foreigners exert strong but dubious influence on village ways while providing the pivot on which the plot turns. Furthermore, Prachakhom's story at first seems to be a predictable tale of tradition versus change, but ends with a telling, humorous, and unexpected twist. The feeling that remains with the reader at the end is nearly identical to that experienced on finishing "Breeding Stock" or other successful stories by Khamsing.

Prachakhom's novel, *Fang Saeng Jan*, is a tale of the lives of fishing boat workers in southern Thailand. Aside from the fact that many Isan people find jobs on such boats, the book has no connection to Isan. However, the book's dedication seems to be an allusion once again to Lao Khamhawm. In *Fa Bo' Kan*, Khamsing famously dedicated his book, "To my mother, who never knew the alphabet."[37] Having a mother who is illiterate is not unusual, especially among Isan writers, but Khamsing was the first to announce it, making it almost a badge of honor (and emphasizing his own achievement at the same time). Other Isan writers have since inscribed their books with similar statements, demonstrating their authentic origins among the people (particularly important during the Literature for Life era). Prachakhom, in his dedication, states, "To my mother, who wrote the tales of her seven children with her life."[38] Thus, Prachakhom honors his mother's achievements and sacrifices, rather than pointing out her inabilities and elevating himself. In this way, he acknowledges Lao Khamhawm but turns the older writer's statement around and improves upon it.

The title story in Prachakhom's collection, *Tua Lakho'n Tok Samai*, is a landmark in contemporary Thai literature, both in technique and content. Although it contains no discernible Isan elements, it nonetheless explores an issue of major relevance to Isan writing specifically and Thai literature in general: the enduring presence (for good or ill) of the Literature for Life movement and its influence on the contemporary literary scene. The story concerns a writer whose thoughts and activities are continually interrupted by the appearance of a fictional character he created, who returns to ask when the writer will put him in a story as previously promised. The writer is busy and preoccupied with other projects and other demands on his time, and thus, although he is sympathetic, keeps delaying, promising to include the character (an old man) in something soon.

The significance of the story is tied to its self-referential quality. The writer who created the character of the old man is himself a character in the story we are reading. The narrative relates the experiences of the writer and his character, who in turn create the narrative. The writer *in* the story mirrors

---

[37] ลาว คำหอม, ฟ้าบ่กั้น. กรุงเทพฯ: แพรว, 2541 p. 4.

[38] ประชาคม ลุนาชัย, ฝั่ง, 2540, p. 6.

the writer *of* the story, while the old man takes on a life of his own. When the writer goes to visit him, the old man has died yet continues to appear to the writer. Meanwhile, the old man's family struggles on in a life of poverty and adversity. Thus Prachakhom's story recognizes: 1), the enduring suffering that Literature for Life aimed to alleviate; 2), the apparent death of the movement (symbolized by the old man); and 3), the persistence of the demands of the movement in the minds of writers today. In the story, as in the real-life Thai literary sphere, the issue is not resolved. At the end of the story, the writer is still putting off the old man, trying to put him out of mind by promising to write about him at a later date. Of course, the writer has already completed a piece about the old man, in the form of the story itself. Perhaps Prachakhom is pointing out that, while writers today may try to get beyond Literature for Life, many have not been successful nor can they be until they acknowledge its persistence in their sensibilities.

Prachakhom has read widely but rejects the notion of influence from earlier writers. In the past when he read, he says, he responded only to select pieces by any given writer:

> I didn't like all of a writer's work. I liked a few stories, or a few novels. Some stories I didn't care much for. [...] Like Wat Wanlayangkul, [...] Riem Eng, or Manas Janyong: I liked some of the their stories. But they didn't really have any influence. I studied the work of older writers who created work before me. I considered it a way of studying, of learning, and they gave me inspiration. But it wasn't to the point of influence. What really had influence on me was all of the work overall. Like Literature for Life during the time after October 14. I consider this to have a lot of influence on both my thinking and my creating work at first. [...] Now the atmosphere of reading and writing, the atmosphere of the Thai literary sphere has developed in a way that is more individualistic. Does [Literature for Life] have influence? Well, it might deep down, in building social consciousness and ways of thinking. [...] It became roots, flowers, branches, leaves, of work that was created afterwards.[39]

While acknowledging the impact of Literature for Life on his work, he nonetheless dismisses suggestions that he is a Literature for Life writer. At the social gathering (described at the beginning of this chapter) that took place in Nonthaburi after the Sirikit Center panel discussion on Literature for Life, Prachakhom was given the microphone and asked to comment. In introducing him, Prida Khaobo' ปรีดา ข้าวบ่อ, a writer and editor from

---

[39] Prachakhom, Interview, 1999.

Isan who came of age during the 1970s, quoted Prachakhom as having once claimed to be "the last Literature for Life writer." On receiving the microphone, the very first thing Prachakhom said was, "I remember that I never said I was the last Literature for Life writer." Prachakhom is known for being unusually direct and not wasting time on social niceties. As this instance and others show, he consistently refuses to be classified or categorized. He is pointedly not a member of the Isan Writers' Association, nor of the Writers' Association of Thailand, as he explains:

> I live on my own. It's not that I don't want to be [a member], or that I do want to be, but there's no factor that makes me want to be. [...] I am a person who doesn't have a group, a cohort, a gang.[40]

Not surprisingly, he does not identify himself as any particular kind of writer, whether Thai, regional, Isan, Southern, or anything else, nor does he pay attention to it in others:

> I'm not interested in that. I'm interested in whether they write well: is it balanced? What are they presenting? After I finish reading it, what do I get from the writing? [...] Similarly, I'm not really interested in whether there is [such a thing as] new or contemporary Northern literature, or Southern. What I'm interested in is, when I read it do I like it? Does it have charm? Can it communicate with my feelings? Other than entertainment, when the reading is finished, does it build something new or spark new ideas for me?[41]

Prachakhom is from Isan, but his literary concerns are more generalized, more universal. His appeal goes beyond boundaries of region, and he seems certain in the coming years to continue gaining popularity, acclaim, and awards, including most likely the SEAWrite award.

Manote Phromsingh

Manote Phromsingh มาโนช พรหมสิงห์ is another highly regarded writer who has won several important awards and in the late 20th century was frequently named as being among the most promising of the new generation of Isan writers. He is less prolific than Phaiwarin or Prachakhom, and further contrasts with them in spending nearly his entire life in Isan.

Manote was born in 1956 in the provincial capital of Nakhorn Ratchasima, where he attended elementary school until 1964, when his father, a

---

[40] Ibid.
[41] Ibid.

soldier, moved the family to Warin Chamrab District of Ubon Ratchathani, where Manote completed elementary and secondary school. With his four siblings, Manote grew up speaking Lao, but with his parents he speaks Korat language. Manote attended Srinakarinwirot University in Mahasarakham (now Mahasarakham University) and narrowly escaped being killed there during the events of October 6, 1976. The following year, he was prevented from graduating on schedule by administrators at the school where he was doing his practice teaching (he was studying to be a math teacher) due to their accusations that he was stirring up students in support of the Left. Manote finally was allowed to finish his degree and graduate, nearly a year late, in 1978, whereupon he took a teaching job in Srisaket. After a year, he returned to Warin and taught eight more years, followed by another year teaching in Phitsanulok. He then quit teaching (in 1989), and thereafter spent his time writing and helping his family grow flowers, which his mother sold in the market.[42]

From an early age, Manote enjoyed books, beginning with comics, which he would narrate from his own imagination before he could read. Later, he spent so much time reading that his father felt the need to forbid it, fearing that Manote's studies would suffer.[43] As a student and aspiring writer, Manote particularly liked the work of Phibulsak Lakhornphol, Ko'n Krailat, and Assiri Thammachot:

> I liked their style of writing, and their ideas. I liked their language, which was beautiful. One thing that I have become attached to up to the present in my writing is language, which some people say is very beautiful and some say is circuitous, overly long, sluggish. But I rather like language that is beautiful.[44]

Manote was also influenced by Lao Khamhawm's *Fa Bo' Kan*. Manote attributes his early interest in literature, at least in part, to a lack of skill in socializing:

> I wasn't so good at talking. So when I was free I liked to go to the library at school. I'd eat quickly to put something in my stomach,

---

[42] Manote Phromsingh, Interview, January 17, 1999, Ubon Ratchathani.

[43] As a child, Manote also began drawing and painting, which he continues to do. He provided the illustrations for his first book, and for Fon Fafang's ฟ้าไกลจะได้ฟ้า, as well as for ฤดูดอกไม้ร่วง (*Season of Falling Flowers*), a collection of five stories by writers living in Isan, including Manote, Fon, Chaiya (see below), and Sanan and Neramit (see Chapter 7).

[44] Manote, Interview, 1999.

and then run to the library and offer to help the librarian put things in order. The librarian introduced me to books, saying, 'Mom Jao Akatdamkoeng's *Lako'n Haeng Chiwit* is good, SriBurapha is good,' and I'd go and read them. And I had special privileges helping the librarian; I could borrow books for many days.[45]

He began writing, he says, in 1977 or 1978, and published his first piece, a short story entitled, *"Nam Ta Lae Khwam Jep Puat"* น้ำตาและความเจ็บปวด (Tears and Pain), in 1978 in the periodical, *Num Sao*, which paid him 300 baht. His first poem, *"Ko'To'Meua Thoe Pen Khabot"* ก็ต่อเมื่อเธอเป็นขบท (If She Rebels), appeared in the same magazine in 1979.[46] In spite of this quick success, he did not publish another piece for 15 years.

In 1994, Manote reappeared on the literary scene with a story in *Do'k Tiw Pa*[47] and another in *Cho'Karaket*. The latter story, *"Khuk Do'k Mai"* คุกดอกไม้ (Flower Prison), won an honorable mention from the *Cho'Karaket* committee. In 1995, Manote published several more short stories, including one in *Cho'Karaket* entitled, *"Rawang Ro'y Mit"* ระหว่างรอยมีด (Between the Knife Marks), which that year won the outstanding short story award from the Language and Book Society of Thailand (PEN International Thailand Center). Among the stories he published in 1996, *"Rang Hae Haeng Wihok"* ร่างแหแห่งวิหค (Net of Birds) received the award for most popular *Cho' Karaket* story of the year.[48] This story also provided the title for Manote's first book, a collection of stories, in 1997. The following year, he again won the prize for most popular story in *Cho'Karaket*, with *"Sai Lom Bon Thanon Boran"* สายลมบนถนนโบราณ (Wind on an Ancient Road). Also in 1998, his book won the Outstanding Book Award from the National Book Development Committee of the Ministry of Education.

Although Manote has lived his life in Isan, he has not been a strongly regional writer, that is, his concerns are wider than Isan *per se*. In the 1980s, he knew Yiem Thongnoi and other Isan writers, and got together with them at times, but he did not join their group, the MRLG. The reason, he says, is that he wanted to be independent, and also that he was not very impressed with the group and its activities:

Instead of talking about topics that seemed creative, mostly they drank alcohol and were rowdy and angry. I'm quiet, not boisterous much, and

---

[45] Ibid.

[46] มาโนช พรหมสิงห์, ร่างแหแห่งวิหค. บุรีรัมย์: บ้านทุ่ง, 2540 (inside back cover).

[47] A periodical published in Surin by a rural development NGO of the same name, under the editorship of Sanan Chusakul (see Chapter 7).

[48] มาโนช, ร่างแห, 2540.

maybe seeing that, I was a bit shocked and afraid. Sometimes they may have done something substantial or useful, but I didn't see it. Or I saw it, but when I saw them relaxing, drinking, making noise, and berating each other, I trembled with fear, maybe that was the way it was. I didn't like that kind of image, I didn't want to drink and then discuss literature.[49]

Eventually, though, Manote did join the IWA:

I joined in '36 [1993], after I left teaching and farmed and wrote poetry that was published. I felt it was time to: since I didn't have a job that interfered with working on the activities of the Association, I should join in order to develop reading and writing and build activities that were useful. So I joined.[50]

By that time, he says, the members had gotten older and were less rowdy and aggressive; also, they had no problem with his not joining them in drinking alcohol. Perhaps, too, as Phisit Phusri (a writer and critic from Udorn, see below) has pointed out,[51] other writers had to acknowledge Manote, who was increasingly being published in respected periodicals (like *Cho' Karaket*) and winning awards. In any case, though Manote at times has participated in IWA activities, he has not felt the need to fill his work with what have been the standard subjects of Isan writing. For example, while at one time he was interested in Literature for Life, the movement has had no discernible bearing on his later work.

Most of his stories, including "Flower Prison" and "Between the Knife Marks," have little or no connection to Isan, and are not concerned with social injustice or political change. Rather than adhering to a strict realism, they take place largely in the minds of the characters. The action or events that occur are merely triggers that evoke people's rich inner lives. The characters are often melancholy and alone, facing the world and their place in it with an injured and uncomprehending doggedness and trying to cling to some beauty or goodness even in circumstances of adversity. In several stories, the main character's past (and defining experiences) are gradually made plain to the reader as the story progresses. Flowers often serve a redemptive purpose in these stories, giving some measure of meaning and hope to lives made forlorn by fate.

"Net of Birds" shows these characteristics, too, but it also contains minor elements that clearly locate it in Isan: a Lao word in the dialogue, a

---

[49] Manote, Interview, 1999.
[50] Ibid.
[51] Phisit Phusri, Interview, January 17, 1999, Ubon Ratchathani.

Lao musical instrument (the *khaen*) in one scene, Lao food in the plot. The story concerns a doctor, married and with a newborn son, who is coming to terms with his adult responsibilities. Once again, the substance of the story occurs in the mind of the main character, in this case the doctor, as he reflects on his life. The dialogue is secondary to, almost obscuring or at odds with, the inner thoughts and internal monologue of the protagonist. The language of the story is descriptive and evocative. The use of Lao is subtle and carefully chosen, adding dimension without drawing attention to Isan merely for its own sake, as some more regionalist writers do. In Manote's words,

> I feel that I am a Thai writer, but as I live in Isan I ought to reflect something about Isan. [...] If you live in Isan, you reflect the feelings that you experience; the environment that you're in is reflected in your work.[52]

By 1999, however, Manote was making Isan a more central focus of his work. The story, "Wind on an Ancient Road," which takes place in the distant past, concerns ill-fated love between a Lao man and a Khmer woman. It contains a number of elements specific to Southern Isan, including the *sanu* kite, which makes a certain singing sound as it flies in the wind and provides a kind of threnody accompanying the plot. The characters in the story are Lao, Khmer, and Kui, and songs and poetry that appear in the plot are quoted in these languages. The Lao characters conduct an ancient ceremony, the *ram phi fa*, which paid homage to *phaya thaen*, or traditional Tai spirits. Manote obtained details of the ceremony from a Masters' thesis at Mahasarakham University.[53] Such research was by 1999 becoming increasingly important for his work:

> In my current book, [...] I depend a fair amount on textbooks. Prinya Phinthong, who is the son of Dr. Preecha Phinthong, who they call 'the sage of Ubon,' started a publishing house to produce his father's books. I know him, and he gave me books with knowledge about [traditional Isan culture]. [...] I think the things that Isan has, whether culture or way of life, [used] in this way, in short stories like this: no one has done it yet. So I should do it. Because doing things that no one has presented before is creating another way.[54]

---

[52] Ibid.
[53] Ibid.
[54] Ibid.

According to Phisit, such efforts gave Manote significant standing:

> I see Manote as perhaps the only one [among current Isan writers] who is outstanding. Not in terms of a mood of nostalgia, but in bringing local people and folk traditions [into his work] and using them in a modern way. [...] What Manote is doing is trying to make present-day people aware of their roots, [which he does] by researching in a scholarly way, not just by using nostalgia.[55]

Suchart further commended Manote's achievements, noting, "If you look at stories like those of Manote, he has characteristics of *tho'ngthin*, but people from other regions who read his work accept that it is a story of their own, too."[56]

Thus Manote's work, though intended for a general Thai audience, has covered a range of subject matter, at times using the products of Isan Studies in order to produce historically accurate context for the psychological exploration that has been his primary interest. His simultaneous concern with the regional and the universal have made him an Isan writer with a national presence.

Phisit Phusri

Phisit Phusri พิสิฐ ภูศรี is a writer and critic of the younger generation living in Udorn. By 1999, he was writing full-time, publishing widely, and often cited as one of the most promising of Isan authors, a skilled writer who continued to improve and impress.

Phisit was born in 1965 in Udorn Thani,[57] where he completed primary and secondary school. He studied art at the Northeast Ratchamongkhol Institute in Nakhorn Ratchasima, after which he worked in Bangkok as a designer, art director, and production manager. Following the events of Black May, 1992, he became interested in being a writer, and practiced over the next two years.[58] His first piece, a short story called "*Kamalaisechan*" กามาไลเซชั่น (or "Kamalization," a play on the word "globalization" and meaning something like "Global Sexualization"), was published in *Writer* magazine in 1994.[59] In 1996, he won two awards from the PEN International

---

[55] Phisit, Interview, 1999.

[56] Suchart Sawatsri, Interview, June 23, 1999, Bangkok.

[57] วิวัฒน์, ed., นักเขียน, 2542a.

[58] พิสิฐ ภูศรี, สัตว์แปลกหน้า. กรุงเทพฯ: ดอกหญ้า, 2539 (inside front cover).

[59] วิวัฒน์, ed., นักเขียน, 2542a.

Thailand Center: a commendation for his story, "*Nak Tak Akat*" นักตากอากาศ (The Rambler), and an Outstanding Short Story Award for "*Khon So Nai Prasat*" คนโซในปราสาท (The Starved in the Castle). That same year, Phisit published his first book, *Sat Plaek Na* สัตว์แปลกหน้า (*Animal Stranger*), a collection of short stories. In 1997, he received a *Cho' Karaket* honorable mention for his story, "*Khu Rak — Khu Ruay*" คู่รัก — คู่รวย (Partner in Love — Partner in Luxury), and the Supha Thewakul Award for another story, "*Maew Mae Luk O'n*" แมวแม่ลูกอ่อน (The Mother of Kittens).[60] Phisit's first novel, *Chai Chana* ชัยชนะ (*Victory*), was also selected for the Supha Thewakul Award when it appeared in 1998. In 1999, Phisit published another collection, which included the award-winning story after which it was named, "*Khon So Nai Prasat*"; the collection was one of seven on the shortlist for that year's SEAWrite Award. At the end of the 20th century, in addition to fiction, Phisit was regularly publishing criticism in *Cho' Karaket* (until its closure), the *Nation Weekend*, the Sunday literature section of *Krungthep Thurakit*, and other periodicals.

After the events of Black May, Phisit moved out of Bangkok and returned to Udorn to write. However, he did not seek to become an Isan writer in the image of those who had preceded him. While acknowledging the influence of the values (rather than the work) of the older generation, he is critical of contemporary writers who, unthinkingly or simply for the sake of nostalgia, follow trends set in previous decades and write about an Isan that no longer exists. As he has stated,

> My work previously was all about Isan problems, but modern Isan problems. [...] Saying that people who write like Khamsing are Isan writers is not the main issue, I think. It's just showing a picture of Isan, which anyone can write. And it's a picture that isn't true, either. Some people write about leading buffalo to plow the fields, [but] in Isan now, nowhere are there buffalo anymore. They're nearly gone. Some people still write about getting up in the morning to take the buffalo to plow. In my mother's village, there aren't any buffalo. They raise cows. When they plow, they use tractors.[61]

Such imitative writers, he says, are "showing the same film and just changing the voices and the actors."[62]

---

[60] วิวัฒน์, ed., นักเขียน, 2542a.

[61] Phisit, Interview, 1999.

[62] Ibid.

In fact, Phisit has rejected the whole notion of "Isan writers":

The term 'Isan writers' that people talk about is a term that does not exist in the dictionary. And there is no way to combine or compound [the words] because they have no connection to each other of any kind.[63]

His attempt to dismiss the term, "Isan writer," it turns out, mirrors an objection to the stereotypes that are connected to it: stereotypes of Isan people as lazy, dull-witted, and unsophisticated, and of Isan writers as repetitive, boring, and plain.[64] Contemporary Isan writers find themselves in a bind, as Phisit insightfully points out:

What can we do? When we write about aridity, about problems of farmers, [people] say that we are repetitious and monotonous; when we write about something else, they say we are mavericks.[65]

Nonetheless, Phisit's work at the end of the 1990s was not about Isan, but was instead concerned with wider issues of more general pertinence to Thailand (including Isan). For example, the stories, "*Khon Tak Akat*" and "*Khu Rak — Khu Ruay*"[66] deal with matters of contemporary society, such as wealth, status, capitalism, integrity, and freedom, and their role in the lives of individuals. Phisit's skill and his interest in going beyond regional considerations perhaps have played a role in the positive critical reception that he has enjoyed.

Chatchawal Khotsongkhram

Chatchawal Khotsongkhram ชัชวาลย์ โคตสงคราม is the youngest of the new generation of Isan writers who by 1999 had gained a significant measure of recognition through their writing.

Born in a Phu Thai village in No'ng Pho'k District of Roi Et Province in 1968, Chatchawal completed his primary and secondary education near his home. He then played in a band called "*Kaen Isan*" (Isan Axis) for a time before attending the Ratchabhat Institute (now University) in Mahasarakham, where he graduated with a degree in Thai. After working

---

[63] พิสิฐ ภูศรี, "นักเขียนระดับภาค," 2542, pp. 17–8, in จดหมายข่าวสโมสรนักเขียนภาคอีสาน 2, 7 (ก.ย.–ต.ค. 2539): 17–9.

[64] Ibid.

[65] Ibid., p. 18.

[66] The title of this story was changed to โรแมนติกตาย (Romantic to Death) for its inclusion in *Khon So Nai Prasat*.

as a proofreader for *Siam Rath* newspaper in Bangkok, he left to become a teacher in Roi Et Province.[67]

Chatchawal's interest in writing began at an early age when he attended a panel discussion put on at his school by members of the Mun River Literary Group.[68] He published his first story, *"Num Khon Puay"* หนุ่มคนป่วย (The Ill Young Man), in *Praew* magazine in 1991. The same year, his story, *"Jao Nok Krajip"* เจ้านกกระจิบ (the title refers to the name of the main character), received an honorable mention from *Cho' Karaket*. Chatchawal's first book, a collection of short stories entitled, *Meuan Rot Fai Ja Ma* เหมือนรถไฟจะมา (*As If a Train Were Coming*), was published in 1994. Thereafter, he continued to write and publish short stories exclusively. His second book appeared in 1999 under the title, *Chao Na Phu Prasop Phai* ชาวนาผู้ประสบภัย (*Imperiled Farmers*).

"Jao Nok Krajip" tells the story of a young woman in Isan whose mother tries to dissuade her from marrying a *mo' lam* who lives on the other side of the nearby river (probably in Laos, although this is never explicitly stated). There is little use of Lao language, but otherwise the story is steeped in Isan Lao culture and laden with symbolism. The main character, Nok Krajip, rejects suitors from the city, while her mother tells her not to cross the river. In the end, Nok Krajip learns of her mother's loneliness in being married to Nok Krajip's father, who is also a *mo' lam*. Another story in *Meuan Rot Fai Ja Ma*, *"Lang Songkhram"* หลังสงคราม (After the War), also deals with the unhappiness of a cross-river marriage, but in this case the Mekong River is referred to explicitly, using its Lao name, *Nam Kho'ng* น้ำของ, rather than the Thai term, *Mae Khong* แม่โขง. Chatchawal's stories give the sense that the world consists entirely of Isan and nearby Laos. There is little indication of a non-Lao world beyond, no acknowledgement of central Thailand. His writing makes the point that Isan has its own validity, that it is not a poorer, lesser adjunct to the rest of the country. Central Thailand simply does not exist for the characters in his work; they have their own cares, their own lives, their own world.

Chatchawal is a member of the Phu Thai ethnic group, who came to Northeast Thailand from Laos in the early 19th century. They lived semi-autonomously until forced under the administrative control of King Chulalongkorn around 1900.[69] Phu Thai language, though closer to Lao than

---

[67] ชัชวาลย์ โคตสงคราม, เหมือนรถไฟจะมา. กรุงเทพฯ: แพรว, 2537 (inside back cover).

[68] Ibid.

[69] William Smalley, *Linguistic Diversity and National Unity: Language Ecology in Thailand* (Chicago, IL: University of Chicago, 1994).

Thai, is a separate language from both, and its use remains strong among the roughly 100,000 Phu Thai people in Thailand.[70] Chatchawal has lived in Phu Thai areas of Roi Et, Yasothorn, and Mukdahan, and although he rarely uses the word, "Phu Thai," in his writing, he clearly has strong feelings about the importance of maintaining Phu Thai tradition and culture. In the 1994 "Author's Foreword" to his first book, Chatchawal states, "I write in the name of the value of ethnicity [...] not of nationality."[71] He describes himself as being, "between the old and the new,"[72] and further declares, "I firmly believe in the original value of the gentle era that has just passed, and agree with the attempt to build a new cultural consciousness."[73] He sees deep social problems related to capitalism, materialism, and the misuse of power, noting that, "We have fallen under a process of development which on the outside appears beautiful but on the inside is rotten."[74] In response to this, he maintains faith in literature, he says:

> I believe strongly in the power of literature, and the legitimacy of the force of writing. [...] Writing in order to communicate our mind's meaning remains something that we should not overlook, as long as our society still has such bad signs and occurrences due to the effects of the central state power structure distorting history and developing a standard of living that intentionally neglects the foundations of culture.[75]

Thus Chatchawal clearly sees and acutely feels the loss of traditional culture and ways of life that result from the central government's narrow pursuit of progress. These are the convictions that have informed his thoughts and his work in his continuing development as an Isan writer.

Somneuk Phanitchakij

Somneuk Phanitchakij สมนึก พานิชกิจ is one of a very small number of 20th-century women Isan writers, for some years writing essays, non-fiction, short stories, and children's books, and maintaining a strong connection to traditional Isan culture.

Somneuk was born in 1949 in Samrong District of Ubon Ratchathani Province. She grew up speaking Lao with her family in Ubon, where her

---

[70] Ibid.
[71] ชัชวาลย์ โคตสงคราม, "คำนำผู้เขียน," 2537a, pp. 14–5, in ชัชวาลย์, เหมือนรถไฟ, pp. 12–5.
[72] Ibid., p. 12.
[73] Ibid., p. 14.
[74] Ibid.
[75] Ibid.

father was a teacher. She enjoyed listening to and studying *mo' lam* until her father forbade it, and thereafter continued to gather stories from her mother's elder sister, a practicing *mo' lam*. After finishing primary and secondary school, Somneuk attended Ratchabhat Institute (now University) in Ubon, where she graduated with a degree in Library Science. In 1999, she was teaching sixth grade in Ubon.[76]

Somneuk began writing seriously in the early 1980s when she returned to school to study contemporary literature, having already married and had children Although she had been writing for some years, she had not attempted to publish her work. Her first publication was a short story that appeared in the women's monthly, *Satrisan*, in 1983. Thereafter, she produced essays and non-fiction articles, but she changed her focus to writing children's books after attending a seminar on the subject.[77] Many of these books, such as *Nithan Pheun Ban Isan* นิทานพื้นบ้านอีสาน (*Isan Folk Tales*), concern Isan topics, and several received awards from the National Book Week Fair.[78] Among her favorite writers were Thommayanti, Wanich Jarungkitanan, and, in translation, Isaac Asimov and O. Henry. She also admired the work of her friend, Somkhit Singsong, who inspired her to write an essay entitled, *"Kho'y ... Pen Khon Isan"*[79] ข้อย ... เป็นคนอีสาน (I ... Am an Isan Person), in which she explains the use of the Lao word *"kho'y"* for "I" and discusses other aspects of Lao Isan language and culture. Her two most frequent pen names are "Euay Nang" เอื้อยนาง (*"euay"* being the Lao word for "older sister") and "Phraewa Phanitchakij" แพรวา พานิชกิจ (*phraewa* being the traditional Phu Thai silk shawl mentioned in Chapter 1).

Much of Somneuk's writing is more reportive than inventive, that is, she has often taken tales and cultural practices from Lao tradition and adapted them for a Thai audience. For example, her essay, "I ... Am an Isan Person,"[80] explains aspects of Isan language and culture, as mentioned above. Her article, *"K. Kai K. Ka"*[81] (C is for Chicken, C is for Crow),

---

[76] Somneuk Phanitchakij, Interview, March 28, 1999, Ubon Ratchathani.

[77] Ibid.

[78] วิวัฒน์, ed., นักเขียน, 2542a.

[79] This essay was published in *Kulasatri* and again in the teachers' publication, *Warasan Pheuan Khru Ubon*. It was written in response to Somkhit's article in *Krungthep Thurakit* entitled "กูเป็นคนอีสาน," in which he expresses pride in his Isan origins.

[80] สมนึก พานิชกิจ, "ข้อย ... เป็นคนอีสาน," กุลสตรี ก.พ. (2540): 160–3.

[81] แพรวา พานิชกิจ, "ก ไก่ ก กา," ศิลปวัฒนธรรม 9, 16 (ก.ค. 2538): 224–5.

is a description of the Lao writing system. *"Songsan Mo' Khaen"*[82] (Pity the *Khaen* Player) discusses the role of *khaen* players and their gradual disappearance in *mo' lam* music. *Mo' Du* หมอดู (Fortune Teller), is a compilation of traditional Lao astrological knowledge "from ancient Isan texts," as its cover states. Somneuk's book, *Nithan Pheun Ban Isan*[83] (*Isan Folk Tales*) (referred to above), retells 18 Lao folktales in condensed Thai versions for young readers. Thus, it is evident that Somneuk has been most interested in acting as an intermediary, drawing on her broad knowledge of Isan Lao literary and cultural traditions and conveying them in a comprehensible form to Thai (including Isan) readers in order to expand people's awareness and appreciation of Isan.

Although at the end of the 20th century, Somneuk was a member of both the Isan Writers' Association and the Writers' Association of Thailand, she rarely attended meetings and generally worked by herself. Isan played a role in nearly all her writing, she said.[84] At the very least, Isan provided the setting, and she was increasingly using Lao language as well, except in the case of her children's books, where there was pressure from publishers to use Central Thai. Somneuk ranked Khamphun, Khamsing, Somkhit, Fon, and Phaiwarin among significant Isan writers, but felt that the most important ones have remained anonymous, such as the author of *Siow Sawat* and other traditional Lao tales. She enjoyed this classical literature, she said, and was able to quote *Khu Lu Nang Ua* from memory. She believed her ancestors were *phibun phibap*, spiritual figures who led millenialist revolts against central Thai authority. The pride and pleasure she has taken in traditional Lao culture has inspired her to emphasize aspects of Isan that differ from what has been chosen by many other Isan writers, especially of her generation or older. As she has stated:

> I don't write about the suffering of Isan. We have fruit trees and fun.
> It's dry in the dry season, but there are still frogs in the cracked mud,
> crickets, etc. It's not just pain and suffering all the time … I don't feel a
> part of those who write about drought and dryness all the time, maybe
> because here we're different. We're close to rivers and so on, not like
> *Thung Kula.*[85]

---

[82] เอื้อยนาง, "สงสารหมอแคน," กรุงเทพธุรกิจ 9 พ.ค. 2540, pp. 10–1.

[83] เอื้อยนาง และ วาสนา, นิทานพื้นบ้านอีสาน. กรุงเทพฯ: ชมรมเด็ก, 2539.

[84] Somneuk, Interview, 1999.

[85] Somneuk, Interview, 1999. *Thung Kula* is the Kula region of south-central Isan, known for its lack of water and harsh living conditions.

Why are there so few women Isan writers? Previously in Isan, only monks (men) were educated and could write, and Somneuk felt that the current lack of women writers was a legacy from that time. Innovative writers tend to be men who think freely and do not bow to society's pressures and norms, she said, whereas women might write but do not allow others to see their work. For example, many of her friends wrote but did not send their writing to be published, and for this reason, she noted, "they don't develop."[86] As she stated:

> To be a writer, one has to have experience, and to read a lot. When I was young, my father didn't allow me to read much. He was afraid it would spoil my innocence. Later I could read what I wanted. But now children are more free.[87]

In 1999, Somneuk was aware of only two other women writers in the IWA, neither of whom wrote creative literature: Sumali Phophayak, a journalist, and Jaruwan Thammawat, an academic. Somneuk herself, though having published widely and successfully, did not refer to herself as a writer. "I am a teacher," she said. "Writing is my hobby."[88]

Raks Mananya

Raks Mananya รักษ์ มนัญญา is an Isan writer who in 1999 was also the senior editor at a major Bangkok publisher. Isan was always significant in his personal life, but waned in importance in his writing, and remained separate from his professional role as an editor.

Raks Mananya is the pen name of Thongsuk Somthep. He was born in 1957 in Phibulmangsahan District of Ubon Ratchathani Province, and grew up speaking Lao in a rural village without electricity or running water, a two-hour boat ride from the nearest town. After finishing elementary school in his village, he attended secondary school in town and then went to Bangkok in 1975 to study at Ramkhamhaeng University. There he became interested in politics and social issues, and then in literature, and he began to make friends with other writers. Although he studied law, Raks spent most of his time at school in the library working on his writing. After October 6, 1976, when many of his friends had gone into the jungle, Raks continued to write,

---

[86] Ibid.
[87] Ibid.
[88] Ibid.

particularly poetry, influenced by the politics and events of the time. He read and was impressed with the work of SriBurapha, Seni Saowaphong, Lao Khamhawm, Malai Chuphinit, and Manas Janyong. Then, around 1981, Raks stopped writing and did not resume until a decade later, when the events of Black May, 1992, occurred.[89] Thereafter, his poetry, essays, and short stories appeared in a wide variety of periodicals. In the 1990s, he published three books of short stories: *Rawang Kan Doen Thang* ระหว่างการเดินทาง (*Along the Way*) in 1992, which received a commendation from the National Committee to Develop Books; *Kem Wisaman* เกมวิสามัญ (*Extraordinary Games*) in 1994; and *Siang Satho'n Kho'ng Khwam Ruseuk* เสียงสะท้อนของความรู้สึก (*Feeling's Reflective Sound*) in 1996. His novel, *Fa Thang Tan* ฝ่าทางตัน (*Surmounting a Dead End*), appeared in 1999.

In the 1970s, when Raks was first writing, his work did not have any obvious connection with Isan, nor did his friends know he was from that region. Soon, though, he says, when he began writing short stories and the majority of them were concerned with Isan issues, he was seen to be an Isan writer. As he says:

> Early on in my writing, there was a strong local trend. But when I came to be working at a certain level, I wanted to be a writer who wasn't limited to a single region, to have more universality. […] So in the work that came afterwards, I took problems from a wider source. […] Even if I took an issue from the region, I tried to expand it to be a problem of the majority, of the center, not individually of the region.[90]

Living in Bangkok brought about changes in his awareness and point of view, which were reflected in his work. In his words:

> A writer who grows up in Isan has direct experience of regionality. But if that writer comes to live in the center, his regionalism, or the problems of the region that he is aware of, decreases. And he knows more about Central problems. This is an observation I've made of others, and of myself.[91]

If such a writer then continues to write about situations in the region, the product will seem contrived, he felt. Thus Isan has little presence in his more recent writing. For example, "*Lokiyawithi*" โลกิยวิถี (The Mundane Path), a long poem he published in a dozen weekly installments in *Than Sapdawijan*

---

[89] Raks Mananya, Interview, May 28, 1999, Bangkok.
[90] Raks, Interview, 1999.
[91] Ibid.

between November 1998 and January 1999, is concerned with metaphysical and spiritual questions related to life, death, and merit. Similarly, in his novel, *Fa Thang Tan*, which involves an attempted land purchase, the land in question is in Ubon, but its location is secondary in importance to the author's exploration of wider issues related to land speculation, materialism, and greed.[92]

Raks in 1999 was managing editor at Dok Ya publishing house. He explained clearly that in making decisions about what authors to publish, he considered only literary quality, not the writers' origins:

> When it comes to doing the work of an editor, I cut out the word, 'locality'. If the writer writes a good story, with good issues and everything, it doesn't matter where they come from. [...] Everyone has the same chance. [...] It's not limited by region.[93]

In the past, Raks noted, some Isan writers sent their work to him perhaps hoping that he might help them publish because of his shared origins with them. However, he discouraged such attempts, making it plain to them that, "I work here in the Center, as a Central person. If your work is good, I'm not interested in what region you come from."[94] Previously Dok Ya published works by Somkhit Singsong, Sangkhom Phesatchmala (see below), and Chaiya Wannasri (see below), but in 1999 Raks himself and Phisit were the only two Isan writers whose books the company published.

Raks gained a wide perspective on contemporary Thai (including Isan) writers through his position as an editor. At the end of the 20th century, he felt that the Isan writers of the current generation whose work was of particular interest and who showed the most promise for the future were Manote Phromsingh, Prachakhom Lunachai, Phisit Phusri, and possibly Chaiya Wannasri. These writers, he said, were likely to "create work that has a new Isan identity."[95]

Sangkhom Phesatchmala

Sangkhom Phesatchmala สังคม เภสัชมาลา joined the Mun River Literary Group in its early period and subsequently continued his involvement with the IWA. His writing consistently treats Isan themes and subjects.

---

[92] ดอกไม้ดำ, "ฟ้าทางตัน," กรุงเทพธุรกิจ 12, 3769 (17 ม.ค. 2542), จุดประกายวรรณกรรม, p. 2.
[93] Raks, Interview, 1999.
[94] Ibid.
[95] Ibid.

Sangkhom was born in 1957 in Manjakhiri District of Khon Kaen Province. After completing the fourth year of elementary school, he was ordained and remained a novice until the age of 17. He then worked a variety of jobs in different places until he turned 21 and was able to be ordained as a monk.[96] His interest in literature began early on, but he did not publish his first short story until 1985, by which time he had already left the monkhood. That story, entitled *"Khru Roniow"* ครูโรเนียว (Roneo Teacher), appeared in the "They Started Here" column of Ajin Banjaphan's *Fa Meuang Thai* magazine, under the pen name, Do'n Jaibum ดอน ใจบุ้ม. Thereafter, his essays, short stories, and a serialized novel appeared in a wide variety of periodicals, including *Fa Meuang Tho'ng*, *Sakun Thai*, and *Matichon Weekend*.[97] His friend Wongdeuan Thongjiow (see below) encouraged him in his writing and brought him into the MRLG in about 1986. Thereafter, Sangkhom participated in many activities of the MRLG and then the IWA, and served as the IWA secretary.[98]

Sangkhom received two awards in 1989: first prize for short stories from the Travelling Literary Fair, and third prize in the October Short Story Contest of the Federation of University Students of Thailand. In 1994, he published two novels, *Rong Rien Nai Phu* โรงเรียนในภู (*School in the Mountains*), and *Huat Hang* หวดฮ้าง (*The Abandoned Rice Steamer*). The title of the latter novel is in Lao, using the word *huat*, which refers to a bamboo rice steamer, and *hang* (cognate with the Thai word *rang* ร้าง), meaning "abandoned, deserted, vacant"; this book is one of the few in Thai literature to bear a Lao title.[99] Like Sangkhom's other books, it has not sold well. In 1995, he published two more books: *Nai Thung Pliow* ในทุ่งเปลี่ยว (*In Remote Fields*), a collection of short stories; and *Ban Rong Si* บ้านโรงสี (*Mill Village*), another novel. At the end of the 20th century, he was teaching at a small school in Chaiyaphum Province, and his short stories appeared most often in the *Nation Weekend*.

Isan plays an essential role in Sangkhom's identity and in his work. In the foreword to *Ban Rong Si*, he declares, "I am an Isan person and a citizen of this country"; he then invites the reader to "open the curtain" (a common opening line used by *mo'lam* singers) and see *"mu hao"* (Lao for

---

[96] สังคม เภสัชมาลา, ในทุ่งเปลี่ยว. กรุงเทพฯ: ดอกหญ้า, 2538a (inside front cover).

[97] Anon., "สังคม เภสัชมาลา," 2530b. ถนนหนังสือ 5, 4 (ต.ค. 2540): 48.

[98] สังคม, ในทุ่ง, 2538a.

[99] The first was Lao Khamhawm's ฟ้าบ่กั้น; Prasert Jandam published two others, คือเก่า and หมู่บ้านเฮา.

"our friends") in Mill Village.[100] One of his goals in writing is to impart an appreciation of Isan people and their lives to city dwellers. He states:

> If you [the reader] come to love and understand the straightforward and foolish ways of life of Isan people who are dispersed in every corner of various large cities, I will consider my dream more than half fulfilled.[101]

Sangkhom's stories are generally set in rural Isan, and incorporate familiar elements of the region. In *"Nai Thung Pliow,"* for example, an old man is left alone by his relatives in a remote hut in the rice fields during the dry season. His only companions are a family of chickens and some children from the next village who come to play practical jokes on him. When an unseasonable storm blows in, the old man dies of exposure. The images and themes of abandoned old people, searing heat, lack of water, callousness to suffering, and lonely or meaningless death are by now all too common in Isan writing. Indeed, Sangkhom views Isan as a rather bleak and static place when he states, "Up to today, nothing much has changed in the lives of Isan people; not only that, they continue to suffer decline unendingly."[102] Such sentiment harks back to Literature for Life attitudes in the 1970s and early 1980s. If Sangkhom's books have not been particularly successful, perhaps readers find them overly conventional or unoriginal. Sangkhom responds to such criticism, stating:

> All of my short stories are somewhat repetitious and repetitive, but what am I going to do when the people around me are ceaselessly repetitive? They are still treading the same old path, still subject to the control of the powerful, still being led by the words and wealth of politicians without end. And they have still never received sympathy from any civil servant at all. This is what I've seen, so this is what I write.[103]

Wongdeuan Thongjiow

Wongdeuan Thongjiow วงเดือน ทองเจียว joined the MRLG soon after it was founded and thereafter consistently participated in its activities and those of

---

[100] สังคม เภสัชมาลา, "คำนำผู้เขียน," 2538c (no page number), in บ้านโรงสี. กรุงเทพฯ: ดอกหญ้า, 2538d.

[101] สังคม เภสัชมาลา, "คำนำผู้เขียน," 2538e, p. 8, in หวดฮ้าง. กรุงเทพฯ: ดอกหญ้า, 2538f, pp. 7–8.

[102] Ibid.

[103] สังคม เภสัชมาลา, "คำนำผู้เขียน," 2538b, in สังคม, ในทุ่ง, 2538a , p. 6.

the IWA. He has a large body of published work extending over more than two decades, but has not gained proportionately wide popularity.

Wongdeuan was born in Yasothorn Province in 1957. His father was a woodcarver, and Wongdeuan learned the trade alongside him, carving oxcarts, temple doors, etc. Until the 1990s, however, Wongdeuan's principal occupation was teaching elementary school, which he did for 12 years in Yasothorn and five years in Kanchanaburi. During this time, he was continuing his studies as well, and in 1992 he received a BA degree from Sukhothai Thammathirat University. He then made his living in art, woodcarving, and writing, and resided in Suphanburi with his family.

Wongdeuan's first publication, a piece entitled, "*Chan Rak Mu Ban*" ฉันรักหมู่บ้าน (I Love My Village), appeared in *Fa Meuang Thai* in 1979. In 1982, he received an award from Srinakharinwirot University in Mahasarakham (now Mahasarakham University) for his short story, "*Wan Dek*" วันเด็ก (Children's Day). In 1984, he won two awards, one from *Praew* magazine for his short story, "*Pang Tai*" ปางตาย (Close to Death), and the other for his serialized novel, *Nithan Phaen Din* นิทานแผ่นดิน (*Tales of the Realm*), from the Patriotic Youth Association of Thailand, Office of the Prime Minister.[104] That same year, he published his first book, *Luk Chang Kae Salak* ลูกช่างแกะสลัก (*Woodcarver's Child*), a collection of short stories. In the following 15 years, he produced seven more books, six of which are novels and short story collections. The other, *Chang Salak Mai* ช่างสลักไม้ (*The Woodcarver*), is described on its cover as, "a sculpture of thoughts and reflections of life and soul."[105]

Chang Salak Mai was published in 1998 and reviewed in *Krungthep Thurakit* later that year.[106] It consists of the musings and experiences of a woodcarver from Isan who goes to an island in the Andaman Sea with his brother and a senior woodcarver to undertake a large project for a temple and its patron. According to the reviewer, who used the pen name "Wijan," Wongdeuan's writing in general until then had been improving:

> I feel that it is stronger and more powerful. His short stories especially have a point of view and a way of thinking from old traditions that bring new awareness, and an Eastern philosophical quality.[107]

---

[104] วิวัฒน์, ed., นักเขียน, 2542a.

[105] วงเดือน ทองเจียว, ช่างสลักไม้. กรุงเทพฯ: ประพันธ์สาส์น, 2541 (front cover).

[106] วิจารณ์ สนามจันทร์,"'ช่างสลักไม้' อธิบายโลกและชีวิตด้วยทฤษฎีความสับสน," กรุงเทพธุรกิจ 12, 3742 (20 ธ.ค. 2541), จุดประกายวรรณกรรม, p. 3.

[107] Ibid.

However, Wijan was disappointed with *Chang Salak Mai* and roundly criticized it, saying, "It [...] is full of confusion, lacks unity and clarity, and I don't know what kind of literature to call it."[108] While the book may not be a success, it does represent an attempt by Wongdeuan to strike out in a new direction and create something innovative. The critical reaction it received would seem to support the comment, made by Phisit (quoted above), that when Isan writers try something new or unconventional, their work is criticized and rejected. Unfortunately, such criticism seems to have had a negative impact on Wongdeuan, causing him to step back into a familiar sanctuary of Isan literature. His subsequent book, a collection of short stories published in 1999 under the title, *Thang Jao Sadet* ทางเจ้าเสด็จ (*The Royal Way*), bears on its cover the designation, "Literature for Life."[109]

Siowjan Raemphrai

Siowjan Raemphrai เสี่ยวจันทร์ แรมไพร is a younger generation writer from Isan who initially associated himself with Isan writing (he joined the MRLG in its early stages) but later effectively erased Isan from his work and identity.

Siowjan was born Kanok Sangimtho'ng in Nong Khrok Village in Srisaket Province in 1962, the only boy among six children. His mother was a teacher and his father a civil servant.[110] After completing elementary school near his home, he moved away from his village permanently, attending secondary school in Khon Kaen[111] and eventually graduating from Ramkhamhaeng University in 1987 with a degree in humanities. Thereafter, he worked for *Lalana* and other publications, including his own printing house, *Rupjan* รูปจันทร์, which he ran in Bangkok with another young Isan writer, Pornchai Saenyamun.[112] In 1990, he published his first book, a collection of poetry called *Ho'ng Mai Mi Saeng Daed* ห้องไม่มีแสงแดด (*Room without Sunlight*). The following year, his second book, also a collection of poetry, appeared under the title, *Anakhet Haeng Khwam Fan* อาณาเขตแห่งความฝัน (*Territory of Dreams*). Two books of short stories, *Lok Chapo'* โลกเฉพาะ (*Particular World*) and *Khap Khan Khang Nai* ขับขานข้างใน

---

[108] Ibid.

[109] วงเดือน ทองเจียว, ทางเจ้าเสด็จ. กรุงเทพฯ: ประพันธ์สาส์น, 2542 (front cover).

[110] เสี่ยวจันทร์ แรมไพร, ขับขานข้างใน. นนทบุรี: บ้านหนังสือ, 2536a (inside front cover).

[111] วชิระ บัวสนธ์,"บรรณาธิการสนทนา," in เสี่ยวจันทร์ แรมไพร, 2536b. โลกเฉพาะ. ธนบุรี: นกสีเหลือง, pp. 6–10.

[112] สัญภูมิ ละออ, "เสี่ยวจันทร์ แรมไพร กับ 'กุดจี่' เจ้าหนี้ผู้ยากไร้," กรุงเทพธุรกิจ 12, 3867 (25 เม.ย. 2542), จุดประกายวรรณกรรม, p. 8.

(*Chanting Inside*), were published in 1993. His story, "*Wan Neung Kho'ng Chiwit*" วันหนึ่งของชีวิต (A Day of Life), won honorable mention from *Cho' Karaket* in 1992 and was reprinted in *Lok Chapo'*.

Siowjan used the pen name Thongkhram Phudetkla ทองคร้าม ภูเดชกล้า until 1982, when he changed it to Siowjan Raemphrai. By early 1983, he had become a member of the newly-formed MRLG. However, his involvement with the group was short-lived, and he stopped associating himself with Isan writing. Although his third book described him as "a young writer of the plateau"[113] and was dedicated to his mother "and my birthplace — 'Ban Nong Khrok',"[114] there is nothing in his work or his activities to differentiate him (regionally) from any other writer in Bangkok. As one Isan writer noted about Siowjan, "He has used his pen name for so long, he doesn't remember what his real name is," the implication being that Siowjan has forgotten, perhaps purposely, his Isan origins as well. Siowjan was not cited among the 73 people described in Wiwat's book of Isan writers,[115] which was issued by the IWA for the *Cho' Karaket* conference in Buri Ram in February 1999. Instead, Siowjan's name appeared in a list at the front of the book under the heading, "Isan writers about whom we have not yet been able to find information."[116] The fact that Siowjan lives in Bangkok and socializes with other writers there suggests that his absence from the IWA's book was a result of his refusal to be included rather than any difficulty in contacting him.

Siowjan's interest in literature began at an early age when, encouraged by his mother, he started to read comic books, followed by the more serious volumes that were kept in the family's locked cabinet. During secondary school, he received guidance in literary matters from one of his teachers, now a SEAWrite Award-winning poet known as Raekham Pradoykham.[117] During that period, Siowjan wrote a story called "*Kheun Deuan Meut*" คืนเดือนมืด (Dark Moon Night), about a fellow student who was murdered while pedaling a *samlo'* in the evenings after school. The story was printed in a magazine put together by the students, and its subsequent publication in the periodical, *Khuruparithat*, gave Siowjan the ambition to be a writer.[118]

---

[113] เสี้ยวจันทร์ แรมไพร, โลก, 2536b (inside back cover).

[114] Ibid., p. 16.

[115] วิวัฒน์, ed., นักเขียน, 2542a.

[116] Ibid., p. 3.

[117] เสี้ยวจันทร์ แรมไพร, "จากนักเขียน," 2536c, in เสี้ยวจันทร์, โลก, 2536b, pp. 11–5.

[118] เสี้ยวจันทร์, "จาก," 2536c.

At Ramkhamhaeng later, Siowjan was influenced for a time by leftist students and read a great deal of Literature for Life, but after a few years he rejected the movement.[119] "And I am still searching," he has said, "searching for new knowledge, searching for life's answers, with doubts that never end."[120] He was clearly determined to avoid being associated with any movement or group, wishing instead to express himself individualistically and unconventionally. "I feel I am special,"[121] he stated simply, and his work reflects that view.

The stories in *Lok Chapo'* show his interest in the odd and unusual, and his efforts to be unorthodox: the book is subtitled, "Deviant Conditions of Urban Humanity." As Wachira Buason suggests,[122] Siowjan's writing is concerned primarily with psychological aspects of life in the city, especially the aberrant and unattractive. For example, in "*Khon Ba Tai Teuk*" คนบ้าใต้ตึก (The Crazy Person Below), a student is more interested in a deranged man outside his window than his university class lecture. The narrator of "*Ngoen Peuan Leuat*" เงินเปื้อนเลือด (Blood-Stained Money) finds a 100-baht banknote with blood on it on Ratchadamnoen Avenue soon after the May 1992 protests. In spite of the obvious political context, however, the story consists of the stream-of-consciousness musings of the apolitical narrator as he imagines the circumstances under which the banknote was dropped. In fact, politics have as little significance as Isan in Siowjan's work. In presenting bizarre thoughts or bodily functions, so common in his writing but otherwise rarely the subject of Thai literature, Siowjan apparently seeks primarily to astonish. The same qualities mark his involvement with experimental theater, an interest that increasingly occupied his energies in the late 1990s. In January 1999, for instance, during the evening of entertainment that followed the literature seminar at Ubon University (described in Chapter 1), Siowjan climbed onto a roof (already something of a stunt) and delivered a monologue about life, crazy people on roofs, and bankruptcy suicides.

In his writing, then, concerned as it is with Bangkok's urban oddities, Siowjan seems to ignore the existence of Isan, and even to deny his own origins. In doing so, he has almost completely transformed himself from an Isan writer into a Bangkok Thai writer.

---

[119] Ibid.

[120] Ibid., p. 14.

[121] Ibid., p. 11.

[122] วชิระ, "บรรณาธิการ," 2536.

Chaiya Wannasri

Chaiya Wannasri ไชยา วรรณศรี is a writer of the younger generation whose background and point of view differ from that of most other Isan writers. In the 1990s, he was active in some IWA activities (including as editor of its *Newsletter* from 1998 on), but also maintained something of an outsider's perspective both on the organization and on Isan in general.

Chaiya was born in Chanthaburi but moved at the age of about nine to Surin Province, where his father's family originated. He grew up speaking Central Thai within his family, but soon learned Lao and some Khmer from his neighbors. After finishing elementary school in a rural village in Sangkha District (later nearly reached by the spread of Surin town), Chaiya was unable financially to continue his studies, so he took jobs at a fish-steaming factory and as a laborer. In his many jobs, he was cheated, mistreated, and persecuted: at one factory he was confined and given only one meal daily; at another job he was threatened with death when he asked for his wages.[123] These experiences caused him to think about society and to become interested in reading. His mother had taught him how to read even before he entered school, and he now rediscovered his earlier interest:

> I started to like to read. At first it was cartoons, during the time I was mistreated. I had the idea that I wanted to write, but I didn't know how, because I hadn't studied. But I knew how to read. I read the newspaper since I was a kid. Then I read *Bangkok* [magazine].[124]

Chaiya attended adult education classes in the evenings, then went to work in a hotel in Pattaya, and eventually enlisted as an army scout in 1985. For seven years, he worked in the jungle, guarding the border and doing village development in Surin, Buri Ram, and Nakhorn Ratchasima provinces. As his interest in literature grew, he became increasingly frustrated with life as a soldier, especially the difficulty in getting reading material and sending his work for publication. In 1993, Chaiya left his position with the army, having decided after the events of Black May that he could no longer be in the military, and moved to Bangkok to devote himself fully to writing.[125] That same year, his first short story, "*Nangseu*" หนังสือ (Books), was published in *Siam Rath Weekly Review*.[126] His first novel appeared in

---

[123] Chaiya Wannasri, Interview, March 31, 1999, Surin.
[124] Ibid.
[125] Ibid.
[126] Anon., "ไชยา วรรณศรี," 2542e, in สนั่น ชูสกุล *et al.* ฤดูดอกไม้ร่วง. บุรีรัมย์: อิงฟ้า, 2542.

1995, entitled *Meuang Jao Pho'* เมืองเจ้าพ่อ (*Mobster Town*), and another, *Phan Meuang* พันเมือง (*Surrounding the City*), came out the following year. Both novels had been written more than ten years earlier when Chaiya was still a soldier, along with other novels and short stories, all of which drew on his various experiences.[127] In 1999, he continued to write and publish poetry, short stories, and non-fiction.

Chaiya's situation as a writer is a distinctive one in a number of ways. The first is the manner in which he came to writing. With limited formal education, he became a laborer at an early age, and it was his personal acquaintance with injustice and exploitation that fueled his desire to write. Only then did he begin to read what would be considered literature. As he noted:

> I'm different from [other writers]. I started writing not from having read. It was the opposite. I started writing from what I experienced and saw: society's exploitation, making trouble for people and mistreating us. It made me write these things.[128]

It also led to an interest in politics, which informed his early writing. As he began to read more, Chaiya was influenced, he says, by Khamphun Bunthawi, Phanom Nanthapreuk, and the periodical Cho' Karaket, with its diversity of stories by new writers.[129]

Another of Chaiya's distinguishing characteristics is his development of a perspective on Isan that is uncommon among Isan writers, perhaps arising out of his move to Isan from the Central region as a young boy. As an outsider might, he takes a critical stance, rather than a nostalgic one, toward Isan and its people. He does not mourn the loss of tradition and custom, but instead questions presumptions that are held by Isan people about themselves and their region, and closely and unsentimentally examines the reality he sees around him. For example, in Chaiya's semi-autobiographical short story, "*Siang Klo'ng*"[130] (Sound of the Drum), a boy tells how his fascination with monks turns to disillusionment after he moves to Isan, where the local temple differs from the one he knew previously and its respected abbot is discovered having sex. Chaiya sets up a contrast in the story in which Isan is compared to the Central region and found to be lacking, at least as far as the protagonist's experience with the Sangha is concerned. Unlike many of

---

[127] Chaiya, Interview, 1999.

[128] Ibid.

[129] Ibid.

[130] ไชยา วรรณศรี, "เสียงกลอง," ดอกติ้วป่า 10, 1 (23) (ก.พ. 2541): 96–101.

his fellow writers, who apparently feel the need to represent Isan positively to their readers, Chaiya feels free to criticize Isan; he is not on a mission of *tho'ngthin niyom*.

The same is true of his story, "*Lao Luang*" ลาวลวง (Deceitful Lao), in which a young man argues with his father at their home in Isan about whether Lao-Isan people cheat and take advantage of one another, especially Isan people in Bangkok. At the end, the young man returns to his job in the capital, where he makes a living meeting Isan people as they arrive at Hualamphong train station and conducting them to worksites. The reader is left to consider the question of exploitation. Chaiya's use of Lao language in the dialogues lends an authenticity to the story and validity to the writer and his views.

Chaiya became active with the IWA at the end of the 20th century, taking on the editorship of its *Newsletter* in 1998, yet still distinguished himself from other members by his beliefs about both the Association and his own role as a writer. He has stated:

> Really I didn't think I would join any group. […] I felt [the IWA] didn't accomplish anything concrete, I mean they didn't have a clear objective, a direction. Their thinking was okay, but they didn't carry it out. I felt they were pointless […] but in the end, I joined to help them. I think I became a subscriber to the *Newsletter* in 1995. […] But from what had passed I saw that it hadn't developed at all. […] They wanted the later generation to see where the *Newsletter* had come from, where it was going, who started it, who worked on it. They were putting too much emphasis on this. They weren't talking about what work to do to make it successful.[131]

Not everyone was happy with his work on the *Newsletter*, he noted:

> Sometimes people criticize me, saying, 'Since Chaiya started to do the *Newsletter* it hasn't had any Isan atmosphere'. […] But you have to make the content universal. You have to make it good. […] The main issue is, what to do to make it survive.[132]

Chaiya's response reflects his conviction that regional affiliation is unimportant.

> Thai writers just flatter and cheer each other on. This is the lack of development, of progress, of Thai literature. [They] cheer each other on, flatter each other, tell each other off, argue with each other, drink together,

---

[131] Chaiya, Interview, 1999.
[132] Ibid.

divide [themselves] into Southern writers, Isan writers, Eastern writers. I don't like it. I'm not a writer of anywhere. [...] [And] I don't look at what region a writer comes from. It's not an issue. I'm not interested.[133]

Such regional labels, he feels, are more confining than meaningful.

It's not that I'm a writer of Isan. I want to be a writer of everything, of anyone who accepts me. If you are an Isan writer who others don't accept, or you're a Thai writer but every region doesn't accept you, doesn't know you, what use do you have? [...] I want people of every level to read [my work]: farmers, *samlo'* pedallers, workers, and so on. And especially teachers, because they teach children.[134]

For these reasons, Chaiya has endeavored to write stories in a straight-forward style that capture the reader's interest and are easy to read,[135] thereby appealing to the widest possible audience.

The Coming Generation

As noted in Chapter 5, the IWA has tried to inspire an involvement with literature among young students by making presentations at elementary and secondary schools across Isan. For the most part, however, as of 1999 the next generation of Isan writers, that is, Isan writers of the future, had yet to be recognized, except perhaps at a very local level. Fon Fafang, for example, fostered literary interest and aspirations among his secondary school students in Srisaket, one of whom he encouraged to enter a national literary contest in 1999. Manote Phromsingh was particularly active in nurturing budding writers in Ubon. He periodically met at his home with a group that called itself, *"Khi Kabo'ng Hil"* ขี้กะบองฮิล (the name, meaning "Ash Hill," uses the local Lao word for ashes, *khi kabo'ng*), consisting of young writers and teachers, most of whom were art and literature students or recent graduates of Ubon University. The group had arisen spontaneously when a few students from the university sought out Manote and, finding him positive and open, began to visit his house regularly, bringing friends. Some continued to attend the gatherings after graduating, while others were replaced by their juniors from the university. The tenor of these gatherings was set by Manote's example: his soft-spoken demeanor, his respect for others, and his serious interest in literature. Thus, as Manote commented, the participants did not

---

[133] Ibid.
[134] Ibid.
[135] Ibid.

bring guitars and sing Songs for Life, drink alcohol and bang on the bottles, or get drunk and expound about literature,[136] all of which are often standard behavior in similar groups.

At one meeting of the group at Manote's house on November 14, 1998, eight people attended. The discussion was led by Manote and conducted in a mixture of Thai and Lao, with each participant speaking as they pleased. The first topic was the recent essay in the *Nation Weekend* concerning the question, "Why Can't Literature Solve Society's Problems?"[137] and included consideration of Literature for Life, gender relations, and the relationship between writers and society. Then the group moved on to examine Manote's short story, "*Saphan*,"[138] also recently published in the *Nation Weekend*.[139] "Forget that I am the author," said Manote, encouraging an exchange that no doubt was useful both to himself and to the others in the group. At the end, tentative plans were made for the next gathering, with Existentialism suggested as a possible discussion topic.

Members of the group who were Ubon University students at the time, including Thatsanai Khotthom ทัสนัย โคตรทม, contributed to a student literary magazine, *Thanon* ถนน (*Road*), that was produced in January 1999 and distributed at the evening performance that followed the January 15, 1999, seminar at Ubon University entitled, "Thai Literature in an Era Without Boundaries" (discussed above). Another student whose work appeared in *Thanon*, Ramok Wo'ratchayako'n ราโมกซ์ วรัชญากร, was a discussant on the panel, "Thai Literature in the Opinion of Students of the New Generation," held at the *Cho' Karaket* conference in Buri Ram on February 13, 1999. The moderator was Manote, and the other panelists included Thiraphong Janprieng ธีรพงษ์ จันทร์เปรียง, a student at Ratchabhat Buri Ram, and Bamphen Chaiyaraks บำเพ็ญ ไชยรักษ์ from Mahasarakham University. In their remarks, these students boldly identified themselves as members of Isan minorities. Thiraphong greeted the audience in Khmer before switching to Thai. Bamphen gave a greeting in Yo' language (related to Lao) and then used Thai to give her presentation, during which she referred to Khamphun's book, *Luk Isan* as "Isan's SEAWrite," as if the award belonged to the region rather than the writer, whose name she did not even mention.

---

[136] Manote, Interview, 1999.

[137] ดวงมน จิตร์จำนงค์, "สืบเนื่องจากคำถาม 'ทำไมวรรณกรรมสะท้อนสังคมจึงแก้ปัญหาสังคมไม่ได้'," เนชั่นสุดสัปดาห์ 8, 366 (10–16 มิ.ย. 2542): 44–5.

[138] มาโนช พรหมสิงห์, "สะพาน," เนชั่นสุดสัปดาห์ 7, 329 (24–30 ก.ย. 2541): 50–2.

[139] In addition to these texts, members of the group also brought along recent issues of *Cho' Karaket* and the *IWA Newsletter*.

After all the members of the panel had spoken, an official from Ratcha-bhat Buri Ram stood up to comment, and his first statement was, "Thai is the paramount language. This is most important." The official, who appeared to be 35 or 40 years older than the students speaking, was expressing the dominant view of an earlier era, and thus exposing a generation gap. It seems very possible that this instance of students' defiant, public pride in their origins, which transcends simply identifying themselves with Isan, might be an indication of a new direction for emerging Isan writers.

Conclusion

The eleven contemporary Isan writers discussed in this chapter demonstrate the great range of diversity of Isan writing at the end of the 20th century. If placed on a continuum according to the importance of Isan in their work, they would be scattered from one end to the other. At one pole would be Chatchawal, Sangkhom, and Somneuk, who were living in Isan and whose writing was entirely about Isan. At the other extreme would be Siowjan, from whose life and work Isan had effectively disappeared; then Raks, who had also ceased writing about Isan; and nearby, Prachakhom, for whom Isan was primarily a distant memory.[140] These three writers were living in Bangkok and generally avoided involvement with other Isan writers or the IWA. At the middle of the continuum, one would find Phaiwarin, whose work exists at the convergence of rural Isan and urban Bangkok and represents a balance of, or bridge between, the two. On one side of Phaiwarin would be Manote, leaning toward the Isan end, and on the other side, Wongdeuan, Phisit, and Chaiya, tending away from Isan. The written work of these latter four writers shows the most variety, sometimes making use of Isan issues, atmosphere, and language, and other times pursuing other concerns.

While earlier Isan writers often wrote with political ends in mind, or with the goal of explaining Isan to the general Thai reader, the newer

---

[140] Why have some writers turned their backs on Isan? For Raks and Prachakhom, it seems that other concerns simply supplanted Isan. By 1999, Raks had lived in Bangkok for many years, and his life and professional interests were based there. Prachakhom gradually lost his connection to Isan by living in other parts of the country for all of his adult life. In Siowjan's case, the answer to the question is largely a matter of speculation. Perhaps his interests were restricted to an urban context, or he felt he no longer shared commonalities with Isan; it is also possible that, like some other Isan people, he preferred to be seen as a Bangkok person rather than be associated with a denigrated population and region.

generation in 1999 seemed more interested in cultivating their literary skills. Thus the latter group produced work that was more diverse, and included the use of stream of consciousness, interior monologue, self-reference, and other techniques for the purpose of satire, social and literary criticism, and general entertainment. As writers, they forged their own identities by which, to a greater or lesser extent, they became publicly known. Phaiwarin was seen as a prolific and skilled poet who achieved major recognition with the SEAWrite Award; Prachakhom was a serious, accomplished writer (and a loner) likely to achieve greater and greater success; Phisit was a satiric and humorous fiction author and a sharp and insightful critic. Manote's life represented an ideal for many writers, as he spent his days farming in Isan and writing psychologically rich (and successful) fiction, while Chatchawal was building a promising career with work that evoked a nostalgic Isan. Somneuk, a woman writer of children's stories, Wongdeuan, a philosopher-woodcarver, and Sangkhom, a Lao language enthusiast, were less well-known but no less distinctive. Raks, a major editor, Siowjan, a purposeful eccentric, and Chaiya, an outspoken individualist, set their own standards and resisted external pressures. As poets, novelists, essayists, and short story writers, these authors, along with their younger compatriots of the future, defied easy generalization as they expanded contemporary Isan (and Thai) writing and literary culture in new and more varied directions at the dawn of the 21st century.

CHAPTER 7

Conclusion:
Isan Writers, Thai Literature

In considering the subject of Isan regionalism in the context of modern Thai literature, three primary issues must be addressed: 1) what makes Isan a region, and how do its distinctive qualities come to play in literature; 2) who is considered an Isan writer and why; and 3) what is the nature of Isan writing, and what role has it played in the development of modern Thai literature?

It is a widely accepted fact that Isan is a region distinct from both the Thai center and the other regions of Thailand. The characteristics that distinguish Isan from the rest of the country can be found in every area of scrutiny, be it geography, climate, history, economics, ethnicity, language, religion, or the oral and written traditions. Influences on the area now known as Isan have over the centuries come primarily from Lao and Khmer civilizations, until around 1900, when Central authorities began to force the square peg of Isan into the round hole of Siamese, and then Thai, nationhood. Foremost among these efforts was the attempt to negate and extinguish linguistic and other cultural practices among the ethnically diverse non-Siamese populations of the region. The process of coercion and repression has given rise to a whole array of reactions and feelings, including distrust, resentment, and revolt on the part of Isan people, and suspicion, contempt, and exploitation by the center. This uneasy relationship between the region and the center continued throughout the 20th century, influencing the content and direction of literature by Isan writers.

Isan writing, in the sense used here, is by definition written by Isan writers.[1] However, the issue of what defines an Isan writer is far more

---

[1] Work related to Isan and written by outsiders would be considered writing about Isan, not Isan writing. The issue of outsiders and insiders is discussed below.

complicated than the question of what makes Isan a region. Contributing factors include where a person was born and grew up, where they have resided as an adult, what they write about, how they identify themselves, and how others (whether Isan writers or the reading public in general) perceive them.[2] None of these elements is by itself either necessary or sufficient to determine an Isan writer. The salient points seem to be that if someone was born (and preferably grew up) in Isan, and their writing is related to Isan, then they are an Isan writer and will be recognized as such. All 24 writers discussed in this thesis (except Chaiya) were born in Isan, and most grew up there. Siowjan transformed himself from an Isan writer into a Bangkok writer by excluding Isan from his work, and a few others, such as Raks and Prachakhom, seemed also to be moving in that direction. All the rest, though, have a recognizable connection to Isan in some, if not all, of their writing.

The issue of birthplace and residence is an interesting one in determining who an Isan writer is. Chaiya was born in the Central region, but with his father's roots in Surin, his own residency there, and his editorship of the IWA *Newsletter*, as well as the fact that some of his work concerns Isan directly, Chaiya has been widely seen as an Isan writer. Khamphun is more strongly associated with Isan than any other writer, even though he left Isan as a young man and spent most of his life in Bangkok and the South. While not all of his work relates to Isan, he is nationally known as an Isan writer, not just because *Luk Isan* explicitly and purposefully breathes Isan on every page, or because the SEAWrite gave him wide publicity, but also because he himself, in his behavior, attitudes, and speech patterns, was clearly recognizable as an Isan person. Yong Yasothorn is a similar case. He was born in Isan and wrote a distinguished novel about growing up there, but later lived in Rayong. While still somewhat active with the IWA, he also started an Eastern Writers' Group, with which he was increasingly associated. However, since he rarely published new work, there was some question whether in the future he would continue to be seen as an Isan writer or would move more toward an Eastern regional affiliation.

What happens when the situation is reversed, and a writer moves to Isan from elsewhere? One example is Phaithun Thanya, who was born and grew up in Phatthalung but moved to Isan in his 30s. Even after living for

---

[2] Some Isan people evidently consider ability to speak Lao as a defining criterion for being an Isan person, even going so far as to criticize Isan people who do not speak Lao as pretentiously insisting on using only standard Thai. In fact, however, some urban Isan people grew up using Thai in their daily lives and never developed fluency in Lao.

several years in Mahasarakham, and teaching literature at the university, he was not considered an Isan writer. He did not write about Isan, he did not identify himself with Isan, and he was not a member of the IWA. On the contrary, with his fiction generally set in the South, and as a member of the Nakhorn Group,[3] he was very much a Southern writer. It is worth noting, however, that his students have included Chatchawal, whom Phaithun cites as a literary friend and inspiration,[4] and Nanthaphorn Phokham, who in 1999 was writing a Masters' thesis on Isan writers.[5]

There are two other writers who moved to Isan from other regions but, in contrast to Phaithun, were considered Isan writers, at least to some extent. Nerimit Praphan, who was born and grew up in Cholburi Province, moved to Isan to work in healthcare and then lived in Buri Ram, his wife's home province. He was an active member of the IWA, wrote a regular column for the *Newsletter*, and was included in the IWA's book of Isan writers. However, Nerimit was not considered, nor would he have claimed to be, an Isan writer in the same way that, for example, Manote or Phaiwarin were. Not only was Nerimit's work not strongly related to Isan, but his knowledge and experience of the region were, as he would have readily admitted, more those of a recent immigrant than a native.

A related situation is that of Sanan Chusakul, who was born and grew up in Nakhorn Sri Thammarat, studied and worked in Bangkok, and then joined a number of development projects in Isan. In 1999, he was living in Surin, where he edited the periodical, *Do'k Tiw Pa*, continued his development work, and participated at times in IWA activities. Sanan's writing reflected his interest in rural Isan and, according to Phisit, was able to "reflect the problems of Isan brilliantly."[6] Furthermore, "If Khamsing had been born in this era," Phisit stated, "he would have to write like Sanan."[7] Sanan was accepted (though perhaps not universally) as an Isan writer largely, it seems, because of his obvious dedication to the region and his skill in depicting it in his writing. At the same time, though, he was still seen as a Southerner as well. Thus, he was not considered simply an Isan

---

[3] An association of Southern writers.

[4] ศิริพร วรรณศิลป์, "บนทางคู่ขนานอิสระ สัมภาษณ์ : ไพฑูรย์ ธัญญา," สยามรัฐสัปดาห์วิจารณ์ 45, 43 (28 มี.ค. –3 เม.ย. 2542): 56–7.

[5] Nanthaphorn, who is from Buri Ram, defines "Isan writers" as those who were born in Isan, although they might subsequently have moved to live elsewhere. Nanthaphorn Phokham, pers. comm., June 10, 1999, Mahasarakham.

[6] Phisit Phusri, Interview, January 17, 1999, Ubon Ratchathani.

[7] Ibid.

writer like others, but rather someone from the South who had become an Isan writer, a Southerner who was practically an Isan person. As he noted in an interview in 1997, "I am not able to reach all the way into Isan culture, to reach its true essence. […] I have become uncertain about my own culture."[8] Elsewhere he stated, "I think and dream of something that is exceedingly difficult: one day I will finally return home."[9] In effect, he maintained a dual identity, a hybrid self, which was neither completely Southern nor completely Isan. Sanan was a kind of adopted or honorary Isan writer; his Isan status was attained by achievement rather than birth. In the world of Isan writing and regionalism (as in the larger realm of nationalism), this is never quite sufficient nor fully legitimate; authenticity lies in the land, but more deeply in the blood.

Clearly, as of 1999, there was a wide spectrum of Isan writers, but was there such a thing as modern or contemporary Isan writing, that is to say, a distinct body of work identifiable as somehow belonging to the Isan region? For most people, including most Isan writers, at the end of the 20th century, the term *wannakam Isan* วรรณกรรมอีสาน (Isan literature) referred to traditional or classical Lao literature written on palm leaves, while *wannakam Isan samai mai* วรรณกรรมอีสานสมัยใหม่ (modern Isan literature) and *wannakam Isan ruam samai* วรรณกรรมอีสานร่วมสมัย (contemporary Isan literature) were not recognized expressions and had no generally understood meaning. Hardly anyone I talked to in Thailand, whether writer, editor, critic, or academic, seemed ever to have conceptualized such a literary category. Kittiwat Sattanakho, an Isan Studies scholar at Mahasarakham University, stated that what is written by authors like those discussed in this book was contemporary general (Thai) writing, not Isan writing.[10] For him, Isan writing was literary composition in Lao classical idiom using the traditional forms handed down over centuries. Somphong Thawi, the Bangkok critic and writer, agreed, further asserting that contemporary Thai literature could not be divided or distinguished according to region.[11] However, Suchart Sawatsri felt that modern Isan literature did exist and that it was distinguishable by the "tone color" of its language,[12] with influence and inspiration from Lao.

---

[8] Anon., "สัมภาษณ์ สนั่น ชูสกุล นักเขียนหรือหัวแถวมือบ," p. 26. จดหมายข่าวสโมสรนักเขียนภาคอีสาน 3, 11 (ก.ย. – ต.ค. 2540): 23–6.

[9] สนั่น ชูสกุล, "เกี่ยวกับผู้เขียน," p. 165, in ช้างเหยียบนา พระยาเหยียบเมือง. สุรินทร์: อิงฟ้า, 2541, pp. 164–5

[10] Kittiwat Sattanakho, Interview, June 9, 1999, Mahasarakham.

[11] Somphong Thawi, Interview, March 1, 1999, Bangkok.

[12] Suchart Sawatsri, Interview, June 23, 1999, Bangkok.

He used the example of Lao Khamhawm's *Fa Bo' Kan*:

> People of every region can understand it all, and they know it's Isan. He
> wrote in language that has the characteristics of the Isan atmosphere,
> but it's language that is understandable. Like *daed ro'n reuang raeng*
> แดดร้อนเรื่องแรง. With the word *reuang raeng* I see the shimmering glare,
> it's arid. Southerners have no way to use this kind of tone color. [...]
> Since then we see that many people have developed a lot, in every
> region. They have tone color in the characteristics of their region but
> using language that everyone, every region, understands.[13]

This element of Isan writing is a relatively minor, subtle one and,
moreover, it is not a feature of all Isan writers' work. In addition to
Khamsing, Suchart mentioned only Manote, Sangkhom, and Pramote as
authors whose writing shows such tone color. There are other characteristics,
though, that are frequently found in Isan writing and which together help
to define it, even if no single feature is common to all of it. For example,
in addition to Lao, words and phrases from other Isan languages, such as
Khmer or Kui, appear in the work of some Isan writers. Heat, drought,
poverty, and deprivation have been frequent subjects of Isan writing since
the 1950s, although some writers have concentrated more on honesty, humor,
and solidarity among Isan people. Suffering, injustice, and exploitation at
the hands of powerful economic and political interests were standard themes
during the Literature for Life era, while later, tradition and social change
became frequent concerns. Although these elements have not been limited
to Isan writing, they do help to give an indication of its nature. Perhaps
as important as the common threads among Isan writers and their work,
though, is the individual contribution that each has made to the total picture
of modern Isan literature.

One of the most widespread elements of Isan writing since its inception
has been the dichotomy of Isan versus Bangkok, rural versus urban, the
region versus the center. This distinction, most highly developed in the
work of Phaiwarin, casts Isan as a pure, honest, dependable, natural, healthy,
loving, nurturing home, a place of freedom, belonging, virtue, and tradition.
Bangkok, by contrast, is seen as the location of power, wealth, artifice, greed,
illusion, selfishness, confinement, dehumanization, loneliness, disattachment,
and alienation. The tension between the region and the center is expressed
in various ways, including the choices that Isan writers make in what they
write, and also where they live, and how they identify themselves.

---

[13] Ibid.

Few Isan writers, especially those working at the end of the 20th century, saw themselves as writing specifically for other Isan people. For writers who wished to draw heavily on Lao or other Isan traditions, the difficulty was that the non-Isan Thai audience might not understand the work, while the Isan readership alone was insufficient to support it. Isan writers recognized that their audience was the Thai reading public in general, and thus their goals were primarily to educate outsiders, to bring about social and political change (and thereby improve the conditions of Isan), or simply to assert the presence and significance of Isan. Some writers supported the opening of bookshop-publishing houses in Isan, such as Ban Thung[14] in Buri Ram and Ing Fa[15] in Surin, in order to provide an alternative to Bangkok's monopoly on the selection, publication, and distribution of literary work, but at the same time they realized that they could not succeed or perhaps even survive as writers if they remained completely outside the capital's literary industry. This fact as much as any other marked them as Thai writers who were part of, and dependent on, the Thai literary sphere, and differentiates their work from the traditional verbal and literary arts of Isan, such as *mo' lam* and palm leaf tales.

The fact that modern Isan literature is not an offshoot of traditional Isan literature but rather a subset of modern Thai literature is an ironic aspect of the conflict between Isan and the Thai center and one that was perhaps recognized but not frequently discussed in Isan literary circles. The genres, conventions, and techniques of modern Isan literature are also those of modern Thai literature; even modern Isan poetry (such as Phaiwarin's) is not based on Lao or Khmer or other Isan traditions, but is written in Thai using Thai poetic forms. While a few Isan writers have managed to incorporate aspects of Isan storytelling techniques (e.g., Khamphun) or traditional Lao tales (e.g., Pramote) in their work, for the most part Isan writers show a high level of deracination, due largely to Central Thai domination. Not many were literate in their native languages or knowledgeable about their literary traditions. This was primarily a result of Central Thai standardized education programs and suppression of local languages and scripts, as well as perhaps a modern drift toward centralized forms of communication. Some contemporary Isan writers responded to the loss of tradition by looking to Laos, only to find that contemporary writers there were often similarly constrained, or their works diluted, due to the edicts of the Lao (and Vietnamese) Communist Party. Other contemporary Isan writers made

---

[14] Founded and operated by Wiwat Rotjanawan.
[15] Operated by a group that includes Sanan Chusakul.

use of materials from scholars of Isan Studies, or from *mo' lam* singers. Nevertheless, in the end what they produced was written in Thai; it can be considered modern Isan writing, or Thai literature with an Isan sensibility.

Modern Isan literature grew up as part of modern Thai literature, with similar influences and evolution, and yet the two are not entirely coincident. Isan writers have played significant and at times decisive roles in the development of Thai literature by treating it as a legitimate forum for reflecting the lives of farmers and villagers, furthering awareness of government misdeeds, encouraging social criticism and political action, and demanding respect for Isan traditions and ways of life. In addition, modern Isan writing has had its own development as well, combining some aspects of national literary trends with influence from the region's own historical, cultural, and political forces. To rephrase Ralph Rusk's observation, when Bangkok (or other central Thai) authors write, they are conscious of being Thai, but when Isan authors write, they are aware of being both Thai and Isan.[16] For example, Somkhit's "*Ku Pen Khon Isan*," Somneuk's "*Kho'y ... Pen Khon Isan*," and Udorn's *Isan Ku* all declare their authors' Isan identity, sometimes using Lao words, but the contents of these works are all written in Thai. Moreover, a Bangkok writer is likely to have a high degree of overlap (in terms of background and culture) with the general reading public, while an Isan writer might have rather less in common with the same audience. This has had direct relevance to the way Isan writers have seen themselves and shaped their work.

It has been noted elsewhere that the word "regional" has two meanings: 1) attached to a locality; and 2) limited, provincial, lacking the desire or ability to appeal to a wider audience.[17] Modern Isan literature has variously demonstrated each of these attributes.[18] What is important, however, is that by 1999 it was no longer a largely homogeneous literary movement or the work of only a few writers. Instead it was (and no doubt remains) an

---

[16] Ralph Leslie Rusk, *The Literature of the Middle Western Frontier*, Vol. 1 (New York: Frederick Ungar, 1962). This book, originally published in 1925, is a study of a particular segment of 19th-century American literature. In contrasting American writers of the Eastern and Western parts of the country, Rusk states, "When an Easterner wrote, he was conscious of the fact that he was an American; but, when a Westerner attempted authorship, he was troubled by the consciousness of the fact that he was not only an American but a Westerner" (p. 272).

[17] E.U. Kratz, "Regional Aspects of Indonesian Literature," *Tenggara* 21, 22 (1988): 57–81.

[18] In Suchart's words, "Some people can see only as far as the flagpole at their school." Suchart, Interview, 1999.

increasingly varied body of writing that is as diverse as Isan itself, continuing to develop along its own path while simultaneously enriching Thai literature overall. Modern Isan literature encompasses the political diatribes of Udorn Thongnoi, the interior monologues of Manote Phromsingh, the historical novels of Khamphun Bunthawi, the Khmer and Kui tales of Fon Fafang, the plotless but evocative stories of Surachai Janthimathorn, the nationally known classicism of Phaiwarin Khaongam, and the still emerging work of students at Ubon University.

In his 1954 study of British regional novelists, Lucien Leclaire delineated five primary and partially overlapping stages (and time periods): 1) "picturesque regionalism," which was "characterized by externals" and exhibited "features [the writers] felt to be unique";[19] 2) "romantic and sentimental regionalism," which "dwell[ed] upon old scenes for remembrance' sake";[20] 3) "realistic and naturalistic regionalism," which showed "little romanticism," suggesting instead that "facts must be faced" in presenting "real people from the ordinary walks of town and village life, unpleasant as they may be";[21] 4) "interpretive regionalism," in which facts were interpreted and conclusions drawn in "the scientific spirit of inquiry";[22] and 5) "present-day regionalism," of which the characteristics were not yet clearly visible, but "the conflict between town and country, nature and industrialization, [was] often emphasized."[23]

Apparent parallels between Leclaire's subject and modern Isan literature can be easily discerned. For example, Leclaire's description of Stage One, picturesque realism, seems to apply rather clearly to Kanchana's *Phu Yai Li Kap Nang Ma* of 1965. Kanchana depicts the farmers' lives in a cheerful and entertaining light, and she describes their festivals and social interactions as honest, simple, and worthy of the reader's attention. Stage Two, romantic and sentimental regionalism, immediately brings to mind Khamphun's *Luk Isan* (1976). Khamphun's evocations of daily practices in Isan in the 1930s are not only nostalgic and picturesque, but they have also influenced many other writers, including Khamman, Yong, and Sangkhom. Stage Three, realistic and naturalistic regionalism, sounds remarkably like

---

[19] Lucien Leclaire, *A General Analytical Bibliography of the Regional Novelists of the British Isles 1800–1950* (Paris: Société D'Édition "Les Belles Lettres", 1954), p. 122.
[20] Ibid., p. 183.
[21] Ibid., p. 223.
[22] Ibid., p. 271.
[23] Ibid., p. 361.

Literature for Life, from the late 1960s to end of the 1970s. As we have seen in Chapters 2 and 3, realistic depiction of unpleasant conditions of life is the standard fare of socialist realist works, for example, Rom's "*Phra Jao Kho'ng O'm.*" Even Stage Five, Leclaire's so-called "present-day regionalism," recalls the work of later writers like Phaiwarin. The problem of reconciling the urban with the rural, and all the aspects and implications of that division, is the primary theme of Phaiwarin's work, as discussed above. The idea is also central to such works as Khamphun's *Luk Thung Khao Krung* (1979), in which unwitting Isan villagers negotiate urban Bangkok, and Chatchawal's "*Meuan Rot Fai Ja Ma*" (1994), in which Isan farmers are faced with a new train line being built through their fields.

However, Leclaire was writing about a period covering 150 years, while modern Isan writing is a relatively new phenomenon (about half a century old) and its study a completely new field. Isan literary regionalism is still in the process (and perhaps the early stages) of developing, and thus is difficult to clearly and conclusively see, analyze, and assess. The present book is merely a first step in a potentially rich realm. Carrying out another study along similar lines 20 or 50 years in the future could help clarify which writers and trends proved to be of lasting resonance, and would also identify new developments. Several writers discussed here merit more in-depth treatment, including Surachai Janthimathorn, Khamphun Bunthawi, Phaiwarin Khaongam, and Prachakhom Lunachai. Other useful topics for further inquiry and potentially valuable comparison include an examination of modern Southern Thai literature, and an investigation of contemporary practices of *mo'lam* and other Isan verbal arts.

Nonetheless, in this book I have tried to show that Isan literary regionalism is a significant and undeniable feature of modern Thai literature. Just as Isan is a distinct region with a complex relationship to the Thai center, so Isan writing is a distinctive literary phenomenon with an important place in the development of the nation's literature. As demonstrated above, Isan writers participated in and often deeply influenced developments in Thai literature during the second half of the 20th century. The role of Isan writing was most prominent in the Literature for Life movement in the 1970s and in the rise of regionalism in the 1980s and 1990s. However, the wide variety of style, content, and goal in Isan writing overall parallels the broad range of what it means to be an Isan writer in the context of contemporary literary culture. For Isan writers, the creative tensions of coming to terms with regional identities and expressing those identities through literature in the national language have given rise to a diverse yet uniquely Isan literary production that is increasingly demanding attention and recognition.

Bibliography

Interviews

Chaiya Wannasri, March 31, 1999, Surin.
Khamphun Bunthawi, June 25, 1999, Bangkok.
Kittiwat Sattanakho, June 9, 1999, Mahasarakham.
Manote Phromsingh, January 17, 1999, Ubon Ratchathani.
Nanthaphorn Phokham, June 10, 1999, Mahasarakham.
Phaiwarin Khaongam, June 22, 1999, Bangkok.
Phisit Phusri, January 17, 1999, Ubon Ratchathani.
Pira Sudham, December 3, 1998, Bangkok.
Prachakhom Lunachai, June 24, 1999, Bangkok.
Pramote Naijit, March 29, 1999, Yasothorn Province.
Raks Mananya, May 28, 1999, Bangkok.
Somneuk Phanitchakij, March 28, 1999, Ubon Ratchathani.
Somphong Thawi, March 1, 1999, Bangkok.
Suchart Sawatsri, June 23, 1999, Bangkok.
Surachai Janthimathorn, May 14, 1999, Bangkok.
_____, March 6, 2000, London.
Wira Sudsang, March 28, 1999, Srisaket.
Yong Yasothorn, October 23, 1998, Bangkok – Chachoengsao.

Western-Language Sources

Anderson, Benedict. 1985. "Introduction." In *In the Mirror*, ed., trans. B. Anderson and R. Mendiones. Bangkok: Editions DK Books, pp. 9–87.

Anderson, Benedict and Ruchira Mendiones, ed., trans. 1985. *In the Mirror*. Bangkok: DK Books.

Anon. 1998. "Network Gives Apology to Lao Athletes." *The Nation* [Bangkok], December 12.

_____. 1999. "The Love of Isan." *The Nation* [Bangkok] 24, 48626 (June 10).

Boccuzzi, Ellen. 2007. "Becoming Urban: Thai Literature about Rural-Urban Migration and a Society in Transition." PhD diss., University of California at Berkeley.

Chai-anan Samudavanija. 1991. "State Identity Creation, State-Building and Civil Society." In *National Identity and Its Defenders: Thailand 1939–1989*, ed. C. Reynolds. Monash University Papers in SEA No. 25, pp. 59–85.

Chulalongkorn University. 1985. *Traditional and Changing Thai World View*. Bangkok: Southeast Asian Studies Program and Chulalongkorn University Social Research Institute.

Cohen, Erik. 1991. *Thai Society in Comparative Perspective*. Bangkok: White Lotus.

Cummings, Joe. 1990. *Thailand: A Travel Survival Kit*. Hawthorn, Victoria: Lonely Planet.

Danerek, Stefan. 2006. *Tjerita and Novel: Literary Discourse in Post New Order Indonesia*. Lund: Lund University Center for Language and Literature.

Davidson, J.H.C.S. and H. Cordell, eds. 1982. *The Short Story in South East Asia: Aspects of a Genre*. London: School of Oriental and African Studies.

Diller, Anthony. 1991. "What Makes Central Thai a National Language?" In *National Identity and Its Defenders: Thailand 1939–1989*, ed. C. Reynolds. Monash University Papers in SEA No. 25, pp. 87–132.

Fallon, Edward. 1983. "The Peasants of Isan: Social and Economic Transitions in Northeast Thailand." PhD diss., University of Wisconsin-Madison.

de Fels, Jacqueline. 1993. *Promotion de le Litterature en Thailande: Vers les Prix Litteraires 1882–1982*. Paris: INALCO.

Gap. 1987. "'Lom Lang' (The Dry Season Wind) … Timeless Lifestyle of Villagers." *Bangkok Post*, February 22. Reprinted in ลาว, 2533, กำแพงลม, p. 6.

Girling, John. 1981. *Thailand: Society and Politics*. London: Cornell University.

Goscha, Christopher. 1998. *Thailand and the Southeast Asian Networks of the Vietnamese Revolution 1885–1954*. London: Routledge.

Grabowsky, Volker. 1995. "The Isan up to its Integration into the Siamese State." In *Regions and National Integration in Thailand, 1892–1992*, ed. V. Grabowsky. Wiesbaden: Harrassowitz Verlag, pp. 107–29.

———, ed. 1995. *Regions and National Integration in Thailand 1892–1992*. Wiesbaden: Harrassowitz.

Hall, D.G.E. 1994. *A History of South-East Asia*, 4th edition. London: Macmillan.

Hamilton, Annette. 1991. "Rumours, Foul Calumnies, and the Safety of the State: Mass Media and National Identity in Thailand." In *National Identity and Its Defenders: Thailand 1939–1989*, ed. C. Reynolds. Monash University Papers in SEA No. 25, pp. 341–79.

Hong Lysa. 1991. "Warasan Sethasat Kanmu'ang." In *Thai Constructions of Knowledge*, ed. Manas Chitakasem and Andrew Turton. London: School of Oriental and African Studies, pp. 99–117.

Ichimura, S., ed. 1976. *Southeast Asia: Nature, Society, and Development*. Honolulu: University of Hawai'i.

Ishii, Yoneo. 1976. "A Note on Buddhistic Millenarian Revolts in Northeastern Siam." In *Southeast Asia: Nature, Society, and Development*, ed. S. Ichimura. Honolulu: University of Hawai'i.

Kampoon Boonthawi. 1991. *Child of the Northeast*, trans. S.F. Kepner. Bangkok: Duang Kamol.

Kanala Eksaengsri. 1977. "Political Change and Modernization: Northeast Thailand's Quest for Identity and Its Potential Threat to National Security." PhD diss., State University of New York at Binghamton.

Kepner, Susan. 2009. "Thai Short Fiction of the Modern Era." In *Modern Short Fiction of Southeast Asia: A Literary History*, ed. T.S. Yamada. Ann Arbor, MI: Association for Asian Studies, pp. 19–41.

Keyes, Charles. 1967. *Isan: Regionalism in Northeastern Thailand*. Southeast Asia Program Data Paper #65. Ithaca, NY: Cornell University.

_____. 1991. "The Case of the Purloined Lintel: The Politics of a Khmer Shrine as a Thai National Treasure." In *National Identity and Its Defenders: Thailand 1939–1989*, ed. C. Reynolds. Monash University Papers in SEA No. 25, pp. 261–92.

_____. 1995. "Hegemony and Resistance in Northeastern Thailand." In *Regions and National Integration in Thailand, 1892–1992*, ed. V. Grabowsky. Wiesbaden: Harrassowitz Verlag, pp. 154–82.

Khammaan Khonkhai. 1984. *Teacher Marisa*, trans. G. Wijeyewardene. Bangkok: Pandora.

_____. 1989. "From the Author on the Publication of the Seventh Printing." In *The Teachers of Mad Dog Swamp*, trans. G. Wijeyewardene. Chiang Mai: Silkworm, pp. xi–xiii.

_____. 1992. *The Teachers of Mad Dog Swamp*, trans. G. Wijeyewardene. Chiang Mai: Silkworm.

Khamsing Srinawk. 1973. *The Politician and Other Stories*, trans. D. Garden. Kuala Lumpur: Oxford University.

Koret, Peter. 1994. "Whispered So Softly It Resounds Through the Forest, Spoken So Loudly It Can Hardly Be Heard: The Art of Parallelism in Traditional Lao Literature." PhD thesis, School of Oriental and African Studies, University of London.

_____. Forthcoming. *Lao Literature of Buddhist Prophecy*. Poughkeepise: Benefit of the Doubt Press.

Kratz, E.U. 1988. "Regional Aspects of Indonesian Literature." *Tenggara* 21, 22: 57–81.

Leclaire, Lucien. 1954. *A General Analytical Bibliography of the Regional Novelists of the British Isles 1800–1950*. Paris: Société D'Edition "Les Belles Lettres."

Luther, Hans. 1995. "Regional Identity versus National Integration — Contemporary Patterns of Modernization in Northeastern Thailand." In *Regions and National Integration in Thailand, 1892–1992*, ed. V. Grabowsky. Wiesbaden: Harrassowitz Verlag, pp. 183–91.

McDaniel, Justin. 2008. *Gathering Leaves and Lifting Words: Histories of Monastic Education in Laos and Thailand*. Seattle, WA: University of Washington.

Manas Chitakasem. 1982. "The Development of Political and Social Consciousness in Thai Short Stories." In *The Short Story in South East Asia: Aspects of a Genre*. ed. J.H.C.S Davidson and H. Cordell. London: School of Oriental and African Studies, pp. 63–99.

Manas Chitakasem and Andrew Turton, eds. 1991. *Thai Constructions of Knowledge*. London: School of Oriental and African Studies.

Mischung, Roland. 1995. "The Hill Tribes of Northern Thailand: Current Trends and Problems of their Integration into the Modern Thai Nation." In *Regions and*

National Integration in Thailand, 1892–1992, ed. V. Grabowsky. Wiesbaden: Harrassowitz Verlag, pp. 94–104.

Morell, David and Chai-anan Samudavanija. 1981. *Political Conflict in Thailand: Reform Reaction Revolution.* Cambridge, MA: Delgeschlager, Guna, and Hain.

Myers, David. 1994. "Pira Sudham and the Rape of the Esarn People of Northeastern Thailand." *Asian Studies Review* 18, 2 (November 1994): 77–87.

The Nation [Bangkok], November 20, 1998.

Phillips, Herbert. 1987. *Modern Thai Literature: An Ethnographic Interpretation.* Honolulu: University of Hawai'i.

Pasuk Phongpaichit and Chris Baker. 1995. *Thailand Economy and Politics.* Kuala Lumpur: Oxford University.

Phaiwarin Khao-Ngam. 1995. *Banana Tree Horse and Other Poems*, trans. B. Kasemsri. Bangkok: Amarin.

Pira Sudham. 1988. *Monsoon Country.* Bangkok: Shire.

_____. 1992. "Voice from the Grass Roots." *Asia Magazine*, April 10–12, p. 50.

_____. 1994. *People of Esarn.* Bangkok: Shire.

Platt, Martin. 2001. "Interview with Fon Fafang, A Kui-Khmer Writer in Thailand." *Udaya* 2: 81–96.

Prakobpong Panapool. 1998. "Isan Paper Good News — For NAP." *The Nation* [Bangkok] 22, 48391 (October 19): 1.

Reynolds, Craig. 1987. *Thai Radical Discourse: the Real Face of Thai Feudalism Today.* Ithaca, NY: Cornell University.

_____. 1991. "Introduction: Thai National Identity and its Defenders." In *National Identity and Its Defenders: Thailand 1939–1989*, ed. C. Reynolds. Monash University Papers in SEA No. 25, pp. 1–39.

_____, ed. 1991. *National Identity and Its Defenders: Thailand 1939–1989.* Monash Papers on Southeast Asia, No. 25. Clayton, Victoria: Monash University, Center of Southeast Asian Studies.

Rowe, Noel. 1994. "Foreword." In Pira S., *People of Esarn.* Bangkok: Shire, pp. 8–10.

Rusk, Ralph Leslie. 1962. *The Literature of the Middle Western Frontier. Vol. 1.* New York: Frederick Ungar.

Silk Magazine, January 1999.

Smalley, William. 1994. *Linguistic Diversity and National Unity: Language Ecology in Thailand.* Chicago: University of Chicago.

Smithies, Michael. 1973. "Introduction." In *Khamsing Srinawk, The Politician and Other*, trans. D. Garden. Kuala Lumpur: Oxford University, p. xiii.

Smyth, David and Manas Chitakasem, trans. 1998. *The Sergeant's Garland and Other Stories.* London: Oxford University.

Sridaoru'ang. 1994. *A Drop of Glass*, trans. R. Harrison. Bangkok: D.K. Books.

Srisakara Vallibhotama. 1997. *A Northeastern Site of Civilization.* Bangkok: Matichon.

Judith Stowe. 1991. *Siam Becomes Thailand.* Honolulu: University of Hawaii.

Suradech Chotiudompant. 2009. "Contemporary Trends in Thai Short Fiction." In *Modern Short Fiction of Southeast Asia: A Literary History*, ed. T.S. Yamada. Ann Arbor, MI: Association for Asian Studies. pp. 43–77.

Streckfuss, David. 2011. *Truth on Trial in Thailand: Defamation, Treason, and LèseMajesté*. London and New York: Routledge.

Stuart-Fox, Martin. 1998. *The Lao Kingdom of Lan Xang: Rise and Decline*. Bangkok: White Lotus.

Tej Bunnag. 1977. *The Provincial Administration of Siam 1892–1915*. Kuala Lumpur: Oxford University.

Thak Chaloemtiarana, ed. 1978. *Thai Politics: Extracts and Documents 1932–1957*. Bangkok: Social Science Association of Thailand.

Thongchai Winichakul. 1994. *Siam Mapped*. Honolulu: University of Hawaii.

Vatcharin Bhumichitr. 1997. *Vatch's Southeast Asian Cookbook*. London: Kyle Cathie.

Wajuppa Tossa. 1996. *Phaya Khan Khaak, the Toad King*. Lewisburg: Bucknell University Press.

Wenk, Klaus. 1995. *Thai Literature: An Introduction*, trans. E. Reinhold. Bangkok: White Lotus.

Wijeyewardene, Gehan. 1992. "Translator's Introduction." In Khammaan Khonkhai, *The Teachers of Mad Dog Swamp*, trans. G. Wijeyewardene. Chiang Mai: Silkworm.

_____. 1984. "Translator's Introduction." In Khammaan Khonkhai, *Teacher Marisa*, trans. G. Wijeyewardene. Bangkok: Pandora.

Winterton, Bradley. 1998. *Thailand Traveller's Companion*. Switzerland: Kümmerly & Frey.

Wolters, O. W. 1999. *History, Culture, and Region in Southeast Asian Perspectives*. Ithaca, NY: Southeast Asian Program Publications, Cornell University.

Thai-Language Sources

Anon. (undated)a. "สถาบันวิจัยศิลปะและวัฒนธรรมอีสาน." มหาวิทยาลัยมหาสารคาม.

_____. (undated)b. "สัมภาษณ์ คำสิงห์ ศรีนอก." Reprinted in Anon., 2537b, หอมคำ, pp. 14–9.

_____. (undated)c. "จากสำนักพิมพ์." In อุดร (undated)b, หมาเน่า, p. 3.

_____. 2518. "รู้จักกับนักเขียน." In คำหมาน, จดหมาย, back cover.

_____. 2520. "วิจารณ์หนังสือ ลูกอีสาน." โลกหนังสือ 1, 1 (ต.ค.): 76–9.

_____. 2521a. "ฟังเขาคุยเรื่อง วรรณคดีอีสาน." โลกหนังสือ 2, 2 (พ.ค.): 6–11.

_____. 2521b. "นายฮ้อยทมิฬ." โลกหนังสือ 1, 12 (ก.ย.): 136–7.

_____. 2521c. "หนังสือชุด 'มรดกอีสาน'." โลกหนังสือ 2, 2 (พ.ค.): 130–1.

_____. 2521d. "รมย์ รติวัน นักรบผู้ขาดเหรียญฯ" โลกหนังสือ 1, 8 (พ.ค.): 115–8.

_____. 2521e. "ผมจะเขียน 'ทุ่งกุลาร้องไห้ …' สัมภาษณ์ คำพูน บุญทวี ผู้เขียน 'ลูกอีสาน'." โลกหนังสือ 1, 4 (ม.ค.): 40–52.

_____. 2521f. "อภิปรายเรื่องนิยายชนะการประกวดใครใครก็ชอบนายฮ้อยทมิฬ." โลกหนังสือ 1, 12 (ก.ย.): 13.

_____. 2522a. "โรงเรียนคือแดนหฤโหด …" โลกหนังสือ 2, 10 (ก.ค.): 21–5.

_____. 2522b. "วัฒนธรรมพื้นบ้านสะท้อนเอกลักษณ์ของแต่ละท้องถิ่นเท่านั้นหรือ." โลกหนังสือ 2, 4 (ม.ค.): 131–2.

_____. 2522c. "คำนำ." In สมคิด, ลาก่อน (no page numbers).

_____. 2523. "พระอริยานุวัตร หัวหน้าศูนย์อนุรักษ์วรรณคดีภาคตะวันออกเฉียงเหนือ." โลกหนังสือ 3: 5 (ก.พ.): 74–7.

_____. 2530a. "รมย์ รติวัน." In รมย์, เสียงแคน, pp. 6–7.

_____. 2530b. "สังคม เภสัชมาลา." ถนนหนังสือ 5, 4 (ต.ค. 2530): 48.

_____. 2532. "เกี่ยวกับผู้เขียน." In ประเสริฐ จันคำ, ดอกคูน, p. 10.

_____. 2533. "'ฟันผมหาย' แผลลึกของชีวิตไทย เรื่องสั้นของลาว คำหอม." In ลาว, กำแพงลม, pp. 7–9.

_____. 2536a. ตำนานชีวิตคาราวาน. กรุงเทพฯ: ดอกหญ้า.

_____. 2536b. "สมคิด สิงสง." *Writer Magazine* 1, 7 (เม.ย.): 69.

_____. 2537a. "วัยเด็ก." Interview published in *Writer Magazine*, April 1993. Reprinted in Anon., 2537b, หอมคำ, pp. 23–31.

_____. 2537b. หอมคำ … ลาว คำหอม. Bangkok: Manager Media Group.

_____. 2537c. "ฟ้าบ่กั้น สวรรณไม่แบ่ง อิสานฮักแพงสืบสานนานมา." ผู้จัดการ 26 ก.ย. 1994. Reprinted in Anon., 2537b, หอมคำ, p. 143.

_____. 2538. "ชีวประวัติ กาญจนา นาคนันท์." In กาญจนา, ผู้ใหญ่ลี, p. 9.

_____. 2539. "กาญจนา นาคนันท์." In ทองเพียน (เรียบเรียง), ประวัติ, pp. 5–9.

_____. 2540. "สัมภาษณ์ สนั่น ชูสกุล นักเขียนหรือหัวแถวมือบ." จดหมายข่าวสโมสรนักเขียนภาคอีสาน 3, 11 (ก.ย.): 23–8.

_____. 2541a. "วรรณกรรม–เพลงเพื่อชีวิต '25 ปี ไม่ใช่การเฉลิมฉลอง แต่เป็นการฟื้นฟู วัฒนธรรม'." เนชั่นสุดสัปดาห์ 7, 33 (22–26 ต.ค.): 56–7.

_____. 2541b. "ทัศนะของเพื่อนมิตร ต่อ 'บทกวีในเสียงเพลง' ของ สุรชัย จันทิมาธร." กรุงเทพธุรกิจ วันอาทิตย์ 13, 3742 (20 ธ.ค.): 8.

_____. 2541c. "เมืองอีสาน' แห่งทุ่งทานตะวัน." เนชั่นสุดสัปดาห์ 7, 333 (22–28 ต.ค.): 4.

_____. 2542a. "รำภูก วาระครบรอบ 5 ปี กับการจากไปของมหากวีศรีปวงชน 'ประเสริฐ จันคำ'." จดหมายข่าวสโมสรนักเขียนภาคอีสาน 5, 21 (พ.ย.–ธ.ค.): 13.

_____. 2542b. "การก่อเกิดของสโมสรนักเขียนภาคอีสาน." จดหมายข่าวสโมสรนักเขียนภาคอีสาน 4, 17 (ม.ค.–ก.พ.): 15.

_____. 2542c. "ดอกไม้มิตรภาพไทย-ลาว เบ่งบานรับลมฝนกลางเขาใหญ่." เนชั่นสุดสัปดาห์ 8, 362 (13–19 พ.ค.): 4–5.

_____. 2542d. "ตามรอย …สุรชัย จันทิมาธร ในวันที่ไร้ 'ดวงตะวันสีแดง' ส่องทาง." เนชั่นสุดสัปดาห์ 8, 352 (4–10 มี.ค.): 4. Reprinted as ภาวิณี, "สุรชัย," p. 3.

_____. 2542e. "ไชยา วรรณศรี." In สนั่น ชูสกุล *et al.*, ฤดูดอกไม้ร่วง. สุรินทร์: องฟ้า.

_____. 2542f. "1 ทศวรรษ 'สโมสรนักเขียนภาคอีสาน'." จดหมายข่าวสโมสรนักเขียนภาคอีสาน 5, 20 (ก.ย.–ต.ค.): 8–13.

กองบรรณาธิการ. 2542. "คุย 3 คดีดังสาละวิน 'บิ๊กป่าไม้' ใครร่วมงานป่า." ฐานสัปดาห์วิจารณ์ 5(6): 246(311) (9–15 ม.ค.): 18–9.

กัณหา แสงรายา และ เจษฎา ทองรุ่งโรจน์, บ.ก. 2546. ปริทรรศน์วรรณกรรมไทย สมัยใหม่. กรุงเทพฯ: มูลนิธิสถาบันวิชาการ ๑๔ ตุลา.

กาญจนา นาคนันท์. (undated). "ผู้ประพันธ์คุยกับผู้อ่าน." In กาญจนา, 2538, ผู้ใหญ่ลี, pp. 5–8.

_____. 2538. ผู้ใหญ่ลีกับนางมา. กรุงเทพฯ: บรรณกิจ.

กานต์มณี ศักดิ์เจริญ. 2538. "บทเสริมท้ายเรื่องผู้ใหญ่ลีกับนางมา." In กาญจนา, ผู้ใหญ่ลี, p. 590–2.

กุหลาบ *et al.* 2538. "คำประกาศของคณะกรรมการตัดสินรางวัลช่อไรท์ประจำพุทธศักราช 2538." In ไพวรินทร์, 2540, ม้า, pp. 6–7.

เกษียร เตชะพีระ. 2540. "จารึกร่วมสมัย." In ไพวรินทร์, ม้า, p. 137–76.

คนเดียว. 2540. "จากนาโพธิ์ถึงโนเบล." สารคดี 148 (มิ.ย.).

คนอุบล ฯ. "คนรุ่นใหม่สนใจ 'พื้นบ้าน'." โลกหนังสือ 6, 3 (ธ.ค. 2525): 6–7.

คำพูน บุญทวี. 2522a. "คำนำของผู้เขียน." In คำพูน, ลูกทุ่ง, pp. 3–4.

———. 2522b. ลูกทุ่งเข้ากรุง. กรุงเทพฯ: บงกช.

———. 2540. ลูกอีสาน. กรุงเทพฯ: บรรณกิจเทรดดิ้ง.

———. 2541a. "คำนำของผู้ประพันธ์ในการพิมพ์ครั้งที่ 4." In คำพูน, นายฮ้อย, pp. 4–6.

———. 2541b. "คำนำของผู้ประพันธ์ในการพิมพ์ครั้งที่ 5." In คำพูน, นายฮ้อย, p. 3.

———. 2541c. นายฮ้อยทมิฬ. กรุงเทพฯ: โป๊ยเซียน.

คำสิงห์ ศรีนอก. (undated)a. "บอกเล่าความเป็นมาของหนังเรื่องทองปาน." Reprinted in Anon., 2537b, หอมคำ, pp. 54–5.

———. (undated)b. Interview with ไทยนิกร: "ทำไมผมออกจากป่า." Reprinted in Anon., 2537b, หอมคำ, p. 20.

คำหมาน คนไค. 2518. จดหมายจากครูคำหมาน คนไค. กรุงเทพฯ: บรรณกิจ.

———. 2521a. "คำนำของผู้เขียน." In คำหมาน, จดหมาย, (no page numbers).

———. 2521b. "คำนำของผู้เขียน." In คำหมาน, บักสีเด๊อ, (no page numbers).

———. 2521c. "จากผู้เขียน." In คำหมาน, ครูบ้านนอก, p. (5).

———. 2521d. จดหมายจากครูบ้านนอก. กรุงเทพฯ: บรรณกิจ.

———. 2521e. บักสีเด๊อ. กรุงเทพฯ: บรรณกิจ.

———. 2521f. ครูบ้านนอก. กรุงเทพฯ: การเวก.

———. 2529a. "คำนำของผู้เขียน." In คำหมาน, ยิ้ม… คนกรุง (no page numbers).

———. 2529b. ยิ้ม… คนกรุง. กรุงเทพฯ: พลพันธ์.

———. 2539a. "คำนำ." In คำหมาน, ผญา, p. 3.

———. 2539b. ผญา ภูมิปัญญาอีสาน. กรุงเทพฯ: ไทยวัฒนาพานิช.

———. 2540a. "คำนำผู้เขียน." In คำหมาน, ข้ามโขง (no page numbers).

———. 2540b. ข้ามโขงไปลาว. กรุงเทพฯ: ต้นอ้อ แกรมมี่.

แคน สาริกา. 2529. "ฝนแรกของวรรณกรรมภูพาน." ถนนหนังสือ 4: 4 (ต.ค.): 19.

จิตกวี กระจ่างเมฆ. 2541. ศึกษาวรรณกรรมเพลงเพื่อชีวิตของ สุรชัย จันทิมาธร. ปริญญานิพนธ์ มหาวิทยาลัยทักษิณ.

เจน อักษราพิจารณ์. 2542. "วรรณกรรมลำน้ำมูลสู่สโมสรนักเขียนภาคอีสาน." กรุงเทพธุรกิจ วันอาทิตย์ 31 ม.ค., p. 3.

เจริญ กุลสุวรรณ. 2542. "ลำนำรำลึก นักเขียนอีสานผู้ล่วงลับการแสดงที่หลายคนยังติดตาม และถามถึง." จดหมายข่าวสโมสรนักเขียนภาคอีสาน 4, 18 (มี.ค.–เม.ย.): 13.

จิตร ภูมิศักดิ์. 1981. "ผีตองเหลือง." โลกหนังสือ 4, 12 (ก.ย.): 40–2.

ช่อการะเกด 39 (ก.ย.–ต.ค. 2541), pp. 197–201.

ช่อเพชร มณีแดง. 2521. "คำพูน บุญทวี เขาจะเลือกเส้นทางสายไหน." โลกหนังสือ 1, 4 (ม.ค.): 49–52.

ชัชวาลย์ โคตรสงคราม. 2537b. "ฟ้าบ่กั้น ในความเก่าหลัง." In Anon., หอมคำ, pp. 140–1.

———. 2537a. "คำนำผู้เขียน." In ชัชวาลย์, เหมือนรถไฟ, pp. 12–5.

———. 2537c. เหมือนรถไฟจะมา. กรุงเทพฯ: แพรว.

ชาญวิทย์ เกษตรศิริ, บ.ก. 2549. ทองปาน. กรุงเทพฯ: มูลนิธิโครงการตำราสังคมศาสตร์และ มนุษยศาสตร์.

ชาติ กอบจิตติ ฯลฯ บก. 2544. ลาว คำหอม *Khamsing Srinawk*. กรุงเทพฯ: นักเขียน.

ชูเกียรติ ฉาไธสง. 2548. กำเนิดในนามพระเจ้าหลังไหล. กรุงเทพฯ: สามัญชน.

ไชยา วรรณศรี. 2541. "เสียงกลอง." ดอกติ้วป่า 10, 1 (23) (ก.พ.): 96–101.

_____. 2542. "ลาวลวง." In สนั่น *et al*, ฤดู, pp. 33–45.

ฉะรงค์ จันทร์เรือง. 2532. "จากณรงค์ จันทร์เรือง ถึง ประเสริฐ จันคำ." In ประเสริฐ จันคำ, ดอกคูน, pp. 8–9.

ดวงมน จิตร์จำนงค์. 2542. "สืบเนื่องจากคำถาม 'ทำไมวรรณกรรมสะท้อนสังคม จึงแก้ปัญหาสังคมไม่ได้'. เนชั่นสุดสัปดาห์ 8, 366 (10–16 มิ.ย. 2542): 44–5.

ดอกไม้คำ. 2542. "ฝ่าทางตัน." กรุงเทพธุรกิจ 12, 3769 (17 ม.ค.). จุดประกาย วรรณกรรม, p. 2.

ดินสอสี. 2541. "'สุรชัย จันทิมาธร' วันนี้ยังมีบทกวีในเสียงเพลง." กรุงเทพธุรกิจ วันอาทิตย์ 12, 3742 (20 ธ.ค.): 8.

_____. 2542. "สัพเพเหระเรื่องงานเขียนกับ สุรชัย จันทิมาธร." กรุงเทพธุรกิจ วันอาทิตย์ 12, 3923 (20 มิ.ย.): 16.

โคม สุขวงศ์. 2533. ประวัติภาพยนตร์ไทย. กรุงเทพฯ: องค์การค้าของคุรุสภา.

ถนนหนังสือ 2: 5 (ธ.ค. 2527), p. 71.

ทรงพันธ์ วรรณมาศ. 2534. ผ้าไทย ลายอีสาน. กรุงเทพฯ: โอเดียนโสตร์.

ทวีศักดิ์ ปิ่นทอง. 2546. นวนิยายกับการเมืองไทย ก่อนและหลังเหตุการณ์ *14 ตุลาคม 2516* (พ.ศ. *2507–2522*). กรุงเทพฯ: รักอักษร.

ทองเพียน สารมาศ (เรียบเรียง). 2539. ประวัตินักเขียนไทย เล่ม 3. กรุงเทพฯ: กรมศิลปากร.

ทีปกร. 2521. ศิลปะเพื่อชีวิต ศิลปะเพื่อประชาชน. กรุงเทพฯ: ต้นมะขาม.

ธนาพล อิ๋วสกุล. 2549. "หนังสือต้องห้าม ความรู้ที่ถูกจองจำ." สารคดี 260: 133–74.

นพพร สุวรรณพานิช. 2535. (untitled). In ลาว, ฟ้า (back cover).

นพพร ประชากุล. 2541. "ทำไมวรรณกรรมสะท้อนสังคมจึงแก้ปัญหาสังคมไม่ได้." สารคดี 162 (ส.ค.).

_____. 2543. "มีอะไรในลูกอีสาน." เนชั่น (online), 19 เม.ย. (no page numbers).

นรนิติ เศรษฐบุตร. 2532. "10 ปี ซีไรท์ คำให้การเรื่องรางวัลวรรณกรรมสร้างสรรค์ แห่งอาเซียน ปี 2522–2531." In ประเสริฐ ไสววรรณ, วิเคราะห์, pp. 221–4.

นฤมิตร ประพันธ์. 2539. "ไปฟังเสวนา 'รำลึก ประเสริฐ จันคำ...' ณ ศูนย์สังคีตศิลป์ ชั้น 4 ธนาคารกรุงเทพฯ ผ่านฟ้า." จดหมายข่าวสโมสรนักเขียนภาคอีสาน 2, 6: 11.

นายผี. 2533. "อีสาน!" In วิมล, รำลึก, p. 6–7.

น้ำพุ แสนสวย. 2542. "'ทำไมวรรณกรรมแก้ปัญหาสังคมไม่ได้'." เนชั่นสุดสัปดาห์ 7, 329 (13–19 พ.ค.): 44–5.

นีลส์ มุลเดอร์. 1980. "การสื่อแสดงความหมายทางวัฒนธรรมของแก่นเรื่องที่เด่นๆ ในวรรณกรรมสมัยใหม่ของไทยและชวา." โลกหนังสือ 4, 2 (พ.ย.): 70–87.

เนาวรัตน์ พงษ์ไพบูลย์. 2540. (untitled). In ไพวรินทร์, ม้า (back cover).

บัญชา เฉลิมชัยกิจ. 2541. "สำนักพิมพ์สุขภาพใจ." In ลาว, ฟ้า, p. 9.

ม.ล. บุญเหลือ เทพยสุวรรณ. 2538 (2511). "คำนำ." In กาญจนา, ผู้ใหญ่ลี, p. 4.

ประชาคม ลุนาชัย. 2540. ฝั่งแสงจันทร์. กรุงเทพ: สหการคนวรรณกรรม.

_____. 2541a. "พันธุ์พื้นถิ่น." In ประชาคม, ตัวละคร, pp. 71–84.

_____. 2541b. ตัวละครตกสมัย. กรุงเทพ: สหการคนวรรณกรรม.

ประทีป ชุมพล. 2525. พื้นเวียง. กรุงเทพฯ: อดีต.

ประทีป เหมือนนิล. 2542. *100* นักประพันธ์ไทย. กรุงเทพฯ: สุวีริยาสาส์น. In ประเสริฐ จันคำ. (undated)a. เมล็ดข้าวคืนรวง. กรุงเทพฯ: แสงดาว.

_____. (undated)b. "จากเมล็ดข้าว — พลัดรวง." In ประเสริฐ จันคำ, (undated)a, เมล็ดข้าว, p. 3.

_____. 2528. ฝอยฝนบนม่านฝุ่น. กรุงเทพฯ: ก่อไผ่.

_____. 2530a. "ถ้อยความจากผู้เขียน." In ประเสริฐ จันคำ, นางไห้ (no page numbers).

_____. 2530b. นางไห้. กรุงเทพฯ: วลี.

_____. 2532a. "จากผู้เขียน." In ประเสริฐ จันคำ, ดอกคูน, pp. 8–9.

_____. 2532b. ดอกคูน เสียงแคน. กรุงเทพฯ: มิ่งมิตร.

_____. 2533a. "ครั้งสุดท้ายระหว่างคนเขียนรูปกับคนเขียนเรื่อง." In ประเสริฐ จันคำ, 2533b, คือเก่า, pp. 5–6.

_____. 2533b. คือเก่า. กรุงเทพฯ: ดอกหญ้า.

_____. 2534. พลิกตำนานเพื่อชีวิต. กรุงเทพฯ: ดอกหญ้า.

ประเสริฐ จันทร์คำ. 2541. "แค่พระองค์ผู้ล่วงลับ." เนชั่นสุดสัปดาห์ 7, 336 (12–18 พ.ย.): 52.

_____. 2542. "สิ่งที่เราเรียกร้อง." เนชั่นสุดสัปดาห์ 8, 354 (18–24 มี.ค.): 52.

ประเสริฐ ณ นคร. 2538. "คำนำ." In มูลนิธิสารานุกรมวัฒนธรรมไทย ธนาคารไทย พาณิชย์, สารานุกรม, p. 4.

ประเสริฐ ไสววรรณ. 2532. วิเคราะห์นวนิยายและเรื่องสั้นที่สะท้อนชีวิตชาวชนบทอีสานของ คำพูน บุญทวี. ปริญญานิพนธ์ มหาวิทยาลัยศรีนครินทรวิโรฒ ประสานมิตร.

ปราโมช ปราโมทย์. 2533a. "หรือคือบุญบั้งไฟ." In ปราโมช, ถิ่นเถื่อน, pp. 99–104.

_____. 2533b. ถิ่นเถื่อน. กรุงเทพฯ: บางหลวง.

พจนานุกรม ฉบับราชบัณฑิตยสถาน กรุงเทพฯ. พ.ศ. 2525.

พระศรีธรรมโสภน. 2500. ภาษิตโบราณอีสาน. อุบลฯ: ศิริธรรม.

พิพัฒน์ บริบูรณ์. (undated tape). รำวงมาตรฐาน ผู้ใหญ่ลี. กรุงเทพฯ: เลบโส้.

พิมลราศ. 2541. "อะคูสติก สุรชัย จันทิมาธร 'เฉพาะกาล' ลานหญ้าหอศิลป์." ฐานสัปดาห์วิจารณ์ 4(5): 243(308) (19–25 ธ.ค.): 40.

พิสิฐ ภูศรี. 2539a. สัตว์แปลกหน้า. กรุงเทพฯ: ดอกหญ้า.

_____. 2539b. "นักเขียนระดับภาค." จดหมายข่าวสโมสรนักเขียนภาคอีสาน 2, 7 (ก.ย.–ต.ค.): 17–9.

ไพฑูรย์ ธัญญา. 2537. "ความประทับใจจากการอ่าน ฟ้าบ่กั้น." In Anon., หอมคำ, pp. 137–9.

ไพลิน รุ้งรัตน์, ed. 2539. ลมหายใจสุดท้ายของประเสริฐ จันคำ. กรุงเทพฯ: ดอกหญ้า, pp. 6–16.

ไพวรินทร์ ขาวงาม. 2538. ไม่ใช่กวีนิพนธ์ จากชายป่าอารยธรรม. กรุงเทพฯ: แพรว.

_____. 2540. ม้าก้านกล้วย. กรุงเทพฯ: แพรว.

แพรวสำนักพิมพ์. 2540. "คำนำสำนักพิมพ์." In ไพวรินทร์, ม้า, p. 14–5.

แพรวา พานิชกิจ. 2538. "ก ไก่ ก กา." ศิลปวัฒนธรรม 9, 16 (ก.ค.): 224–5.

ฟอน ฝ้าฟาง. 2530a. "กันจัญเจกวับ." In ฟอน, เหตุการณ์, pp. 36–44.

_____. 2530b. *1986* เหตุการณ์ที่ท่าช้าง. ศรีสะเกษ: ชาวอักษร.

_____. 2540. "รำฟ้อนย้อนกฤษณา เป็นตายากหัว (1)." มติชนสุดสัปดาห์ 17 เม.ย, p. 69.

ภาค พิเรทร. (untitled excerpt from ฟ้าเมืองไทย ฉบับ 968). Reprinted in ลาว, 2531, ลมแล้ง, p. 7.

ภาวิณี อินเทพ. 2542. "สุรชัย จันทิมาธร กับ 'ตะวันสีแดง'." กรุงเทพธุรกิจ วันอาทิตย์ 12, 3832 (21 มี.ค.): 3.

ภิญโญ กองทอง. 2546. "จาก 'พระจันทร์เสี้ยว', 'หนุ่มเหน้าสาวสวย' ถึง วรรณกรรม เพื่อชีวิต." In กัณหา และ เจษฎา, บ.ก., ปริทรรศน์, pp. 89–109.

มนัส พูลผล. 2526. "คนเพลงพื้นบ้านกับงานวันเกิดชูเกียรติ." โลกหนังสือ 6: 6 (มี.ค.): 12–5.

มาโนช พรหมสิงห์. 2540a. "ร่างแหแห่งวิหค." In มาโนช, ร่างแห, pp. 130–75.

_____. 2540b. ร่างแหแห่งวิหค. บุรีรัมย์: บ้านทุ่ง.

_____. 2440c. "สายลมบนถนนโบราณ." ช่อการะเกด 34 (ก.ย.–ต.ค.): 109–33.

_____. 2541. "สะพาน." เนชั่นสุดสัปดาห์ 7, 329 (24–30 ก.ย.): 50–2.

มาร์ติน. 1999. "คนละภาษาเดียวกัน." จดหมายข่าวสโมสรนักเขียนภาคอีสาน 4, 17 (ม.ค.–ก.พ.): 28.

มาลี ร้อยสีพันใบ. 2541. "อีสานคือต้นแบบวรรณกรรมเพื่อชีวิต." เนชั่นสุดสัปดาห์ 7, 332 (15–21 ต.ค.): 49.

มูลนิธิสารานุกรมวัฒนธรรมไทย ธนาคารไทยพาณิชย์. 2538. สารานุกรมวัฒนธรรมไทย ภาคอีสาน. กรุงเทพ: ธนาคารไทยพาณิชย์.

โมน สวัสดิ์ศรี. 2541. "สัญจรพบ 'นักเขียนอีสาน' 5 จังหวัด (2)." เนชั่นสุดสัปดาห์ 8, 343 (31 ธ.ค.–6 ม.ค.): 48.

ยงค์ ยโสธร. 2539. คำอ้าย. กรุงเทพฯ: มิ่งมิตร.

รงค์ วงษ์สวรรค์. 2541. "รงค์ วงษ์สวรรค์ เขียนถึง สุรชัย จันทิมาธร." In สุรชัย, ความบ้า, pp. 17–8.

รมย์ รติวัน. 2519a. "ครับ, แม่ผมชื่อแพรว โสเภณี." In รมย์, หยัด, pp. 71–83.

_____. 2519b. หยัดอยู่สู้โลกพาลา. กรุงเทพฯ: ผ่านฟ้าพิทยา.

_____. 2523. โทน เทวดา นักสู้จากที่ราบสูง. กรุงเทพฯ: โคมทอง.

_____. 2530. เสียงแคนและเปียนโน. กรุงเทพฯ: ประพันธ์สาส์น.

ร้อย รวีวรรณ. 2522. "เราจะเริ่มต้นกันใหม่... บทวิเคราะห์ 'นักเขียนรุ่นใหม่' หลังเหตุการณ์ 6 ตุลา." โลกหนังสือ 3, 1(ต.ค.): 47.

รักษ์ มนัญญา. 2542. ฝ่าทางตัน. กรุงเทพ: ดอกหญ้า.

รัญจวน อินทรกำแหง. 2521a. วรรณกรรมวิจารณ์ ตอนที่ 1. กรุงเทพ: ดวงกมล, pp. 137–9.

_____. 2521b. "ลูกอีสาน." In รัญจวน, วรรณกรรม ... 3, p. 117.

_____. 2521c. วรรณกรรมวิจารณ์ ตอนที่ 3. กรุงเทพฯ: ดวงกมล, p. 19.

รื่นฤทัย สัจจพันธุ์, ไพลิน รุ้งรัตน์. 2541. หนังสือฝ่ายวรรณกรรม รำลึก 25 ปี 14 ตุลา: พ.ศ. 2516–2541. กรุงเทพฯ: ชนนิยม.

ลันนา เจริญสิทธิชัย. 2546. "ปราชญ์อีสาน" คำพูน บุญทวี. นนทบุรี: โป๊ยเซียน.

ลาว คำหอม. 2531. ลมแล้ง. กรุงเทพ: สุขภาพใจ.

_____. 2533. กำแพงลม. กรุงเทพ: ใบบัว.

_____. 2535. ฟ้าบ่กั้น (พิมพ์ครั้งที่เก้า). กรุงเทพฯ: กำแพง.

_____. 2541. ฟ้าบ่กั้น. กรุงเทพฯ: แพรว.

ลาวัณย์ สังขพันธนนท์. 2529. ภาพสะท้อนสังคมไทยจากเรื่องสั้นร่วมสมัย. ปริญญานิพนธ์ มหาวิทยาลัย ศรีนครินทรวิโรฒ พิษณุโลก.

ลูกข้าวนึ่ง. 2543. "ชัยอนันต์ สมุทวณิช มองลอดแว่น... มีอะไรใน 'ลูกอีสาน'." เนชั่น (online) 12 เม.ย. (no page numbers).

วงเดือน ทองเจียว. 2541. ช่างสลักไม้. กรุงเทพฯ: ประพันธ์สาส์น.

_____. 2542. ทางเจ้าเสด็จ. กรุงเทพฯ: ประพันธ์สาส์น.

วรรณฤกษ์. 2542. "ฐานวรรณกรรม." ฐานสัปดาห์วิจารณ์ (245) 2–8 ม.ค., p. 60.

วัชระ บัวสนธ์. 2533. "ข้อสังเกตของบรรณาธิการ." In ลาว, 2535, ฟ้า, p. 18.

_____. 2536. "บรรณาธิการสนทนา." In เสี่ยวจันทร์, โลก, pp. 6–10.

วัลยา วิวัฒน์ศร. 1994. "เขียดขาคำ." In Anon., หอมคำ, p. 124.

วานิช จรุงกิจอนันต์. 2540. "กฤษณาสอนน้อง (2)." มติชนสุดสัปดาห์ 20 พ.ค., pp. 70–1.

วาสนา ไชยรัตน์. 2534. การวิเคราะห์เรื่องสั้นของสุรชัย จันทิมาธร. ปริญญานิพนธ์ มหาวิทยาลัย ศรีนครินทรวิโรฒ ประสานมิตร.

วิจารณ์ สนามจันทร์. 2541. "'ช่างสลักไม้' อธิบายโลกและชีวิตด้วยทฤษฎีความสับสน." กรุงเทพธุรกิจ 12, 3742 (20 ธ.ค.): 3.

วิมล พลจันทร์. 2533. รำลึกถึงนายผี จากป้าลม. กรุงเทพฯ: ดอกหญ้า.

วิทยากร เชียงกูล. 2517a. "คำนำเชิงวิจารณ์ จากฉบับพิมพ์ครั้งที่ 3 พ.ศ. 2517." Reprinted in ลาว, 2535, ฟ้า, p. 236.

_____. 2517b. "บันทึกของผู้เขียนในการพิมพ์ครั้งแรก." In วิทยากร, 2517c, p. (39).

_____. 2517c. ฉันจึงมาหาความหมาย. นนทบุรี: พระจอมเกล้าวิทยาลัยเทคนิค.

วิวัฒน์ โรจนาวรรณ, ed. 2542a. นักเขียนอีสาน. บุรีรัมย์: สโมสรนักเขียนภาคอีสาน.

_____. 2542b. "'สโมสรนักเขียนภาคอีสาน' สู่ทศวรรษที่ 2 สู่ชนบทอย่างถึงรากถึงโคน." จดหมายข่าวสโมสรนักเขียนภาคอีสาน 5, 20 (ก.ค.–ต.ค.): 8–13.

วีระ สุดสังข์. 2542a. "คำนำ." In วีระ, ความ, pp. 3–4.

_____. 2542b. ความไม่เอาไหนของคนไม่เอาไหน. กรุงเทพฯ: ชมรมเด็ก.

_____. 2542c. "ลึจู แซ่อึ้ง สาวแก่ค้างบ้านของชาวกวย." In สนั่น et al, ฤดู, p. 47–57.

วีระศักดิ์ สุนทรศรี. 2536. คาราวาน: ตำนานทัพหน้าวงดนตรีเพื่อชีวิตของไทย. กรุงเทพฯ: กำแพง.

ศิริพร วรรณศิลป์. 2542. "บนทางคู่ขนานอิสระ สัมภาษณ์: ไพฑูรย์ ธัญญา." สยามรัฐสัปดาห์วิจารณ์ 45, 43 (28 มี.ค.–3 เม.ย.): 56–7.

สนั่น ชูสกุล. 2541a. "เกี่ยวกับผู้เขียน." In สนั่น, ช้าง, pp. 164–5.

_____. 2541b. ช้างเหยียบนา พระยาเหยียบเมือง. สุรินทร์: อิงฟ้า.

_____. 2541c. "'บ้านเมืองจะไม่ฉิบหายได้ยังไง… อย่างนี้ดีกว่า…'." จดหมายข่าวสโมสรนักเขียนภาคอีสาน (พ.ย.–ธ.ค.): 20–1.

สนั่น ชูสกุล et al. 2542. ฤดูดอกไม้ร่วง. สุรินทร์: อิงฟ้า.

สมคิด สิงสง. (undated). "ฟ้าบ่กั้น และ ลาว คำหอม ที่ผมรู้จัก." In Anon., หอมคำ, 2537b, p. 118.

_____. 2515. มโหรีแห่งชีวิตอิสระ. ขอนแก่น: รุ่งเกียรติ.

_____. 2518. "เรายังไม่ชนะดอกหรือ พ่อ." In สุชาติ ส., ed., แล้งเข็ญ, p. 304.

_____. 2522. ลาก่อนนาวังเหล็ก. กรุงเทพฯ: ปิยะสาส์น.

_____. 2536a. "คำนำผู้เขียน." In สมคิด, ข้าว, p. 5.

_____. 2536b. ข้าวเขียว. กรุงเทพฯ: ดอกหญ้า.

สมนึก พานิชกิจ. 2540. "ข้อย…เป็นคนอีสาน." กุลสตรี ก.พ, pp. 160–3.

สมรม สทิงพระ. 2536. "คำพูน บุญทวี." In บนถนนนักเขียน. กรุงเทพฯ: ไรเตอร์, pp. 99–102.

_____. 2537. เส้นทางนักเขียน. นนทบุรี: ไรเตอร์.

สมาคมนักเขียนแห่งประเทศไทย. 2528. 100 ปี เรื่องสั้นไทย. กรุงเทพฯ: ประพันธ์สาส์น.

สังคม เภสัชมาลา. 2538a. ในทุ่งเปลี่ยว. กรุงเทพฯ: ดอกหญ้า.

_____. 2538b. "คำนำผู้เขียน." In สังคม, ในทุ่ง, pp. 5–6.

_____. 2538c. "คำนำผู้เขียน." In สังคม, บ้าน, (no page number).

_____. 2538d. บ้านโรงสี. กรุงเทพฯ: ดอกหญ้า.

_____. 2538e. "คำนำผู้เขียน." In สังคม, 2538f, หวด, pp. 7–8.

_____. 2538f. หวดฮ้าง. กรุงเทพฯ: ดอกหญ้า.

สัจภูมิ ละออ. 2541. "ฝันของศิลปินแห่งชาติ ลาว คำหอม และ 2 ซีไรท์เรื่องสั้น." กรุงเทพธุรกิจ 12, 3728 (6 ธ.ค.): 8.

_____. 2542. "เสี่ยวจันทร์ แรมไพร กับ 'กุดจี่' เจ้าหนี้ผู้ยากไร้." กรุงเทพธุรกิจ 12, 3867 (25 เม.ย.): 8.

_____. 2546. 25 ปี ซีไรท์. กรุงเทพฯ: สยามอินเตอร์บุ๊คส์.

_____. 2551. ซีไรท์ไดอารี่. กรุงเทพฯ: สุขภาพใจ.

สัญญาลักษณ์ คอนศรี. 2529. "กลุ่มวรรณกรรมลำน้ำมูล เป้าหมายใหม่ของ กอ. รมน. อีสาน?" ถนนหนังสือ 4, 3 (ก.ย.): 18–20.

สำนักพิมพ์โคมทอง. 2523. "คำนำ." In รมย์, โทน, p. 4.

สำนักพิมพ์บรรณกิจ. 2540. "จากสำนักพิมพ์." In คำพูน, ลูกอีสาน, (no page number).

สำนักพิมพ์ผ่านฟ้าพิทยา. 2519. "คำนำของสำนักพิมพ์." In รมย์, หยัด, p. 7.

สีพลอย มณีรัตน์. 2540. "เรื่องสั้น ประเวณี." จดหมายข่าวสโมสรนักเขียนภาคอีสาน 3, 9 (ม.ค.–เม.ย.): 24.

สุกัญญา ภัทราชัย. 2526. "ตาโบ นักเจรียง." โลกหนังสือ 6, 4 (ม.ค.): 12–3.

สุชาติ ภูมิบริรักษ์. 2514. อีสาน ดินแดนแห่งเลือดและน้ำตา. กรุงเทพฯ: ชมรมหนังสือเปลวไฟ.

สุชาติ สวัสดิ์ศรี, ed. 2518. แล้งเข็ญ. กรุงเทพฯ: ดวงกมล.

_____. 2542. "กูคือประเสริฐ จันคำ." เนชั่นสุดสัปดาห์ 8, 346 (21–27 ม.ค.): 46.

สุเนตร ชุตินธรานนท์. 2533. "เมื่อฝรั่งมอง ลาว คำหอม." In ลาว, กำแพง, pp. 10–6.

สุมาลี โพธิ์พยัคฆ์. 2540. "สามแพร่งชีวิต – สมคิด สิงสง." จดหมายข่าวสโมสรนักเขียนภาคอีสาน 3: 8 (ม.ค.–ก.พ. 2540), pp. 4–9.

สุรชัย จันทิมาธร. 2528. "คิดถึงบ้าน คิดถึงนายผี ..อัศนี พลจันทร์." ถนนหนังสือ 3: 4 (ต.ค. 2528), pp. 16–9.

_____. 2531a. "จากผู้เขียน." In สุรชัย, ก่อนฟ้า, pp. 9–16.

_____. 2531b. ก่อนฟ้าสาง. กรุงเทพฯ: กำแพง.

_____. 2532a. "จากผู้เขียน." In สุรชัย, ข้าง, pp. 12–4.

_____. 2532b. ข้างถนน. กรุงเทพฯ: สามัญชน.

_____. 2533a. "จากผู้เขียน." In สุรชัย, มาจาก, pp. 11–4.

_____. 2533b. มาจากที่ราบสูง. กรุงเทพฯ: กำแพง.

_____. 2536a. "คนกับควาย." In Anon., ตำนาน, pp. 100–2.

_____. 2536b. "บ้านนาสะเทือน." In Anon., ตำนาน, pp. 218–9.

_____. 2541a. "ลมหายใจของท้องทุ่ง." In สุรชัย, ความบ้า, p. 63.

_____. 2541b. "จากผู้เขียน." In สุรชัย, ความบ้า, pp. 9–14.

_____. 2541c. ความบ้ามาเยือน. กรุงเทพฯ: สามัญชน.

เสนอ กลิ่นหอม. 2542. "ห้องสุนทรภู่ ฝันที่ใกล้จะเป็นจริง." ฐานสัปดาห์วิจารณ์ 5(6): 245(310) (2–8 ม.ค.): 65.

เสถียร จันทิมาธร. 2518a. "ก่อนจะเป็น ครูคำหมาน คนไค." In คำหมาน, จดหมาย (no page numbers).

_____. 2518b. "คำนำ." In อุดร, อีสาน, p. (9).

_____. 2527a. "วรรณกรรมในยุค 'แสวงหา' ของคนหนุ่มสาวรุ่นใหม่." In เสถียร, สายธาร, pp. 375–414.

_____. 2527b. "วรรณกรรมยุค 14 ตุลา 2516." In เสถียร, สายธาร, pp. 459–60.

_____. 2527c. สายธารวรรณกรรมเพื่อชีวิตของไทย. กรุงเทพ: เจ้าพระยา.

เสี้ยวจันทร์ แรมไพร. 2536a. ขับขานข้างใน. นนทบุรี: บ้านหนังสือ.

_____. 2536b. โลกเฉพาะ. ธนบุรี: นกสีเหลือง.

_____. 2536c. "จากนักเขียน." In เสี้ยวจันทร์, โลก, pp. 11–5.

ใหม่ รักหมู่. 2521. "ครูบ้านนอก." โลกหนังสือ 1, 10 (ก.ค.): 109.

อิงอร สุพันธุ์วณิช. 2548. นวนิยายนิทัศน์. กรุงเทพฯ: ภาควิชวภาษาไทย, คณะอักษรศาสตร์, จุฬาลงกรณ์มหาวิทยาลัย.

อิสรีอิน. 2542. "'คนกับควาย' สมคิด สิงสง และหมู่บ้านซับแดง ยุคขี้ข้าฝรั่ง." เนชั่นสุดสัปดาห์ 8, 361 (6–12 พ.ค.): 62.

อุดร ทองน้อย. (undated)a. "หมาเน่า อีแร้ง และแมลงวัน." In อุดร, (undated)b, หมาเน่า, p. 69.

_____. (undated)b. หมาเน่า อีแร้ง และแมลงวัน. กรุงเทพฯ: แสงดาว.

_____. 2518. อีสานกู. กรุงเทพฯ: ประพันธ์สาส์น.

_____. 2519a. "คำนำ." In อุดร, สายเลือด, p. 1.

_____. 2519b. "เพื่อนผู้สู้ในป่า." In อุดร, สายเลือด, p. 10.

_____. 2519c. สายเลือด หนังเนื้อ และกระดูกของคนยากไร้. กรุงเทพฯ: สัญญาน.

เอื้อยนาง. 2540. "สงสารหมอแคน." กรุงเทพธุรกิจ 9 พ.ค. pp. 10–1.

เอื้อยนาง และ วาสนา. 2539. นิทานพื้นบ้านอีสาน. กรุงเทพฯ: ชมรมเด็ก.

Index